Saturn's
Children

In Memory of
James Grant Duncan
Who Loved Freedom
and for
Ivo, Clementine and Nathaniel Hobson
Who We Trust Will Cherish It

Alan Duncan and Dominic Hobson

Saturn's Children

How the State Devours Liberty, Prosperity and Virtue

The authors and publishers are grateful for permission to reproduce
material in this book as follows: Lawrence Stone,
The Road to Divorce 1530–1987, OUP, 1990, by permission of Oxford
University Press; C. A. R. Crosland, *The Future of
Socialism*, Jonathan Cape, 1956, by permission of the Estate
of C. A. R. Crosland.

This paperback edition published in Great Britain in 1998
by Politico's Publishing
8 Artillery Row
London SW1P 1RZ

First published in hardback in 1995 by Sinclair Stevenson

Copyright © 1998 by Alan Duncan and Dominic Hobson

A CIP catalogue record of this book is available at the British Library

ISBN 19023 0104 8

Typeset in Berkeley OS by FSH Ltd.
Printed and bound in Great Britain by the St Edmundsbury Press

Until August 1914 a sensible, law-abiding Englishman could pass through life and hardly notice the existence of the state, beyond the post office and the policeman. He could live where he liked and as he liked. He had no official number or identity card. He could travel abroad or leave his country for ever without a passport or any sort of official permission. He could exchange his money for any other currency without restriction or limit. He could buy goods from any country in the world on the same terms as he bought goods at home. For that matter, a foreigner could spend his life in this country without permit and without informing the police. Unlike the countries of the European continent, the state did not require its citizens to perform military service. An Englishman could enlist, if he chose, in the regular army, the navy, or the territorials. He could also ignore, if he chose, the demands of national defence. Substantial householders were occasionally called on for jury service. Otherwise, only those helped the state who wished to do so. The Englishman paid taxes on a modest scale: nearly £200 million in 191314, or rather less than 8 per cent of the national income. The state intervened to prevent the citizen from eating adulterated food or contracting infectious diseases. It imposed safety rules in factories, and prevented women, and adult males in some industries, from working excessive hours. The state saw to it that children received education up to the age of 13. Since 1 January 1909, it provided a meagre pension for the needy over the age of 70. Since 1911, it helped to insure certain classes of workers against sickness and unemployment. This tendency towards more state action was increasing. Expenditure on the social services had roughly doubled since the Liberals took office in 1905. Still, broadly speaking, the state acted only to help those who could not help themselves. It left the adult citizen alone.

A. J. P. Taylor, *English History 1914–1945*

Contents

Preface

We always plan too much and think too little. We resent a call to thinking and hate unfamiliar argument that does not tally with what we already believe or would like to believe. We walk into our future as we walked into the war, blindfolded.

Joseph A. Schumpeter[1]

And thine ears shall hear a word behind thee, saying, This is the way, walk ye in it, when ye turn to the right hand, and when ye turn to the left.

Isaiah 30:21

This book is an epistle to our countrymen. As a work of political polemics, addressed to a people not much given to politics, it must number vanity among its authors. But its origin lies less in our conceit than in our apprehension at the indifference of our fellow citizens towards the despotism under which they are obliged to live. It is a despotism spawned by egalitarian democracy, and it is primarily of the mind rather than of the body. This spectral guise; has allowed it to encroach relentlessly but imperceptibly on the private lives, liberties and property of the British people for over one hundred years; Our account of the paradox of a democratic despotism is scarcely original – it was first identified by Alexis de Tocqueville a century and a half ago – but we believe it is timely. As with syphilis, the last stages of such a despotism are worse than the first. State power, hallowed initially as liberator and benefactor, does not disclose its true nature until its charges are so mesmerised by its permanence and ubiquity that they can neither recognise it nor resist it. In the end, the power of the State becomes so pervasive that people do not merely cease to find it irksome but yearn for their subjection to it to be completed. This is the stage which we may have reached in Britain today.

After a decade and a half of repeated assaults on the outworks of the State, public expenditure is as high as at any time since the war. The overall burden of taxation is heavier than it was in 1979. One in every five workers is still employed by the State. There are more officials and regulators and policemen, enforcing more laws and more regulations, than in any previous era. Yet it is rapidly becoming the received opinion, even among conservatives, that the country is at the fag-end of an extreme and ill-judged experiment in economic and political freedom. The crusade to diminish the State is popularly assumed to have over-reached itself, and to have expired at last of natural political causes on the steps of the General Post Office. Acceptance of capitalism as the surest route to material prosperity may be widespread, but conviction of its low morals and ignorance of its unseverable connection to liberty is almost universal. Virtually nobody disagrees that all of the social ills of our time unemployment, crime, drug-taking, truancy, divorce, illegitimacy, homelessness and the corruption of public and private morals – are the handiwork of fifteen years of untrammelled individualism.

Communitarian ideas, with their forceful appeal to false memories of the *Gemeinschaft und Gesellschaft* of yesteryear, are in the ascendant. What kind of Society is this, asks every journalist or politician in pursuit of applause, which allows people to sleep in the streets and pensioners to freeze to death? They know their answer. It is to resume the steady goose-step of the State, until it has taxed and spent and legislated and regulated and policed its way into the last redoubts of private life and liberty. Far from dying in the last ditch in defence of their traditional way of life, the British people are already out in No Man's Land, ushering their oppressors in. The prospect of renewed State power has achieved great contemporary popularity precisely because it promises to restore in full measure the blamelessness and carelessness of a political servitude which it is imagined was lost. This book – which endeavours, however inadequately, to question communitarian values – is our frail offering in opposition to the dominant political tendency of our times.

We wish we had executed it better. Like any text composed by two laymen in the interstices of their busy lives, it is bound to contain some errors, misunderstandings and misrepresentations. There will be contradictions too. Some will be accidental, but several were left unresolved deliberately. They reflect our genuine bewilderment at the intractability of some of the problems we encountered, and our consequent willingness to consider virtually any means of escape from the present impasse. Perhaps the most depressing aspect of our contemporary socio-political culture is its fearfulness, its aversion to risk, its craving for conformity and its inveterate hostility to experiment, spontaneity, innovation and variety. The apparent irreversibility of State power rests largely upon its own capacity to deaden the spirit and dull the imagination. Its enemies being few in number, lightly armed and lacking as yet the support of the people – must retain at least the element of surprise.

The book includes unusually lengthy historical analyses. Although the final chapter is devoted exclusively to policy recommendations, it might be thought that the book dwells too much on the past or favours analysis over prescription. This is one aspect of the book for which we see no need to apologise, except where we are rightly indicted of repetition or of labouring our points. It is politically convenient for communitarians to confine their diagnosis of our current predicament to the brief interlude of the last fifteen years, but we believe that their myopia has persuaded them to propound superficial solutions to bogus dilemmas. The relentless presentation of unarguable fact is anyway a necessary antidote to the tempting delusions of collectivist psychopathology. Nor do we see any shame in the brevity of our prescriptions. It is our chief boast that, unlike the collectivists, we have no detailed blueprint for a future order of society. In our estimation, the main task facing contemporary statesmen is not to 'reinvent' government but to liquidate it. It is to release the moral power and creative force of individuals, both born and unborn, to fashion their own diverse and unknowable posterities.

It will be objected that individualism of this kind is too methodical, and wilfully ignorant of the role played by group loyalties and social institutions in the moralisation of the individual. It is certainly our view that methodological individualism is the only reliable prophylactic against the perennial temptation to treat people as means rather than ends. As soon as the individual is subsumed in the seductive collective abstractions of communitarian ideology, he or she becomes easier to coerce. But our aversion to sociological argument is far from complete. This book makes much use of its insights into poverty, crime and the disintegration of the family. It is also one of our principal contentions that it is the State and not the possessive individualism of the last fifteen years which has corrupted ordinary men and women. By expropriating the tens of thousands of intermediar institutions which once stood between the citizen and the State, successive governments have robbed the individual of all the private schools of virtue. Our ambition was to describe a way to be free which relies on neither an irresponsible libertarianism nor an oppressive moral authoritarianism. We are conscious of how far we have fallen short of it.

We are grateful to Claire Gagneux and Nicholas Woolf, and to Robert Twigger of the House of Commons Library, for their research. Hermione Parker offered invaluable counsel on our Basic Income proposal, and Holly Sutherland, the Director of the Microsimulation Unit at the Department of Applied Economics in the University of Cambridge, gave freely of her time to help us test its plausibility on the POLIMOD computer model of the tax and benefits system. Samuel Brittan and the Reverend Andrew Studdert-Kennedy read parts of the first draft, and made many helpful comments. Dick Hobson read and edited the whole of the first draft, and prepared the index. Our editor, Christopher Sinclair-Stevenson, once again showed the courage and imagination which was lacking in others.

---

1 Joseph A. Schumpeter, *Capitalism, Socialism a Democracy*, Preface to the Second Edition, George Allen and Unwin Ltd, 1957, page xi.

Saturn's Children

Introduction

CHAPTER ONE

The New Despotism

A people among whom there is no habit of spontaneous action for a collective interest – who look habitually to their government to command or prompt them in all matters of joint concern – who expect to have everything done for them, except what can be made an affair of mere habit and routine – have their faculties only half developed; their education is defective in one of its most important branches...Such a system, more completely than any other, embodies the idea of despotism.

John Stuart Mill, *Principles of Political Economy*[1]

Despotism is particularly to be feared in ages of democracy. I think that at all times I should have loved freedom, but in the times in which we live, I am disposed to worship it.

Alexis de Tocqueville, *Democracy in America*[2]

What I fear is that both our political parties will bid for the support of the working man; that both of them will promise to do what he likes if he will only tell them what it is...*Vox populi* will be *Vox diaboli* if it is worked in that manner.

Walter Bagehot[3]

People are perplexed. The constant economic change of the last decade and a half has failed to deliver a decisive rise in the standard of living. It seems instead to have spread economic insecurity from its traditional domains into the once-prosperous suburbs and shires. But the sense of unending upheaval reaches far beyond the merely economic. No cherished institution, public or private, seems immune to the incessant quest for value-for-money. Schools, universities, hospitals, regiments, municipalities, charities, churches, clubs, even political parties, are under attack as inefficient or old-fashioned. The Welfare State, collapsing slowly under the weight of its inflated obligations, seems increasingly unable to contain an explosion of poverty and homelessness. The dissolution of the family and of traditional moral values have unleashed an epidemic of crime, drug-taking, divorce and illegitimacy. Thoughtful citizens are increasingly afraid that the depraved, violent and trivial ways of life depicted around the clock by the great engines of popular communication – radio, television, and especially newspapers – may be a true representation of the existence and character of the British people at the close of the second millennium. Familiar features of the social and political landscape are badly eroded. The monarchy has lost the respect of its subjects. Cabinet ministers are popularly assumed to be drunk with uninterrupted power, implementing ill-thought-out policies, routinely defying the judiciary and carelessly misleading Parliament. The elected representatives of the people – divided, powerless, arrogant and mired in sleaze – have never sunk lower in the estimation of the voters. Civil servants, once admired around the world for their probity and neutrality, are seen to have colluded in ministerial misdeeds. In the courts, a series of spectacular miscarriages of justice, compounded daily by the petty miscalculations of elderly judges, have forfeited the confidence of the public in the entire system of criminal justice.

The political posturings, theological contortions and sexual peccadilloes of clergymen, at every rank in every church, have reduced organised religion to a bleak irrelevance. The police, lumbered with impossible responsibilities and increasingly alienated from the people they serve, have lapsed into a sullen trade unionism. Doctors and nurses have succumbed to a Pecksniffian greed, never hesitating to couch their crude financial demands in the soothing vocabulary of patient care. The teachers, the once respected custodians of knowledge and opportunity, have spent a decade locked in chronic industrial conflict with the government. Despised, even attacked, by their pupils, they are an apt symbol of the universal collapse of authority.

Individualism versus 'Community'

This formidable catalogue of evil is a popular analysis of the British predicament today. Vote-grubbing politicians, ever-ready to ply the British people with alibis, assign sole authorship to a supposed war of all against all unleashed by the possessive individualism of the 1980s. 'No number other than one. No person other than me. No time other than now. No such thing as society, just "me" and "now",' as Neil Kinnock put it to the Labour Party conference in 1988. The unforgiving pursuit of self-interest is alleged to have undermined the respect for authority, tolerance of others, public spiritedness and fair-mindedness which were the hallmarks of the pre-Thatcherite way of life in Britain. By subjecting the country to an unprecedented ordeal by market economics, the governments of the 1980s are popularly judged to have smashed a myriad congenial and altruistic private and public 'communities' into millions of competing, atomistic individuals driven only by greed and selfishness.

Belief in the culpability of a destructive individualism is common across the political spectrum. The Labour Party leadership, drawing on a long tradition of Christian Socialism, believes the promise to rebuild 'communities' shattered by fifteen years of individualism is the vision which can resurrect the corpse of State collectivism for a new generation. The Liberal Democrats, who have of necessity taken greatest pride in local political visions, now also believe that 'community' politics can be translated successfully to the national stage. A string of senior Conservative politicians have rediscovered the One Nation, communitarian traditions of; Carlyle and Disraeli after twenty years of obeisance to the supposedly alien ideology of Manchester liberalism. One former prophet of free market liberalism, John Gray, has gone so far as to argue that market forces have destroyed even Conservatism itself as a viable political platform and electoral force, by undermining the self-governing institutions, autonomous professions and 'communities' which it was intended to conserve.[4]

One of his former pupils at Oxford, the Conservative MP David Willetts, believes his erstwhile tutor exaggerates the destructive impact free market economics has had on the British way of life. But even he accepts the force of the communitarian argument, advocating a kinder and gentler 'civic Conservatism' which incorporates the useful mechanisms of the marketplace without undermining the shared values of 'communities'. In his view, Conservatives value free markets because they work. They work because Conservatives uphold the institutions – private property, the law of contract, monetary stability, free trade, an independent judiciary – which enable them to work. But Conservatives also treasure the national, neighbourhood and parental affiliations of pub, club, church, regiment and family because they save people from the anomy and alienation of a mere atomistic individualism. 'The conservative,' he writes, 'thus stands between the two errors of socialist collectivism and liberal individualism and, indeed, understands that they are mutually dependent. Big government undermines community. Rampant individualism without the ties of duty, loyalty and affiliation is only checked by powerful and intrusive government.'[5]

This new consensus on the importance of rebuilding 'communities' does not translate easily into a distinctive set of new policies. The Labour Party has kept its prescriptions deliberately vague, confident that the appeal of 'community' will be stronger in the abstract than in the reality. A leitmotif runs through the policies which the party has disclosed – using the power of Society to advance the Individual – but the policies themselves have the familiar ring of taxation, subsidy and transfer by the State. Likewise, the new model Conservatism of David Willetts turns out to be what the Conservative government is doing already. In his most recent pamphlet, which is actually entitled civic Conservatism, Willetts applauds the 'targeting' of social security benefit, tougher sentences for criminals, de-regulation, competitive tendering, market testing, internal markets, purchaser/ provider splits, decentralised pay bargaining, private finance for public sector projects and opted-out schools.[6] It is a more or less complete list of the policies of the present government.

John Gray is not confident that a country ravaged by market economics can ever be at ease with itself. 'Human beings need, more than they need the freedom of consumer choice, a cultural and economic environment that offers them an acceptable level of security and in which they feel at home,' he writes.

'The challenge for thought and policy is that of abandoning once for all the project of any such [free market] utopia and of applying the genuine insights of conservative thought to the novel circumstances in which we find ourselves...for us, in Britain today, individualism and pluralism are an historical fate. We may reasonably hope to temper this fate, and thereby to make the best of the opportunities it offers us; we cannot hope to escape it.'[7] He argues that an unavoidable inheritance of free market economics must be turned into a new set of shared values. Accordingly, he advocates the introduction of a Citizen's Income – a basic national minimum income paid to all irrespective of need – and the adoption of protectionist policies to safeguard jobs from technological change and cheap foreign competition. He also favours tighter planning controls to protect cities from motor traffic and unsightly drive-in supermarkets, and the introduction of vouchers to make schools and welfare organisations more sensitive to families and 'communities'. His solution, in other words, is to subordinate the excesses of free market economics to expressly political control. This may or may not create a new moral consensus which can be called 'community.'[8]

In other words, for most advocates of community' politics, communitarian policies turn out to be the policies they would have adopted anyway. This is not surprising. 'Communities' do not exist. The new communitarianism shares the contradiction which bedevils all collectivist philosophies. It is that collective activities are not practicable much above the level of the family or the team-sport and even family life and team games are more readily comprehensible in terms of the individuals which make them up than any normal sense of the 'group'. Likewise, the 'community' has no objective reality except as a collection of individuals, whether or not they are members of the same club or working for the same employer. The term is harmless enough on the factory floor or the sports field. But once it is applied to political entities, as small as neighbourhoods or boroughs or as large as nations or continents, 'community' becomes an instrument of terrifying coercive power

This is because a community cannot exist beyond the unity of purpose of the individuals which make it up. Unity of purpose is maintained reasonably easily in a family or a cricket team but it is maintained only with the greatest of difficulty in any collection of individuals much larger than a rugby fifteen. At the level of the nation, it is maintained only by the coercive power of the State. Even during the two great wars of this century, when 'community' feelings were particularly intense, unity of purpose was maintained only by extensive State coercion of the individual. Over a third of the five million men who served in the First World War had to be forced to do so. There were massive expropriations of private property, through requisitioning, regulation and taxation, to prosecute and pay for the war. The standard rate of income tax was quintupled. Opponents of the war were jailed. Key workers were told where to go and what to do. Public houses were closed during working hours. The gravity of beer was reduced to save grain and prevent drunkenness. The price of food was fixed, and its distribution decided by the State. Strikes and lock-outs were declared illegal. 'Daylight saving' was introduced, giving the State control even over the time of day. Censorship and propaganda were used to manipulate public opinion, with government officials actively circulating lies and suppressing the truth to bolster unity of purpose. By the end of the First World War the State not only told people what to do, where to work, what to eat and drink, and how to spend their time and money. It told them what to think as well.

The Second World War, revered then as now by socialists as a great and highly instructive collective endeavour, was in reality the period when Britain came closest to totalitarianism. Male conscription was introduced immediately, and female conscription in 1941. The Minister of Labour was empowered to direct 'any person in the United Kingdom to perform any service required in any place'. By the end of the war, the daily lives of a quarter of the adult population were dictated by the State. Food was rationed from the outset, and distributed on generous terms only to those the State considered especially needy or meritorious. For the first time in British history, the standard rate of income tax made individual taxpayers minority shareholders in their own income. The higher rates reached 97½ per cent. Savings schemes were compulsory, and there was a forced sale of foreign private investments. Many innocent people were detained without trial. The press was censored, and recalcitrant newspapers closed down. Regional Commissioners, comparable with the gauleiters of Nazi Europe, were given sweeping powers over local government.

In war, the interests of the individual are rightly subordinated to those of the 'community' or the State. The mistake is to think that methods suitable to a dire national emergency – when the aim is to defeat the enemy, irrespective of the cost in individual life and liberty – are appropriate to peacetime conditions. As soon as the 'community' is deemed to be an objective reality with ends which are independent of and superior to those of the individuals which make it up, only those individuals which work for the same ends can properly be regarded as members of the 'community'. It follows that the dignity of individual men and women stems only from their membership of a group, and not from their individual humanity. They can earn the respect of others only by working for the collective aims and ends of the 'community'. This is an idea which comes straight from the German metaphysical tradition, in which the individual cannot properly 'realise' himself except as a member of a larger group. The whole species of totalitarian thought, from Rousseau to Rosenberg, is infected by metaphysical nonsense of this kind.[9] And it is the common philosophical thread which links not only fascism and communism, but all forms of modern communitarian thinking. Christian Socialism, High Toryism, One Nation Toryism, Civic Conservatism and Liberal Democracy – of the Paddy Ashdown kind as much as the Vladimir Zhirinovsky brand – share this common, disreputable origin.

The metaphysical properties of the idea of 'community' are apparent as soon as a description of a 'community' is attempted. An elderly and much-loved inhabitant of a village dies. Is it a 'community' which grieves for her, or her friends and fellow-villagers? What do journalists mean when they refer to the 'black community'? Does it include Africans as well as West Indians, Jamaicans as well as Barbadians, Pakistanis as well as Indians? When ill or elderly people are released into 'community care', can they expect a bed, food and care from a neighbourhood, or even a family or an individual? An impressive attempt by one pamphleteer to translate communitarian rhetoric into practical achievement exposes the same insubstantial qualities. No new realities are created by his proposals to make schools and colleges self-governing, or to switch political control of public services from Whitehall departments or borough councils to neighbourhood councils.

Creating 'communities' seems actually to consist of making existing entities – families, schools, colleges, housing associations, churches, employers, surgeries, family centres and charities – talk to each other,-perhaps electronically. Architectural modifications on council estates and in the municipal parks might impart a sense of communal ownership. Ordinary language proves incapable of capturing and describing the new reality which results, and the pamphlet expires eventually in the dispiriting jargon and diagrams of modern managerialism. In the end, the 'community' turns out to be individuals bringing up their children responsibly, becoming school governors, paying local taxes and supporting local charities, sweeping the street, serving on juries and the neighbourhood council, setting up development trusts and urban academies, and buying the modem which enables them to join the electronic 'community.'[10]

If there is one genuinely novel strand in communitarian thinking, it is a renewed interest in the means of politics rather than its ends. This is where the true purpose of the idea of 'community' becomes evident. Events in east and central Europe and repeated electoral defeats in this country have persuaded the majority of British collectivists of the popularity and usefulness of market economics, and of the impossibility of securing an electoral majority for a high-taxing, high-spending State of the traditional socialist kind. The redistribution of wealth through the electoral system over the last one hundred years has ended in a democratic impasse, in which shearers and shorn are of roughly equivalent size. It has become impossible to increase public expenditure or taxation, except at the margin, without courting electoral defeat.

The obvious solution to this conundrum is to alter the electoral system to make it more friendly towards high-taxing, high-spending political programmes. This explains the growing interest on the left of British politics in direct rather than representative democracy, in which voters pass their verdict on local or national spending programmes in a referendum rather than buying indiscriminate packages of policies from party representatives at periodic general elections. The same search for new ways to legitimise higher public expenditure and taxation animates the growing interest in regional devolution and in earmarked or hypothecated taxes, in which particular revenues are assigned to particular spending programmes. Local referendums, local taxes, and local spending projects blend easily with communitarian political ideas. This is why constitutional reform is the one firm policy commitment the modern Labour Party is prepared to make. 'Community' is an electorally useful euphemism for renewed State power.

Freedom versus Security

The idea of 'community' is either a meaningless metaphysical abstraction, a banal shorthand description of existing social realities, or a euphemism for State power. No coherent policy proposals can be derived from it. Its only appeal lies in its electoral usefulness. 'Community' offers an illusion of thought and vision at a time when virtually all politicians and political commentators agree that both are in short supply. But the truth is that the choice facing the country is a drearily familiar one. Policymakers are not staring into an intellectual and policy vacuum created by the collapse of socialism on the one hand, and the implosion of a failed experiment in market economics on the other. There is no political or electoral space waiting to be filled by a new notion of 'community', or any other innovative Big Idea or Vision Thing. The essential political choice is the same as it always was: freedom or security.

The appeal of the idea of 'community' lies precisely in its promise of security. Like all collectivist ideas, it is nostalgic, atavistic, backward-looking, irrational rather than rational. 'Community' is a safe and mythical place, where people can be free of redundancy notices, public expenditure cuts, failed examinations, vandalised telephone booths, teachers on strike, ram-raiders, burglaries, muggings, cheap imports, VAT on domestic fuel and all the other travails and tribulations of life in a modern urban civilisation. It is a place where people can lay down the burden of care and personal responsibility, and where they can set aside for a while their duty to use their powers of reason to improve their own lot. It is a place of peace, where the world and its ceaseless clamour of change will stop. Its significance is almost religious: 'Come unto me, all ye that labour and are heavy laden, and I will give you rest.'[11] Service to the community, to adapt the words of the collect, is perfect freedom.[12] That is the promise, as Karl Popper warned fifty years ago, of every millenarian and demagogue and totalitarian in history.

In the powerful closing passage of the first volume of *The Open Society and Its Enemies*, Popper explained why the temptations of the retreat into the security of the collective must be resisted:

> We can never return to the alleged innocence and beauty of the closed society. Our dream of heaven cannot be realised on earth. Once we begin to rely upon our reason, and to use our powers of criticism, once we feel the call of personal responsibilities, and with it, the responsibility of helping to advance knowledge, we cannot return to a state of implicit submission to tribal magic. For those who have eaten of the tree of knowledge, paradise is lost. The more we try to return to the heroic age of tribalism, the more surely do we arrive at the Inquisition, at the Secret Police, and at a romanticised gangsterism. Beginning with the suppression of reason and truth, we must end with the most brutal and violent destruction of all that is human. *There is no return to a harmonious state of nature. If we turn back, then we must go the whole way – we must return to the beasts.* It is an issue which we must face squarely, hard

though it may be for us to do so. If we dream of a return to our childhood, if we are tempted to rely on others and so be happy, if we shrink from the task of carrying our cross, the cross of humaneness, of reason, of responsibility, if we lose courage and flinch from the strain, then we must try to fortify ourselves with a clear understanding of the simple decision before us. We can return to the beasts. But if we wish to remain human, then there is only one way, the way into the open society. We must go on into the unknown, the uncertain and insecure, using what reason we may have to plan as well as we can for both security and freedom; [13]

It was once the chief glory of the English political genius to have devised just such a method. During the two centuries which separate the Glorious Revolution and the Third Reform Act it delivered unparalleled prosperity and, through its example, inspired most of the states of modern Europe and America.

The method is classical liberalism, or what used to be known as Whiggism. Its inventors and heroes were men like Edmund Burke, Thomas Babington Macaulay, William Gladstone, Alexis de Tocqueville, and Lord Acton. It was the creed to which Friedrich von Hayek confessed he properly belonged, in his famous postscript to *The Constitution of Liberty*, 'Why I am not a Conservative.'[14] Whiggism was overtaken by the rising tide of collectivism in the twentieth century, at first intellectually and then electorally. But its instincts and ideas are still there, awaiting rediscovery and redeployment by a new generation of imaginative men of public affairs. Its watchwords were Liberty, Property, Free Trade, Individualism, Capitalism. Its adherents believed in the value of Religion and Public Service, and in the application of an informed intelligence to the great political and social problems of the day. They favoured adaptation to new circumstances through the considered and piecemeal Reform of institutions; in private Charity over public Largesse; in Voluntarism, not Compulsion; in the Retrenchment of public expenditure, and the mitigation of Taxation; in the value of Education; in Prosperity, Peace and the morally responsible Individual. 'In truth, Whiggism is not a creed, it is a character,' wrote Walter Bagehot in the mid-Victorian heyday of Whiggery in 1855. 'Perhaps as long as there has been a political history in this country there have been certain men of a cool, moderate, resolute firmness, not gifted with high imagination, little prone to enthusiastic sentiment, heedless of large theories and speculations, careless of dreamy scepticism; with a clear view of the next step, and a wise intention to take it; a strong conviction that the elements of knowledge are true, and a steady belief that the present world can, and should be, quietly improved. These are the Whigs.'[15]

There is no instantaneous method by which the values and ideas of Whiggism can be insinuated once again into the British body politic. It is certain only that they cannot be revived without a drastic shrinkage of their twentieth-century Nemesis: the collectivist State. In Britain the State has grown slowly and discontinuously throughout the last hundred years, gradually devouring the spontaneous virtues and institutions which were the insignia of the ways of life of the British in their heroic age. The love of liberty; the respect for privacy; the pride, independence, character and individuality of ordinary men and women; the sense of personal responsibility, the preference for the private over the public; the gifts of enterprise, initiative and self-reliance; the deep-rooted respect for property; the toleration of the different and the eccentric; the distaste for grandiose political schemes; a Church wise enough to 'keep the Mean between Two Extremes'; the grammar schools and the independent Universities; the independent man of business; the friendly societies, the endowed charities, and the members-only club, are all going or gone, hammered flat and lifeless by the steamroller of the State. Even the fabled British sense of humour – author of the laugh which Ruskin called the 'purest and truest in the metal that can be minted' – no longer preserves *homo Anglianus* from the petty tyrannies of the politically correct. As the twentieth century draws to a close, ordinary British men and women are more coerced by the State than at any time in history.

The Despotism of Democracy

The paradox is that the British people do not feel themselves to be unfree. This is partly a matter of habituation. A man or woman would need to be over one hundred years old to have witnessed the whole of the period in which the State has encroached on private life, though the irruption was vastly accelerated by British involvement in the two global conflagrations of this century. Total war is a formidable engine for the extinction of liberty as well as life, making both coercion and death routine. It is also in the nature of the despotism under which the British people currently labour to appear beneficent. The liberal, majoritarian democracy of today appears to treat government as a matter of trial and error. It seems to regard all public institutions as pragmatic contrivances of fallible men, which change or get changed when they cease to work well. It is also thought to recognise that there are many different kinds of public and private endeavour and enterprise, and many areas of life which are personal rather than political or public. In short, the shape of the British democratic State appears spontaneous, historical, haphazard, accidental, happy-go-lucky and entirely lacking in despotic characteristics.

In fact, the modern British State has developed far more systematically than constitutional mythology suggests. Liberal democracy in Britain has been accompanied by a steady accretion of State power, egalitarianism and bureaucratic centralisation at the expense of individual liberty, private property and self-governing institutions. This is a second paradox, the paradox of democratic despotism. The phenomenon was first identified by the great liberal thinker, Alexis de Tocqueville, during his visit to the United States in the early 1830s. He admits himself that his attempt to compose a systematic presentation of democratic despotism, as he encountered it in the first liberal democracy on earth, does not entirely succeed. But it is still worth quoting:

The type of oppression which threatens democracies is different from anything there has ever been in the world before. Our contemporaries will find no prototype of it in their memories. I have myself vainly searched for a word which will exactly express the whole of the conception I have formed. Such old words as 'despotism' and 'tyranny' do not fit. The thing is new, and as I cannot find a word for it, I must try to define it. I am trying to imagine under what novel features despotism may appear in the world. In the first place, I see an innumerable multitude of men, alike and equal, constantly circling around in pursuit of the petty and banal pleasures with which they glut their souls. Each one of them, withdrawn into himself, is almost unaware of the fate of the rest. Mankind, for him, consists in his children and his personal friends. As for the rest of his fellow citizens, they are near enough, but he does not notice them. He touches them but feels nothing. He exists in and for himself, and though he still may have a family, one can at least say that he has not got a fatherland. Over this kind of men stands an immense, protective power which is alone responsible for securing their enjoyment and watching over their fate. That power is absolute, thoughtful of detail, orderly, provident, and gentle. It would resemble parental authority if, father-like, it tried to prepare its charges for a man's life, but on the contrary, it only tries to keep them in perpetual childhood. It likes to see the citizens enjoy themselves, provided that they think of nothing but enjoyment. It gladly works for their happiness but wants to be sole agent and judge of it. It provides for their security, foresees and supplies their necessities, facilitates their pleasures, manages their principal concerns, directs their industry, makes rules for their testaments, and divides their inheritances. Why should it not entirely relieve them from the trouble of thinking and all the cares of living? Thus it daily makes the exercise of free choice less useful and rarer, restricts the activity of free will within a narrower compass, and little by little robs each citizen of the proper use of his own faculties. Equality has prepared men for all this, predisposing them to endure it and often even regard it as beneficial. Having thus taken each citizen in turn in its powerful grasp and shaped him to its will, government then extends its embrace to include the whole of society. It covers the whole of social life with a network of petty, complicated rules that are both minute and uniform, through which even men of the greatest originality and the most vigorous temperament cannot force their heads above the crowd. It does not break men's will, but softens, bends, and guides it; it seldom enjoins, but often inhibits, action; it does not destroy anything, but prevents much being born; it is not at all tyrannical, but it hinders, restrains, enervates, stifles and stultifies so much that in the end each nation is no more than a flock of timid and hardworking animals with the government as its shepherd.[16]

De Tocqueville foresaw the creation of a Leviathan which would consume all intermediate sources of economic and social power and turn individual citizens into soulless employees and pensioners of the State. The democratic despotism has not turned out exactly like that. De Tocqueville could not have foreseen the role played by the giant but private bureaucratic corporations, which, by trapping people in nine-to-five routines, PAYE and occupational pensions, have become the handmaiden of the over-mighty State.'[17] The passage is still a remarkably prescient description of the workings of the modern democratic process.

The retention of power in a liberal democracy depends upon a constant sensitivity to the minutest cares and concerns of the electorate. The government endeavours to spare its citizens the need to husband their own resources against hard times; to educate their children; tend their sick; regulates the terms and conditions of their employment; and floods their workplaces, shops and streets with laws, regulations, officials, policemen and cameras to insulate them from the chance of accident, robbery, assault, or death. Even the private household is not immune to inspection by the State, whose officials are empowered to check the quality of the brickwork, the windows and the doors for signs of shoddy workmanship or fire hazards.

'Housewives as a whole cannot be trusted to buy all the right things where nutrition and health are concerned,' wrote Douglas Jay in 1939, in a remark which remains the most candid statement of the new despotism. 'This is really no more than an extension of the principle according to which the housewife herself would not trust a child of four to select the week's purchases. For in the case-of nutrition and health, just as in the case of education, the gentleman in Whitehall really does know better what is good for people than the people know themselves."[18] The man in Whitehall still knows best what people should eat. In November 1994 the little-known Committee on Medical Aspects of Food Policy published a list of dietary recommendations whose detail extended to the advice that people eat 31½ slices of bread a week, and make sure that seven of them are wholemeal.

Democracy, because it teaches men to value security more highly than freedom, encroaches on liberty piecemeal, slowly, unseen and in a beneficent guise, applying a remedy to each grievance, meeting each claim and solving every problem without regard for the freedoms it consumes. This makes it even more dangerous than more overt forms of tyranny. 'It is seldom,' warned David Hume, 'that liberty of any kind is lost all at once.' The social worker, the traffic warden, the ubiquitous 'counsellor', the hygiene policeman, the health and safety inspector, the borough surveyor, the health warning, the fluoridation of water, the sex education booklet, the helmet laws, anal dilatation technique, Satanic abuse and the motorway camera are all characteristic inventions of the liberal democratic State.

Its sensitivity to every need and whim of its charges has given to modern politics a Pavlovian aspect. After some horrifying attacks on children by Rottweilers, the decree went forth from the Home Office that all such animals were to be slain. The so-called Hungerford massacre was followed by sweeping controls over the ownership and distribution of guns. The threatened Prime Ministerial 'crackdown' has become the standard Downing Street response to virtually any instance of public unease. But democratic despotism does its most ruinous work through the constant but unseen pressure it exerts on the whole of the political system to remedy each subtraction from human happiness as and when it appears. Contrary to popular wisdom, British politicians are not 'out of touch' with the voters. Nor do they refuse to listen. On the contrary, they are constantly in touch with the voters, and listen to them obsessively.

The Unlimited Power of the Democratic State

It is a second characteristic of modern liberal democracy to be impatient of any constitutional obstacles to the immediate satisfaction of the demands of the voters. A majoritarian democracy is not constrained by any theory of the role and limits of government. The democratic State, armed with the unanswerable mandate of a majority of the people, is merely a mechanism for enacting the popular will. It was for this reason that the earliest socialists welcomed the advent of democracy, since the majority of voters were bound to support candidates promising a redistribution of wealth. 'It appears to me,' wrote the Fabian Sidney Webb in 1892, 'that if you allow the tramway conductor to vote he will not forever be satisfied with exercising that vote over such matters as the appointment of the Ambassador to Paris, or even the position of the franchise. He will realise that the forces which keep him at work for sixteen hours a day for three shillings a day are not the forces of hostile kings, of nobles, of priests; but whatever forces they are he will, it seems to me, seek so far as possible to control them by his vote. That is to say, he will more and more seek to convert his political democracy into what one may roughly term an industrial democracy, so that he may obtain some kind of control as a voter over the conditions under which he lives.'[19] Equality, as Sidney Webb explained, is merely the economic obverse of democracy.

This is not always understood. Democracy and liberty are often juxtaposed, as if they mean the same thing. But democracy is in fact the ally not of liberty but of equality, or what is sometimes called 'positive liberty'.[20] Most modern politicians, but particularly those of a collectivist inclination, see the State not as a tool for protecting people from things but as a device for enabling people to do things or become things. This is what Tony Blair means when he promises to use Society to advance the Individual, or the Liberal Democrats are saying when they promise to make 'everybody a somebody'. They want to give people freedom to do things by redistributing wealth in both cash (through tax or social security benefits) and kind (through health, education, training and other public services). Some socialist thinkers even believe that economic needs can be turned into legally enforceable welfare 'rights' with the same power of enforcement as civil and political rights such as the right to vote or freedom of speech.'[21] Social security, education and free health care are obvious candidates for this kind of treatment, and the plausibility of the idea has to some extent been admitted already. Industrial tribunals and statutory redundancy payments, for example, do make a partial reality of the legally enforceable job.

When the Labour Party set about reformulating its aims and values in 1985 the ideas of democracy and 'positive' liberty were the ones the Party's thinkers chose, and yoked together. Shortly before the 1987 general election the then deputy leader of the Labour Party, Roy Hattersley, published a book whose title, *Choose Freedom*, embodied both ideas. 'The true object of socialism,' read its opening sentence, 'is the creation of a genuinely free society in which the protection and extension of individual liberty is the primary duty of the State.'[22] He was in fact writing not about liberty at all, but equality.

A more equal distribution of wealth, achieved peacefully through the democratic system, was probably necessary, if only to avoid a sudden and violent expropriation of the rich by the poor. But democratic egalitarianism has also overturned completely the traditional British conception of the State, detaching it from the values which formally constrained the reach of its power. All of the classical liberal thinkers – Thomas Hobbes, John Locke, David Hume, Adam Smith, Edmund Burke – thought that the proper role of the State was not to arbitrate in the distribution of wealth but to protect the lives and possessions of people from expropriation by others. In their minds, individual liberty and private property were not at war with each other but inextricably linked. Unless a man or woman could control their own wealth, and transfer it to others, prosperity was a chimera and liberty a myth. The ownership of private property conferred power economic power – and it was because it dispersed that power among many millions of individuals that no one person or institution could accumulate an overwhelming concentration of power. Economic independence also gave men the confidence to express their personal values and ideals, even when these were antipathetic to the interests of the prevailing political order.

It is customary now to see the right to own property as merely one among several rights which make up the classical or 'negative' conception of liberty. It ranks alongside equality before the law, immunity from arbitrary arrest and freedom of movement and labour in the litany of rights which limit the ability of the democratic State to interfere with the private life of the individual. But this disaggregation is new. Locke and the other classical liberal thinkers saw liberty and property as indissoluble and interchangeable. They referred routinely to their 'propriety', by which they meant all the properties that made up their individuality.[23] Locke did not see property merely as the ownership of possessions but as the 'lives, liberties and estates' of each and every citizen. Liberties like freedom of speech were not civil rights granted by the State but natural rights actually owned by the individuals prior to the establishment of the State.[24] Their only reason for agreeing to submit to the State was its pledge to protect these natural rights from others, and their obligation to the State ceased at the point where the government failed to uphold them. Agreeing to live under a State which took away the natural rights it was set up to defend was, in the words of Locke, 'too gross an absurdity for any man to own'.[25]

The modern democratic State, by contrast, has dispensed with the tiresome constraint of natural rights. Its role is not to uphold the high doctrine that men have rights which are granted to them by Nature rather than the State. It is the humdrum, utilitarian task of finding out what most people want, and giving it to them. The purpose of government, in the estimation of the utilitarian school, is merely 'the greatest happiness of the greatest number'. Its chief advocate, Jeremy Bentham, dismissed the whole of the natural rights argument as an 'anarchical fallacy'. If private property was a natural right, he argued, the State could not raise taxes to pay for the upholding of the law to protect property and there would be no property. It is this view – that property is the creation of the State, and not a natural right of man – which has prevailed in the twentieth century. Once property was seen as a creation of man-made laws it was open to expropriation by the State, since State-made laws can be changed by the State. It effectively reduced the rule of law to whatever a passing Parliamentary majority decided it was and, by exposing the whole of the national wealth to expropriation by the State, equipped modern government with formidable economic power. Any private asset or practice or institution which made enough people unhappy could be remedied by State taxes, laws or regulations. This was the great gift of utilitarianism to socialism. 'The individual has no absolute rights,' wrote one of the main authors of English socialism, R. H. Tawney. 'They are derived from the end or purpose of the society in which they exist.'[26]

The Benthamite attack on natural rights transformed the role of the law. It was no longer rooted in natural rights, but merely a system of man-made rules backed by the coercive powers of the State with no need for justification by any external criterion. This was probably the most significant institutional change in Britain between the Angevins and Queen Victoria. As Geoffrey Elon put it:

> Until the nineteenth century, the law had been thought of as an independent force within the organising of life and of rights, independent of other aspects of society and absolute in its claims over its own area of operation. In the wake of Benthamite reform it came to be changed conceptually into an instrument of social control in the hands of government, at the service of whatever larger social purposes might be thought desirable at any given time. The sceptre turned into a screwdriver…The law became a weapon for winning whatever new theory and new people's power asked to see put through.[27]

Law – which from medieval times aimed solely to guarantee to every individual his life, liberty and property – was transformed from an independent standard of justice into a mere instrument of government, to be judged only by the standards of democratic legitimacy (was it passed by a duly elected Parliament?) and social utility (does it make more people happy than unhappy?).

Unprincipled Government by Experts

It is these changed conceptions of the role of the State and of the nature of the law which have, despite occasional appearances to the contrary, made the government of Britain a technocratic rather; than a political business. It is a recurrent curiosity of British politics that people believe them to be needlessly adversarial, when in fact the differences between the major parties are invariably matters of form rather than substance. The adversarial myth is so deeply rooted in the English political psyche that Roy Jenkins and some former colleagues from the Labour Party started a new political party to put an end to it. Occasionally some other political gadfly, usually from the world of business, will appear to promise that he will form a new political party which will choose ideas on their merits rather than their ideological approval rating. But he is too late. It is already being done. Those commentators who disparage current politics as not adversarial enough have mistaken a norm for an aberration. They attribute the 'managerial' nature of modern politics, in which the major parties seem to exist only to seek office, to the demise of ideology in the wake of the material, moral and intellectual collapse of socialism. In fact, the utilitarians drained British politics of ideology a century and a half ago.

Modern Britain was and is governed by a utilitarian clique of intellectuals, politicians and officials who rarely view problems in the light of fundamental values or principles, and who regard disagreement as an inevitable but ultimately escapable hindrance to the making of compromises. The business of government, for this class, is a matter of management – adjusting expenditure, administering policy, fine-tuning regulations – without reference to awkward superstitions like natural rights or the principle of liberty. They, not the ideologues, are the principal architects of the gargantuan State. 'The only rational foundation of government,' argued one of the early Victorian pioneers of the utilitarian approach to government, Nassau Senior, 'is expediency- the general benefit of the community. It is the duty of a government to do whatever is conducive to the welfare of the governed.'[28] This is a surprisingly powerful formula for increasing State interference in the private lives of individuals.

The reformist public officials of the early Victorian period, like Edwin Chadwick, James Kay-Shuttleworth and Nassau Senior, were inspired directly by the prevailing Benthamite orthodoxy. They regarded themselves as practical men engaged in the solution of practical problems, commissioning surveys and reports to ascertain the facts on which effective legislation could be based. It meant that, even at the height of the era of *laissez-faire*, experts an: officials were engaged in an unnoticed and unplanned expansion of the power of the State. The private telegraph system, for example, was nationalised as early as 1869, purely on grounds of efficiency.[29] The socialist Fabians, popularly associated with the creeping municipalisation of private life and enterprise in late Victorian Britain, in fact drew on a long tradition of official busybodying. They too used surveys, and particularly the sociological investigations of men like Charles Booth and Seebohm Rowntree, to decide policy from facts rather than principles. Booth was a wealthy shipowner who devoted a large part of his life to compiling a factual survey of work and poverty in London, convinced that if the facts were uncovered he could devise more 'efficient' ways of relieving poverty.[30] It was Booth who erased the old distinction between the deserving and the undeserving poor by inventing relative deprivation, or the 'poverty line'. Rowntree was of similar ilk. A pioneer of 'scientific' management techniques and industrial welfare, he thought industry could be made more efficient by making it more human. The social historian Harold Perkin has charted the gradual emergence in England from 1880 of what he calls the Professional Society. He argues that State aggrandisement was both a characteristic expression of a 'professional' social ideal and the specific creation of a group of self-appointed professional experts – politicians, social thinkers and civil servants like the Webbs, Robert Morant, William Beveridge and others drawn from Tory imperialism as well as New Liberalism and Fabian Socialism whose consciences were affronted by the 'waste' and 'inefficiency' of unbridled capitalism.[31] All of the Edwardian social reforms like old age pensions, school meals and medical inspection, education, unemployment and health insurance, were devised and implemented by these essentially non-ideological experts. Maynard Keynes and Douglas Jay, who between them drew up complete blueprints for the post-war Welfare State and the demand-management economy, were drawn from the same intellectual tradition. They assumed that, through the application of their superior intellects to the social and economic problems of the day, they could make the free society and the capitalist economy more efficient. Keynes distrusted markets precisely because he trusted the application of disinterested expertise by a self-appointed elite. In economic policy he looked forward to the 'euthanasia of politics' and a 'willingness to entrust to science those things which are properly the concern of science'.

Keynes wanted, in the words of his biographer, to 'decentralise and devolve only down to the level of the Top People'.[32]

Contemporary socialists thought along the same lines. In *A Grammar of Politics*, published in 1925, Harold Laski argued that the complexities of the modern collectivist State were too great for its management to be left in the hands of amateurs:

> Any system of government, upon the modern scale, involves a body of experts working to satisfy vast populations who judge by the result and are careless of, even uninterested in, the processes by which these results are attained...A democracy in other words must, if it is to work, be an aristocracy by delegation.[33]

Morally speaking, men like Laski and Keynes were traditional English utilitarians. They saw the merits of an action entirely in its consequences, especially for the happiness of the greatest number, and not in terms of its motive or in the merits and demerits of its beneficiaries. Efficiency, not social justice, was their watchword. 'The case for socialism and planning in a free society,' wrote Douglas Jay in 1946, 'is nothing more than a plea for the application of reason and intelligence to the job of producing and distributing the good things of life.'[34]

The search for efficiency through the application of undistracted Reason to the practical problems of society and the economy was the main instrument in Britain of ever-increasing State involvement and ever-decreasing interest in the liberty of the individual. This was partly a matter of temperament. Economists, sociologists, politicians, civil servants and other members of the intellectual and policymaking elite are always more comfortable dealing with social groups and with society as a whole than they are with individuals and the Welfare State gave them ample scope for experiment. Many of the early socialist thinkers, like H. G. Wells, D. H. Lawrence and William Morris, were utterly contemptuous not only of the toiling proletarian masses on whose behalf they were struggling to inaugurate Utopia but also of their immediate circle of wives, friends, colleagues and girlfriends. Morris confessed in a lecture in 1879 as his wife slid into epilepsy, that he needed to be with others who 'meet to forget their own transient personal and family troubles in aspirations for their fellows and the days to come'.[35] Theirs was a special kind of telescopic philanthropy, which dabbled more than occasionally in eugenics and death camps as the final solution to the 'revolt of the masses'.[36]

The urge of self-appointed experts to interfere and to correct inefficiencies did not stop at unemployment, poverty, sickness and physiognomy. They wanted to run the economy too. In *The Acquisitive Society* (1920), a book which had a profound influence on post-war socialists of the Gaitskellite stamp, R. H. Tawney advocated the replacement of the chaos of the free market economy by a professionally managed alternative reorganised to perform its 'social functions' more efficiently:

> The application to industry of the principle of purpose is simple . . . It is to turn it into a Profession. A Profession may be defined most simply as a trade which is organised, incompletely, no doubt, but genuinely, for the performance of function . . . The difference between industry as it exists today and a profession is, then, simple and unmistakable. The former is organised for the protection of rights, mainly rights to pecuniary gain. The latter is organised, imperfectly indeed, but none the less genuinely, for the performance of duties.[37]

It is in the thinking of men like Tawney, with their desire for efficient management by disinterested elites, and not the wilder shores of Marxism-Leninism, to which can be traced the intellectual origins of the British economic holocaust – nationalisation, regional policy, economic planning, 'picking winners', and all the other forms of subsidy and intervention. 'Only if public ownership replaces private monopoly,' claimed the 1945 Labour Manifesto, 'can industry become efficient.'[38] The case for nationalisation was based primarily; upon the belief in its efficiency. The same brand of thinking secured British entry to the European Economic Community in 1972. At the time, the arguments adduced for British membership were almost entirely those of economic efficiency. Europe, it was argued, would promote growth and productivity in the British economy. Efficiency, not sovereignty, was the issue.

This unprincipled, utilitarian approach to policy questions is not limited to ministers and officials. A complete detachment from wider considerations is the chief characteristic of the modern solution-monger, and can be found just as easily among ostensibly independent observers of the political and administrative scene. A senior journalist on the *Financial Times*, for example, argued recently for the introduction of a national identity card. His case was as follows:

The absence of any recognised form of identity is an anachronism which harks back to some mythical bygone era when society was purely composed of private individuals. The reality today is a mass society where everybody has frequent, multiple and almost unavoidable transactions with different parts of the state system, and in which both sides of those transactions have an interest in being able to establish the identity of the individual. The libertarians try to scare us with the danger that a menacing police force would constantly be stopping people to check their identity cards, but this is just a trumped up bogey. In five years in France I was not stopped on the street for an identity check, and never met anyone who was. In place of this bogey, there may be other cases where an identity card system might actually improve the quality of civil society. Young blacks who could easily prove that they were born in Britain and were not illegal immigrants might be better protected against police harassment; and the rest of us might be better off if Irish terrorists found it more difficult to remain underground. For either of these benefits, I should gladly be prepared for the trivial inconvenience of being required to admit to my identity.[39]

This is an almost perfect example of the uncluttered professional policymaking mind at work. It is always a well-travelled mind, convinced that they do these things better abroad. It also knows of a minor administrative reform, from which immediate, concrete, politically correct and wholly congenial efficiencies will flow in exchange for some trifling infraction of liberty. But, if the era of the private individual is gone, it was certainly not mythical. A Victorian or Edwardian Englishman would not have looked to a revolutionist regime like France for political advice, and would have considered it contemptible to adopt the methods of a Salazar or a Mobutu to defeat terrorism. Nor would he have valued the public face of an individual more highly than his better and private self. 'Society' has always consisted of nothing but private individuals, and still does. They are just less private than they used to be, and for precisely the reason identified: the frequent, multiple and almost unavoidable transactions they have with the State. The proper task of politicians today is not to facilitate those transactions, but to reduce their number and frequency.

The Propriety of the Individual

'This nation,' wrote Montesquieu of the eighteenth-century English, 'is passionately fond of liberty.'[40] It is difficult to believe the same of a country in which the members of the ruling party submit to their annual conference nearly fifty separate resolutions calling for the introduction of a national identity card, and then heckle the Home Secretary for shilly-shallying when he proposes the introduction of a voluntary scheme. A formidable array of advantages is adduced reductions in crime, savings in social security fraud, less under-age drinking, fewer illegal immigrants, a smaller number of cards to carry and so on – which is liable to reduce anyone not prepared to sacrifice liberty to administrative convenience to the status of a criminal, a drunk, an illegal immigrant or a crank.

Yet the introduction of a national identity card would be the biggest extension of State power since the introduction of income tax. A card incorporating modern data-storage technology would allow State officials instant access to tax, welfare, educational, criminal, driving, employment, marital and personal financial records. It is an apt measure of the degradation of the British political character by the democratic, egalitarian and utilitarian State that such a powerful instrument of social control should actually be popular.

A political culture more hospitable to individual liberty will take time to create. It is tempting to believe that the limits to State power can be codified in a single constitutional document, like a Bill of Rights. This solution appears to attack the problem directly, by distinguishing between means and ends. Democracy is a method but liberty is a principle and, as a method, democracy is highly corrosive of the principle of liberty. Since democracy is thought to place power in the hands of the people, the powers of the democratic State are theoretically unlimited, unless they are divided or constrained. The ability of an elected Parliament to claim the sovereignty of the people means that an interfering liberal democracy may actually curtail liberty to a far greater extent than a monarch, an oligarchy or even a dictator. It is not inconceivable that an electorate might consent unanimously to the extinction of all their remaining liberties. Without an alternative source of constitutional power like a supreme court, or a Bill of Rights which gave citizens legally enforceable claims against the State, nothing could alter the fact that liberty had been destroyed.

A new constitutional settlement that entrenched individual rights, and made them enforceable through a proper separation of powers, appears to resolve the democratic paradox that no rights can be above the law because it is the State which makes the law. In effect, utilitarian democracy replaced the rule of law by the rule of arbitrary power and discretionary authority. A Bill of Rights promises to restore the rule of law by ensuring that governments cannot exercise power without express regard to rights that are outside, above and independent of the law. These expectations are vain. The pressure to include an immense variety of welfare and other politically correct social and economic 'rights' would be irresistible. It is in practice impossible to limit the civil and political rights described in such a document to traditional natural rights. A modern Bill of Rights would not limit the power of the State but would enlarge the claims that citizens can make upon it.

Any attempt in a modern democracy to write down the rights of individuals, and to establish institutions to enforce them, would be self-defeating. Individual rights need to be imbued with moral, not constitutional, power, and entrenched in the hearts and minds of men and women. This is not as remote a prospect as it seems. All reasonable people can see that murder; rape an theft are wrong, without the need to consult a statute book that lists them as criminal offences. In other words, the rights to life, liberty and prosperity are the essential rights that the State must guarantee. But making them a vital part of a new political culture will involve a fundamental change in mentality, of precisely the opposite kind to that indicated by the current enthusiasm for the specious idea of 'community'.

If people are to be treated as ends, and not as means, the only true repository of rights is the individual. The individual has three great rights, which are sacred from arbitrary interference by the State. These are the right to life, the right to liberty and the right to property. They are indivisible. To allow a man to live, but to deny him his liberty, is to rob his life of meaning. To give him liberty, but expropriate his property, is to make his liberty meaningless. These three rights are in practice one right, which Locke and seventeenth century contemporaries called Propriety. Propriety is not as peculiar or anachronistic an idea as it at first seems. The word property was once synonymous with nature. In the Book of Common Prayer, for example, mercy was a 'property' of God. The term personality, now used to describe the distinctive characteristics which give an individual his or her personal existence and identity, was originally used by lawyers to describe personal possessions. They still use the term personality to describe the personal belongings of an individual. The things which a person owns – his car, or his books, or his CD collection – are always expressions of a distinctive personality. Propriety captures in a single word the absolute necessity of life, liberty and property to the full flowering of each irreplaceable human personality.

Robert Nozick used a similar idea of 'self-ownership' to show that all rights are property rights, only individuals can have property rights, and that property rights cannot be eroded by the State without infringing the rights of individuals. In the preface to his influential *Anarchy, State and Utopia*, Nozick wrote:

Individuals have rights, and there are things no person or group may do to them (without violating their rights). So strong and far-reaching are these rights that they raise the question of what, if anything, the State and its officials may do. How much room do individual rights leave for the State? . . . Our main conclusions about the State are that a minimal State, limited to the narrow functions of protection against force, theft, fraud, enforcement of contracts, and so on, is justified; that any more extensive State will violate persons' rights not to be forced to do certain things, and is unjustified; and that the minimal State is inspiring as well as right. Two noteworthy implications are that the State may not use its coercive apparatus for the purpose of getting some citizens to aid others, or in order to prohibit activities to people for their own good or protection.[41]

One result of Nozick's theory is to demonstrate that the taxation of earned income is on a par with forced labour. But his ultimate conclusion is more striking. To the extent that the State coerces people through redistributive taxation it is acquiring a right of property in the individuals concerned.[42] Through taxation, the State actually begins to possess the individual.

Propriety, or self-ownership, is the most plausible grounding for natural rights in a modern liberal democratic state. In a sense, the rediscovery of Propriety would mark no more than a return to the Whig tradition of British politics. Some think that such a journey, like time-travel, can be made only in the mind. John Gray is fond of quoting Wittgenstein's remark that 'trying to repair a broken tradition is like a man trying to mend a broken spider's web with his bare hands'. But this is precisely the kind of High Tory pessimism which the Whigs – with their clear view of the next step, and wise intention to take it – have always rejected. The idea of working towards a country of free, propertied individuals, governing their own choices and behaviour by a compelling personal code of morals, is not a doomed attempt to re-create the past but a powerful vision of the future. It cannot take root in the heart and mind until it has become a part of the daily routine, and that will not happen until the State embarks on a wholesale retreat from the positions it now occupies in the private lives of ordinary men and women. This book analyses how the State came to occupy the country of the mind as well as of the flesh, in order to understand how best to expunge it. It proposes a series of initial steps towards the realisation of a nation of individuals who prize self-ownership, self-reliance, self-control and self-government as the highest of political virtues. It was written in the knowledge that it will take far longer to build the new tradition than it took to destroy the old one but it is, at bottom, a work of hope and not of despair.

References

1   John Stuart Mill, Principles of Political Economy, Books IV and V, Penguin Classics Edition, 1985, pages 3113.
2   Alexis de Tocqueville, Democracy in America, translated by George Lawrence and edited by J. P. Mayer, Fontana, 1994, page 695.
3   Walter Bagehot, Introduction to the 1872 Edition, in The English Constitution, Fontana, 1973, page 277.
4   John Gray, The Undoing of Conservatism, The Social Market Foundation, June 1994, page 7.
5   David Willetts, Modern Conservatism, Penguin, 1992, pages 94-5.
6   David Willetts, Civic Conservatism, The Social Market Foundation, June 1994, pages 39–53.
7   John Gray, The Undoing of Conservatism, The Social Market Foundation, June 1994, pages 30 and 39.
8   The Undoing of Conservatism, pages 414.
9   See Chapter 8, pages 197-207.
10   Dick Atkinson, The Common Sense of Community, Demos, 1994.
11   Matthew 11:28.
12   Book of Common Prayer, Order for Morning Prayer, Second Collect, for Peace.
13   K. R. Popper, The Open Society and Its Enemies, Volume 1: Plato, Routledge & Kegan Paul, 1984, pages 200–1.
14   'The more I learn about the evolution of ideas, the more I have become aware that I am simply an unrepentant Old Whig.' See F. A. Hayek, 'Why I am not a Conservative', in The Constitution of Liberty, Routledge, 1960, page 409.
15   From 'The First Edinburgh Reviewers', National Review, 1855, quoted in Ruth Dudley-Edwards, The Best of Bagehot, Hamish Hamilton, 1993, page 264
16   Alexis de Tocqueville, Democracy in America, translated by George Lawrence and edited by J. P. Mayer, Fontana, 1994, pages 691–2.
17   See Chapters 7 and 8.
18   Douglas Jay, The Socialist Case, Faber & Faber, 1946, page 258.
19   Quoted in Bentley B. Gilbert, The Evolution of National Insurance in Great Britain: The Origins of the Welfare State, Michael Joseph, 1966, pages 25-6.
20   See Isaiah Berlin, 'Two Concepts of Liberty', in Four Essays on Liberty, OUP, 1992,

pages 130-1.

21   See Raymond Plant, 'Citizenship and Rights', in Citizenship and Rights in Thatcher's Britain: Two Views, pages 3–32, IEA Health and Welfare Unit, June 1990. The belief that social and economic 'rights' can be added to civil and political rights is partially grounded in a traditional socialist medievalism. C. B. Macpherson, who was an enthusiast for legally enforceable welfare rights, likened them to the just prices, usury laws, detailed social hierarchies and State monopolies of the medieval economy. See C. B. Macpherson, The Rise and Fall of Economic Justice and Other Essays, OUP, 1987, page 83. See also Chapter 6.

22   See Colin Hughes and Patrick Wintour, Labour Rebuilt: The New Model Party, Fourth Estate, 1990, pages 64–75.

23   Hobbes described the laws of property as 'Rules, whereby every man may know, what Goods he may enjoy and what Actions he may doe without being molested by any of his fellow subjects: And this is it men call Propriety.' Quoted in C. B. Macpherson, The Rise and Fall of Economic Justice and Other Essays, OUP, 1987, page 143.

24   Alan Ryan, Property and Political Theory, Blackwell, 1984, page 22.

25   John Locke, Two Treatises of Government, II, Sections 134–8, quoted in The Locke Reader: Selections From the Works of John Locke, edited by John W. Yolton, CUP, 1977, pages 303–4

26   R. H. Tawney, The Acquisitive Society, G. Bell & Sons, 1922, pages 53–4.

27   Geofrey Elton, The English, Blackwell, 1992, pages 232–3.

28   Quoted in Derek Fraser, The Evolution of the British Welfare State, Second Edition, Macmillan, 1984, page 120.

29   S. G. Checkland, The Rise of Industrial Society in England 1815–1885, Longman, 1964, page 17

30   'Booth,' writes Bentley Gilbert, 'taught the entire nation to be practical, rather than sentimental, about poverty.' See Bentley B. Gilbert, The Evolution of National Insurance in Great Britain: The Origins of the Welfare State, Michael Joseph, 1966, page 56.

31   Harold Perkin, The Rise of Professional Society: England Since 1880, Routledge, 1989, pages 155-70

32   Robert Slidelsky, John Maynard Keynes: The Economist As Saviour 1920–1937, Macmillan, 1992, page 228.

33   Quoted in Harold Perkin, The Rise of Professional Society: England Since 1880, Routledge, 1989, page 393.

34   Douglas Jay, The Socialist Case, Faber & Faber, 1946, pages 278-9.

35   Fiona MacCarthy, William Morris: A Life for Our Time, Faber & Faber, 1994, page 371

36   See, for example, John carey, The Intellectuals and the Masses: Pride and Prejudice Among the Literay Intelligentsia 1880–1939, Faber & Faber, 1992.

37   R. H. Tawney, The Acquisitive Society, G. Bell & Sons, 1922, pages 106–8.

33   Quoted in Cento Veljanovski, Selling the State: Privatisation in Britain, Weidenfeld & Nicolson, 1988, page 52.

39   Financial Times, 27 October 1993.

40   From The Spirit of the Laws. Quoted by Alan Macfarlane, The Origins of English Individualism, Blackwell, 1979, pages 168 9.

41   Robert Nozick, Anarchy, State and Utopia, Blackwell, 1974, page ix. 4

42   'End-state and most patterned principles of distributive justice institute (partial) ownership by others of people and their actions and labour. These principles involve a shift from the classical liberals' notion of self-ownership to a notion of (partial) property rights in other people.' See Robert Nozick, Anarchy, State and Utopia, Blackwell, 1974, page 172.

PART ONE

The Loss of Liberty

CHAPTER TWO

The Rise of Public Expenditure

It is the mark of a chicken-hearted Chancellor when he shrinks from upholding economy in detail...He is not worth his salt if he is not ready to save what are meant by candle-ends and cheese-parings in the cause of the country.

W. E. Gladstone, ex-Liberal Prime Minister, 1874[1]

Nervos belli, pecuniam infinitam.
The sinews of war, unlimited money.

Cicero

A spirit of public extravagance is a great moral and material canker, which during the course of the twentieth century has spread to all parts of the British body politic. Throughout the eighteenth and nineteenth centuries it was axiomatic that public expenditure was confined to the defence of the realm, the maintenance of internal law and order, the servicing of the national debt, certain local government infrastructural projects and the relief of some forms of social distress. The need for economy in public expenditure was not seriously disputed by either of the main political parties, and Parliamentary exchanges were confined mainly to the best means of financing regrettable but unavoidable spending. The classical truism about British public finance - that expenditure determines policy- indicated that expenditure should be reduced, to ensure policy was directed by politicians rather than by its beneficiaries. 'The cost of any policy,' argued Gladstone, 'would generally be about the sole element in deciding its desirability.'[2]

It was the collectivist thinkers who emerged from the 1880s who first peddled the delusion that policy could determine expenditure, even in the long run. As Table 1 shows, as late as 1890 the government spent less than 9 per cent of the national income, well down from its nineteenth-century peak of 29 per cent at the height of the Napoleonic Wars in 1814. A large proportion of even this modest figure was devoted to the defence of the empire, and the repayment of debts incurred in the past. Once defence and interest on the national debt are excluded, the State of 1890 spent just 5 per cent of the national income.[3] If grants and transfers to the private sector are excluded, the State actually 'consumed' just 6.7 per cent of the national income. Table 1 also shows how rapidly this modest role was expanded over the three decades which separate the assassination of the Archduke Franz Ferdinand from the dropping of the first atomic bomb on Hiroshima. The proportion of the national income pre-empted by the State climbed from 12.4 per cent on the eve of the First World War to 24.2 per cent in 1923, 30 per cent in 1938, and 40.6 per cent in 1948. Between 1890 and 1948 public expenditure rose by 78.5 per cent in real terms, eighteen times as fast as the growth of real output and twenty-four times as fast as the increase in the population.[4] It was an astonishing transformation in a remarkably short period, and one which owed remarkably little to conscious political choices by voters or governments.

The Sinews of War

Public expenditure on the modern scale is largely the creation of the two extraordinary national emergencies between 1914 and 1918 and 1939 and 1945. As Table 1 shows, the growth in public expenditure was not a steady aggrandisement but rather a series of plateaus, each higher than the last, separated by periodic jumps in the volume; of government spending around each of the major conflicts of the twentieth century. Total public expenditure rose eight-fold from £305.4 million in 1913 to £2,427 million in 1918, or from an eighth of the national income to nearly half of it. It increased six-fold during the Second World War from £1 billion in 1938-39 to over £6 billion in 1944-45, or from just over a quarter to nearly two thirds of the national income.[5]

But warfare is expensive not only while it continues. It also leaves a legacy of indebtedness which can only be fully discharged through taxation or inflation (another form of tax) long after peace is agreed.

The sale of assets, the death and mutilation of potentially productive labour, the destruction of property and the burden of war pensions and compensation schemes reduce taxable wealth at just the time when a dire national emergency also makes possible taxes which were previously politically unthinkable, and so enlarges the taxable capacity of the country. Wars also uncover social problems, like poverty and poor health and education, which appear to be susceptible to State action. Both the Boer War and the First World War exposed the unhealthy and malnourished condition of much of the urban working class. The combination of new social facts with the overriding need to formulate exciting war aims then encourages political leaders to promise to build Utopia once victory is assured. The Foreign Secretary, Lord Halifax, gave this account of a discussion with Ernest Bevin and others about using the promise of social reforms to bolster morale at the beginning of the Second World War:

> We were all conscious as the talk proceeded of the contrast between the readiness of the Nation, and particularly of the Treasury, to spend £9 million a day in war to protect a certain way of life and the unwillingness of the administrative authorities in peace to put up, shall we say, £10 million to assist in the reconditioning of Durham unless they could see

the project earning a reasonable percentage.[6]

Table 1   General Government Expenditure From 1890 to 1931[1]

Year	GDP At Market Prices	GGE At Market Prices	GGE As a Per Cent of GDP	Year	GDP At Market Prices	GGE At Market Prices	GGE As a Per Cent of GDP
1890	1,473	130.6	8.9	1944	10,272	6,307	61.4
1891	1,496	136.1	9.1	1945	9,831	5,781	58.8
1892	1,489	142.9	9.6	1946	9,959	4,587	46.1
1893	1 459	145.9	10.0	1947	10,655	4,184	39.3
1894	1 541	154.1	10.0	1948	11,835	4,381	37.0
1895	1,548	156.8	10.1	1949	12,565	4,459	35.5
1896	1 631	184.3	11.3	1950	13,112	4,522	34.5
1897	1 620	204.1	12.6	1951	14,612	5,371	36.8
1898	1,738	231.1	13.3	1952	15,764	5,962	37.8
1899	1,871	258.2	13.8	1953	16,906	6,172	36.5
1900	1 932	280.8	14.5	1954	17,890	6,145	34.3
1901	2054	.277.3	13.5	1955	19,304	6,466	33.5
1902	2,016	266.1	13.2	1956	20,766	7,041	33.9
1903	1 995	257.4	12.9	1957	21,920	7,633	34.8
1904	2028	251.5	12.4	1958	22,853	7,971	34.9
1905	2,092	241.7	11.6	1959	24,213	8,461	34.9
1906	2,116	247.6	11.7	1960	25,887	8,944	34.6
1907	2156	254.4	11.8	1961	27,432	9,756	35.6
1908	2119	264.9	12.5	1962	28,812	10,400	36.1
1909	2,168	268.8	12.4	1963	30,586	10,979	35.9
1910	2,223	272.0	12.2	1964	33,435	12,007	35.9
1911	2,328	284.0	12.2	1965	36,035	13,322	37.0
1912	2,380	295.1	12.4	1966	38,370	14,474	37.7
1913	2,535	305.4	12.0	1967	40,400	16,684	41.3
1914	2 540	624.8	24.6	1968	43,808	18,307	41.8
1915	3 392	958.1	28.2	1969	47,153	19,030	40.4
1916	3,770	1,297	34.4	1970	51,770	20,918	40.4
1917	4,642	1,515	32.6	1971	57,748	23,529	40.7
1918	5,378	2,427	45.1	1972	64,663	26,453	40.9
1919	5,598	–	–	1973	74,257	30,540	41.4
1920	5,845	1,592	27.2	1974	83,862	39,264	46.8
1921	5134	1,430	27.9	1975	105,852	51.560	48.7
1922	4 579	1,177	25.7	1976	125,247	58,651	46.8
1923	4,385	1,025	23.4	1977	145,983	62,027	42.5
1924	4,419	1,027	23.2	1978	168,526	72,431	43.0
1925	4,644	1,072	23.1	1979	198,221	85,729	43.2
1926	4,396	1,106	25.2	1980	231,772	104,290	45.0
1927	4,613	1,106	23.9	1981	254,927	117,101	45.9
1928	4 659	1,095	23.5	1982	279,041	128,755	46.1
1929	4 727	1,107	23.4	1983	304,456	138,521	45.5
1930	4,685	1,145	24.4	1984	325,852	147,305	45.2
1931	4,359	1,174	26.9	1985	357,344	157,851	44.2
1932	4,276	1,138	26.6	1986	384,843	162,431	42.2
1933	4,259	1,066	25.0	1987	423,381	169,331	40.0
1934	4,513	1,061	23.5	1988	471,430	178,319	37.8
1935	4 721	1,11	23.7	1989	515,957	197,169	38.2
1936	4 905	1.18	24.2	1990	551,118	215,633	39.1
1937	5,289	1,304	24.7	1991	575,674	228,425	39.7
1938	5,572	1,587	28.5	1992	598,916	254,584	42.5
1939	5,958	1,960	32.9	1993	631,003	273,094	43.3
1940	7,521	3,903	51.9	1994	669,069	286,042	42.8
1941	7,521	4,543	60.4	1995	704,156	304,892	43.4
1942	9,591	5,860	61.1	1996	742,090	306,236	41.3
1943	10,208	6.268	61.4	1997	786,308	312,239	39.7

1 General Government Expenditure (GCE) is a measure of the combined spending of central

and local government. See footnote 22, page 51, for a full definition.
The facile nature of the comparison – the country never recovered, financially and economically, from the cost of the Second World War – is characteristic of war, in which all other considerations are subordinated to victory. Wartime public expenditure tends to rise without displacing other forms of spending, because the demands of war propaganda create new social and political expectations which are expensive to fulfill. Dreams of a better world in general, and the Beveridge Plan in particular, were an integral part of the war effort.

War also familiarises people with unprecedented levels of State expenditure and taxation, accustoming them to higher levels of both in peacetime too. The ruinous costs of waging war make it easy for collectivists to ask the voters rhetorical questions about why similar amounts cannot be put to more constructive purposes. Public expenditure has not taken less than 33 per cent of the national income in any year since 1945 and the standard rate of income tax did not dip below 30 per cent again until 1986. The establishment of new plateaux for public expenditure and taxation is the most destructive long-term consequence of war. It was why Gladstone added Peace to Retrenchment and Reform as one of the main planks of his political programme.

Micro-Economic Interventionism

Another unfortunate side-effect of war is to make collectivist ideas more plausible. The principal socialist superstition- the efficiency of public ownership – was imbued with a spurious plausibility by the wartime reorganisation of private industries. The private railway companies were effectively nationalised on the outbreak of war in August 1914, though they continued to be run by private managers. Legislation to nationalise the railways was introduced to the House of Commons in 1919, but they were eventually privatised as regional monopolies instead. The coal mines were gradually brought under State control between 1915 and 1917. In 1919 a government-appointed commission chaired by a High Court judge, Sir John Sankey, endorsed the idea of the nationalisation of the mining industry on grounds of efficiency alone.

The Socialist thinker R. H. Tawney, who had served on the Sankey Commission, rightly identified its report as a turning point in the history of nationalisation. He wrote at the time:

> Up to 1919 it might fairly be said that the nationalisation of foundation industries was an aspiration rather than a policy...Henceforward no government and no party will be able to pretend that nationalisation is one of the questions with regard to which politicians can keep an 'open mind.' It will be impossible to assert in the future that it is a wanton disturbance of a smoothly running industrial system, or that it is a 'mere theory' with no solid body of economic and technical argument behind it...For the first time, the evidence for and against capitalism in one great industry has been marshalled and presented to the public, not by private individuals, but by a public body appointed by Act of Parliament. For the

first time, its economic wastefulness has been laid bare, not by reformers, but by technical experts, administrators, men of science and officials, including two blameless baronets whom the mine-owners found it hardest to forgive. For the first time, all the business men on a Commission, not directly concerned in the industry under investigation, have affirmed that 'the present system of ownership and working...stands condemned, and some other system must be substituted for it.' For the first time, the case for transferring to public ownership property worth not less than £135,000,000, and the methods by which, when transferred, it is to be administered, have been worked out in detail not by socialists, but by that most venerable of British institutions, a judge of the High Court...The policy of nationalisation occupies today a position of vantage which it has never held in the past. The burden of proof no longer rests upon its supporters, but upon its opponents. The case for it has been made out. What is needed now is that the general public should master it, and should end a situation which is as objectionable from the standpoint of the consumer of coal as it is from that of the mine-workers.[7]

It took nearly thirty years to accomplish the public ownership of the mining industry, but it was during and after the First World War that nationalisation made the transition from Utopian blueprint to practical policy.

Until 1919, public ownership was reserved for industries regarded as vital to national security. This was the justification for Disraeli's purchase of the Khedive's shares in the Suez Canal Company in 1875, and for Winston Churchill's acquisition of a controlling stake in the Anglo-Persian Oil Company (later British Petroleum) in August 1914. It is true that local authorities had supplied gas, water and electricity services from Victorian times, but private companies were still free to offer them as well. The increasing acceptability of nationalisation, on grounds of industrial efficiency rather than national security or municipal socialism, was largely a twentieth-century phenomenon. Churchill had nationalised the Thames dockyards as early as 1908, ostensibly to overcome ruinous competition and under-investment by their private owners. After the Sankey Report, even Conservative-dominated governments were happy to establish public corporations. The Forestry Commission was set up in 1919. The first State electricity commissioners were appointed the same year, and the Central Electricity Generating Board was set up in 1926 to build power stations. A nationalised National Grid was recommended in an official report of 1936. The British Broadcasting Corporation was formed in 1926 nationalising what was then a State-regulated private monopoly of radio broadcasting. The objective was the more efficient management of the electromagnetic spectrum. The London Passenger Transport Board was formed between 1931 and 1933. In 1939 overseas air services were placed in the hands of a new public corporation, British Overseas Airways. But the great bulk of the important nationalisations – coal, aviation, road transport, railways, gas, electricity and steel – took place in a burst of activity between 1945 and 1951 when belief in the efficiency of public ownership, fuelled by a naive faith in the efficacy of economic planning, was virtually uncontested.

Nationalised industries ostensibly differed from other forms of publicly financed activity, in that they could charge for the services they provided and so generate a trading income as well as tax revenues on their profits and the wages of their staff. It was also thought that they could borrow freely in the capital markets without increasing the burden of public sector debt. In fact, the nationalised industries were from the outset a burden on the taxpayer. Subject to arbitrary interference by politicians, intimidated by highly unionised workforces, and free of the disciplines of both competition and bankruptcy the nationalised industries consistently produced a lower return on capital than their counterparts in the private sector. They also shed jobs rather than created them. The net trading and tax revenues enjoyed by the Treasury were probably lower than they would have been if the industries had stayed in the private sector. As heavily unionised monopolies, nationalised industry prices also tended to increase more rapidly than prices generally in order to cover mounting labour costs and millions of days lost to strikes. The price rises were a disguised tax burden on the private sector.

Nationalisation eventually degenerated in the 1960s and 1970s into the rescue of unviable industries in exchange for votes: It is true that the nationalisations of the 1940s were in part the redemption of political pledges the Labour Party had issued to trade unions, but the main impetus behind the taking of industries into public ownership was the belief that it would be more efficient. By the 1970s nobody believed that any more. But employees of troubled private sector businesses did believe that the State had a role to play as a hospice for dying manufacturing companies like British Leyland and Rolls-Royce. This drew the State into a wholly new area of public expenditure: rescuing failing companies from their creditors. British Leyland had absorbed £2.9 billion of taxpayers' money by the time it was returned to the private sector in August 1988. In the Keynesian era, governments were also seduced into using investment in nationalised industries as a counter-cyclical weapon. The ultimate effect of nationalisation was not to revolutionise the performance of the economy but to add massively to the liabilities of the State. At the beginning of the 1980s the total cost to the taxpayer of the nationalised industries, in capital write-offs and grants, was put at £40 billion in current prices. The £94 billion of taxpayers' money invested in them was yielding an average return to the Exchequer of minus 1 per cent.[8] A sum of that magnitude might then have earned £10 billion a year if it had been simply left in the bank.

Macro-Economic Interventionism

Another important influence over the increase in public expenditure was a naive faith in the power of economics, a pseudo-science accorded (like nuclear fission) a special reverence in the post-war era. Most of modern economics was invented by Maynard Keynes, an undoubted genius whose versatile ideas proved a fertile source of arguments for those who wanted to transform public expenditure from a means of defraying the public expenses into an instrument of economic policy without frightening the voters with the threat of full-blooded Socialism. In the inter-war years, the orthodox response to a downturn in the economy was to reduce taxation and public expenditure. The Geddes Axe imposed severe economies in 1921 and the May Committee – appointed by the second Labour Government – inspired another round of major cuts in 1931. A balanced budget was considered essential to business confidence, public expenditure a diversion of resources from private enterprise and government borrowing the surest route to inflation, a run on the pound and the collapse of the export trade.

Retrenchment was in line with traditional economic theory and endorsed by conservative-minded politicians in all parties, yet at bottom the policy was rooted not in abstract theory or reactionary politics but in the practical budgetary considerations of the Treasury. Keynes, who had worked there, understood this well. In January 1939 exasperated by his failure to persuade the Treasury mandarins of the benefits of counter-cyclical spending, he wrote in an article in the New Statesman:

> There has been nothing finer in its way than our nineteenth-century school of Treasury officials. Nothing better has ever been devised, if our object is to limit the functions of Government to the least possible and to make sure that expenditure, whether on social or economic or military or general administrative purposes, is the smallest and most economical that public opinion will put up with. But if that is not our object then nothing can be worse. The Civil Service is ruled today by the Treasury school, trained by tradition and experience and native skill to evenly form of intelligent obstruction . . . We have experienced since the war two occasions of terrific retrenchment and axing of constructive schemes This has not only been a crushing discouragement for all who are capable of constructive projects, but it has inevitably led to the survival of those to whom negative measures are natural and sympathetic.[9]

Keynes had battled in vain throughout the inter-war years to overturn the balanced budget constraint and the dogmatic cuts in expenditure on public works, wages and unemployment benefits. Although the governments of the 1930s intervened increasingly in the economy at the micro-economic level, mainly in response to producer lobbies, the sophisticated arguments of Keynes about the beneficent macro-economic effects of government expenditure singularly failed to dislodge the resolute pragmatism of the 'Treasury view' until the vast expenditures of the war seemed to have put the theory to a successful practical test.'[10]

The publication by the wartime coalition in May 1944 of the White Paper Employment Policy marked a partial public acceptance of the ideas of Maynard Keynes, though they had influenced government policy since the outbreak of war. Their acceptance and survival into peacetime conditions reflected less an intellectual conviction that they were right than a recognition of their political usefulness. Keynes provided a theoretical support for direct government intervention in the economy – at a time when public sector ownership and activity and economic 'planning' were much in vogue, and apparently vindicated by the wartime experience which did not rely on the physical controls of traditional socialist economics. The contemporary appeal of such a course was obvious. The 'Treasury view' was utterly discredited by its association with the mass unemployment and appeasement politicians of the 1930s, even if the Great Depression was actually caused less by domestic retrenchment than by post-war financial dislocation, the revival of protectionism, and the failure of any one of the major economic powers to give a decisive lead in international economic and financial policy.[11] For post-war politicians interested in avoiding a socialist revolution – which included the then leadership of the Labour Party – the origins of the slump were less important than the likely political consequences of an abrupt end to the full employment of the wartime years. In short, the management of aggregate demand through periodic adjustment of the fiscal and monetary levers offered a moderate collectivist alternative to full-blooded socialism. Robert Skidelsky rightly sub-titles the second volume of his life of Keynes 'the economist as saviour'.[12]

Sir Kingsley Wood's Budget of April 1941, which used the notion of an inflationary gap between demand and supply, is generally regarded as the first of the Keynesian budgets. It was a portent of the future that Wood found the idea of an inflationary gap a useful way to present an increase in the rate of income tax and a reduction in the personal allowances: prices would go up unless consumer expenditure was contained by tax increases. The tax increase was meant to be repaid after the war, when a slump was anticipated. In other words, the 1941 Budget was the first in which the government promised to manipulate the fiscal and monetary levers to restrain inflationary levels of aggregate demand and to expand deflationary levels of aggregate demand. This approach to government expenditure stood the Gladstonian doctrine of Retrenchment on its head, implying that State spending was not the curse of economic stability and prosperity but its source. In the Keynesian economy, the national income ceases to belong to the individuals who earn it, since they cannot be trusted to use it wisely. They save in a recession, when they should be spending; and they spend in a boom, when they should be saving.

The value of these ideas to high-spending and high-taxing interventionist politicians is not hard to understand, but they proved unexpectedly useful in other ways too. The deficit financing Keynesian ideas inspired was the major cause of the post-war inflation, especially after inflationary expectations took root and the Bretton Woods system of fixed exchange rates (which Keynes had helped to devise) broke down. Inflation is a gift to any government seeking to reduce the political consequences of excessive public borrowing and taxation. Inflation not only progressively reduces the real cost of government debt, but also allows the State to raise taxes by stealth. Under progressive income tax systems, tax revenues will rise in line with output even if the tax rates remain unchanged. If inflation is simultaneously eroding the real value of rising incomes, the higher earnings may also drag taxpayers into higher tax brackets even though their real standard of living is falling. In most cases, an insufficient number of voter-taxpayers are aware of this sleight-of-hand to demand the government return the additional tax revenues to them by raising the income tax thresholds. Deficit financing both reduced the real cost of State borrowing and enlarged taxable capacity.

Though Keynes himself never doubted the importance of monetary policy – he was, after all, a monetary economist - his growing band of disciples among the younger generation of economists assumed that economic growth could be secured by a fiscal stimulus alone. On the whole, monetary policy followed fiscal policy passively. Even as inflation began to accelerate in the 1960s Keynesian politicians and economists treated it as a separate problem, to be contained by the physical controls that demand management was originally intended to escape. By 1961 the government was sufficiently alarmed by the impact of wage inflation on the international competitiveness of British exports to add an incomes policy to the instruments it used to steer the economy. State regulation of personal incomes was tried in a variety of statutory, voluntary and exhortatory guises before the idea was discredited completely in the celebrated Winter of Discontent in 1978–79. Government intervention did not stop at the wage-packet, but strayed into dividend warrants and heating bills as well. Over the; two decades of pay policy, controls on wages and salaries were supplemented by physical controls over prices and dividends, and the subsidisation of labour costs and politically sensitive services like energy and water. Keynesian economics, which had begun by promising to save capitalism from socialism, ended up as a powerful ally of the collectivist State.

The Castration of the Treasury

The main casualty of the Keynesian revolution was the traditional Treasury. The historic 'Treasury view' that public expenditure should be confined to the minimum necessary, in order to allow the private sector to make best use of limited resources, was regarded as laughably unsophisticated in the age of State-designed economic equilibrium. Instead of minimising State command over resources, the revised role of the Treasury was to achieve the optimum disposition of resources between the public and the private sectors by adjusting the balance of taxation and public expenditure. From one point of view, this made the Treasury more powerful than ever. The wider economic role assigned to the State by Keynesianism-certainly enlarged the importance of the department both in Whitehall and in Westminster. The problem was that, by making public expenditure and taxation the principal instruments for securing economic growth and full employment, Keynesian policies were bound to allow public expenditure to grow faster than the economy. Spending was ostensibly geared to the gyrations of the trade cycle. But thanks to the in exactitudes of economic policymaking – especially in a democratic political system plagued by ambitious politicians, scheming bureaucrats and dozens of consumer and producer pressure groups – spending tends to rise steeply in recessions and fall slowly if at all in the upturns.

The method of determining public expenditure priorities does not make it any easier for the Treasury to contain the rate of growth of public expenditure. As early as 1918 Stanley Baldwin complained that Cabinet ministers no longer supported the Treasury:

> In nine cases out of ten [the Cabinet] would back the Treasury. The whole outlook today is changed...and all large items are controlled, not by the Treasury, but by the policy of the Government, and if the Chancellor raises objections, and the Minister takes the matter to Cabinet, the natural bias will not be against the expenditure but in favour...the House of Commons itself would in nearly every case support the Government which was spending the money on purposes of social amelioration.[13]

The modern ministerial career depends in large part on success in extracting extra money from the Treasury. Whether he or she succeeds depends less on the merits of the programme than on the minister's powers of persuasion, his personal relations with the Chancellor and the Prime Minister, and his standing in Cabinet. The Conservative Governments of the 1980s settled the division of public expenditure by agreeing a global total in advance, which was then apportioned in bi-lateral meetings between the Chief Secretary to the Treasury and spending Ministers. Unresolved disagreements were referred to an ad hoc Cabinet committee popularly known as the Star Chamber, and ultimately to the Cabinet itself. Nigel Lawson has described this process as 'as near to a coherent system as any government has achieved'.[14]

From 1992 the Star Chamber was replaced by a committee of senior ministers chaired by the Chancellor, charged with taking decisions within a fixed cash total for public expenditure. But the new system still relies on the interplay of politics and personalities rather than principle, which makes it virtually impossible to effect real cuts in departmental budgets. Departmental ministers submit exaggerated bids to the Treasury for extra money, conscious that the initial bid will be whittled down to a more realistic figure. As the Treasury scales down the increases demanded by departmental ministers, the cry of 'cuts' goes up. In reality, bids are cut but expenditure continues to rise, so the Treasury is able to affect only the rate of deterioration.

The Treasury has never really recovered the authority it shed during the high Keynesian period, when its power in relation to other departments was significantly diluted. During the Wilson years an attempt was made to replace it altogether by a Department of Economic Affairs interested solely in output and employment, leaving economy to a demoted Treasury. But it was the manifest failure of Keynesian economic policies, and the unpopularity of the increasingly desperate expedients used to support them, which undermined the morale of Treasury of ficials and the respect of the public. In the mid-1970s, after both the Heath and Wilson governments had tried to inflate the economy out of mounting; unemployment, the Treasury lost control of public spending completely. The battered authority of the department was partially restored under Margaret Thatcher in the first half of the 1980s, when public expenditure was contained successfully if not reduced. But the restored standing of the Treasury was squandered again in a series of bizarre and disastrous miscalculations in the management of monetary policy in 1986–88 and 1990–92. The Treasury misjudged inflationary conditions badly from 1986. It then took the pound into the Exchange Rate Mechanism (ERM) of the European Monetary System at the wrong time and the wrong price, and spurned every opportunity to adjust within the ERM until currency speculators finally forced sterling out of the mechanism altogether in September 1992.

It is often argued that the Treasury has too many responsibilities to discharge any of them well. Certainly, the Treasury is almost unique among Western governments in retaining responsibility for monetary management and economic policymaking as well as control of taxation and public expenditure. It is now rightly ceding at least some of its responsibility for monetary policy to the Bank of England. This will allow the department to concentrate on the less glamorous task of matching public expenditure to the available tax revenues, rather than vice-versa. Economic forecasting is being downgraded, and may eventually be left to the private sector. The Treasury also believes that it can improve its control of public expenditure if it ceases shadowing every detail of departmental budgets, and delegates more of the responsibility for detailed spending decisions to the spending departments. Reforms intended to achieve this were announced by the Treasury in October 1994. It may be that freedom from immersion in detail will facilitate control of the overall total, but past experience is not encouraging.

The whole of post-war history shows that any relaxation of Treasury vigilance over spending departments ends in disaster. The recommendation of the Plowden Report of 1961 that public expenditure programmes be planned for five years ahead in the prices of the starting year was intended to enable spending departments to plan real resources – numbers of teachers, or miles of motorway built – without worrying about inflation. In practice, spending plans simply increased in line with prices. It was to stop this cost-plus approach to public spending that cash limits were introduced for the first time in 1976–77, after the 'funny money' of the Plowden years had taken public expenditure to what was believed at the time to be 60 per cent of the national income.[15] The effectiveness of cash limits was mitigated by the fact that they did not apply to the most expensive, demand-led programmes like social security. But, even after complete cash planning of public expenditure was introduced in 1981, the Treasury still lost control of public expenditure for a second time in the early 1990s.

The Role of Democracy in Heightening Expectations

Of course, this was not entirely the fault of the Treasury. Public expenditure is largely a question of political rather than bureaucratic management, and both of the periods in recent history where the Treasury has lost control of public spending – in the mid- 1970s and the early 1990s – were characterised by prolonged election campaigning. The competition for votes in a welfare democracy is a powerful engine of public expenditure. 'The widening of the franchise,' write Peacock and Wiseman, 'increased the political importance of the group most likely to believe that public expenditures should be increased for their benefit, but that the necessary revenues should be raised from others (the richer) by such means as progressive taxation.'[16] The desire for equality – which de Tocqueville saw as the main characteristic of democracy – necessitates the redistribution of wealth through the fiscal system, especially when equality is sought over a large geographical area. Democracy turned Parliament into an assembly representative mainly of those who imagined themselves to be the expropriators, ending the traditional role of the legislature as the guardian of the taxpayer against the demands of the government. The result was to transform the Mother of Parliaments into a pork barrel, in which the wealth of some voters was churned around in order to benefit other and larger classes of voter.

The Gladstonian doctrine of Retrenchment could not survive the introduction of a democratic legislature of this kind. The second major Victorian extension of the franchise in 1884, which introduced a universal male suffrage, was followed immediately by the; first auction of spending commitments for votes. Joseph Chamberlain and his henchman in the cause of land reform, Jesse Collings, claimed to have won the November 1885 election for Gladstone by buying the newly enfranchised farm labourers' votes with the slogan 'three acres and a cow'. Gladstone himself was driven in 1891 to adopt the so-called Newcastle Programme, which promised to expropriate land and industrial property for political gain. It was aptly described by one biographer as 'a demagogic hotch-potch...hastily compiled with the object of attracting as many votes from as many different sources as possible'.[17] The political programme of every political party in every general election since 1884 has had the same objective: to assemble a coalition of voters sufficiently large to secure office by offering supporters what less scrupulous Third World politicians are prone to call 'free things.'

The central political purpose of the annual Budget is no longer to match expenditure to income, but to churn the national income in such a way that it guarantees there are more 'winners' than 'losers'. The political economy of democracy is as simple as that, and it is a powerful upward ratchet on public expenditure. The sensitivity of the democratic mechanism to the electoral consequences of public expenditure decisions is now so great that spending is even used to offset the cost of taxes. In 1994, for example, 5.25 million Britons received £1.81 billion from the Treasury to compensate them for the likely cost of the Council Tax. The abortive introduction of the second stage of VAT on fuel in the autumn of 1994 was accompanied by similar promises of State largesse.

The public discussions which precede the Budget are characterised by assessments of how much the Government has to 'give away', and those which follow it by complaints about its meanness to some groups and generosity to others. Tax-cutting Budgets, in which the State returns income to its owners, are routinely described as electoral 'bribes', even if they are preceded by a series of Budgets which took away a far greater sum than that which is being returned.

It is not uncommon for non-taxpayers to write to the Chancellor of the Exchequer after a tax-cutting Budget to complain that he has 'done nothing for them'. Similarly, pensioners and other savers suffering from money illusion (in which nominal increases in income are mistaken for real ones) will frequently write to complain about cuts in interest rates.

Eventually, it comes to seem as if nobody owns anything any more; that the entire national income belongs to the State; and that it is the task of elected politicians to decide upon its distribution. The State takes on a human shape, capable of generosity to some deserving groups and of meanness to others. Samuel Brittan has dubbed this modern democratic phenomenon 'the Wenceslas Myth', after the tenth-century Bohemian king who gave alms to a poor man on St Stephen's Day:

> If the 'government' – that is citizens acting through a central collective agency – spends more on roads or military hardware, it has less available for health services or pensions or cutting taxes. These latter foregone benefits are the cost of the expenditure- money being just a conventional token or measuring rod. The Wenceslas myth is simply the neglect of this truism in nearly all debates on public policy...The government has no resources, but is simply an agency for carrying out those decisions which, rightly or wrongly, are taken collectively rather than left to the market or voluntary action. To ask the 'government' to be less mean towards a particular deserving cause is a bad shorthand way of asking for some of our fellow citizens to be 'less mean'.[18]

The classic instance of the Wenceslas Myth is the annual Christmas Bonus for State pensioners, first introduced to boost aggregate demand in the still-Keynesian days of recession in 1972. Although it is a fiction that the Chancellor 'gives' the bonus – it is money transferred from one set of taxpayers to another – it has become impossible to 'take it away' without huge political cost. In 1994 12.9 million pensioners received £10 each, at a cost of £129 million.

William Harcourt, Chancellor of the Exchequer from 1892 to 1895, thought within less than a decade of the passing of the franchise extension of 1884 that 'a Chancellor preaching against extravagance is the voice of one crying in the wilderness'.9 He foresaw that in a democracy the proportion of the national income consumed by the State is restrained only by the willingness or otherwise of voters to pay for additional taxes. 'Governments,' as Peacock and Wiseman put it, 'like to spend more money...citizens do not like to pay more taxes, and... governments need to pay some attention to the wishes of their citizens.'[20] Superficially, democratic control of this kind is a comforting constraint on public largesse. But in reality war, and the increasing dependency of a large part of the population on the transfers and services of the Welfare State, have so blunted the intolerance of higher taxation that it is now regarded as reasonable for a single man or woman to start to pay income tax after he or she has earned just £67 a week. This has fixed the upward limit on public expenditure at nearly half the total national income. The unrealistic expectations generated by the competition for votes remains the principal upward pressure on public expenditure. The pressure is most obvious in the field of health, where early hopes that the National Health Service would actually reduce the costs of health care by eliminating poverty-induced diseases have given way to despair over a demand for high technology medicine whose costs have no ceiling. Technological pressures have also pushed up defence spending. A century ago aeroplanes, tanks and intercontinental ballistic missiles were not yet invented, but the modern military establishment expects to have all of these weapons. The electorate also expect the State to provide universal secondary school education and an ever-expanding number of university places. Education, which once consisted of little more than a teacher and a blackboard in a draughty room, now requires purpose-built classrooms, up-to-the-minute textbooks and equipment, computer technology and whole new universities.

But it is within the social security budget where rising expectations have done their deadliest work. The range of benefits has risen as social investigators have uncovered new pockets of poverty; the take-up of benefits has increased as the shame of pauperism has diminished, higher unemployment has acquainted more people with the range of benefits on offer, and the activities of charities and other social security lobbyists have enlarged. public understanding of their entitlements; the dissolution of the family has increased the number of single parents, who inevitably rely on benefits to a greater extent than two-parent families; economic change has stranded many unskilled workers in unemployment; others have been pushed into early retirement on sickness or invalidity benefits; and the growing gap between the standard of living of elderly people who made provision for their old age and those who dinot has increased massively the pressure for higher spending on State pensions.

Of course, demographic forces are partially responsible for the increase in social security expenditure. An ageing population is increasing the number of pensioners. Pensions were paid to 8.25 million people in 1977 but there are now nearly 10 million pensioners, and pensions account for a third of all social security spending. But people are also becoming habituated to living on State benefits, and adept at negotiating the bureaucratic maze which separates them from their entitlements. In 1948 a million people were living on national assistance; today, the estimated average number of people on Income Support at any one time is put at 5.3 million. Claimants (and their employers and doctors) have learnt to arbitrage between high and low cost benefits, notably by opting for Invalidity Benefit rather than Sickness or Unemployment Benefit because it is paid at a higher rate. The number of people claiming Invalidity Benefit has nearly tripled since 1979, without a corresponding increase in the number of genuine invalids, to 1.6 million.[21]

These various pressures have turned social security into the biggest single item of public expenditure today. The total cost in 19934 was over £87 billion, or roughly one and a half times the total yield from Income Tax in the same year. It accounts for nearly one third of general government expenditure and just under 14 per cent of GDP.[22] In 1945, social security consumed only 4.7 per cent of GDP. In the last sixteen years alone, social security expenditure has grown at an average rate of 3.7 per cent a year in real terms, more than twice as fast as the average rate of growth of the economy as a whole.23 Between 1979 and 1993 94 social security spending rose in real terms by £37.1 billion, or 78 per cent, and it is projected to climb to £93.1 billion by the end of the century unless there are radical reductions in unemployment.[24]

The massive growth of social security is at the heart of the public expenditure problem. It is crowding out other, more desirable, forms of spending. Being demand-driven, it is difficult to control. Its sheer size and momentum forces the government to choose continuously between accommodating unforeseen increases through extra borrowing or cutting other programmes. Social security expenditure rises inexorably in recession and so imperceptibly creates room for spending in other areas when it falls in the boom, a problem the government has tried to tackle by earmarking 'cyclical' social security expenditure. With much of it based on a notional 'insurance' principle – retirement pensions and unemployment, sickness, maternity and invalidity benefits are all supposedly funded by contributions – it is difficult to reform the system without denying people benefits which they feel, however erroneously, that they have paid for. People are being pauperised.

The large number of people who depend on State welfare has created a powerful lobby in favour of higher public spending. The Department of Social Security estimated in 1993 that the number of people receiving at least one form of social security benefit totalled 46 million.[25] Benefits are payable in a large array of different circumstances. Cash is given to pensioners; pregnant mothers; all families with children, regardless of income; low-income families in employment, but in need of help with housing costs, council tax payments or major purchases; the sick and the disabled; those injured at work or on active service; the unemployed; and widows (though not widowers) and the elderly. The needs of almost all of these groups are articulated by well-funded and well-organised lobbyists, like the Child Poverty Action Group, Age Concern and Shelter. The same groups also provide claimants with advice on how to make the most effective use of the benefits on offer, making a reasonable living for themselves by acting as brokers between their clients and the taxpayer. Charities of this kind can expect taxpayer support themselves. Shelter, for example, received one fifth of its total income in 1992 in the form of grants by local, central and European government. In the same year, Age Concern received 28 per cent of its total income from government.[26] Only half of all social security benefits are conditional on contributions paid and, even if the fiction that employers' and employees' National Insurance contributions are a form of saving rather than a tax is indulged, general taxation still provides half of the money to fund the social security programme.

How the Public Payroll Increases Public Expenditure

Welfare dependants are not the only group with a vested interest in higher public expenditure. As public spending has expanded, so have the numbers employed in the public sector. In 1891 just 3.6 per cent of the working population was employed by central government, but by the late 1940s nearly a quarter of the workforce was in the public sector. In 1979 over 29 per cent of the employed population, nearly 7½ million people, worked on a full or part-time basis for central or local government, the public services, the armed forces or the nationalised industries. The Labour government of 1974–79 used public sector employment quite deliberately to provide jobs at a time when the private sector was shedding labour. Between 1973 and 1977 the numbers employed in the private sector fell by 775,000, but the numbers employed by favoured public sector organisations like the National Health Service, government departments and the nationalised industries rose by 564,000.[27]

The Conservative governments of the 1980s managed to prevent public sector employment rising any further and, through a mixture of rationalisation, privatisation and job cuts in the civil service, actually to reduce the numbers employed by the nationalised industries and in Whitehall. But, as Table 2 shows, the numbers employed by central government as a whole remained remarkably stable and the numbers employed by local authorities actually carried on rising until 1988. As a result, the total number of full-time equivalent jobs provided by central and local government fell by just 2 per cent between 1979 and 1988. Since 1979 the public sector has shed 2.2 million full-time jobs, but two thirds of the decline occurred in the nationalised industries, the majority of which were transferred wholesale to the public sector. Another tenth of the job losses fell upon teachers, which largely reflected declining school rolls. Only the Civil Service, which has lost nearly a tenth of its numbers, has shrunk significantly without a major change in the scale of its responsibilities. The numbers of policemen and people working in local authority social services has actually gone up. In 1994 5.3 million people (4.3 million full-time equivalents), or roughly one in every five workers, were still employed in the public sector. Once privatisations and other reclassifications are taken into account, public sector employment is probably at much the same level as it was in its heyday in the mid-1970s.[28]

Public sector pay is one of the largest single elements in public expenditure. In 1992 the total public sector pay bill was £92½ billion, a sum equivalent to one third of general government expenditure that year.[29] It is impossible to contain the rate of growth of public spending, let alone cut it in real terms, without controlling public sector manpower and pay. Historically, this has proved difficult to achieve. Between 1961 and its peak in 1976 the number of full- and part-time workers employed in the public sector climbed by over 25 per cent, or well over 1½ million people, to a total payroll of nearly 7½ million (6½ million full-time equivalents). The bulk of the increases were in the National Heath Service and in local government education, social security and administration.[30] The relative security of public sector employment meant the cost of public sector pay had to be controlled almost entirely by the level of settlements the government managed to achieve, rather than by alterations in the numbers employed. Because pay tended to be set by national bargaining between trade unions and employers' organisations, or by centralised pay review bodies which made comparisons with the private sector, pay increases were difficult for the government to resist.

Table 2   Public Sector Employment in the United Kingdom
Full-time Equivalents   000's

Year	Total Central Government	Total Local Authorities	Total General Government	Total Pubic Corporations	Total Public Sector
1979	2,388	2,997	5,385	2,065	7,450
1980	2,394	2,956	5,350	2,038	7,388
1981	2,420	2,899	5,319	1,867	7,186
1982	2,401	2,865	5,266	1,756	7,022
1983	2,384	2,906	5,290	1,663	6,953
1984	2,359	2,942	5,301	1,599	6,900
1985	2,360	2,958	5,318	1,251	6,569
1986	2,337	3,010	5,347	1,187	6,534
1987	2,312	3,062	5,374	985	6,359
1988	2,323	3,081	5,404	912	6,316
1989	2,314	2,940	5,254	832	6,086
1990	2,300	2,967	5,267	786	6,053
1991	2,178	2,947	5,125	724	5,849
1992	2,008	2,898	4,908	874	5,780
1993	1,606	2,679	4,321	1,158	5,443
1994	1,185	2,646	3,827	1,467	5,298
1995	1,058	2,639	3,697	1,527	5,224
1996	981	2,637	3,618	1,512	5,130

Even today, despite the reorganisation in recent years of many public sector institutions into executive agencies and hospital trusts and – in the case of recently nationalised or about-to-be-privatised industries like the coal industry and the railways and the Post Office – the adoption of a more commercial approach, less than one in a hundred public sector employees can expect to agree his remuneration directly with his immediate superior. The pay of police officers, firemen and some other public sector workers is still set by simplistic indexation formulae. Attempts to tamper with pay mechanisms established in the 1960s and 1970s usually provoke a strike, or the threat of a strike, as the teachers' unions have demonstrated repeatedly in recent years. In 1993 the police trade unions, whose members are not allowed to strike, waged an expensive and highly successful propaganda campaign against government attempts to reform some of the more egregious anomalies in their system of pay and perks. Like the British Medical Association campaigns against reforms of the pay and working practices of the medical profession, the police did not hesitate to make extravagant claims about the effects of reform on the quality of their service to the public.

Inevitably, public sector pay tends to be set by 'comparability' with the private sector. Between 1955 and 1992 the public sector pay bill increased at an average annual rate of 9.7 per cent, considerably faster than inflation (7.2 per cent a year) and over four times as fast as the rate of growth of the economy as a whole (2.3

per cent), but much the same as the annual average increase in private sector pay (9.9 per cent).[31] The rate of increase, however, is somewhat misleading. As Table 3 shows, the average public sector worker is consistently better off in cash terms than the average private sector worker, except during extraordinary booms like that at the end of the 1980s. On a crude calculation – dividing the public sector paybill by the number of public sector employees – public sector workers remained better of even during those years.[32] This is true at all levels of pay except the highest decile, where the private sector consistently outperforms the public.

Table 3 Annual Increases in Average Gross Weekly Earnings

Year	Public Sector Annual Increase	Public Sector Average Wage	Private Sector (Percentage Increase)	Private Sector Average Wage (Loss)	Public Sector Gain/ (Loss)	Public Sector Gain/
1974	5.6%	£42.9	13.6%	£41.0	2.0%	£1.9
1975	34.3%	£57.6	26.8%	£52.0	7.5%	£5.6
1976	21.4%	£69.9	18.3%	£61.5	3.1 %	£8.4
1977	6.6%	£74.5	9.9%	£67.6	(3.3%)	£6.9
1978	9.4%	£81.5	14.8%	£77.6	(5.4%)	£3.9
1979	11.8%	£91.1	14.2%	£88.6	(2.4%)	£2.5
1980	25.7%	£114.5	21.4%	£107.6	4.3%	£6.9
1981	15.3%	£132.0	11.2%	£119.6	4.1 %	£12.4
1982	8.3%	£143.0	10.8%	£132.5	(2.5%)	£10.5
1983	7.9%	£154.3	8.1%	£143.2	(0.2%)	£11.1
1984	5.8%	£163.2	9.6%	£157.0	(3.8%)	£6.2
1985	6.4%	£172.1	7.8%	£170.3	(1.4%)	£1.8
1986	8.0%	£186.1	8.1%	£183.9	(0.1%)	£2.2
1987	6.9%	£197.3	8.1%	£199.7	(1.2%)	(£2.4)
1988	9.5%	£216.0	9.8%	£219.5	(0.3%)	(£3.5)
1989	9.4%	£235.6	9.6%	£241.4	(0.2%)	£(5.8)
1990	8.9%	£256.4	10.1%	£265.8	(1.2%)	(£9.4)
1991	11.1%	£283.0	7.2%	£285.4	3.9%	(£2.4)
1992	8.8%	£307.8	6.3%	£303.3	2.5%	£4.5
1993	4.3%	£321.0	4.0%	£315.3	0.3%	£5.7
1994	2.5%	£329.3	2.8%	£324.2	–0.3%	£5.1
1995	2.8%	£338.5	3.0%	£333.9	–0.2%	£4.6
1996	3.3%	£349.7	3.2%	£344.6	0.1%	£5.1
1997	2.8%	£359.5	3.2%	£355.6	–0.4%	£3.8

Source: IRS Pay Intelligence – various

The lowest paid public sector workers are considerably better off than the private sector equivalent.[33] Some groups, notably the firemen and the police, have done exceptionally well. Public sector pay also tends to rise without regard to the economic cycle. Table 3 suggests it is actually counter-cyclical, falling relative to private sector earnings when the economy is booming but catching up rapidly as the economy enters a downturn. Public sector pay rose rapidly during the recessions of 1975–76, 1980–81 and 1990–91, in each case driving up public expenditure just as tax receipts were falling. According to the Confederation of British Industry, total public sector pay costs rose during the recent recession from 13 per cent of the national income in 1990 to 14.3 per cent in 1993. At a time when private sector pay was static or falling, public sector pay was rising at around 4 per cent a year.[34] The result in each case is to crowd out productive investment by the public sector, and store up a legacy of debt to be recouped from the private sector in the upturn.

The counter-cyclical pattern reflects the politicisation of the public sector pay process, in which governments seek to buy off public sector discontent with the fall in relative earnings ahead of an election, or redeem pledges made to public sector voters in the aftermath of an election victory. The massive surges in public sector pay in the mid-1970s and the early 1980s both followed general elections in which public sector pay was a major issue, and the increases in the early 1990s occurred during a prolonged pre-election period. Between 1988–89 and 1993–94 – a particularly bad period for taxpayers, when a mistaken decision to enter the ERM crucified large parts of the productive economy, pushed up pay claims to keep pace with high mortgage rates and coincided with two pre-election spending rounds, rather than the usual one- public expenditure rose by 16.3 per cent in real terms. The economy grew by just 1.6 per cent in the same period. Yet throughout that period the public sector trade unions and their Parliamentary client, the Labour Party, campaigned assiduously to persuade the public that public spending was being subjected to swingeing cuts and that many public sector workers were on the breadline. The truth is that public expenditure is as high as it was fifteen years ago, and lower paid public sector workers are actually considerably better of than their private sector counterparts.

Various attempts have been made to depoliticise public sector pay, through the establishment of independent pay review bodies like the Top Salaries Review Body and latterly by mimicking private sector pay practices through the creation of executive agencies and NHS Hospital Trusts, but it is ultimately impossible to prevent public sector pay being determined mainly by political choice. For the first time since the war, this may be turning against public sector employees and in favour of taxpayers. For the first thirty years after the war they were treated with great respect, enjoying both job security, pay which at least kept pace with the private sector and generous pension arrangements Until the 1970s the public sector payroll expanded continuously, since it was used explicitly to soak up surplus labour at times of recession. There is a; case for stability and even generosity in public sector pay and recruitment- particularly, but not exclusively, in areas like the police force and the armed forces – but no case at all for using it as a tool of macro-economic management. Yet the public sector trade unions still maintain that the civil service, the local authorities and the public corporations should be used to create jobs, and there is every reason to expect a Labour government to try and achieve full employment by exactly this method. It would be better to give the private sector room to create the extra jobs by lifting the enormous tax burdens imposed on employers by the need to finance public expenditure which is driven in large measure by the payroll costs of the public sector.

The burden on employers and employees of National Insurance contributions and Income Tax has reduced the take-home pay, particularly of unskilled labour, to the level where many jobs are uneconomic to employers to provide or uneconomic to the unemployed to perform. The taxpayer is then obliged to pay unemployment benefit and means-tested benefits to the unemployed, or to subsidise their employment, or to pay for training places in the hope that they can acquire skills which will command a higher price in the labour market. In 1993, for example, 2.9 million were registered as unemployed and another 321,000 were on work-related government training programmes. Meanwhile, the private sector exports production abroad, and at home turns increasingly to part-time and self-employed labour in an effort to reduce the tax and National Insurance costs of employing people.[35]

This is the final absurdity of public expenditure: it becomes a circular process which feeds on itself. First, the State makes creating or taking a job uneconomic. This reduces tax revenues. Then it subsidises individuals or employers instead, so raising public expenditure. To pay for the extra spending, a smaller tax base has to be squeezed still harder. This makes even more jobs, especially unskilled and full-time ones, uneconomic. The State job destruction machine rotates once more, but the problems it creates do not end there. Unemployed people lose hope, and the habit of work. They get sick more often, demoralised, and desperate. Their demands on the health and social services increase. Some of them turn to crime, taxing employers still further and driving up public expenditure on the police service and the prisons.

The taxpayer is on a treadmill. High public spending necessitates high taxation, which damages economic growth. This leads to greater unemployment, poverty and crime, which necessitates still more public spending and taxation. Getting off the treadmill requires a complete rethinking, from first principles, of the entire agenda of government.

References

1   Edinburgh, 29 November 1874. Quoted in Philip Magnus, Gladstone, John Murray, 1963 page 149
2   Quoted in A. T. Peacock and J. Wiseman, The Growth of Public Expenditure in the United Kingdom, OUP, 1961, page 64.
3   The Growth of Public Expenditure in the United Kingdom, pages 37–8.
4   Calculated using indices published in Tables A-2, A-5, and A-6 in The Growth of Public Expenditure in the United Kingdom.
5   John Stevenson, British Society 1914–45, Penguin, 1984, page 447.
6   Halifax to Duff Cooper, 30 July 1940. Quoted in Paul Addison, The Road to 1945, Quartet, 1977, page 122.
7   R. H. Tawney, 'The Nationalisation of the Coal Industry, Labour Party pamphlet, 1919, reproduced in R. H. Tawney, The Radical Tradition, Pelican, 1966, pages 123–6.
8   Hansard, 9 November 1982, Col. 456.

9   New Statesman, 28 January 1939. Quoted in Paul Addison, The Road to 1945, Quartet, 1977, pages 34–5.
10   On the rise of producer lobbying, see Chapter 7, page 1781.
11   See Charles P. Kindleberger, The World in Depression 1929–1939, Pelican, 1987, pages 288–305.
12   Robert Skidelsky, John Maynard Keynes: The Economist As Saviour 1920–1937, Macmillan, 1992.
13   Quoted in David Galloway, The Public Prodigals, Temple Smith, 196, page 20.
14   Nigel Lawson, The View From No. 11, Bantam, 1992, page 291.
15   See Chapter 3, footnote 1, page 59.
16   A. T. Peacock and J. Wiseman, The Growth of Public Expenditure in the United Kingdom, OUP, 1961, page 67.
17   Philip Magnus, Gladstone, John Murray, 1963, page 396.
18   Samuel Brittan, The Role and Limits of Government, Temple Smith, 1983, pages 5–6.
19   Quoted in A. T. Peacock and J. Wiseman, The Crowth of Public Expenditure in the United Kingdom, OUP, 1961, page 65.
20   The Growth of Public Expenditure in the United Kingdom, page xxiii.
21   Invalidity Benefit is being replaced from April 1995 by a new Incapacity Benefit subject to more rigorous medical tests. This is expected to save £210 million in 1995–6; £700 million in 1997; and £1 billion in 1997–8.
22   General government expenditure is the combined spending of central and local government including both capital and current spending plus net lending and minus privatisation proceeds. It is a measure of the amount the government has to raise through taxation and borrowing.
23   Social security expenditure rose in real terms from £47.3 billion in 1978–79 to £84.4 billion in 19994, or a compound growth rate of 3.68 per cent a year. GDP at factor cost grew by an average of 1.76 per cent a year between 1979 and 1992. Even when the cyclical costs of unemployment are removed from the calculation, the social security budget still grew by 3 per cent a year in real terms.
24   See Department of Social Security, The Growth of Social Security, H.M.S.O., 1993, Table 5, page 11.
25   See The Growth of Social Security, Table 13, page 34.
26   Charity Trends 1993, 16th Edition, Charities Aid Foundation.
27   The Public Sector and Full Employment,' Employment Policy Institute Economic Report, Vol. 7. No. 7, March 1993, Table 3.
28   See People, Paybill and the Public Sector, CBI, February 1994, page 5.
29   Public Finance Foundation, Pay Forecasting Service 1994, Volume 4. Number 1, January 1994, Table A29 and Public Expenditure: Statistical Supplement to the Financial Statement and Budget Report 1994–95, H.M. Treasury, Cm 2519, February 1994, Table 1.1, page 8.
30   Economic Trends, January 1995, Table D.
31 Public Finance Foundation, Pay Forecasting Service 1994, Volume 4, Number 1, January 1994, Table A31
32 Pay Forecasting Service 1994, Volume 4, Number 1, January 1994, Table A30.
33 Pay Forecasting Service 1994, Volume 4, Number 1, January 1994, Tables A9 to A21.
34 CBI, People, Paybill and The Public Sector, February 1994, page 4 and Exhibit 4, page 6.
35 See Chapter 9, page 227.

CHAPTER THREE

Choosing Priorities in Public Expenditure

I take it as a starting-point that it is not the duty of Government to provide any class of citizens with any of the necessaries of life.

R. A. Cross, Home Secretary, 1875

The division of the national income between the Individual and the State is the closest a single political decision can come to choosing between liberty and subjection for the voters. Yet there is no single principle or set of objective criteria by which it is possible to decide how much of the national income should be spent collectively, or even which goods and services should be provided by the State. When in January 1976 the Public Expenditure White Paper disclosed that government spending had risen to 60 per cent of the national income, the Labour Home Secretary Roy Jenkins admitted:

I do not think that you can push public expenditure significantly above 60 per cent and maintain the values of a plural society with adequate freedom of choice. We are here close to one of the frontiers of social democracy.[1]

Most non-Socialists would argue that the free society was extinguished at the considerably lower level of half of the national income, and severely circumscribed at some far lower percentage than that. Where the private sector is no longer the majority shareholder in the national income, the scope for individual decision-making is so far reduced that it is reasonable to conclude that such a society can no longer be properly described as free.

But below this point there is no agreement on the appropriate level of public spending, or on the activities which it is appropriate for the State to undertake. The Keynesian consensus among postwar economists discouraged exploration of the dynamics of public spending. Economists were more interested in the use of public expenditure as a policy instrument than they were in containing or financing it. The subsequent absorption of many economists in the minutiae of econometrics – the use of mathematical models to describe economic relationships – further discouraged interest in a major question of political economy like public expenditure. When Alan Peacock and Jack Wiseman came to write their groundbreaking *Growth of Public Expenditure in the United Kingdom* thirty-odd years ago, they had to turn to a nineteenth-century German Professor of Political Economy called Adolph Wagner for an initial theory of why public expenditure increases.

The Gladstonian approach to public finance – that every expropriation of private property by the State was a defeat for freedom and prosperity- rested on a political consensus which failed to survive the transition to democracy. Today, only a libertarian would argue that collective provision is unjustified in every instance. There is a lack of a politically usable principle or rule-of-thumb by which to restrain the rise of public spending. It is a gap in the armoury of individual freedom which has favoured the emergence, through the incremental increase of government expenditure over many decades, of a powerful collectivist State.

What Should the State Provide?

Adam Smith thought the State should confine its activities to three key functions: external defence, internal law and order and any other goods and services which it would not pay individuals to supply. In a justly famous passage in *Wealth of Nations*, he wrote:

> According to the system of natural liberty, the sovereign has only three duties to attend to; three duties of great importance, indeed, but plain and intelligible to common understandings: first, the duty of protecting the society from the violence and invasion of other independent societies; secondly, the duty of protecting, so far as possible, every member of the society from the injustice or oppression of every other member of it, or the duty of establishing an exact administration of justice, and thirdly, the duty of erecting and maintaining certain public works and certain public institutions, which it can never be for the interest of any individual, or small number of individuals, to erect and maintain; because the profit could never repay the expense to any individual or small number of individuals, though it may frequently do more than repay it to a great society.[2]

The first two duties of government he outlined are the classic 'public goods' – those which no individual or group of individuals have an incentive to produce because they cannot exclude others from enjoying the benefits – identified by economists, and they are not (at least in theory) especially problematic.[3]

No reasonable individual could argue that society is wholly unfree or unjust if it taxes its citizens to pay for defence and the system of justice, though he is certainly less free as a result. Although parts of the structure of defence – like army housing, to take an obvious example – are amenable to being priced and performed by the private sector, at bottom nobody can escape the protection of the armed forces even if they wanted to. Similarly, much of the responsibility for law and order is already borne by the private sector. Even the public police force charges private clients for keeping order at pop concerts and football matches. But the protection of the forces of law and order is still inescapable, and it is therefore reasonable to charge all taxpayers for the service. Education, on the other hand, would be relatively easy to divide and price to consumers in the marketplace. But many would argue that public benefits flow from the collective provision of education: everybody gains if children receive school and university educations which their parents are unwilling or unable to pay for. The same might even be said of free medical care, where the State is better able to restrain costs than the private sector despite the fact that a thriving private sector already exists.

It is the third category identified by Adam Smith which is most troublesome. He had in mind roads, canals, harbours and the like what would today be called the transport infrastructure – and public services like the coinage, the Post Office and the diplomatic service. The Georgian and Victorian State largely confined its nondefence and nonjustice activities to these areas, with some relief of social distress through the Poor Laws as well. It also relied heavily on local forms of government to carry them out, not least because contemporary communications made it impossible to centralise the administration of public services. Victorian public expenditure consisted almost entirely of spending on defence, law and order, debt repayments and subsidies to local government. But, in the changed ideological climate[4] and improved communications of the twentieth century, 'erecting and maintaining certain public works and certain public institutions' has become a licence for the extension of State power into any area where a so-called 'market failure' is identified. The main features of the modern Welfare State like State-sponsored unemployment and health services and pension provision are obvious instances, but State correction of market failures is an unending, and often trivial, business.

The driver who obstructs a thoroughfare by parking his van outside a shop where he is making a delivery will eventually encourage State interference in the shape of double yellow lines, traffic wardens and State fines despatched by post to his home, the address supplied by a computer system in Cardiff which matches his registration number to his home address. Businesses are prime candidates for the correction of market failure. The manufacturer who tips waste matter into a river can eventually expect to be notified of new State regulations forbidding him to do so, to be enforced by the threat of a fine, or to receive an invitation through the post to purchase a licence entitling him to carry on. Similarly, an employer willing to take on unemployed trainees but unable to afford to do so can expect (especially if he asks) to receive a tax break in his annual return to the Inland Revenue or a cheque through the post from the Department of Employment if he elects to take some on. But these rectifications of 'market failure' are far from cost less. Every action the State takes has what economists call third-party or external or neighbourhood effects, or what Milton Friedman has called 'government failure'. One man's subsidy is another man's tax rise, and one man's regulation is another man's price rise.

Almost any government rule, regulation or subsidy is redistributive, in that it imposes costs or benefits on some people at the expense of others. The Manchester Business School, for example, estimated in 1991 that an average business spends 20 per cent of its pre-tax profits dealing with company law and tax regulations. The proportion is undoubtedly higher for many small businesses. Each Finance Act adds another 200–300 pages of complicated tax legislation every year, forcing businessmen to turn to costly professional advisers, buy software packages or simply spend more time on compliance. Similarly, an Enterprise Zone might regenerate a run-down inner-city site, but only by attracting existing businesses from another part of the same town. Or planning permission for a hypermarket on the edge of a town may destroy the high street shops in the same conurbation. Listed building regulations may enhance the appearance of a village, but they oblige owners to abstain from cost-saving improvements and to take out expensive insurance to cover the cost of rebuilding in the appropriate style. A clean atmosphere might be thought to be an unarguable public good, but cleaning up pollution imposes heavy private costs. In such cases the State is merely working to particular political definitions of the public good, and obliging private individuals to bear the costs of its decisions. It is, in other words, taxing them.

It is impossible to avoid the conclusion that there are no goods or services which can be classified as purely public or wholly private. The demarcation between public and private goods is a matter not of principle, but of political judgment. In his memoirs, the former Chancellor Nigel Lawson has agreed that public expenditure priorities are largely a matter of political opinion:

> There is clearly no grand principle which wili yield an answer in terms of a specific percentage of the national income as the appropriate level for public spending. There are some goods identified by economists as 'public goods'... There is also a generally accepted case for raising public funds to relieve poverty and provide for the needs of the sick and disabled which many economists misleadingly describe as 'redistribution'... These objectives, however, can only be a general guide. They still leave the most important issues a matter of opinion... Where to draw the line is a political more than a technical issue. Moreover, even if there were universal agreement on the proper scope of State provision, this would still not determine how much should be spent on these agreed objectives... Just as revealed choice in the market place is a standard way of assessing consumer preferences, so the political market place is the only known method of making choices between different types of collective spending, or between the collective and private variety.[4]

He eventually settled for reducing public expenditure as a proportion of GDP. This was a rule-of-thumb which at least ensured that government spending did not rise faster than the growth of the economy – a sure formula for incremental collectivism – but it also marked a sad retreat from the high hopes which followed the election of the first Thatcher government in May 1979.

Why the Conservatives Failed to Cut Public Expenditure

The policy document published in October 1977 *The Right Approach to the Economy*, promised to 'reduce the share of the nation's wealth consumed by the

State'.[5] The manifesto on which the Government was elected promised 'to make substantial economies, and there should be no doubt about our intention to do so'.[6] Geoffrey Howe said in his first Budget speech that 'finance must determine expenditure, not expenditure finance'. The government's first published public expenditure plans, released in November 1979, stated frankly that 'public expenditure is at the heart of Britain's present economic difficulties...The Government's economic strategy must be to stabilise public spending for the time being.'[7] It is true that in 1979 there was a great deal of misplaced optimism about the savings which could be made through the elimination of waste, bureaucracy, overmanning and industrial and employment subsidies. Ministerial briefing papers prepared in Opposition envisaged public expenditure cuts of £624 million in the first year in office, £2½ billion in the second year, £3¾ billion in the third year and nearly £5 billion in the fourth year. Efficiency gains alone were expected to produce savings of between £700 million and £2 billion.[8] In fact Derek Rayner, head of the Cabinet Office Efficiency Unit from May 1979 to December 1982 managed to save just £39 million in one-off economies and £107 million in annual savings.[9]

At bottom, this naive reliance on the elimination of waste and inefficiency was a political judgment. The Conservative Party in Opposition knew it could not win an election by promising to cut the Welfare State. It had not only to pledge to maintain the real value of welfare payments but to honour the massive pay increases in the public sector, which the Labour Government had negotiated to end the Winter of Discontent. The outgoing Government had already committed its successor to large real increases in defence spending and the Conservatives were determined to inflate expenditure on law and order too. These commitments narrowed the scope for cuts still further, but were relatively trivial by comparison with the welfare undertakings. Although it eventually proved possible to link welfare increases to prices rather than earnings (which rise much faster than prices generally) re-election in 1983, 1987 and 1992 still necessitated an unwavering commitment to the maintenance of the Welfare State in its present form.

Yet real cuts in public expenditure are difficult to achieve unless a government is prepared to cut welfare spending. As Table 4 shows, welfare spending now accounts for nearly two thirds of total public expenditure, and the traditional domain of defence and law and order accounts for less than a fifth. Although privatisation and the reduction of industrial subsidies has reduced the direct role of the State in the economy, government is still sufficiently involved in the economy to make the withdrawal of the remaining subsidies mainly to agriculture, industry, the national heritage and the developing world – impossible without immense short-term economic and political disruption. It is not surprising that successive Conservative governments have fund it difficult to contain public spending, let alone effect real reductions.

No Chancellor in modern times was more committed to the reduction of public expenditure than Nigel Lawson. Yet even he now thinks that real

Table 4   Public Spending Programme as a Proportion
of General Government Expenditure

Function	1978/79 percent of total	1997/98 percent of total (d)	Real change '78/9–'97/8
Traditional Domain			
Defence	10.6%	6.8%	–12%
Law, Order& protective services	3.6%	5.5%	107%
Central administration (b)	3.9%	2.1%	–27%
Welfare State			
Social security	23.5%	31.5%	84%
Health	10.7%	13.6%	75%
Education	12.7%	11.7%	27%
Personal social services	1.9%	3.4%	140%
Housing	6.3%	1.1%	–75%
Mixed Economy			
Debt Interest	6.1%	7.6%	71%
Other environmental services	3.8%	3.1%	14%
Transport	4.2%	2.9%	–4%
Trade, industry, energy, emply't & training	5.8%	2.8%	–34%
Agriculture, fisheries & food	1.4%	1.7%	65%
International development & other employment & training	1.5%	1.1%	–4%
Culture, media & sport	1.0%	0.9%	24%
Adjustments (c)	3.1%	4.3%	91%
Total	100.00	100.00	37

Notes: (a) General government expenditure less privatisation receipts, lottery funded
expenditure and interest and divident receipts.

(b) Including net contributions to EC budget.

(c) Amount necessary to reconcile public expenditure data to national accounts
concepts. Including allowance for shortfall in 1997/98.

(d) Estimated outturn

Source: HM Treasury. 'Public Expenditure Statistical Analyses 1998/99, Cm 3801 table 3.5 –
HM Treasury

reductions in public expenditure are politically unachievable. In one dispiriting passage in his memoirs, he writes:

There was one basic principle which guided my own efforts. Much writing on social choice and welfare economics implicitly assumes that all income belongs in the first instance to the State, and is then allocated by the State to individuals... The Tory belief should be the opposite one: that income or property belongs to the people who earn it or who have legitimately acquired it; and that a case has to be made for taxing it away. When the trumpets and drums are silent, and the last revisionist tract is off the Press, this is the abiding rift which still remains between Left and

Right. With that principle in mind, real world Tory politicians have to start off from where they find themselves: from existing structures, institutions, beliefs, political pressures and (sometimes unwelcome) manifesto commitments. Nevertheless, despite these handicaps, it is possible, with difficulty, to reduce public expenditure as a share of GDP.[10]

It is significant that none of the major spending institutions – the defence establishment, the National Health Service, the teachers, the educationalists, and the paraphernalia of the social security system – was subjected to searching reform during the 1980s.[10]

Though the real value of the defence and education budgets dipped here and there, and the defence budget is now on a pronounced downward trend, virtually every major area of public expenditure saw substantial increases in real spending between 1979 and 1994 (see Tables 4 and 5).

No effective way has yet been found to cut welfare expenditure, except at the margins, and win elections. Politics has become not a matter of competing principles but a dispute over which party is best equipped to manage the State. One economic commentator has estimated, on the basis of an analysis of the Family Expenditure Survey, that 46 per cent of households gain from the Welfare State and 54 per cent lose. He thinks this explains the political paralysis over the cost of the Welfare State. 'A government proposing either spending cuts or tax hikes,' he wrote, 'runs the risk of being thrown out of office... Political paralysis is a dear possibility.[11] Professor Harold Perkin, at the end of an exhaustive survey of society in England since the 1880s, concluded that the conflict between the public and the private sectors was the 'master-conflict' of modern politics.'[12] Marxist writers have rightly adumbrated a 'legitimation' and a 'fiscal' crisis of the liberal democratic State, in which the welfare activities of the government become so extensive that it is unable to deliver either the prosperity or the tax revenues which would enable it to deliver on its promises to either the productive or the dependent parts of the electorate.'[13]

The Bias Against Capital Expenditure

Restraining public expenditure as a proportion of GDP without cutting welfare payments meant, in practice, that public expenditure cuts were concentrated on less politically sensitive areas and especially on capital spending. This was precisely the approach for which the Conservative Party had castigated the Labour government in Opposition, underlining yet again the inescapable short-termism of the democratic State under governments of all persuasions. As Tables 4 and 5 show, the housing budget was cut substantially in real terms. Although the standard accounting treatment of the sale of council houses as negative public expenditure exaggerated the fall, the number of houses built by local authorities did fall by 93.9 per cent between 1979 and 1992. The slack was not completely taken up by an increase in building by private housebuilders and housing associations, though it was obviously easier to make economies in public expenditure where a private sector alternative was readily available.[14]

Table 5   Public Expenditure From 1978-79 to 1993-94

Function	Real change (d)
Personal social services	140%
Law, order & protective services	107%
Social security	84%
Health	75%
Debt interest	71%
Agriculture, fisheries & food	65%
Education	27%
Culture, media & sport	24%
Other environmental services	14%
International development & other int. services	−4%
Transport	−4%
Defence	−12%
Central administration (b)	−27%
Trade, industry, energy, emply't & training	−34%
Housing	−75%
Adjustments (c)	91%
Total	37%
GDP	48%

Notes: (a) General government expenditure less privatisation receipts, lottery funded expenditure and interest and dividend receipts.
(b) Including net contributions to EC budget.
(c) Amount necessary to reconcile public expenditure data to national accounts concepts. Including allowance for shortfall in 1997/98.
(d) Relative to GDP deflator. Estimated outturn for 1997/98
Sources: HM Treasury, 'Public Expenditure Statistical Analyses 1998/99, Cm 3801 table 3.5 HM Treasury

The reduction in trade and industrial subsidies was a sensible and well-considered act of policy, and reflected in large part the successful restructuring and sale of the nationalised industries as well as the demise of regional policy and other wasteful subsidies. But success in making these economies reflected their low political cost. It was also relatively easy, at least in the short term, to cut public expenditure on the transport infrastructure. Although arguably part of the traditional domain of government, and certainly seen as such by Adam Smith, it was badly neglected until the end of the 1980s. Between 1978-79 and 1988-89 the transport budget actually shrank by 9.6 per cent in real terms. Although transport expenditure included a large element of unwarranted subsidy, one consequence of squeezing the budget was undeniably a lack of investment in public transport. Expenditure has since recovered, but it is still insufficient to pay for the backlog of investment which accumulated on the railways during the 1980s.

It is principally the squeeze on capital spending which has fed allegations that the public expenditure constraints of the 1980s created a country of 'private affluence and public squalor' . As Table 6 shows, State capital spending fell in eleven out of the last fifteen years. But then it has fallen in nineteen out of the last twenty-eight years under governments of both parties. This is just one more melancholy effect of the democratic pressure to maintain current spending in popular areas like health, education and law and order at almost any cost. It is in the nature of capital spending that the costs are incurred immediately whilst the benefits are long postponed, and a government seeking re-election is naturally anxious to ensure that the benefits of its largesse are enjoyed immediately and the pain deferred for as long as possible.

It is sometimes thought, usually by people outside the modern political process, that there must be an objective (or at least a better) way of choosing between public expenditure priorities. Calls are made periodically for greater clarity in Treasury accounting between current and capital spending, or for greater use of cost-benefit analysis, or for an end to the bi-lateral haggling between departmental ministers and the Treasury, which tends to preserve departmental current budgets at the expense of a searching overall consideration of the best way of achieving policy goals through the optimum mixture of capital and current spending. The Treasury does now separate public sector capital and current spending in the Financial Statement and Budget Report published at the time of the Budget, but the policy of attracting private capital to public sector projects has made it an increasingly misleading indicator.

Cost-benefit analysis is used to determine priorities within particular programmes – a recent example was choosing the route of the rail link to the Channel Tunnel – but, as the inhabitants of various parts of Kent well know, it cannot eradicate political factors altogether. Nor can cost-benefit analysis help the government choose the Channel Rail link rather than a squadron of Tornado fighter-bombers or six new prisons. In the end public sector capital investments like new roads, schools and hospitals lack the simple test of a cash return, which the private sector uses to choose where to invest. In a democracy, collective spending is determined by politicians, and to complain that the process is inefficient is to misunderstand the nature of democratic politics.

Yet the criticism that the public expenditure system favours current spending over capital expenditure persists precisely because the popular intuition – that capital spending is superior to current spending – is right. Treating £1 spent on child benefit in exactly the same way as £1 spent on a new motorway, ignoring the fact that a stream of future benefits will stem from the road, is counter-intuitive. New roads, like new schools, increase the stock of public sector assets which can be set against public sector liabilities in determining the creditworthiness of the State. The central government balance sheet calculated by the Central Statistical Office shows net assets of minus £25 billion at the end of 1992, and the public sector as a whole with net wealth of only £200 billion, most of it owned by local authorities.[16] But one guesstimate is that the road network alone is worth £90 billion gross (or rather less, net of maintenance, policing, environmental damage and accident costs).[17] Likewise, the Ministry of Defence owns one of the largest freehold land estates in the United Kingdom, consisting of nearly 561,000 acres of land and foreshore.[18] There are plenty of other physical assets of the same kind.

Table 6   Public Sector Capital Expenditure

Financial year	Real GDP growth (a)	Gross capital spending (£bn)	GCS at 1996/97 prices (b) (£bn)	Real CGS net of depreciation (£bn)	Change in GCS at 1996/97 prices
1965/66	2.6%	3.0	32.5	21.0	n.a.
1966/67	1.9%	3.6	36.8	24.9	13.2%
1967/68	2.8%	4.3	43.3	30.6	17.6%
1968/69	3.8%	4.4	41.8	28.4	–3.4%
1969/70	2.2%	4.6	41.3	27.4	–1.2%
1970/71	2.3%	5.2	43.9	29.3	6.2%
1971/72	1.5%	5.3	41.0	25.7	–6.6%
1972/73	5.0%	5.8	40.9	24.9	–0.1%
1973/74	3.9%	7.0	46.7	28.7	14.0%
1974/75	0.0%	9.2	50.8	31.5	8.8%
1975/76	–0.1%	11.2	49.6	30.3	–2.3%
1976/77	3.0%	11.8	45.9	25.9	–7.5%
1977/78	2.4%	11.1	38.1	18.0	–16.9%
1978/79	2.7%	12.0	36.9	16.4	–3.2%
1979/80	2.9%	13.8	36.5	15.7	–0.9%
1980/81	–3.5%	14.8	33.1	11.8	–9.5%
1981/82	0.3%	13.8	28.1	6.9	–15.2%
1982/83	2.2%	16.0	30.4	10.2	8.4%
1983/84	3.7%	17.6	32.0	11.8	5.2%
1984/85	1.6%	17.3	29.8	10.7	–6.8%
1985/86	4.4%	15.9	26.1	8.8	–12.4%
1986/87	4.3%	14.9	23.7	6.7	–9.3%
1987/88	4.9%	14.7	22.2	6.3	–6.5%
1988/89	4.3%	14.6	20.7	4.6	–6.8%
1989/90	1.8%	20.3	26.8	11.3	29.8%
1990/91	–0.3%	20.7	25.4	12.0	–5.4%
1991/92	–1.9%	21.6	24.9	13.4	–1.9%
1992/93	0.2%	23.5	26.0	15.4	4.4%
1993/94	2.7%	21.3	22.9	12.6	–11.8%
1994/95	4.6%	21.7	22.9	12.2	0.0%
1995/96	2.3%	20.8	21.4	10.3	–6.7%
1996/97	2.6%	17.4	17.4	6.8	–18.6%

Notes: (a) Changes in GDP at constant factor cost.
            (b) Revalued using the adjusted GDP deflator.
Source: ONS – CSDB database

The Chancellor of the Exchequer did announce a switch to so-called 'resource accounting' in his 1993 Budget speech. This will enable the State to make better estimates of its net worth and so decide whether the public sector balance sheet (and, by implication, the physical infrastructure of the country) is deteriorating or not. But resource accounting is not expected to affect the whole of the public sector until the turn of the century, and even after it is introduced there will still be no ready means of measuring whether a new road (or school or hospital) built by the public sector is a worthwhile investment for the taxpayer. Public investment rarely yields an income, and it is hard to describe any investment which fails to produce a measurable return as an asset. The cost of maintaining it may even turn it into a financial liability for the taxpayer, whether or not in his alter ego of motorist or mature student he enjoys the unquantifiable benefits of easier access to a sociology course or his mother-in-law.

It is nevertheless true that the public balance sheet does eventually receive a return in the shape of less unemployment or pollution, a healthier population or higher tax revenues from the greater economic growth which stems from more schools and hospitals and from goods and services moving around the country more easily. But these benefits are too difficult, or too long term, to play much role in the short-term political calculus of the universal franchise. State-financed investment in human capital – through education, training and health care, for example – is a concept which fits snugly with the 'positive' conception of freedom preferred by high-spending Socialists and Liberal Democrats, but it is even harder to measure. As Samuel Brittan has frequently pointed out, expenditure on school lavatories counts as capital spending but expenditure on science teachers is current. If the entire education budget was treated as investment in human capital, the taxpayer invested £33.7 billion in human capital in 1993–94. Another £3.6 billion went into employment and training measures.[19] But it is impossible to decide what proportion of these budgets was genuinely new or value-adding investment, and what proportion was consumed merely in maintaining existing educational and training standards.

It is for these sorts of reasons that Nigel Lawson was so withering in his contempt for people who try to import private sector standards into the public sector. 'Those who seek to assimilate the system of public expenditure control to the conventions and methods used in the private sector,' he wrote, 'always remind me of small children playing at shops. It has little relationship to the real thing.'[20] This explains why the distinction between capital and current spending does not feature prominently in public expenditure decisions. Indeed, it is an area where Treasury accounting is at its most arcane.[21] This blurring of the distinction between capital and current spending in the public sector – both in reality and in accounting terms – has reinforced the baleful effects of democracy on the pattern of public expenditure. Nearly seventy years ago in The End of Laissez-Faire, Maynard Keynes argued that 'the important thing for Government is not to do things which individuals are doing already, and to do them a little better or worse; but to do those things which at present are not done at all'. He had in mind the embellishment of cities and the construction of buildings like concert halls and art galleries to make use of unemployed labour. He thought the private sector had lost its nerve, and needed the external stimulus of public works to restore its confidence. 'When we have unemployed men and unemployed plant and more savings than we are using at home, it is utterly imbecile to say that we cannot afford these things. For it is with the unemployed men and the unemployed plant, and with nothing else, that these things are done' as he put it in 1928, long before the General Theory was published.[22]

There is still a strong case for using public works to counter the effects of the trade cycle, especially now that the lifting of exchange controls has freed the State to borrow in the international capital markets. Capital projects provide employment, boost the morale of entrepreneurs and create valuable infrastructural assets. Unfortunately, the whole momentum of the modern democratic State tends to the opposite course. As Table 6 shows, in both of the last two recessions public capital expenditure tended to shrink. As a result, many thousands of men and women have sat out all or part of the recessions on unemployment or social security benefits. In a welfare democracy, it is politically more rewarding to pauperise the unemployed than it is to put them to work. This is another consequence of a system which lacks any set of objective criteria to which an appeal can be made to decide whether or not the State should spend the taxpayers' money on a particular service or project.

The government has now effectively admitted that a bias against capital expenditure exists, and that it cannot be solved by orthodox political methods. In 1992 it launched an initiative to attract private capital into projects previously regarded as exclusively the preserve of the State, like roads, railways, prisons, hospitals, schools and public sector computer projects. Because the State can always borrow more cheaply than a private company, the private finance initiative implicitly recognises that in a welfare democracy infrastructure will never be given priority over the salaries of doctors and teachers or expenditure on social security benefits. In theory, the initiative will reduce the role of the State to that of regulator, or at most to the status of a partner in joint venture projects. But, however limited the involvement of the State, its deadening influence will continue to be felt. The Treasury, which is concerned to ensure privately financed projects have as little impact as possible on the public finances, is anxious to ensure that private investors bear and manage the whole of the planning, construction and financial risks. But private investors are understandably reluctant to assume planning and other political risks which they cannot control at all. These are real enough, as the proponents of the CrossRail link between east and west London found when a handful of MPs sank the project in May 1994.

Any planning or expenditure decisions made by politicians and State officials are bound to be influenced mainly by their own interests. These include retaining or extending their own power and patronage and advancing cherished ideological objectives. The village in a marginal constituency may get its bypass, but the suburb in the nearby town may never be politically important enough to get its much-needed flyover. The bridge over the Humber estuary, promised by a government desperate to win a by-election in Hull, has passed into political memory as the classic instance of an infrastructural project which was justifiable only on political grounds. Occasionally, the political or bureaucratic interest in a decision is even more direct. It was recently disclosed, for example, that the choices made by a Ministry of Defence official in charge of weapons procurement had for many years corresponded exactly to the size of the bribes he was offered by arms manufacturers.

The political mediation of infrastructural investment decisions reduces some of the most important questions of economic prosperity and fiscal policy to an annual round of horse-trading between the Chief Secretary to the Treasury and departmental ministers. If Nigel Lawson is right, elected governments are now perpetually hemmed in by the spending institutions and commitments they inherit, and the best the country can expect is for public spending to be held somewhere around its current share of the national income. In those circumstances, there will always be more votes in current spending than in long-term capital projects. It is not hyperbolic to describe life under this system, which condemns hundreds of thousands of able-bodied people to live at the public expense while the infrastructure of the country falls apart, as absurd. Some entirely new method has to be found to break the democratic deadlock.

References

1   In a speech to the Anglesey Labour Party, 23 January 1976, reported in The Times, 24 January 1976.See also Maurice Mullard, The Politics of Public Expenditure, Routledge, 1993, page 21. The figure of 60 per cent was subsequently reduced to 511/2 per cent by removing from the public expenditure total self-financed investment and borrowings by the nationalised industries and central government subsidies to local authority borrowing for house construction. By recalculating GDP on the basis of market prices (the price actually paid for goods and services bought from the economy) rather than factor cost (market prices less expenditure taxes plus subsidies) it was reduced still further to 46 per cent. For a full description of the changes see Leo Pliatzky, Getting and Spending, Blackwell, 1982, pages 161–6.

2   Quoted in The Essential Adam Smith, edited by Robert L. Heilbroner, W. W. Norton, 1986, page 289.

3   Leo Pliatzky defines a public good as 'available to everybody; it costs no more to supply it to everybody than to only some people; and nobody can contract out of its benefits'. From Leo Pliatzky, Paying and Choosing, Basil Blackwell, 1985, page 126.

4   Nigel Lawson, The View From No. 11, Bantam, 1992, pages 299–300.

5   Geoffrey Howe, Keith Joseph, James Prior and David Howell, The Right Approach to the Economy, Conservative Central Office, October 1977, page 10.

6   Conservative Manifesto, 1979.

7   Cmnd 7746, November 1979.

8   Ministerial Dossier: Dossier for Government, Conservative Research Department, 2 May 1979.

9   Peter Hennessy, Whitehall, Fontana, 1989, page 598.

10   Nigel Lawson, The View From No. 11, Bantam, 1992, page 300.

11   Brian Reading, Sunday Times, 22 August 1993.

12   See Harold Perkin, The Rise of Professional Society: England Since 1880, Routledge, 1989.

13   See C. B. Macpherson, The Rise and Fall of Economic Justice, OUP, 1985, pages 62–75.

14   In 1979 88,495 council houses were built, compared with 5,410 in 1992. See Annual Abstract of Statistics 1993, Table 3.10.

15   Real terms in this case means adjusted by the GDP Deflator, a general measure of domestic costs uninfluenced by import prices or interest rate changes. It is a reasonable measure of what a public service costs to finance in real terms, which is the essential question from the point of view of the taxpayer if not the recipient of public services. Some economists would prefer to see each, public expenditure

programme deflated by an index specific to that type of spending. Because specific deflators can gauge the 'relative price effect' – the extent to which pay and prices affecting a particular programme are rising at a faster or slower rate than pay and; prices in other programmes, or in the economy as a whole – they are felt to be a better gauge of the actual level of service or output being achieved. Since pay is the biggest cost element in any public expenditure programme (at least half of it in most instances) specific deflators can measure the extent to which extra spending is dissipated in pay rises rather than a higher level of service or output but they are over-influenced, from the point of view of a government seeking to contain public expenditure, by the fact that pay tends to rise faster than prices generally. The effect of using specific deflators in public expenditure planning is therefore to build pay inflation into the system. Politically, of course, elected ministers also prefer to announce cash increases or real increases in terms of the GDP deflator, which may actually conceal decreases in real terms. One recent analyst has used specific deflators to demonstrate that public expenditure in all major areas – defence, law and order, education, health, environment housing, roads, trade and industry – was lower between 1983 and 1990, both in real terms and as a proportion of GDP, than in the 1960s and 1970s. This was achieved, in his view, mainly by cutting capital spending but also by containing public sector pay rises. See Maurice Mullard, The Politics of Public Expenditure, Routledge, 1993, pages 22-41.

16   CSO National Accounts, Table 12.9-12.2.

17   Financial Times, 13 February 1993.

18   The National Audit Office has criticised both the Ministry of Defence and the Department of Transport for inadequate management of landed assets. See National Audit Office, Department of Transport: Acquisition, Management and Disposal of Land and Property Purchased for Road Construction, Number 492, June 1994, and Ministry of Defence: Management and Control of Army Training Land, Number 218, February 1992.

19   Public Expenditure: Statistical Supplement to the Financial Statement and Budget Report 1994–95, Cmnd 2519, H.M.S.O., February 1994, Table 1.2, page 9.

20   Nigel Lawson, The View From No. 11, Bantam, 1992, page 298.

21   The Treasury uses two different measures of capital spending. The National Accounts definition, drawn from the data published by the CSO in Financial Statistics, adds up Gross Domestic Fixed Capital Formation (spending on schools hospitals roads, prisons, computers, plant and machinery etc) net of sales of assets (like council houses and surplus land), grants to support capital spending by the private sector (mainly science and technology) and stocks in hand (in the case of government, mainly food mountains). In some cases the Treasury deducts a measure of depreciation, to take account of wear and tear, but it is hard to agree on a measure which is accurate. The second definition is the so-called Public Sector Asset Creation (PSAC) measure, which excludes things the State already owns and concentrates on the purchase of new assets. It also includes receipts from asset sales and counts much more of the military budget as capital rather than current. PSAC makes no attempt to measure depreciation. It therefore tends to be higher than the National Accounts definition.

22   See Robert Skidelsky, John Maynard Keynes: The Economist As Saviour 1920–1937, Macmillan, 1992, pages 298 and 529.

CHAPTER FOUR

The Changing Nature of Taxation

There is…in almost all forms of government agency, one thing which is
compulsory; the provision of the pecuniary means.
John Stuart Mill, *Principles of Political Economy*[1]

No one need be afraid of any taxes being taken off in my time.
David Lloyd George

The Inland Revenue is the largest business in the country.
Elizabeth Filkin, Inland Revenue Ombudsman[2]

If you are a Social Democrat, you think it is terrific to pay taxes. For me,
taxes are the finest expression of what politics are all about.
Mona Sahlin, Party Secretary,
Swedish Social Democrats[3]

Public expenditure has to be financed. Since the State has no income of its own,
save a handful of rent-producing properties, it can pay for its activities only by
confiscating the income and wealth of its citizens. That the State can subsist
only by taking what belongs to others is the single most important reason why
excessive public expenditure threatens individual liberty, economic prosperity
and social harmony. Taxation necessitates the invasion and expropriation of
private property by paid officials of the State, lumbers industry and enterprise
with imposts to pay for the public sector and reduces millions of individuals to
a condition of debilitating dependency on the limited ability of elected
politicians to extort unlimited sums of money from their constituents.

Taxation divides the people of a country into two great and antagonistic
classes. Montesquieu called them the shearers and the shorn. The main political
struggle in Britain today is being fought between those who benefit from public
expenditure and those who pay for it with taxes. As the State has grown, a
paradox has arisen: these two classes are often embodied in the same person. In
its modern, climactic absurdity taxation has at last fused the shearers and the
shorn into one. Everyone pays taxes and everyone receives them, turning the
State from the guardian of property into a giant and malevolent matriarch

whose task it is to decide exactly what portion of the whole wealth of the land each of its infants shall have.[4] In the structure and incidence of taxation today can be found the causes of the decline of liberty and the declension of material prosperity.

After the police baton, taxation is the principal expression of State power in modern democratic societies. It is as unlikely to disappear completely as that blunt instrument of the general will. Wherever a State exists, it will tax. The verisimilitude of Benjamin Franklin's celebrated aphorism that in this world nothing can be said to be certain except death and taxes has magnified, rather than diminished, over the two centuries which have elapsed since he made it. The task of political economy is therefore not to eradicate taxation, but to ensure that taxes are well-chosen. For, if taxation is not levied judiciously, it can expunge freedom, diminish the standard of living and rot the ties of duty and reciprocity that bind individuals together.

The task of devising a wise system of taxation becomes progressively more complicated the higher the volume of expenditure it is intended to finance, and the greater the number of individuals and organisations which acquire a stake in the outcome of the negotiations between taxpayers and tax-receivers. The vast and complex kaleidoscope of modern taxation is the end-result of countless compromises between them over the course of the last one hundred years or so, and it demonstrates more completely than any other single collection of facts the unplanned and unnoticed revolution which has taken place in the twentieth century in the relationship between the Individual and the State. 'Public finances,' the great Austrian economist Joseph Schumpeter once wrote, 'are one of the best starting points for an investigation of society. The spirit of a people, its cultural level, its social structure, the deeds its policy may prepare – all this and more is written in its fiscal history, stripped of all phrases. He who knows how to listen to the message here discerns the thunder of world history more clearly than anywhere else.'[5] The modern fiscal history of Britain is the story of the unceasing aggrandisement of individual liberty and private property by the State.

The Original Purpose of Taxation

It used to be different. Until the close of the nineteenth century, taxation had one overwhelming purpose: to protect private property from criminals and foreign invasion. When Robert Nozick likens the taxation of earned income to forced labour the notion seems at first rather startling, but the earliest English taxes took precisely this form.[6] In return for military protection, the inhabitants of a town or region were expected to maintain roads and forts, house and feed the military and serve in the army themselves. It was only later that scutage ('shield money') was introduced as a cash alternative to military service. Feudal dues, initially paid in kind as well, were also expected to cover the costs of administering the primitive system of justice. In Saxon days, when Kings and Courts were peripatetic, landowners also paid the form, or food-rents, to the monarch when he came to stay. In exchange for surrendering a portion of their labour and the fruit of their labour, the Anglo-Saxon settlers expected their life and property to be protected from foreign and domestic marauders. The State was seen not as a useful actor in their daily life and fortune, but merely as a licensed bandit to which they paid a form of protection money. The essential nature of the State has not changed since – Mancur Olsen has rightly described it as a 'stationary bandit' – but the kinds of security it is prepared to offer now extend far beyond what John Locke and his contemporaries would have called their Propriety.[7] Indeed, it is the central purpose of the modern Welfare State to insulate men and women from *all* forms of adversity, and not just the threats of war, violence and crime.

Armed conflict remained the central preoccupation of the State until the late nineteenth century. Between 1689 and 1815 military expenditure accounted for over two fifths of total public expenditure in peacetime and well over two thirds in wartime. Most of the rest was consumed in interest payments on war debts, with civil government accounting for an average of less than 15 per cent of total expenditure even in peacetime.[8] Until the end of the eighteenth century public expenditure was funded largely through deferred rather than direct or indirect taxation, or by borrowing on the growing London capital market. Taxes were used mainly to meet the interest payments on the debts incurred. Between 1702 and 1783 taxes accounted for an average of just over one fifth of the extra revenue needed to fight wars, but interest payments to holders of government debt accounted for an average of one third of total public expenditure.[9]

The financing of the wars waged by Georgian England provided an early lesson in State expropriation by subterfuge. Taxation grew faster than the economy throughout the eighteenth century, but by using borrowing to avoid sudden and politically unpopular rises in taxation the State was able to increase the real burden of taxation eighteen times between the Restoration in 1660 and victory at Waterloo in 1815 without risking an uncontainable popular revolt. The demands of war finance also strengthened the ability of the State to extort taxes from the people, by increasing the size and efficiency of the bureaucracy and its coercive powers. It was during these years that the first political lobbyists and corporate parasites began to swarm around the enlarged fiscal machine in search of subsidies, tax breaks and rake-offs from the public procurement process. During the eighteenth century the government was transformed from an ineffective and semi-feudal regime into what one historian has called a powerful 'fiscal-military State'.[10]

It was fortunate for the success of the first industrial nation that Victorian Britain was mainly at peace with its neighbours, and the fiscal-military State created by the Georgians went largely unused. The share of the national income consumed by the State in taxes rose from just 3.4 per cent in 1660 to 10.8 per cent in 1720 and to 18 per cent at the climax of the Napoleonic Wars in 1815.[11] But the share of the national income taken in taxes fell sharply after Waterloo. At the beginning of the collectivist era in the 1880s taxation absorbed just 6–7 per cent of the national income and, even at the height of the Boer War at the turn of the century, it took less than a tenth.[12] As Table 7 shows, the peak rate of income tax in the Victorian era was 6.67 per cent, levied in 1856–7 to pay for the Crimean War, and it was paid by just 500,000 people, or rather less than 4 per cent of the adult population.

The national income grew rapidly during the nineteenth century enlarging the resources of the State even though the fiscal burden on the economy was low. But Victorian Chancellors also abjured the Georgian technique of deferring the political impact of taxation by borrowing. Peel reintroduced an income tax in 1842 – the first time it was ever levied in peacetime – to tackle the national debt as well as to relieve the tariffs. His protege Gladstone, despite a deep detestation of income tax, refused to borrow to finance the Crimean War and prolonged and increased income tax instead. 'The expenses of war,' he observed in 1854, 'are a moral check.'[13] Even Harcourt, infamous for introducing Death Duties in 1894, did so not to redistribute wealth but to cover a mounting budget deficit. In Victorian Britain there was also, of course, a widespread objection to government interference, expenditure and taxation. This was rooted not so much in the various theoretical justifications of *laissez-faire* as in the common human objection to paying taxes, a profound reverence for the rights of private property and a widespread belief that governments were invariably incompetent, corrupt and apt to centralise. The governments of the collectivist era have operated in a quite different climate of ideas to that of the Victorians, or even the Hanoverians. Eighteenth-century commentators were obsessed with the waste and extravagance of Georgian government, Tom Paine contrasting the steadily declining taxation of the first four hundred years after the Conquest with the steady increase since Elizabeth with horror:

> The people of England of the present day, have a traditionary and historical idea of the bravery of their ancestors; but whatever their virtues or vices might have been, they certainly were a people who could not be imposed upon, and who kept government in awe as to taxation, if not as to principle. Though they were not able to expel the monarchical usurpation, they restricted it to a republican economy of taxes...It would have been impossible to have dragooned the former English, into the excess of taxation that now exists; and when it is considered that the pay of the army, the navy, and of all the revenue officers, is the same now as it was above a hundred years ago, when the taxes were not above a tenth part of what they are at present, it appears impossible to account for the enormous increase in expenditure, on any other ground, than extravagance, corruption, and intrigue.[14]

Unfortunately, the parsimony of the Victorians created a quite different kind of folk-memory in English radical circles. In their view, the State was a culpable bystander as industrial capitalism progressively impoverished the working classes.

Table 7   Standard Rate of Income Tax in the United Kingdom 1799–1994

Year	Rate	Year	Rate	Year	Rate
1799-1802	10.00	1881	2.50	1938	25.00%
1804-1805	5.00	1882	2.08	1939	27.50%
1806	6.25	1883	2.52	1940	35.00%
1807-1816	10.00	1884	2.08	1941	43.00%
1843-1853[1]	2.92	1885	2.50	1942–1946	50.00%
1853	4.38	1886–1887	3.33	1947–1951	45.00%
1854	5.83	1888	2.92	1952–1953	47.50%
1855	6.67	1889–1893	2.50	1944–1955	45.00%
1856-1857	2.92	1894	2.92	1956–1959	42.50%
1858	2.08	1895–1900	3.33	1960–1965	38.75%
1859	3.75	1901	5.00	1966–1969	40.68%
1860	2.92	1902	5.83	1970–1971	41.25%
1861	2.50	1903	6.25	1972–1973	38.75%
1862-1863	1.67	1904	4.58	1974[3]	30.00%
1864	2.08	1905–1909[2]	5.00	1975	33.00%
1865	2.50	1910–1914	5.83	1976	35.00%
1866-1867	1.67	1915	8.33	1977	34.00%
1868	2.08	1916	15.00	1978	33.00%
1869	2.50	1917–1918	25.00	1979–1985	30.00%
1870	2.08	1919–1922	30.00	1986	29.00%
1871	1.67	1923	25.00	1987	27.00%
1872	2.50	1924–1925	22.50	1988–1995	25.00%
1873	1.67	1926–1930	20.00		
1874	1.25	1931	22.50		
1875-1876	0.83	1932–1933	25.00		
1877-1878	1.25	1934–1935	22.50		
1879-1880	2.08	1935–1937	23.75		

1 There was no income tax in force in 1803 and from 1817 to 1842.
2 The Lloyd-George Budget of 1909 introduced progressively higher rates at different income levels for the first time.
3 From 1974 the Standard Rate became the Basic Rate and high rates were applied to the higher income bands.
Source: B. R. Mitchell, British Historical Statistics.

The Redistributive Purpose of Modern Taxation

It was during the Liberal regime of Asquith before the First World War that the Victorian conception of using taxation for revenue purposes only was superseded by the collectivist idea of using the fiscal system to make socio-political adjustments to an unfair economic dispensation. It was Asquith himself who first introduced a progressive income tax of sorts in 1907, and his successor Lloyd George who sparked a constitutional crisis with his Budget to wage war on poverty in 1909. This notorious Budget introduced the progressive taxation of incomes in a thoroughly modern form for the First time. Income tax was levied at 9d in the pound (3.75%) on incomes up to £2,000 a year, 1s in the pound (5%) on incomes up to £3,000 and 1s 2d (5.83%) on incomes above £3,000 a year. A new 'super-tax' (later abbreviated to surtax) of 6d (2.5%) was levied on every pound of earned income above £5,000 a year and of 9d in the pound (3.75%) on unearned Income in excess of £2,000 a year. There was also a new tax on land values, designed to tap the capital of landowners.[15] Asquith made the purpose of the Budget plain: 'If we are to have social reform we must pay for it and when I say we, I mean the whole nation, the working and consuming classes as well as the wealthier class of direct taxpayers.'[16]

But it was that old enemy of public economy – total war – which finally changed the intellectual and political appreciation of the purposes of taxation out of all recognition. Vastly inflated expenditure on soldiers, sailors, airmen and armaments was accompanied by savage increases in all forms of taxation. The standard rate of income tax quintupled from 1s 2d in the pound (5.83 per cent) in 1914 to 6 shillings in the pound (30 per cent) by 1918. Coupled with a lowering of the income tax threshold from £160 to £130, at a time of surging inflation, the number of taxpayers multiplied nearly eight-fold from just over a million in 1914 to 7.8 million in 1919.[17] When the war began the average workman, clerk or small shopkeeper paid no income tax at all, but by the time it was over he or she was probably surrendering at least a seventh of their income to the State. The war also encouraged the view that the cost of the conflict should be borne by those most 'able to pay', giving progressive taxation a veneer of moral respectability. The surtax reached a peak of 6s 10d (34.17 per cent) during the war. The richest in the land – those earning over £10,000 – were losing over two fifths of their income to the Treasury by the end of the war.

The Second World War merely accelerated these developments. Income tax peaked at 10s in the pound (50 per cent), and the surtax reached 19s 6d in the pound (97½ per cent).[18] The first Socialist majority government elected in 1945 inherited a system of taxation which was no longer bound by any considerations of equity and efficiency, and turned it into the formidable instrument of social engineering which it has remained ever since. 'Taxation,' admitted Douglas Jay in 1946, 'is just as effective as violence or outright confiscation, and at the same time lacks all their disadvantages.'[19] The unprecedented wartime rate of 50 per cent was cut by just one shilling to 45 per cent by Hugh Dalton in 1946. In 1939 less than a fifth of the working population paid income tax, but in the post-war Welfare State even the unemployed find themselves having to pay it. Today, an estimated 24.5 million people, or well over two thirds of the entire adult population aged between 16 and 65, pay income tax.

The Conservative Failure to Cut Taxes

It was not until the 1970s that the political and intellectual tide of collectivism began to ebb, and the election of a government confident enough to reverse nearly a century of rising taxation was postponed until 1979. But it is a measure of the numbing effects of chronic and excessive taxation that even four successive Conservative governments over sixteen years, the longest period of single party government since Lord Liverpool, have failed to reduce the burden of taxation. Table 8 shows that, once local authority and other tax receipts –

principally North Sea oil taxes – are excluded, the burden of tax as a proportion of the national income is actually higher in 1994-95 that it was in the last year of Labour government in 1978-79. There was a modest redistribution of the burden from income to spending, which enabled the higher rate of income tax to be cut from 83 per cent to 40 per cent and the basic rate from 33 per cent to 25 per cent. A new lower rate of 20 per cent was introduced in 1992.

Table 8   General Government Receipts
As percent of GDP adjusted for the abolition of domestic rates

Source of revenue	1978/79	1979/80	1980/81	1981/82	1982/83	1983/84
Income tax	11.0%	10.1%	10.4%	11.2%	10.8%	10.2%
VAT	2.8%	4.0%	4.8%	4.6%	4.9%	5.0%
Social security contributions (a)	5.9%	5.7%	6.0%	6.2%	6.7%	6.9%
Corporation tax	2.3%	2.3%	2.0%	1.9%	2.0%	2.0%
of which: ACT	0.8%	0.9%	0.8%	0.8%	0.8%	0.9%
Local taxes (b)	3.4%	3.4%	3.7%	4.3%	4.3%	4.0%
Fuel duties	1.4%	1.4%	1.5%	1.8%	1.9%	1.8%
Tobacco duties	1.4%	1.3%	1.2%	1.3%	1.2%	1.3%
Alcohol duties	1.4%	1.2%	1.1%	1.2%	1.1%	1.3%
Capital gains tax	0.2%	0.2%	0.2%	0.2%	0.2%	0.2%
Inheritance tax/CTT	0.2%	0.2%	0.2%	0.2%	0.2%	0.2%
Other receipts	8.6%	9.1%	9.6%	10.7%	10.3%	9.9%
Total	38.7%	38.8%	40.7%	43.7%	43.7%	42.9%
of which: oil & gas revenues	0.3%	1.1%	1.6%	2.5%	2.8%	2.9%

Table 8 continued

Source of revenue	1985/86	1986/87	1987/88	1988/89	1989/90	1990/91
Income tax	9.9%	10.0%	9.7%	9.1%	9.4%	9.9%
VAT	5.4%	5.5%	5.7%	5.7%	5.7%	5.6%
Social security contributions (a)	6.8%	6.9%	6.8%	6.8%	6.4%	6.4%
Corporation tax	3.0%	3.5%	3.7%	3.9%	4.2%	3.9%
of which: ACT	1.1%	1.2%	1.2%	1.3%	1.4%	1.4%
Local taxes (b)	3.9%	4.1%	4.0%	4.1%	4.0%	4.1%
Fuel duties	1.8%	1.9%	1.8%	1.8%	1.7%	1.7%
Tobacco duties	1.2%	1.2%	1.1%	1.0%	1.0%	1.0%
Alcohol duties	1.2%	1.1%	1.0%	1.0%	0.9%	0.9%
Capital gains tax	0.3%	0.3%	0.3%	0.5%	0.4%	0.3%
Inheritance tax/CTT	0.2%	0.3%	0.3%	0.2%	0.2%	0.2%
Other receipts	8.7%	6.7%	6.7%	6.2%	6.3%	5.4%
Total	42.3%	41.4%	41.1%	40.3%	40.1%	39.3%
of which: oil & gas revenues	3.2%	1.2%	1.1%	0.7%	0.5%	0.4%

Table 8 *continued*

Source of revenue	1991/92	1992/93	1993/94	1994/95	1995/96	1996/97
Income tax	9.9%	9.4%	9.1%	9.3%	9.5%	9.2%
VAT	6.1%	6.1%	6.1%	6.1%	6.0%	6.2%
Social security contributions (a)	6.2%	6.2%	6.1%	6.2%	6.2%	6.2%
Corporation tax	3.1%	2.6%	2.3%	2.9%	3.3%	3.7%
of which: ACT	*1.4%*	*1.4%*	*1.2%*	*1.2%*	*1.4%*	*1.6%*
Local taxes (b)	3.7%	3.6%	3.4%	3.2%	3.2%	3.4%
Fuel duties	1.9%	1.9%	2.0%	2.1%	2.2%	2.3%
Tobacco duties	1.1%	1.0%	1.0%	1.1%	1.0%	1.1%
Alcohol duties	0.9%	0.8%	0.8%	0.8%	0.8%	0.7%
Capital gains tax	0.2%	0.2%	0.1%	0.1%	0.1%	0.2%
Inheritance tax/CTT	0.2%	0.2%	0.2%	0.2%	0.2%	0.2%
Other receipts	5.0%	4.8%	4.7%	4.8%	5.2%	4.9%
Total	38.3%	36.7%	35.9%	36.9%	37.9%	38.0%
of which: oil & gas revenues	*0.2%*	*0.2%*	*0.2%*	*0.3%*	*0.3%*	*0.5%*

Table 8 *continued*

Source of revenue	1997/98 (prov)	1998/99 forecast
Income tax	9.6%	10.1%
VAT	6.4%	6.4%
Social security contributions (a)	6.3%	6.4%
Corporation tax	3.8%	3.6%
of which: ACT	*1.5%*	*1.4%*
Local taxes (b)	3.2%	3.2%
Fuel duties	2.4%	2.6%
Tobacco duties	1.0%	1.1%
Alcohol duties	0.7%	0.7%
Capital gains tax	0.2%	0.3%
Inheritance tax/CTT	0.2%	0.2%
Other receipts	5.3%	5.0%
Total	39.3%	39.6%
of which: oil & gas revenues	*0.4%*	*0.3%*

Notes: (a) Excluding national insurance surcharge.
              (b) Rates, national non-domestic rate, community charge and council tax.
Sources: ONS–CSDB database; FSBR March 1998; Inland Revenue Statistics

But the falling value of personal allowances in relation to earnings, which have risen faster than the inflation to which the allowances are usually indexed; the shrinkage of the marriage allowance and mortgage interest relief; and the steep increase in National Insurance contributions has meant that the real burden of taxation has increased despite the cuts in the headline rates of income tax. There was a brief fall in the proportion of earnings taken by the State after the 1979 Budget. But, as Table 8 shows, between 1980-81 and 1987-88 each of the four major classes of taxpayer were actually paying more of their gross earnings in taxes than in the last year of the Labour Government. Table 10 shows that it was not until 1988 that the burden of income tax and National Insurance, the main target of the tax-cutting programme, fell for any class of taxpayer. Table g shows that only three out of twelve groups of taxpayers have paid less of their gross earnings in taxes than they did under the last Labour government for more than half of the years the Conservatives have held office. The family was the main victim of the failure to cut taxes effectively in the 1980s. In the worst cases, a family with two children on average earnings was worse off under the Conservatives in fourteen out of the eighteen years the party has held office and even a relatively poor family on three quarters of average earnings was worse off for the same number of years. On average, taxpayers were worse off under the Conservatives for nearly two thirds of the period they have held office. Table 10 shows that, even when the shift in the burden of taxation towards indirect taxes is taken out of the calculation, over two fifths of taxpayers (and especially families) were still worse off under the Conservatives for more than half of the period the party has held office. The burden of tax has now started to rise again and, as Tables 9 and 10 show, the average family with two children will actually pay more in taxes in 1995–96 than they did in 1978–79, when the Labour Party was last in office. Despite the cuts in the headline rates of income tax, marginal taxes rates remain far too high. If the government seeks an explanation of why the family is disintegrating it will find a large part of the answer in its own tax policies.[20] Apart from the undesirable social effects of punishing the average family through the tax system, the burden of taxation also blunts economic incentives. If employers' and employees' National Insurance contributions are added to the basic rate the marginal rate of taxation - the amount of tax paid on every extra pound of income – has fallen, for the great majority of taxpayers, from 53 per cent in 1978–79 to just 44 per cent in 1995–96.[21]

There is good reason to think that the burden of taxation could get heavier yet. North Sea oil revenues and privatisation proceeds flattered the taxation and public expenditure record of the Conservative governments of the 1980s. As these receipts shrink, the burden of taxation will have to rise elsewhere to maintain spending at current levels. It also seems likely that inflation is at last defeated. Throughout much of the last twenty years inflation has acted as a hidden tax, because the tax system is linked only to price increases and not to increases in real income. As economic growth accelerates, so do tax revenues. Inflation also taxes holders of government debt, expropriating them surreptitiously by reducing the real value of their investment. Total government debt of £250 billion would shrink by £25 billion a year in real terms if inflation was running at 10 per cent a year but by only one fifth of that sum at 2 per cent a year. With inflation under control, the cost to the taxpayer of carrying the same burden of debt is much higher. Debt interest is already the fifth most expensive government spending programme, behind only social security, health, education and defence.

Table 9   Tax, NIC and indirect taxes as percent of gross earnings

Financial year	Single person			Married no children			Married two children			Married both working no children		
	Percentage of average earnings			Percentage of average earnings			Percentage of average earnings			Percentage of average earnings		
	75	100	150	75	100	150	75	100	150	75	100	150
1978/79	44.0	45.6	46.5	40.1	42.6	44.4	30.9	35.3	38.9	33.2	36.6	40.7
1979/80	43.8	45.3	45.8	40.0	42.3	43.7	30.6	34.8	38.0	34.2	37.5	41.0
1980/81	45.3	46.5	46.8	41.5	43.5	44.7	33.0	36.8.	39.6	36.2	39.3	42.3
1981.82	47.7	48.7	49.1	44.4	46.1	47.2	35.8	39.1	41.9	40.0	42.5	44.8
1982/83	48.0	49.0	49.6	44.4	46.2	47.6	35.6	39.2	42.3	39.8	42.4	45.0
1983/84	47.7	48.9	49.5	43.9	45.9	47.3	34.8	38.7	41.9	39.0	41.9	44.8
1984/85	47.6	48.7	49.0	43.7	45.7	47.0	34.5	38.6	42.0	38.4	41.5	44.5
1985/86	47.5	48.5	48.7	43.7	45.6	46.7	34.6	38.7	42.0	37.3	40.8	44.2
1986/87	46.8	47.9	48.1	43.0	44.9	46.1	34.3	38.3	41.6	37.3	40.2	43.8
1987/88	45.6	46.6	46.4	42.1	43.8	44.5	33.8	37.6	40.3	37.2	39.7	42.9
1988/89	44.3	45.2	44.5	41.0	42.6	42.7	33.3	36.8	38.8	36.6	38.9	41.8
1989/90	43.3	44.3	43.7	40.0	41.8	41.9	32.8	36.4	38.3	35.3	37.9	40.9
1990/91	42.3	43.0	41.9	41.8	42.7	41.8	34.9	37.5	38.2	36.1	38.3	40.5
1991/92	41.7	42.5	41.8	40.6	41.8	41.5	33.7	36.7	38.1	34.9	37.5	40.0
1992/93	41.0	42.0	41.3	39.8	41.2	41.0	33.1	36.2	37.7	34.7	36.5	39.5
1993/94	na	na	na	na	na	na	na	na	na	na	na	na
1994/95	41.5	42.8	42.9	40.6	42.0	42.3	35.0	37.3	38.4	33.9	36.9	40.2
1995/96	41.9	43.1	43.2	41.7	42.8	42.9	36.2	38.2	39.1	35.1	37.9	40.9
1996/97	41.5	42.7	42.6	41.3	42.4	42.2	35.9	37.8	38.5	35.0	37.6	40.5
1997/98	na	na	na	na	na	na	na	na	na	na	na	na

Source: HM Treasury, 'Tax/Benefit Reference Manual 1997/98' table 13.7

The cash accounting methods used by the Treasury to prevent public expenditure rising automatically in line with prices also have a perverse effect when inflation is low, by boosting real spending. And the State has accumulated a number of other long-term liabilities which will need to be financed. An ageing population will increase the cost of maintaining the value of the unfunded State pension. One survey estimated that unfunded pension liabilities in the United Kingdom were worth £450 billion, or 70 per cent of the national income.[22] If State pensions had retained a link to earnings rather than prices, they would already be costing another £8 billion a year.[23] If the link with earnings was re-established, the State pension might easily be costing another £17 billion a year within twenty-five years and up to £50 billion more a year by the middle of the next century.[24] Another large long-term liability is the cost of decommissioning nuclear reactors, variously put at £18–20 billion. In the face of liabilities of this magnitude, it is time to reconsider the design of the entire tax system.

The Arbitrary Structure of Modern Taxation

The present system has many objectionable features. One is its completely arbitrary structure. Revenue is no longer raised according to any set of agreed or identifiable principles. Its sole purpose is to finance expenditures which are already made, and to do so in ways which minimise the political cost. The designers of the system of taxation ceased long ago to look for a fair, just, uniform, equitable or even an efficient structure. They are concerned solely with how much revenue a particular tax will raise; what damage raising it will do to productive activity; and whether or not it is administratively achievable and politically possible. At Somerset House senior officials of the Inland Revenue are engaged constantly in the search for opportunities to widen the scope of taxation. Nigel Lawson relates in his memoirs how Inland Revenue officials came to him shortly before the 1987 Budget with a 'long list of allegedly taxable benefits, ranging from corporate Christmas presents (diaries, calendars and the like) to the provision of car parking spaces for employees on the company's premises…The Revenue was always a rich source of odd and usually counter-productive revenue proposals which would have required large numbers of extra staff to monitor for little revenue and at the cost of considerable annoyance to the taxpayer.'[25] The airport departures tax, like the tax on mobile telephones before it, was a characteristic product of Somerset House.

Table 10 **Tax and NICs as percent of gross earnings**

Financial year	Single person			Married no children			Married two children			Married both working no children		
	Percentage of average earnings			Percentage of average earnings			Percentage of average earnings			Percentage of average earnings		
	75	100	150	75	100	150	75	100	150	75	100	150
1978/79	28.9	31.5	33.3	23.8	27.8	30.8	14.6	20.9	26.2	14.1	19.8	26.4
1979/80	27.4	29.7	30.8	22.8	26.3	28.5	13.1	18.9	23.6	14.0	19.5	25.1
1980/81	28.7	30.7	31.6	24.2	27.3	29.4	15.5	20.8	25.0	16.1	21.3	26.4
1981.82	30.5	32.3	33.5	26.4	29.3	31.4	17.4	22.5	26.9	19.2	23.8	28.5
1982/83	31.1	33.0	34.3	26.8	29.8	32.2	17.5	22.8	27.5	19.2	24.1	29.0
1983/84	31.0	33.0	34.2	26.4	29.6	32.0	16.9	22.4	27.2	18.4	23.5	28.7
1984/85	30.7	32.7	33.9	25.9	29.2	31.5	16.3	22.0	26.8	17.5	22.9	28.3
1985/86	30.5	32.6	33.7	25.6	29.0	31.3	16.3	22.0	26.7	16.1	22.1	28.0
1986/87	29.9	31.9	32.9	25.3	28.5	30.6	16.4	21.8	26.2	16.4	21.6	27.6
1987/88	28.8	30.6	31.0	24.8	27.6	29.0	16.5	21.4	24.8	16.8	21.4	26.8
1988/89	27.5	29.1	28.9	23.8	26.3	27.0	16.2	20.7	23.2	16.4	20.6	25.6
1989/90	26.9	28.7	28.4	23.3	25.9	26.6	16.4	20.8	23.1	15.8	20.2	25.1
1990/91	26.3	28.2	28.1	22.7	25.5	26.2	16.4	20.8	23.1	15.0	19.8	24.5
1991/92	26.1	28.1	28.2	22.7	25.6	26.5	16.2	20.7	23.2	14.8	19.6	24.4
1992/93	25.5	27.6	27.7	22.3	25.2	26.1	15.6	20.2	22.5	13.8	18.8	23.9
1993/94	25.5	27.6	28.2	22.4	25.3	26.2	15.7	20.3	22.9	14.1	19.0	24.0
1994/95	26.3	28.5	29.3	23.9	26.7	28.1	17.3	21.7	24.8	15.5	20.2	25.1
1995/96	26.4	28.5	29.3	24.6	27.2	28.5	18.0	22.3	25.2	16.3	20.8	25.5
1996/97	25.5	27.6	28.2	23.7	26.3	27.4	17.1	21.4	24.1	15.6	19.9	24.6
1997/98 (a)	24.8	26.9	27.5	23.1	25.6	26.6	16.6	20.7	23.4	15.3	19.5	24.0

Note: (a) Consistent with November 1996 Budget

(b) Percentage of years (including 1978/79) in which tax burden is at or above 1978/79 level.

Source: HM Treasury, 'Tax/Benefit Reference Manual 1997/98' table 13.7

Politicians and even independent students of public finance fall easily into the same pattern of thinking as that of the official mind, fussing over the economic effects of changes in the tax code without pausing to consider the moral and political implications for liberty, property and equality before the law. 'My task is simple,' said the Chancellor of the Exchequer in his November 1993 Budget speech. 'I need to raise revenue, but to do so in a way which does least damage to the economy.' If he had added the political standing of the government, the Chancellor would have offered a complete explanation of an otherwise arbitrary selection of tax increases. John Kay and Mervyn King, in their admirable book *The British Tax System*, are clearly in favour of radical reform. But the book itself is ultimately no more than a dispiriting search for a well-designed tax system, as if the Inland Revenue and the Customs and Excise owned the national income and it was the job of the State to decide on its distribution. The 'principles of taxation they outline are economic rather than moral.

Likewise, the Institute of Fiscal Studies bases all of its work on finding more efficient systems of taxation rather than questioning the moral validity of public expenditure and taxation altogether.[26] Its recently established Tax Law Review Committee is pledged only to scrutinise the efficiency and complexity of tax legislation, and not its rationale.[27] Even Nigel Lawson, whose heroic Budget of 1988 was the first serious attempt to reverse the century-long drift of the income tax system towards ever-higher rates, describes taxation in purely mechanical terms and concedes that expenditure determines finance rather than vice-versa:

> The tax system enables the State to take money in the simplest, least economically damaging and fairest way it can devise in order to finance necessary Government spending, with no 'social' dimension of any kind.[28]

This argument, advanced in the course of an attack on the idea of integrating the tax and social security systems as philosophically incompatible, has a limited validity in that narrow sphere. But since most of the public expenditure the tax system is called upon to finance is specifically 'social' in intent, it would be absurdly unbalanced to ignore entirely the moral, social and political consequences of the taxes raised to pay for it. Too much public discussion of the fiscal system is mired in a pointless debate over the ways in which taxes redistribute money between individuals or make the economy more or less efficient. It would be gratifying to see politicians talk more often about who the money actually belongs to.

The Withdrawal of Consent to Taxation

A second objectionable feature of the current structure of taxation is that taxes are clearly no longer being levied with the consent of the taxpayers. The fact that Parliamentary representatives vote periodically for individuals to pay taxes is usually adduced as evidence that people have consented to taxation, but it is questionable how meaningful consent of this kind actually is. It is in the nature of the democratic political system that a majority will always be voting to expropriate the property of a minority without their consent. Even the periodic use of a referendum to approve increases in taxation, now advocated by some progressive thinkers, cannot circumnavigate this fact.[29] Political choices will always differ from market choices, in that they cannot be made with the agreement of all the parties. 'What property have I in that which another may take when he pleases himself?' asked John Locke. It is a question too few modern politicians bother to ask themselves, though the taxpayers they serve are already giving their answer.

There is in Britain today a secret army of waiters, cleaners, salesmen, prostitutes, baby-sitters, mini-cab drivers, builders and decorators whose labour would not be purchased at all on a fully- taxed basis. Many people are subsidising their meagre wages by claiming unemployment or social security benefits at the same time. Employers occasionally collude, unable to afford to pay a fully-taxed or even untaxed wage themselves. Unconventional retailing, and the enormous increase in part-time work and self-employment, are further causes of the undoubted increase in untaxed economic activity. The black economy is now thought to be worth between 5 and 7½ per cent of the national income, or between £38 billion and £50 billion. This is modest by comparison with countries like Greece, Italy, Spain and Portugal, where the black economy may be as large as 20 or 30 per cent of the national income, but the estimates are necessarily unreliable and it is likely that informal economic activity is actually taking place on a far larger scale. But even if the estimates are accurate, the black economy is still a significant symptom of popular resistance to excessive taxation.

The traditional solution to over-taxation – emigration – is still a viable option, especially for the rich or those with portable skills. One author has estimated that more British citizens (not Irish) went to North America in the fifty years after 1870, as the tax burden began to climb steeply for the first time, than in the preceding two and a half centuries. Even in the 1980s, when the burden of direct taxation fell marginally, the United States received 159,000 British emigrants. In 1990 16,000 Britons were admitted to the country as 'workers of distinguished merit and ability'. Many of them are academics and scientists. The continuing 'brain drain' is symptomatic of a tax system which is still hostile to the gifted and the successful. Australia remains a popular destination, and an unknown number of employees of British-based banks and multinationals choose to work abroad largely because of the tax advantages.

Other forces are at work – the weather and unemployment among them – but the principal cause of emigration from these islands is unchanged: to seize the opportunities to make good which are squeezed out by excessive taxation at home. With marginal tax rates of 44 per cent for most people, the tax system is still the most obvious demonstration of a well-attested national resentment of success. It is not just individuals who are emigrating either. Companies are increasingly adept at receiving income and profits in jurisdictions where taxes are lowest or even non-existent. Unofficial and 'emigrant' economic activity on this scale indicates the untaxed economy does not consist solely of transactions which would not take place on a fully taxed basis, though there are doubtless plenty of those. A great, if unspoken, tax rebellion is in train.

Some find this regrettable. But they must face the fact that excessive taxation has undermined the moral force of the entire fiscal system and, as it continues to grow, even the most honest taxpayers are beginning to question whether the claims of the State can continue to take precedence over those of themselves and their families. A recent television documentary pointed out, for example, that it can be cheaper to pay the fines for driving a lorry illegally than paying the taxes (and the State-supervised insurance and maintenance costs) to run it legally.[30] Even people in senior and responsible positions – such as John Birt, the director-general of the BBC – are driven by an iniquitous system of taxation to engage in complicated avoidance strategies. Employers are reduced to paying salaries in gold bars or life policies to avoid National Insurance contributions, until legislation obliges them to find some other method of achieving the same effect. By forcing otherwise law-abiding people into petty felonies, excessive taxation reduces respect for the law, criminalises a significant section of the population and makes it harder for people to distinguish between real crimes and offences against an onerous administrative law.

Taxpayers are also increasingly suspicious of the uses to which money is put. Increases in health expenditure, for example, are popularly supposed to be funding lavish new foyers for hospitals and large salaries, carpets and company cars for the new breed of National Health Service manager. Almost everybody has heard of the year-end scramble throughout the public sector to spend a budget, to avoid it being cut in the following year. The National Audit Office uncovers inept management of public sector resources in almost every report it publishes. A recent examination of the Ministry of Transport, for example, found that officials frequently bought far more land than they needed to build roads, and then sold the surplus too cheaply. In recent years both a West Country health authority and the ambulance service have spent millions on ambitious computer systems which failed to work. Revelations of misappropriation and fraud at every level of public life – the Welsh Development Agency, Lambeth Council and the Ministry of Defence are only three of the most prominent recent examples – reinforce the long-standing popular suspicions of official corruption and incompetence. During the late summer of 1992 the government itself squandered billions of pounds in a vain and foolish attempt to maintain the parity of the pound against the Deutsch Mark. 'In those corrupted governments where there is at least a general suspicion of much unnecessary expense and great misapplication of the public revenue,' observed Adam Smith, 'the laws which guard it are little respected.'[31]

This growing disregard of the law is increased to the extent that the State seeks to enforce tax evaders to pay by criminalising their activities. Tax evasion is the creature of excessive taxation, and it cannot be eradicated or even reduced without diminishing the overall burden of taxation. Whilst it remains high, the incentive to evade is too valuable to forgo. 'The law, contrary to all the ordinary principles of justice, first creates the temptation, and then punishes those who yield to it,' was the verdict of Smith.[32] The great economist described a smuggler as 'a person who, though no doubt highly blameable for violating the laws of his country, is frequently incapable of violating those of natural justice, and would have been, in every respect, an excellent citizen had not the laws of his country made that a crime which nature never meant to be so'.[33] He had in mind the expansive trade in goods smuggled into England to avoid the onerous duties levied on them by the government.

The history of smuggling in the eighteenth century is a reminder not only of the self-defeating nature of excessive taxation, but of the violent forms which popular resistance to taxation can take if the State is overly inclined to press its case. The most draconian methods and punishments – gun battles, naval patrols, official bribing of informers, threats to jurymen, the creation of a new Coast Guard, the possibility of transportation and even the death penalty – did not prevent men killing to protect their profits (which far exceeded most legitimate forms of trade) without improving the government's revenues from custom duties a tenth as much as lifting the taxes altogether.[34] Excessive levels of duty on internationally traded commodities in Georgian England had much the same practical effect as Prohibition in America. The Georgian customs regime created armed gangsters as vicious as Al Capone, which fought bitter territorial battles with their rivals and terrorised the ordinary inhabitants of southern England.[35] The smugglers preferred to describe themselves as Free Traders, and they did not disappear completely until Britain adopted Free Trade in the 1840s. As the economist Nicholas Kaldor put it in 1980: 'The existence of widespread avoidance is evidence that the system, not the taxpayer, stands in need of radical reform.'[36]

If taxation presses too hard upon people their resistance does not, of course, stop at avoidance, smuggling and evasion. The Poll Tax riot of March 1990 was in a long tradition of extra-Parliamentary resistance to excessive taxation. Lady Godiva rode naked through Coventry in 1040 to persuade her husband Leofric, Earl of Mercia, to lift the heavy taxes he had imposed on his tenants. The Magna Carta of 1215 was in large part an attempt by the barons to restrain the tax burden imposed by John. The Poll Taxes of 1377–81 were resisted initially by evasion and eventually by popular revolt. Henry VIII also had to abandon a Poll Tax. The efforts of Charles I to raise Ship Money was a primary cause of the Civil War and the excise duty introduced to pay for the New Model Army provoked such 'very foul riots' that it had to be abandoned on food and clothing. The Hearth Tax of 1660, under which State officials were empowered to enter private houses to count the number of fireplaces, was denounced by Parliament as 'a badge of slavery upon the whole people, exposing every man's house to be entered and searched at the pleasure of persons unknown to him'.[37] Its unpopularity persuaded the authorities to try a window tax (they could be counted from outside) but the 'surveyors' despatched in 1696 to count the windows in the houses of the wealthier sections of the community found many were bricked up, and reopened after they had left.

In 1733 Robert Walpole's attempt to widen the Excise – another tax which was deeply unpopular, because the excisemen were empowered to force their way into business premises – provoked a wave of pamphleteering and riots which forced him to abandon the idea completely for fear of causing a civil war.[38] When the news broke, bonfires were lit, bells were rung and people danced in the street.[39] Until the last quarter of the eighteenth century there was a smuggling epidemic, caused by high rates of duty on imports. It is estimated that 20,000 people, out of a total population of eight million, were engaged full-time in this form of tax resistance.[40] In some decades of the eighteenth century smuggling probably reduced State customs revenues by as much as a quarter.[41] The vast size of the industry thrived on popular resentment of the customs duties, and riots, commotions and the mugging and murder of tax inspectors were commonplace.

Why Progressive Taxation is Not Fair

A third disquieting feature of the modern fiscal system is its lack of fairness. This arises primarily because incomes are taxed at progressive rather than proportional rates. A proportional tax is one which is levied at the same rate at all income levels. Until the twentieth century it was an unquestioned assumption among all mainstream political and economic thinkers that a progressive tax – a tax which becomes progressively heavier as a taxpayer moves up the income scale – was inherently unjust. Adam Smith likened the nation to a great landed estate, to which individuals contributed money for maintenance in proportion to the stake they owned. A taxpayer who owned twice as much of the national wealth as somebody else was obliged to pay twice as much towards its upkeep. If tax was levied at 10 per cent, the man who earned £10,000 paid £1,000 in tax but the man on £20,000 paid twice as much, or £2,000. 'In the observation or neglect of this maxim,' thought Smith, 'consists, what is called the equality or inequality of taxation.'[42] Yet Britain has exactly such an unequal system in place today. A man earning £10,000 and a man earning £20,000 pay income tax at quite different rates. The first loses 14.6 per cent of his income to the State, and the second 16.6 per cent.[43]

Once the State abandons the principle that every taxpayer should contribute the same proportion of his or her income or profits the tax system is bound to become arbitrary and unequal. Progressive taxation makes people unequal before the law on grounds of wealth alone. Once a tax system is based on 'ability to pay', which is not a principle of justice in taxation but merely a subjective assessment of means, the State is effectively licensed to tax without limit. The Labour Government of 1974-79, for example, thought a top marginal tax rate of 98 per cent was fair in terms of 'ability to pay'. In some countries, the top marginal rate has exceeded 100 per cent. 'When the rule of arithmetical proportion is broken, ' forecast Adam Smith in *The Wealth of Nations*, 'the door is open to extortion.' It is in the progressive system of taxation that Englishmen have become most accustomed to their loss of liberty – not only in the expropriation of their property, but in the loss of equality before the law- and where the State has moved closest to purely arbitrary powers. Elected politicians now claim the consent of a majority of the people – and in Britain only one government this century has mustered more than 50 per cent of the vote on a single party ticket – to the application to a minority of a discriminatory law which the majority is unwilling to impose upon itself.[44]

Progressive taxation is also a powerful instrument for the redistribution of wealth, which is why it was favoured by revolutionaries from Tom Paine to Karl

Marx. In *Rights of Man* Tom Paine reproduced tables showing a progressive income tax rising steadily from 15 per cent on the first £500 of income to 100 per cent on anything above £22,000.[45] In *The Communist Manifesto* Marx and Engels advocated a 'heavy progressive or graduated income tax' specifically to facilitate the elimination of private property.[46] Gladstone agreed that a progressive income tax 'tended to Communism', and advised that an income tax should only be used at all in extremis. He called it 'an engine of gigantic power for great national purposes'.[47] John Stuart Mill described progression in his *Principles of Political Economy* as 'a mild form of robbery'. Unlike Gladstone, he thought an income tax was justifiable in principle, but bound in practice to degenerate into arbitrariness. It was therefore best 'reserved as an extraordinary resource for great national emergencies, in which the necessity of a large additional revenue overrules all objections'.[48]

This was in fact the accepted usage of income tax in England until the middle of the last century. From the Glorious Revolution until deep into the Victorian era an income tax was bracketed with a standing army as one of the two main threats to liberty, and therefore both militarisation and the taxation of incomes were to be sampled only in a dire national emergency like the threat of invasion by France. Pitt introduced the first income tax in January 1799 to finance the war against Napoleon, and at a time when the burden of debt incurred in the American war was so threatening to the public credit that there were doubts whether the army and navy could be financed at all. The tax was a progressive one, but diluted with generous allowances and ample scope for evasion and limited to a maximum of lo per cent of total income. Pitt also made it clear that it was purely an emergency measure which would be repealed once Napoleon was defeated. Addington duly abolished it after the Treaty of Amiens in 1802, but had to revive it (at half Pitt's original rates) in the following year when hostilities resumed. As Table 7 shows, even after subsequent increases the rate never exceeded 2 shillings in the pound (10 per cent) and it was finally abolished in 1816, after victory at Waterloo had eliminated the Napoleonic threat for good.

It was because the Napoleonic experience had established the income tax so firmly in the public mind as a war tax that Robert Peel's decision to reintroduce it in the peacetime conditions of 1842 caused such an immense shock. Of course, direct taxes were nothing new even in 1799, but they too were always reserved for extraordinary circumstances. The first direct tax on land, the Danegeld, was the symbol of Saxon humiliation at the hands of the Danes. It was retained after the Conquest only to pay for war, until Henry II replaced it by an indirect impost on moveables to fund the Third Crusade. Poll taxes were levied in 1377, 1379 and 1380. The last of them was a progressive tax, with rates ranging from 4 pence to 20 shillings a head. The land tax, levied in various forms during the seventeenth and eighteenth centuries, was more akin to a wealth tax than an income tax. From 1692 it was levied on the capitalised value of property. Likewise, the various other forms of direct taxation were merely levies on further manifestations of personal wealth like houses, windows, servants, clocks and watches, silver plate, shooting and gamekeepers, race-horses and carriages.

Table 11   Tax Thresholds
                        Percent of average male manual earnings

Fiscal year	Single person	Married man Without Children (a)	Married man With two Children (a)	Married man With four Children (a)
1949/50	39.9	63.7	101.2	135.1
1959/60	27.8	46.3	80.3	1 23.6
1969/70	25.8	37.9	53.2	67.3
1979/80	22.5	35.0	35.0	35.0
1989/90	23.7	37.3	37.3	37.3
1992/93	24.4	36.5	36.5	36.5
1993/94	23.8	35 7	35 7	35 7
1994/95	23.0	34.5	34.5	34 5
1995/96	22.9	31.3	31.3	31.3
1996/97	23.6	32.1	32.1	32.1
1997/98 (b)	24.3	32.5	32.5	32.5
1998/99 (c)	24.1	32.3	32.3	32.3

Notes: (a) Assuming man receives full MCA. Children aged under 11.
          (b) Provisional
          (c) Assuming earnings grow by 4.5% om 1998/99
Source: 'Inland Revenue Statistics' 1997 table 2.7 & earlier editions Library calculations

Between 1793 and 1802 Pitt added dogs, hair powder and armorial bearings. It was the failure of his attempt to use such signs of conspicuous consumption as a crude measure of personal wealth – the idea was to levy a multiple of the direct taxes paid in the previous year-to produce the revenues anticipated that obliged Pitt to introduce the income tax. 'This repugnant tax,' writes one historian, 'only entered the statute book in highly exceptional circumstances.'[49] Gladstone fought an election on a pledge to abolish the income tax as late as 1874 and his opponent in that contest, Benjamin Disraeli, told the electors of Aylesbury in February that year that 'I think the income tax is a war tax, and should not exist except when we are in a position of war'.[50]

But by the 1880s the collectivists had already identified a progressive tax on incomes as a means of redistributing the wealth of the people for political advantage. Initially smuggled on to the statute book as an emergency measure at a time of grave national crisis, a progressive income tax was initially transmuted into an 'equality of sacrifice' (a notion thought to rest upon the ability to pay) and then into a solution to the problem of inequality. This was a frankly political claim, unsupported by any principled or even utilitarian piece of reasoning. Proportionality is a principle; progressiveness is purely the arbitrary choice of politicians enjoying a temporary Parliamentary majority, with all the moral force of a shopkeeper charging different prices for the same goods according to the wealth of the customer. A proportional tax, by contrast, is intuitively just. Under it, each taxpayer surrenders the same proportion of his wealth. A proportional tax has the further advantage that it forces governments to make all adjustments to the distribution of wealth through expenditure rather than taxation decisions. Progressive taxation, by taking more from some than others, enables governments to alter the distribution of wealth through revenue rather than expenditure decisions. It allows a government to concentrate the financial burdens of its promises on one group in order to buy the votes of another. It reduces fiscal policy to the art of balancing punishment and reward sufficiently to ensure its political survival.

As the franchise was gradually extended, it was comparatively simple for politicians to argue – as the Labour Party is still inclined to do today – that the burden of increased taxation would fall on those voters most able to bear it, and the bulk of the electorate is naturally inclined to believe that they do not fall into that class. It is a curious characteristic of all opinion polls on the subject of public expenditure that overwhelming majorities believe that there should be more of it, but that it should be financed by 'the rich' because the burden of taxation on low and middle income earners is already too high.[51] In fact, there are never enough rich people to bear the whole burden of rising public expenditure. As Table 11 shows, as recently as the 1950s a married man on average manual earnings with two children paid no income tax at all. Forty years later he was paying income tax after earning just 30.5 per cent of average manual earnings. His counterpart on average manual earnings, but with four children, did not start to pay income tax until 1967, but now also pays it after earning less than a third of the average.[52] It is the cruellest of the many fallacies of egalitarian democracy that ever-rising taxes will always be paid by somebody else. The natural extravagance of democratic States guarantees higher rates of income taxation at all income levels.

References

1   John Stuart Mill, Principles of Political Economy, Books IV and V, Penguin Classics Edition, 1985, page 307.
2   Quoted in Financial Times, 13 April 1994.
3   Quoted in Financial Times, 7 September 1994.
4   Although a majority of individuals in Britain both pay and receive taxes or benefits-in-kind, the exchange is an unequal one. A progressive tax system ensures that the rich pay more, and State employees and dependants gain more from additional public expenditure than they lose in higher taxes.
5   Quoted in Geoff Mulgan and Robin Murray, Reconnecting Taxation, Demos, 1993, frontispiece. Also by Patrick K. O'Brien, 'The Political Economy of British Taxation, 1660–1815', Economic History Review, 2nd ser. XLI, 1 (1988), pages 1–32.
6   'Taxation of earnings from labour is on a par with forced labour.' See Robert Nozick, Anarchy, State and Utopia, Blackwell, 1974, page 169.
7   See above, Introduction, pages 19–20 and 27–30.
8   Patrick K. O'Brien, 'The Political Economy of British Taxation, 1660-1815', Economic History Review, 2nd ser. XLI, 1 (1988), Table I, page 2.
9   'The Political Economy of British Taxation, 1660–1815', Tables I and 3, pages 2 and 4.
10 John Brewer, The Sinews of Power: War, Money and the English State 1688–1783, Alfred A Knopf 1988, page xvii.
11 Patrick K. O'Brien, 'The Political Economy of British Taxation, 1660-1815', Economic History Review, 2nd ser. XLI, 1 (1988), Table 2, page 3.
12 Thelma Liesner, One Hundred Years of Economic Statistics, Economist Publications

1989, Tables UK.2 and UK.18.

13   Quoted in B. E. V. Sabine, A History of Income Tax, George Allen & Unwin Ltd, 1966, page 77.

14   Thomas Paine, Rights of Man, Penguin, 1971, pages 252–3.

15   B.E.V. Sabine, A History of Income Tax, George Allen & Unwin Ltd, 1966 page 146.

16   Quoted in A History of Income Tax, page 146.

17   John Stevenson, British Society 1914–45, Penguin, 1984, page 92.

18   A History of Income Tax, page 196.

19   Douglas Jay, The Socialist Case, Faber & Faber, 1946, page 202.

20   For more on taxation and the family, see Chapter 11, pages 327-31.

21 Marginal rate calculated as follows:
     Basic Rate 33% 25%
     Employers' National Insurance Contributions 10%   10.2%
     Employees' National Insurance Contributions 6.5%   8.9%
     National Insurance Surcharge   3.5%
     Marginal Rate   53%   44.1%

22   CS First Boston Economics Research, 'The Remaking of Europe: Employment and the Hidden Debt', November 1993.

23   Hansard, 26 January 1994, Col. 268.

24   National Insurance Fund Long Term Financial Estimates – Report of the Government Actuary on the Second Quinquennial Review Under Section 137 of the Social Security Act 1975, House of Commons Paper 582, July 1990, Tables 13 and 14, pages 29–30.

25   Nigel Lawson, The View From No. 11, Bantam, 1992, page 822.

26   The introduction to a recent paper issued by the Institute was characteristic: 'From the middle of the 1980s until the end of that decade the government experienced a growing economy and consequently buoyant tax revenues. In addition to cutting the PSBR and increasing spending, these revenues were used as a means of financing massive tax cuts, and in particular cuts in income tax rates. By the early 1990s, however, it had become clear that tax revenues had been cut to an unsustainably low level as recession led to a PSBR which threatened to run out of control.' An alternative view is not that taxes were cut too much, but that public spending was not cut enough. The use of the adjective 'massive' to describe a modest redistribution of taxation from direct taxes to indirect taxes is indicative of the views of the authors. See Christopher Giles and Paul Johnson, Taxes Down, Taxes Up, Institute for Fiscal Studies, Commentary No. 41, February 1994, page 1.

27   The Committee, financed by the Bank of England and a number of banks, accountants and legal firms, was set up in October 1994 amid widespread concern about the increasing volume and complexity of tax legislation. Financial Times, 28 October 1994.

28   Nigel Lawson, The View From No. 11, Bantam, 1992, page 598.

29   See Geoff Mulgan and Robin Murray, Reconnecting Taxation, Demos, 1993, pages 26–9.

30   An example highlighted by the Channel Four programme, Dispatches, on 2 November 1994.

31   Quoted in Charles Adams, For Good and Evil: The Impact of Taxes on the Course of Civilization, Madison Books, 1993, page 280.

32   Quoted in For Good and Evil: The Impact of Taxes on the Course of Civilization, page 286.

33   Quoted in Frank McLynn, Crime and Punishment in Eighteenth Century England, OUP, page 172.

34   See Crime and Punishment in Eighteenth Century England, pages 172–201.

35   See Geoffrey Morley, The Smuggling War: The Government's Fight Against Smuggling in the 18th and 19th Centuries, Alan Sutton, 1994, pages 70-116.

36   Quoted in J. A. Kay and M. A. King, The British Tax System, Fifth Edition, OUP, 1990, page 60.

37   Charles Adams, For Good and Evil: The Impact of Taxes on the Course of Civilization,

Madison Books, 1993, page 252.

38 Ian Gilmour, Riots, Risings and Revolution: Governance and Violence in Eighteenth Century England, Hutchinson, 1992, pages 83–92.

39 Geoffrey Morley, The Smuggling War: The Government's Fight Against Smuggling in the 18th and 19th Centuries, Alan Sutton, 1994, page 7.

40 Frank McLynn, Crime and Punishment in Eighteenth Century England, Oxford, 1991, page 172.

41 Patrick K. O'Brien, 'The Political Economy of British Taxation, 1660–1815', Economic History Review, 2nd ser. XLI, 1 (1988), page 25.

42 The Essential Adam Smith, edited by Robert L. Heilbroner, W. W. Norton, 1986, page 313.

43 Assuming a personal allowance of £3,525; tax at 20 per cent on the first £3,200 of taxable income; and tax at 25 per cent on the next £21,100.

44 The Conservatives won 51.1 per cent of the total vote in 1900. The party secured 55.2 per cent of the vote in 1931 and 53.7 per cent in 1935, but on both occasions as part of a National Government coalition.

45 Thomas Paine, Rights of Man, Penguin, 1971, pages 274–5.

46 Karl Marx and Friedrich Engels, The Communist Manifesto, Penguin, 1978, page 104.

47 Sir Llewellyn Woodward, The Age of Reform 1815–1870, OUP, Second Edition, 1962, page 167.

48 John Stuart Mill, Principles of Political Economy, Penguin Classics Edition, 1985, page 184.

49 Patrick K. O'Brien, 'The Political Economy of British Taxation, 1660-1815', Economic History Review, 2nd ser. XLI, I (1988), Table 2, pages 20-1.

50 B. E. V. Sabine, A History of Income Tax, George Allen & Unwin Ltd, 1966, pages 110.

51 See, for example, Fiscal Studies, November 1994. Nearly half of respondents thought taxes on high incomes were too low or much too low, but hardly anyone thought taxes on middle or low incomes were too low; 96 per cent of respondents described themselves as on low or middle incomes. Reported in Financial Times, 15 December 1994.

52 See Inland Revenue Statistics 1992, Appendices, Tax Thresholds. Part of the table are reproduced in Table 11. See also Hansard, 18 January 1995, Cols 490–1.

CHAPTER FIVE

Prosperity:
The Growing Burden of Taxation

Money is preferable to politics. It is the difference between being free to
be anybody you want and being free to vote for anybody you want.

P. J. O'Rourke

The modern British constitution is incapable of restoring balance to the system
of taxation. The historic separation of executive and legislative power, in which
Parliament was the guardian of the taxpayer against the depredations of the
Crown, has given way to the domination of Parliament by the Executive. This
is an entirely modern development. In the Middle Ages the King – and the
Crown was then co-terminous with the executive arm of the State – was
expected to 'live of his own', or to meet the costs of government out of the
rental and other income of his own estates and additional feudal dues like the
fines levied in the Courts and the income of estates where he had wardship of
a minor or an heiress seeking a suitable marriage. The great fifteenth-century
jurist, Sir John Fortescue, regarded it as axiomatic that the normal expenses of
government were paid for out of 'grete lordshippes, maners, feeffermys and
other such demaynes' owned by the King. The Treasury was originally no more
than a chest containing the King's money, and taxes were for extraordinary
expenditure only.[1]

As late as the eighteenth century it was a normal constitutional convention to
distinguish between the 'ordinary' revenues of the monarch, derived from the
Crown estates and elsewhere, and the 'extraordinary' revenues derived from
taxation and levied only at times of dire national emergency.[2] Government and
judicial posts were generally held by members of the Royal Household, and many
of the titles which survive today – First Lord of the Treasury, Chancellor of the
Exchequer, Lord Privy Seal, Master of the Rolls – are reminders that the position
was originally on the Royal payroll. The King retained responsibility for paying the
salaries of the Diplomatic Service, the Judiciary, the Chancellor of the Exchequer
and the Prime Minister until 1760 when George III finally completed a long
process of increasing dependence on the taxpayer by surrendering to the Treasury

the revenues of the Crown Estate and a variety of other taxes (including customs and excise duties and the income of the Royal Mail) in exchange for a fixed annual subsidy from Parliament now known as the Civil List.[3]

The Lack of a Constitutional Constraint on Taxation

Modern political sensibilities rebel at the notion of the State paying for the government of the country out of its own resources, but at a time when the Crown and the executive arm of the State were indistinguishable it was a perfectly comprehensible arrangement. Its main advantage was to force the executive to secure the support of the legislature before it could levy additional taxes. In other words, the power to spend was separated from the power to tax. 'The Security of our Liberties are not in the Laws but by the Purse being in the Hands of the People,' was how John Carteret (1690–1763), later Earl Granville, described it.[4] By the People he meant the taxpayers represented in Parliament. 'All historical experience,' writes Ferdinand Mount, 'suggests that the separation of powers is indispensable to liberty.'[5] The .fusing of the executive and the legislative arms of the English Constitution is one of the principal causes of rising taxation, because it allows the executive to claim the mandate of the people. The Cabinet is drawn from Parliament, and uses the systems of party discipline to ensure that the legislature bends to its will. The power to tax and the power to spend are thereby subsumed in Parliamentary sovereignty, with the Cabinet acting as what Bagehot called 'a committee of the party majority'.

This constitutional pattern, which now seems so unbreakable, is in fact of relatively modern origin. As the role of the State expanded during the eighteenth century, Parliament became increasingly reluctant to enlarge royal patronage by increasing the number of government posts at the disposal of the King. It gradually assumed responsibility for the payment of official salaries through miscellaneous 'supply grants', which increased in size from £177,000 in 1770 to £848,000 in 1799.[6] This increase of Parliamentary patronage at the expense of Crown patronage was the mechanism by which the executive arm of government came to derive from Parliament rather than the Crown. It blurred and eventually dissolved the separation of executive and legislative power. This changed the role of Parliament from guardian of the liberty and property of the people against the arbitrary power of the State – the feature of the English constitutional system so much admired by the American constitution-makers – into the legislative agent of their destruction.

In fact, it is reasonable to see the whole of the constitutional development of England as a battle between the executive and the legislature over the power to tax. It was the excessive tax demands of King John which led to the baronial rebellion which was concluded by Magna Carta in 1215. Though this document was proclaimed by subsequent generations as a 'charter of liberties', to the medieval mind 'liberty' meant principally the right to the enjoyment of property without excessive taxation. 'The taxpayers had combined to control the tax-imposer,' as Sir Arthur Bryant once wisely described the events at Runnymede.[7]

Resistance to royal taxation was a feature of all subsequent baronial rebellions. The claim that the King should 'live of his own' was first voiced – though not in those exact words - by the Great Council in 1242.[8] Fifteen years later, on the eve of the Barons' Wars, the barons insisted that the King desist from reducing his income by selling land and resume control of assets he had alienated.[9] In the Ordinances the barons imposed on Edward II in 1311, the demand that the King 'live of his own without recourse to prises other than those due and accustomed' was heard for the first time. By insisting on annual Parliaments the barons also introduced the concept of Parliamentary scrutiny of royal expenditure, accelerating the process by which Parliament came gradually to negotiate acceptable levels of taxation with the wealthy mercantile classes on behalf of the Crown. It was the financial demands of the incessant warfare of the Middle Ages – and especially of the Hundred Years' War, during which royal revenues doubled – which increased the constitutional importance of Parliament as guardian of the interests of the taxpayers. The right of Parliament to approve royal taxation was customary by 1300, and was confirmed in statutes of 1340 and 1362.[10] And, although the costs of warfare made the demand increasingly unrealistic, Parliament continued to insist that the King 'live of his own'. The notion did not disappear completely until the eighteenth century. Various Parliamentary Acts of Resumption, obliging Kings to 'resume' alienated lands to relieve the tax burden, were passed in 1404 and 1406, between 1450 and 1456 and again in 1465 and 1473. Henry VII approved three Acts of Resumption in the ten years after Bosworth. His extravagant son, Henry VIII, was eventually forced to dissolve the monasteries rather than test the patience of the taxpayers any further. The great and enduring popularity of his daughter, Elizabeth I, owes much to her rigid fiscal discipline. Like her grandfather, she was a careful steward of the royal finances. Throughout the whole of her reign annual taxation averaged less than £80,000 a year, and in her first thirty years on the throne just £50,000 a year.[11] On the eve of war with Spain she had managed to accumulate a budget surplus of £300,000.[12]

It was the Stuart contempt for the accepted constitutional practice that no new sources of revenue could be tapped without Parliamentary consent which plunged the country into civil war in the seventeenth century. James I dissolved Parliament rather than accede to this convention and the arbitrary and extra-Parliamentary taxes he and his son levied – notably customs dues and Ship Money – were at the heart of the Parliamentary resistance to the Crown. The Petition of Right submitted to Charles I in 1628 was in large part an attempt to reassert the supremacy of Parliament in matters of taxation. Its first clause appealed to statutes granting Parliament the sole right to sanction new taxes agreed in the reigns of Edward I and Edward III, and it concluded:

They do therefore humbly pray your most excellent Majesty that no man hereafter be compelled to make or yield any gift, loan, benevolence, tax or such like charge without common consent by act of parliament, and that none be called to make answer or take such oath or to give attendance or be confined or otherwise molested or disquieted concerning the same or for refusal thereof.[13]

Before the dissolution of 1629 the Speaker was held in his chair while the House passed a resolution declaring anybody who paid a tax not sanctioned by Parliament an enemy of King and Kingdom.[14] The Long Parliament denounced the collection of Ship Money as 'contrary to and against the laws and statutes of the realm, the right of property, the liberty of the subjects, former resolutions in Parliament and the Petition of Right'.[15]

Complete Parliamentary control of taxation was settled eventually by force of arms, and by the Bill of Rights which gave Parliament complete control over the army and the fiscal system. It took another century before Parliament assumed control of the executive arm of government as well, though attempts were made to place the King on the public payroll at the end of the seventeenth century. In the end the English constitution failed to maintain the separation of powers, though the last Act of Resumption was passed as late as 1702. From the time of the Glorious Revolution the essential elements of the system – the sovereignty of Parliament and party discipline – which turned Parliament from the friend of the taxpayer into his enemy were in place. The last constitutional obstacle to excessive taxation was not removed until the reform of the House of Lords in 1911. Until the granting of the universal franchise it was possible to rely on public opinion to exercise fiscal restraint. Taxpayers and property owners were, after all, the same people. In the introduction to the second edition of *The English Constitution* Walter Bagehot argued that the Parliamentary sensitivity to public opinion was the best safeguard against excessive taxation. He compared it favourably with the Presidential system in the United States, which he thought had allowed the State to accumulate a substantial budget surplus:

> In truth taxation is so painful that in a sensitive community which has strong organs of expression and action, the maintenance of a great surplus is excessively difficult. The Opposition will always say that it is unnecessary, is uncalled for, is injudicious; the cry will be echoed in every constituency; there will be a series of large meetings in the great cities; even in the smaller constituencies there will be mostly smaller meetings; every member of Parliament will be pressed upon by those who elect him; upon this point there will be no distinction between town and country, the country gentleman and the farmer disliking high taxes as much as any in the towns. To maintain a great surplus by heavy taxes to pay off debt has never yet in this country been possible, and to maintain a surplus of the American magnitude would be plainly impossible...If America was under a Parliamentary government, she would soon be convinced that in maintaining this great surplus and in paying this high taxation she would be doing herself great harm. She is not performing a great duty, but perpetrating a great injustice. She is injuring posterity by crippling and displacing industry, far more than she is aiding it by reducing the taxes it will have to pay...[It is] contrary to and worse than what would have happened under a Parliamentary government...The sort of taxation tried in America, that of taxing everything, and seeing what everything would yield, could not have been tried under a Government delicately and quickly sensitive to public opinion.[16]

Britain today has just such an American system of taxation. The purpose of taxation is to raise the revenue to pay for public expenditure, and no area of individual endeavour or industry, trade or commerce is safe from the scrutiny of the State for its tax-yielding potentialities. Indeed, for three financial years, between 1987–88 and 1990–91, the country endured exactly what was unknown and unthinkable to Bagehot: the retention of heavy taxation for the purposes of redeeming the public debt. It was regarded at the time not as unnecessary or injudicious, or better spent on tax cuts, but as a great feat of prudent public financing. Ironically, some United States Congressmen have advocated a constitutional amendment requiring the federal budget to be balanced, because a political system dominated by vested interests creates too great a temptation to borrow rather than to tax. The proposal is regarded as unsophisticated in the absence of a plan to achieve fiscal balance, but the criticism misses the point. Once a balanced budget is a constitutional obligation, the means will have to be found. The Cost and Inefficiency of the Tax Bureaucracy The weakening of Parliamentary control of the tax-raising powers of the government has exposed ordinary men and women to the most degrading inquisitions into their private lives and means. Adam Smith laid it down as one of his four principles of a judicious tax that it should not require a vast bureaucracy, or an odious inquisition, to administer and collect. It cannot be said that the modern Inland Revenue satisfies either of these requirements. In 1992-93 the 62,700 staff of the Inland Revenue collected £76.3 billion at a cost of £1.59 billion, or over 2 per cent of the proceeds. It is an unavoidable characteristic of rising taxation that it is accompanied by an expansion of the State bureaucracy. Until the Restoration, taxes were normally collected by tax-farmers, who were allowed to keep a proportion of whatever sums they managed to collect. This proved too inefficient to raise the funds needed to finance the succession of wars Englishmen fought during the eighteenth century.

One historian has estimated that the total fiscal bureaucracy in England expanded nearly seven-fold between the Interregnum and the Napoleonic era, from perhaps 2,524 posts in 1690 to 8,292 in 1782.[17] More people worked for the Customs and Excise- then the main revenue-raising department- than all the other arms of government put together. But after taking account of the venality, corruption, patrimony and pluralism of the Georgian age – many office-holders did no work at all, relying on deputies and remitting taxes only after taking a cut or leaving them on deposit for their personal account – it was, by the standards of the day, remarkably efficient. The running expenses of the Hanoverian fiscal bureaucracy were much the same as they are today: just over 2 per cent of revenues.[18]

In an age of relative probity in public administration, and of powerful technology, an expense ratio equivalent to that of two centuries ago – and twice as high as that of Sweden or Canada, and four times as high as that of the United States – suggests the Inland Revenue is far from efficient. Of the 140 million items of post received by the Inland Revenue, only 55 million come from taxpayers. The remaining 85 million consist of correspondence between the various tax offices. Paper-shuffling on this scale is bound to cause mistakes.

According to the National Audit Office half a million taxpayers, or one tenth of self-employed taxpayers and one fourteenth of those on PAYE, received incorrect assessments last year because of mistakes made by the Revenue. Two thirds of the 5 million taxpayers who receive assessments have the tax demand reduced at least once each year, on one in ten occasions because the Revenue makes a mistake.

That is equivalent to making 500,000 mistakes. The commonest error is to deny taxpayers their correct allowances and reliefs, and errors are not usually discovered until a taxpayer points them out. The Revenue routinely fails to meet its own target of answering all correspondence within twenty-eight days. Sir Anthony Battishall, the chairman of the Board of Inland Revenue, told the House of Commons Public Accounts Committee in June 1994 that some self-employed taxpayers paid £100 million too little in tax in 1993–94 while others paid £70 million too much. Similarly, some of those on PAYE paid £330 million too little, while others paid £260 million too much. The net effect of Revenue mistakes, in other words, was a £100 million shortfall in the public revenues. But IFAP, the lobbying group for independent financial advisers, reckons tax errors by the Inland Revenue cost the public £865 million a year.[19] This huge, blundering bureaucracy operates a system of taxation of such bewildering complexity that taxpayers are unable even to take full advantage of legitimate tax reliefs.

The tax bureaucracy also reflects the inquisitorial nature of any tax. The astonishing detail of the Domesday Book reflects the fact that it was an assessment of the wealth of England for tax purposes. Likewise, the enormous expansion of the tax bureaucracy in the eighteenth century reflected the reliance of the revenue from excise duties on a sinister expansion of State surveillance. By 1780 the excise-men were policing 33,000 brewers and victuallers, 36,000 public houses, 35,500 tea and coffee dealers, several thousand chandlers and countless calico printers and paper-makers. In all, the Excise had 10,000 businesses within its purview. It was known to contemporaries as 'the monster with 10,000 eyes', and its unpopularity was unsurpassed.[20] Excise-men tended to try their own cases, denying people their historic right to trial by jury and any appeal to a higher court. But if a case was tried by jury, almost the only way the excise-men could secure a favourable verdict in court was to bribe the jurymen.

Blackstone said 'the rigour and arbitrary proceedings of excise-laws seem hardly compatible with the temper of a free nation'.[21] Equipped with large numbers of officials – there were nearly 6,000 excise-men in 1778 – and sweeping powers, the Excise was highly successful at extracting revenue. But it took the full mobilisation of all the repressive powers of the State before the customs men were able to make any meaningful impact on the illicit import trade. 'There is no evidence,' writes one historian, 'that the government managed to raise the share of taxable imports falling into the net for government revenue, until the Royal Navy at sea and the militia on land came to the aid of the Customs Service during the long wars with France from 1793 to 1815.'[22] There is no clearer example in modern British fiscal history of the capacity of the tax system to spawn measures which are at once repressive and ineffective.

Indirect taxes are on the whole less inquisitorial than their direct counterparts. They are also more efficient. In 1992–93 the 25,000 staff of the Customs and Excise collected £63.4 billion at a cost of £672.6 million, or 1.06 per cent of the revenue collected. This was half the cost of their counterparts at the Inland Revenue for the collection of only 16 per cent less. These revenues were acquired at a far lower cost in privacy, albeit by shifting much of the administrative load on to the taxpayer. It is therefore doubly unfortunate that the modern Customs and Excise men should have been equipped with powers which are encouraging them to follow the oppressive example of their Georgian predecessors. Customs and Excise officials make over 400,000 'control visits' a year. No business they choose to visit can refuse them, and they are entitled to examine the premises, the stocks, the accounts, bank statements, invoices, cash books and any other documents they deem to be relevant. Severe financial penalties can be imposed, even when innocent mistakes were made which cost Customs and Excise nothing. Because it is simpler and easier than taking a trader to court to recover unpaid VAT, the Customs and Excise often used bailiffs to seize assets as a weapon of first rather than last resort. One authority estimates that in 1993 alone bailiffs were used in 30,000 separate instances.[23] Once considered no more than licensed thugs, bailiffs are now among the highest earners in the country. They, like so many others, have turned State regulation into an enormously profitable business.

But it was the relaxation in January 1993 of the quantities of duty-free alcohol which returning travellers can bring into the country which gave the Customs and Excise fresh opportunities to oppress their countrymen. Coupled with lower excise duties on alcohol in France, the lifting of personal import limits has created a lively cross-border trade arbitraging the different tax regimes. Hard data on the nature and scale of the imports is lacking, but alcohol industry lobbyists argue the trade cannot possibly be for personal consumption only and that it could be worth over £1 billion a year. This is thought to be relieving public houses and off-licences of trade, and to be 'costing' the Customs and Excise upwards of £340 million in lost VAT and excise duties.[24] In November 1994 the Treasury Select Committee, after taking evidence from many different sources, concluded that the trade was not seriously undermining excise duty receipts and that it was impossible to distinguish the loss of sales directly attributable to cross-border shopping from a host of other factors affecting the drinks industry. Claims of a link, the MPs concluded, 'have to be treated with considerable caution'.

Despite this, the Customs and Excise has not hesitated to over- react. In order to prevent people re-selling personal imports at a profit the excise-men have equipped themselves with powers more sweeping even than those of the police. They are now able to issue themselves with warrants to enter private homes and businesses, and are seeking fresh powers to prevent people ordering goods from abroad by telephone. In June 1993 the Customs persuaded the courts to fine one trader, Mr Ashok Patel, £1,200 for selling duty-free goods bought in France. Customs officers had raided his shop in Bristol to assemble the evidence.[25] Three so-called 'bootleggers' from Wolverhampton were jailed for six months after admitting evading duty on imports of alcohol and tobacco. In South Wales, the Customs secured the conviction and jailing of three men for terms of between three and nine months, after they accumulated evidence by tracking the men from Kent to Cardiff. 'We hope these jail sentences will be a big deterrent to help tackle this widespread crime, which is causing concern to the retail industry,' said the Customs and Excise men after the verdict.[26]

The whole history of taxation shows that this is a hopeless aspiration. The only effective and lasting solution to an illicit cross-border trade driven exclusively by differential rates of taxation is to reduce taxes. Mr Patel and his ilk should not be pilloried and jailed, but congratulated for bringing a fiscal absurdity to the attention of the government. They are fit to rank with Isaac Gulliver, the famous 'gentle smuggler' of the Napoleonic era, who died full of riches and honour in his native West Country in 1822.[27] After all, harmonisation of tax regimes is precisely what the raising of the duty-free allowance was intended to achieve. In the single European market, the activities of arbitrageurs are fully expected to force governments to harmonise differential rates of taxation in neighbouring geographical areas. Once the cross-border trade does begin to have a significant impact on State revenues from excise duty, and on employment in public houses and off-licences, domestic excise duty on alcohol will be reduced.

But until then the Customs and Excise will continue to lobby the State for additional powers to harass importers. They will, of course, have the full support of domestic producers anxious to protect themselves from foreign competition. This was how Sir Paul Nicholson, the head of the Vaux brewing group, recently described the cross-channel alcohol trade:

> A scandal...strong criminal element...We have evidence of vans crossing the Channel and transferring to 40 foot wagons...The Customs are showing a remarkable reluctance to do anything about it. I suspect that's because they're afraid that if they brought a case they'd lose it...I don't think the government really understands how much duty they're losing...If they let it go on, they will destroy a huge swathe of British brewing and pubs. Then they will lose revenue, panic, reduce duty, and allow. a further wave of French beer in.[28]

This is the authentic voice of the rent-seeking businessman, anxious to see the excise duty on domestic sales reduced, the customs duty on foreign imports maintained and the Customs and Excise equipped with draconian powers to protect his business from 'unfair' competition.

The Threat Taxation Poses to Liberty

Most modern Parliamentarians are too degraded by the yearning for office, or by the marsupial relationships they enjoy with public sector trade unions and domestic producers, for the House of Commons to be expected to voice its outrage at the worrying expansion of the powers of the Customs and Excise men. Yet one of the main reasons governments were unable to introduce an income tax until 1799 was that Parliament abhorred the idea of a personal declaration of income, with penalties for non-disclosure, as an unthinkable infringement of liberty and privacy. Pitt knew the imposition of the tax would be desperately unpopular in Parliament and in the country, and he introduced it only when all alternatives were exhausted and with ample mitigating allowances and considerable scope for evasion. The new tax caused one naval officer to expostulate in January 1799:

> It is a vile, Jacobin, Jumped up Jack-in-Office piece of impertinence – is a true Briton to have no privacy? Are the fruits of his labour and toil to be picked over, farthing by farthing, by the pimply minions of bureaucracy?29

Evasion of the tax was endemic and in remote parts of the country like Wales and Scotland its collection proved almost impossible. When the income tax was finally repealed in 1816 the tax authorities were obliged to destroy the records of individual incomes, and there was a popular belief at the time that Brougham himself stoked a bonfire of the hated returns in Old Palace Yard.[30] The tax was described by the Court and Alderman of the City of London that year as 'hostile to every sense of freedom, revolting to the feelings of Englishmen and repugnant to the principles of the British Constitution'.[31] Such feelings had not abated by the time Peel reintroduced the tax in 1842. The writer Harriet Martineau declared that there was 'something transcendentally disgusting in an Income Tax, which not only takes a substantial sum immediately out of a man's pocket, but compels him to confide his affairs to a Party whom he would by no means choose for a confidant'.[32]

The modern Inland Revenue inspector is no less unwelcome a confidant. The Revenue employs a number of so-called 'ghost-busters', or tax Policemen. whose task is to Patrol the streets in search of expensive cars, scan local newspapers, peer over garden walls and peek into private houses to assess whether the income and assets of the occupants match the figures on their tax return. Nobody can expect to see his business affairs discussed in the pages of *Private Eye* without the Inland Revenue using gossip as the pretext for launching an official investigation. The 'ghostbusters' are said, in a near-parody of the belief that all income belongs to the State, to pride themselves on the fact that the money they recover is 'spent on building roads, hospitals and schools rather than being salted away by selfish tax evaders'.[33] The Revenue revealed recently that it was even prepared to pay informants. The sums involved are rarely large, but are related to the size of tax recovered and can range up to £20,000.[34] These paid officials of the state – who are prepared to spy on private citizens, use statutory powers to extract confessions and to bribe informants – are the moral equivalents of the Stasi, the Gestapo and the KGB.

The Inland Revenue persuaded the Chancellor to include in the 1994 Finance Bill a clause empowering officials to raid the premises of accountants and seize documents purely on suspicion that some of their clients were evading their tax obligations. This outrageous demand, which exposed all the records of an accountancy firm to official scrutiny without the need to present any evidence of wrongdoing, was rightly resisted by Parliament.[35] A report commissioned by the government after the proposals were rejected by Parliament concluded that the powers sought by the Inland Revenue were 'far too wide', and recommended some restriction of them. But even under the revised proposals Revenue officials will still have the power to demand documents from accountants they suspect of being involved in tax evasion.[36] Unfortunately, the civil liberties lobby takes no interest in the draconian powers of the tax police. They generally applaud any extension of revenue-raising capabilities, imagining that if all tax loopholes were closed and tax evaders prosecuted their clientele, which is reliant on ever-rising public expenditure, would benefit. One recent left-wing survey of the over-mighty State, provocatively entitled *The Coercive State: The Decline of Democracy in Britain*, only mentioned the monstrous tyranny of the Inland Revenue at all in order to compare its ineffectiveness at tackling tax evasion with the ruthlessness of the Department of Social Security in extirpating benefit fraud.[37] Yet the Inland Revenue has the power to intimidate everyone, and not just social security claimants. Reports of tax inspectors issuing threats of litigation and onerous financial penalties are commonplace, and the Revenue has acquired a reputation for bullying people into paying sums they do not owe because they cannot afford the legal costs of resistance.[38] An internal manual on investigation procedures caused such a furore when it was leaked to the press that a copy was placed in the House of Commons library.[39] The Inland Revenue itself admits that a tenth of taxpayers – 2 million people – are unhappy with the way it deals with them. Elizabeth Firkin, the Inland Revenue Ombudsman, decided in favour of the taxpayer in two thirds of the cases brought to her since she started work in July 1993.

'It is very difficult,' as Charles Adams points out, 'for officials even with the best of intentions to administer with humanity an inquisitorial law.'[40] Between 1985 and 1993 the Inland Revenue mounted an average of 74,000 investigations a year into possible tax frauds, and secured money in over nine tenths of all the cases it explored.[41] The tax Ombudsman had recently to call upon Inland Revenue officials to be less zealous and more 'sensitive' in their dealings with the public, who are often frightened, confused and bullied into surrendering monies they do not owe:

> Sometimes the Revenue has been aggressive and shown little imagination in realising what it is like to be a taxpayer. It doesn't take into account the fright it causes to small business.[42]

A number of self-employed people, partnerships and small businesses are being forced to agree to Revenue assessments, or to take out insurance against spot-check investigations, knowing that they cannot afford the costs of defending themselves against the authorities even when they know they are in the right.[43] In other words, the Inland Revenue has become its own judge and jury.

The self-employed, who have to make deductions for expenses and resist incorporation into the PAYE system, are naturally the main target of Revenue investigations. Like the worst sort of totalitarian spy networks, the tax inspectors are quite happy to rely on anonymous tip-offs from hostile neighbours, or even jealous husbands or wives or jilted lovers. The Revenue waged a sustained campaign over several years to treat some freelance workers as employed rather than self-employed, and was prepared to contest two cases in Court to prove it was right. It eventually lost, but not all taxpayers have the means to resist the Revenue in the courts. Undeterred by that defeat, the Inland Revenue recently issued a series of dire threats against self-employed people hoping to use the switch from the current preceding-year basis of tax assessment to a current-year basis for tax planning purposes, including a warning that tax deemed overdue would be taxed at rates far in excess of those agreed by Parliament.[44] The Inland Revenue today exhibits every symptom of a bureaucracy that has broken free of all constitutional constraints, and that is working to a self-interested agenda of its own. It is assisted in this by the pusillanimous attitude of Treasury ministers, who are generally disinclined to resist Revenue advice on apparently 'technical' matters.

Like any State functionaries, the self-interest of tax-collectors lies in expanding their own numbers and powers. Reports surface periodically in Parliament and the press suggesting that the government is not spending enough on enforcing compliance, and promising the recovery of fantastic sums in unpaid tax if only there were more Inland Revenue 'ghostbusters' at work. Similarly, the opening of European border controls was accompanied by a series of dire warnings from Customs and Excise of the plague of hard drugs, unlicensed firearms and rabid dogs which would flood into the country if the number of customs officers at airports and harbours was reduced. When the Chancellor announced in his November 1994 Budget speech that the Customs and Excise was to shed 4,000 jobs over the next five years, mainly because they were engaged in routine compliance and surveillance work which was not worth doing, the National Union of Civil and Public Servants and the Civil and Public Servants Association warned that a smuggling epidemic was bound to ensue.

It was in order to avoid the attentions of intrusive, inquisitorial and self-interested bureaucracies such as the modern Inland Revenue and the Customs and Excise that voters long insisted that the State fund its activities largely through indirect rather than direct taxes. Previous generations regarded direct taxation as utterly inconsonant with liberty. From the time of John Locke to the advent of the collectivist age, when Natural Rights were supplanted with the administrative right of the government to levy whatever taxes it judges fit or necessary, most people in Britain regarded their right not to be taxed as rooted in the Natural Law. History had taught them that it is taxation which enables the State to crush the liberty of the individual – that infinite money is the sinews of all forms of State power, and not just of war – and that well-financed governments are even more capable of pursuing policies which are dangerous, misguided or foolish than poorly-financed ones

Throughout history people resisted those taxes – Poll Tax, Hearth Tax, even a universal excise or an accurate wealth tax – which necessitated an unconscionable invasion of personal privacy and freedom. They knew from bitter experience that the essence of any tax is the taking of money, property or a service by the State without paying for it, and that transactions of that kind can be sustained only by a mixture of fear and punitive sanctions. All taxation was of necessity tyrannical, and a great tax was a great tyranny, but a direct tax was potentially the most tyrannical of all. It was the point of naked confrontation between the individual and the State, where the State had the power to ask how much money each individual had, how he earned it and how he chose to spend it. If they were to be taxed at all, most people preferred to be fleeced indirectly. But they also knew that the sole and dubious virtue of indirect taxation was, as Montesquieu put it, that it bore 'not so direct a relation to the person'.[45]

Until Pitt introduced an income tax in 1799, in the middle of a profound political and financial crisis, Chancellors of the Exchequer confronted what one historian has called 'insurmountable opposition to the reform of direct taxes...Even then the greatest chancellor of the age, whose recommendations on matters of fiscal and financial policy were rarely questioned by Parliament, hesitated to introduce a full-blown income tax ...Eighteenth-century chancellors did not face anything like the same political opposition when they raised or imposed customs duties.'[46] At the time of William and Mary a century before, direct taxes on various forms of wealth and property accounted for nearly half of the public revenue but this fell steadily to an average of only a fifth between 1765 and 1795. The balance was supplied by a mixture of excise duties on domestic production of goods and services and customs duties on imports. Throughout the eighteenth century, taxes fell mainly and increasingly on expenditure rather than wealth or income. The introduction of the income tax in 1799 partially reversed this trend – in the closing years of the Napoleonic Wars direct taxes yielded over a third of total revenues – but the normal pattern was resumed after Waterloo.[47] Direct taxes contributed 28.8 per cent of total public revenues in 1815, but only 8.8 per cent ten years later.[48] Free trade narrowed the indirect tax base – in the same Budget that he reintroduced the income tax in 1842 Peel cut the tariffs on 450 items – and prevented Gladstone from fulfilling his dream of abolishing the income tax. But it led to a healthy obsession with keeping public expenditure to the minimum. This ensured that direct taxes did not return to Napoleonic levels even during the Crimean War.[49] In 1874, the year Gladstone promised to abolish the income tax if he was re-elected, direct taxes (including the new death duties introduced in 1870) yielded just 18 per cent of total revenues. But as the collectivist era opened and progressed the proportion of the public revenues contributed by direct taxes crept steadily upwards, to 25 per cent in 1885, 29 per cent in 1895 and 37 per cent at the peak of the Boer War in 1902. In 1911, the first year in which the taxes imposed by Lloyd George's 'People's Budget' of 1909 were levied, direct taxation accounted for 45 per cent of the total tax take.[50] By the end of the First World War in 1918–19 the direct taxes collected by the Inland Revenue accounted for 79.3 per cent of total government revenue.[51]

During the subsequent decades Britain has gradually reverted to a more balanced pattern of taxation, shifting the burden from income back to spending, but the relentless rise of public expenditure has made it impossible to reduce the impact of direct taxes to Georgian or Victorian levels. Inland Revenue direct taxes as a proportion of the whole fell from a post-war peak of 64.6 per cent of revenues under Labour in 1975-76 to 51.9 per cent in 1993–94[52] The biggest single switch was the consolidation of the two rates of Value Added Tax (VAT) – 12½ per cent on so-called 'luxury' items and 8 per cent on everything else – into a single rate of 15 per cent in the first Budget of the incoming Conservative government in June 1979. There were modest extensions of the range of goods liable to VAT in the 1984 Budget (hot takeaway foods and building improve- ments) and a highly significant and unpopular extension of the tax to domestic fuel in the first of the 1993 Budgets.[53] The rate was then increased to 17½ per cent in the Budget of March 1991 to pay for the Poll Tax fiasco. The recent introduction of taxes on insurance premiums and aeroplane journeys are also part of a shift towards indirect taxation. As Table 8 shows, the main direct taxes on individuals – income tax and National Insurance contributions – fell from 17.3 per cent of GDP in 1979–80 to 15.2 per cent in 1993–94. Table 8 also shows that VAT rose in the same period from 4 per cent of GDP to 6.1 per cent. In terms of liberty and public efficiency, this shift was undoubtedly a gain. But some believe indirect taxation is unfair.

Are Indirect Taxes Unfair?

It is a commonplace of fiscal theory that indirect taxes are regressive, and fall with disproportionate severity on poorer families, whose demand for taxable commodities like tea, sugar, beer and fuel tends to be inelastic. A tax which is levied on commodities is paid in equal amounts by individuals at all income levels alike. A rich man and a poor man may pay the same amount to the Treasury for their consumption of beer, though the value of the money surrendered is far higher to the poor man than to the rich one. This is why indirect taxes are often thought to offend against another principle of a wisely designed tax system – that the burden should not fall upon the poor – and why collectivists planning the redistribution of wealth have preferred to effect their plans through the direct and progressive taxation of incomes. The last socialist government also retained an upper rate of VAT on so-called luxuries, or what Denis Healey called 'things we can do without'. These included petrol, boats, caravans and electrical appliances.

The luxury rate of VAT was one aspect of modern tax policy the Georgians would have understood readily. The Hanoverian governments managed, through a process of trial and error, to ensure that the 'necessities of the poor' like grain, butter, meat and cheese were taxed lightly or even exempted altogether. Indirect taxes, and especially rising indirect taxes, tended to fall with greatest severity on the luxuries of the rich like coffee, tea, tobacco, spirits and silk. Likewise, the old Purchase Tax was imposed at various different rates on a narrow range of goods designed to exclude the necessities of the poor. VAT, introduced in 1972, was never levied universally. The massive areas of food, fuel, housing and transport were exempted, and successive governments regarded any commitment to extending the coverage of the tax as a form of electoral suicide. When the Conservative administration elected in April 1992 was finally driven by fiscal necessity to levy VAT on domestic fuel, it unwisely introduced the impost in two stages. Parliament carried VAT on fuel at a rate of 8 per cent, but in late 1994 voted against the second stage of the increase to 17½ per cent.

The second stage of VAT on domestic fuel was lost despite the fact that it was accompanied by a generous package of subsidies to poorer families, and the VAT net still does not extend to food, children's clothes and (perhaps oddly) newspapers, magazines and books. It is undeniable, as Table 12 shows, that the burden of indirect taxation on the poor has increased since 1978–79. But it has increased for everybody. The main objection to the shift from direct to indirect taxation of the last fifteen years is that it was not accompanied by real reductions in public expenditure. It was therefore not an exchange of one method of financing public expenditure for another, but merely a further extension of the tax base. As Table 10 showed, the burden of direct taxation has gone up for many people as well, though not for the lower paid. The main victims are families, whose wider responsibilities mean they need a larger income but whose stability renders them easy prey for the tax-collectors. The low levels of income at which people, and especially families with dependent children, begin to bear the burden of direct taxation may be a better measure of the unfairness of the current system of taxation than the long-standing concern about the regressive effects of indirect taxation.

In a modern economy without large concentrations of personal wealth which can be taxed for redistribution to the poor, the heavy burden of direct and progressive taxation is arguably far more unfair than any number of regressive indirect taxes. This was well- put by a young Labour MP in the House of Commons nearly fifty years ago:

> As we get…more and more to the stage where men will start life equal as far as possible and will rise by merit in the sphere in which they can offer the maximum contribution to the country's welfare, I do not think we ought necessarily to persist in a system of taxation which will tax higher remuneration at a higher rate. Indeed, in a fully developed Socialist economy, I would expect to see indirect taxation replacing direct taxation as the main source of revenue, because in a Socialist society, where men start equal and rise by merit, there is no point at all in giving them a substantial wage to reward the contribution they are making to the national economy, and then taking it away by taxation.[54]

Table 12   VAT and other indirect taxes as percent of gross earnings

Financial year	Single person			Married no children			Married two children			Married both working no children		
	Percentage of average earnings			Percentage of average earnings			Percentage of average earnings			Percentage of average earnings		
	75	100	150	75	100	150	75	100	150	75	100	150
1978/79	11.7	11.0	10.4	12.9	11.9	11.1	12.8	11.4	10.0	15.0	13.5	11.8
1979/80	12.9	12.4	12.0	13.7	13.1	12.7	14.0	12.8	11.6	15.9	14.6	13.3
1980/81	12.8	12.3	12.0	13.6	13.0	12.6	13.7	12.6	11.6	15.6	14.4	13.2
1981.82	13.1	12.6	12.2	13.9	13.3	12.8	14.3	13.0	11.8	16.0	14.7	13.4
1982/83	12.6	12.2	11.8	13.4	12.8	12.3	13.9	12.6	11.4	15.5	14.3	13.0
1983/84	12.8	12.3	12.0	13.6	13.0	12.5	14.0	12.7	11.6	15.8	14.5	13.2
1984/85	13.1	12.5	11.9	14.0	13.2	12.6	14.3	13.2	12.2	16.2	14.8	13.4
1985/86	13.2	12.4	11.8	14.3	13.4	12.6	14.5	13.3	12.3	16.6	15.0	13.4
1986/87	12.9	12.3	11.9	13.7	13.0	12.5	13.9	13.0	12.3	16.1	14.8	13.3
1987/88	12.8	12.4	12.1	13.4	12.9	12.6	13.5	12.8	12.4	15.6	14.5	13.3
1988/89	12.8	12.4	12.3	13.3	12.9	12.7	13.2	12.7	12.5	15.3	14.4	13.3
1989/90	12.4	12.0	11.9	12.8	12.4	12.3	12.6	12.1	12.0	14.7	13.8	12.8
1990/91	12.3	11.8	11.7	12.7	12.2	12.1	12.4	11.9	11.7	14.6	13.6	12.7
1991/92	12.8	12.3	12.1	13.3	12.8	12.7	13.2	12.6	12.3	15.3	14.3	13.2
1992/93	12.8	12.2	12.0	13.2	12.7	12.6	13.1	12.5	12.3	16.4	14.2	13.1
1993/94	12.8	12.2	11.9	13.2	12.7	12.5	13.1	12.5	12.3	15.3	14.2	13.1
1994/95	12.6	12.3	12.2	13.3	12.6	12.1	14.6	13.1	11.8	15.0	14.1	13.2
1995/96	12.9	12.5	12.4	13.6	12.8	12.3	14.9	13.4	12.0	15.3	14.4	13.5
1996/97	13.4	13.0	13.0	14.1	13.3	12.8	15.6	14.0	12.6	15.8	15.0	14.0
1997/98 (a)	13.7	13.4	13.3	14.4	13.6	13.1	16.0	14.3	12.9	16.2	15.3	14.4

Note: (a) Consistent with November 1996 Budget
Source: HM Treasury, 'Tax/Benefit Reference Manual 1997/98' table 13.7

His name was James Callaghan, and it was his privilege as Prime Minister to preside over the highest rates of income tax in the history of his country. When he joined the Inland Revenue as a Civil Service clerk in 1929, the poor did not pay income tax at all. Their main interest in the annual Budget, as Callaghan later recalled in his memoirs, was whether or not it increased the excise duties on beer, cigarettes and tea.[55] It is a measure of what has happened since that they are now having to pay for those pleasures out of taxed income.

The Need for Tax Neutrality

Another weakness of the present system of taxation is its want of elegance and simplicity. There are essentially two systems of taxation which governments can choose. The best is one which is broadly based, with low rates of tax and few if any tax breaks. The other is a selectively based system, with high rates of tax and a great many tax breaks. The simpler system minimises the economic distortions which result when people are forced, purely for tax reasons, to earn, save or spend in particular ways. It also reduces the susceptibility of the government to lobbyists seeking equivalent or compensatory tax breaks. Most departures from tax neutrality reflect the accumulation over many years of concessions to particular pressure groups at various times. Lastly, a simple system discourages the growth of a counter-productive tax avoidance industry. Complicated tax systems spawn endless opportunities for tax lawyers and accountants to exercise their ingenuity, and draw the tax authorities into a tiresome battle of wits with taxpayers and their advisers.

Unfortunately, the current system of taxation exhibits all of the worst features of a complex and selectively based system. It is both complicated, and riddled with tax breaks. Two of its most distinguished analysts, John Kay and Mervyn King, thought it lacked any rational or consistent architecture at all:

> The present state of the British tax system is the product of a series of unsystematic and ad hoc measures, many undertaken for excellent reasons – for administrative convenience or to encourage deserving groups and worthy activities – but whose overall effect has been to deprive the system of any consistent rationale or coherent structure.[56]

They are too sanguine. In fact, the reasons for the current structure of tax reliefs were rarely excellent. They were the result of a high- taxing and high-spending welfare democracy, in which politicians seek to reward interest groups which they think might help them get elected or re-elected. Home owners, occupational pension scheme members, shareholders and the like could all expect fiscal favours from a Conservative government, just as public sector workers could always look forward to a massive increase in public spending under a Labour government. Interest groups have also proved adept (as Nigel Lawson found when he pondered the extension of VAT to books and newspapers and the reform of the taxation of pension funds in 1984 and 1985) at defending privileges once they are granted.[57] In other words, the tax system is the arbitrary product of power-broking among politicians and their supporters.

Kay and King penned their assessment of the tax system after the modest tax reforms of Geoffrey Howe and Nigel Lawson during the 1980s but before the Budgets of the early 1990s injected further complexities into the system. Between 1979 and 1988 eight different rates of income tax were steadily reduced to just two – 25 per cent and 40 per cent – and disincentives to employment and savings like the National Insurance Surcharge and the Investment Income Surcharge were abolished. The system of Corporation Tax was comprehensively reformed in 1984 to end the subsidisation of investment at the expense of labour. But in the 1992 Budget a third 20 per cent rate of income tax was added, purely for the short-term political gain of wrong-footing the Parliamentary Opposition and the illusory long-term political gain of appearing to contain the level of direct taxation.[58] In the second Budget of 1993 the married couple's allowance was restricted to a wholly arbitrary 15 per cent, and equally arbitrary levies were imposed on insurance premiums and aeroplane travel. A year later, the video games played by children were singled out for special taxation. But they can't vote.

The dismantling of the undeniably excessive (though completely coherent) tax privileges of the pension fund industry is proceeding without any strategic direction at all. Rather than taxing pension funds to make room for compensating reductions in income tax, which would enable people to save more in a greater variety of ways, the pension funds are being soaked for the simple reason that the State needs the money and can acquire it from savings for the future at a lower political cost than taxing individuals on their present income. A raid on pension fund surpluses in March 1993, for example, was disguised as a change in the treatment of Advance Corporation Tax. This was part of a series of surreptitious attacks on the tax privileges of the pension funds – admittedly prompted in large part by the refusal of the pension fund industry to countenance wholesale reform of its privileges – stretching back to 1986. The ambitious hopes of the mid-1980s that the tax system was evolving towards a so-called 'fiscal neutrality' – in which the decisions of workers, consumers and savers are not distorted by tax considerations – are now completely dead. The tax system, far from becoming simpler, more elegant or more principled, is driven more than ever by purely political considerations.

The Threat Taxation Poses to Prosperity

But perhaps the most depressing feature of the modern structure of taxation in Britain is its violation of one of the classic rules of any sensible fiscal policy: taxes should never discourage enterprise. All of the miracle economies of world history – the United States, Japan, Hong Kong, Singapore, South Korea, Taiwan – were or are characterised by low rates of taxation on productive activity. It was true also of Britain, the first miracle economy. The combination of commercial enterprise and unusually low levels of public expenditure and taxation in Elizabethan times, for example, was not a mere coincidence. Barely a twelfth of the population paid any direct taxes at all, most trade was free of duties and internal tolls and purchase taxes were unknown. England was, until at least the Civil War, a lightly taxed country. Sir Francis Bacon had ample justification for saying, even after the war with Spain, that 'the Englishman is most master of his own valuation and the least bitten in purse of any nation in Europe'.[59]

During the eighteenth century, the tax-eating English State scarcely benefited at all from the vast expansion of shipping, shipbuilding, banking and insurance. Peter Mathias, the historian of the Industrial Revolution, has observed of fiscal policy in the late eighteenth and early nineteenth centuries:

> Virtually no taxation fell upon business profits or business capitals and relatively little upon landed capital or farming profits. Increments to national capital were not effectively tapped, and particularly capitals in trade, business and industry...Hence, taxation did not prejudice capital accumulation or investment levels by competing for investment funds or reducing incentives. The main sources of investment capital - the savings of businessmen, merchants, farmers and landowners – were relatively unscathed.[60]

Throughout the Industrial Revolution, and down to the First World War and beyond, industry funded itself primarily through family wealth and retained profits rather than by borrowing in the capital markets. It was the effects of death duties, high personal taxation, and especially corporate taxation after the Second World War, which prevented companies saving enough to fund their own expansion and investment. This increased their reliance on the outside sources of capital which many businessmen, politicians and officials agree have made British capitalism damagingly 'short- termist'.[61] Taxation helped to institutionalise the economy, making business reliant on City institutions which emphasise immediate earnings reliant on City institutions which emphasise immediate development.

The heavy burden of taxation borne by productive capital and labour is arguably the biggest single threat to long-term prosperity. Industry and workers in the rapidly developing economies of East Asia (and even in Japan) pay considerably lower taxes than their counterparts in Britain today. But the taxes themselves are only part of the burden imposed on business by the Inland Revenue and the Customs and excise. During income tax from employees is already a major administrative burden for employers. From 1996– 97 the Inland Revenue is shifting the rest of the administrative burden of income tax assessment to the taxpayer as well, by insisting that the four million self-employed people assess their own income for tax. The change to self-assessment will be accompanied by the loss of the last major tax advantage of self-employment – the taxation of profits earned in the previous rather than the current year – and may well lead to an otherwise undesirable increase in incorporations. It will certainly increase the number of self-employed and small businessmen and women who experience cash flow problems.

The Customs and Excise has always relied on taxpayers to do most of the work for it, confining it own activities to banking cheques and periodic spot-checks of traders it believes are not declaring tax payments they have received. This obliges all traders turning over more than £46,000 to keep detailed records exclusively for tax purposes and to make informed judgments about what is zero-rated for VAT purposes and what is not, under the threat of severe penalties for any miscalculations. For many VAT-registered businesses, the cost of administration is actually higher than the tax they pay. Undeterred, the Customs and Excise is now superimposing data collection responsibilities as well. In November 1994 its officials took a company to court for failing to supply information on trade with other countries in Europe. The data was needed not for tax purposes, but to compile the official trade statistics. The offending company, which pleaded it did not have time to scrutinise 2.000 invoices a month on behalf of the official statisticians, was fined £11,550.[62] According to Customs and Excise, 30,000 companies, or a fifth of those trading with Europe, now have to fill in special forms for statistical purposes.[63] Another estimate suggests senior managers now spend up to ten hours a month filling out statistical data collection forms.[64] Yet the figures which are derived from all this work are not even reliable.

The exact costs imposed by tax collection bureaucracies on productive businesses and individuals are unknown. But the net cost to the American economy of tax collection in the United States – in terms of form-filling, litigation, professional advice and legal and accountancy fees – is put at between 5 and 10 per cent of national income.[65] If the proportion is the same in Britain, the true cost of the tax system in wasted time and effort could easily be £30 to £60 billion. These are sums which only the biggest welfare budgets can rival for scale. The United States does not operate a system of PAYE, which might be thought to be more efficient, but in fact surveys have shown that British taxpayers are in correspondence with the Inland Revenue more often than their American counterparts.[66] Graham Bannock, a small business analyst, has put the cost of tax compliance at 2 per cent of national income (plus another 2 per cent for complying with other business regulations).[67] Even that lower figure implies wastage of over £12 billion simply in paying taxes, and the greater use of self-assessment announced in the March 1993 Budget is bound to increase it. And these costs are incurred even before taking account of the disincentive effects of high marginal rates of tax on production and consumption.

Since the almost universal abolition of exchange controls, capital is no longer trapped behind national barriers. Investors can switch funds to lightly taxed securities markets, and companies can re- locate if taxes are allowed to rise too far. Countries are already obliged to compete for international investment by offering low rates of corporation tax and cheap, lightly taxed labour. Multinational companies are increasingly able to adjust their tax liabilities through essentially bogus transactions which ensure they pay tax in low-tax countries while operating in high-tax ones. This has unfortunate side-effects. As international competition to attract capital through low-tax policies shrinks the corporate tax base, the tax burden on property, jobs and consumption is likely to increase still further. This tends to extend high taxation to the most enterprising individuals, who then choose to live and work abroad. But it is true not only of entrepreneurs. A great many talented managers and financiers are forced to consider working abroad, at least for a few years, in order to amass a modest amount of capital in a lightly taxed jurisdiction.

The evidence of the disincentive effect of high marginal rate a of taxation is notoriousiy patchy and difficult to interpret. The celebrated curve identified by Professor Arthur Laffer – in which lower taxes, even without compensating cuts in public expenditure, lead to lower prices, higher output and therefore higher government revenues – is as yet empirically unproven, except perhaps at the highest rates of income tax. The share of total income tax paid by the top 1 per cent of taxpayers increased from 11 per cent in 1978–79 to 15 per cent in 1993–94, and that of the top 5 per cent from 24 per cent to 32 per cent. This reflects the reduced attractions of tax avoidance in a less penal tax regime, though it may also be symptomatic of the falling number of tax breaks. Early retirement, emigration and especially non-monetary forms of remuneration are all reduced where overall tax rates are lower. In this way, a reduction in high marginal rates can lead to a smaller loss of tax revenue than superficial analysis might suggest, and in most cases to an increase.

The link between taxation and effort is nevertheless complex. Some academic economists are persuaded that lower taxes can lead to less effort. If a man can have the same standard of living for 30 hours' work rather than 40, they say, he will choose to work less. This is reminiscent of Walpole's argument that the excise duties were the only thing which kept the poor at work. On the other hand, people do seem to be working longer hours. Part of the explanation may be that workers can now keep a larger proportion of the money they earn from every extra hour of work. The link between effort and marginal rates of taxation is so blurred because the vast majority of people are now employees working in large corporate hierarchies, where they are simply not able to do more work if they pay a lower marginal rate of tax or earn higher rewards if they do. Pay rises and promotion, especially in middle-class occupations, are more likely to be linked to a mixture of office politics and a willingness to 'put in the hours' than increased output. Even in the professions – policing, medicine, accountancy and the law – pay is determined largely by ascending the ladder of promotion by competitive examination or admission to a partnership. The incentive effects of lower taxes in this kind of corporate-cum-hierarchical economy are bound to be much reduced.[69] A fall in marginal rates of less than 10 per cent since 1979 for the vast majority of taxpayers is also far too small to induce any radical changes in behaviour.

It is in the less secure areas of the modern economy where the disincentive effects of high marginal rates are most pronounced. The first is at the lower end of the earnings spectrum, especially at that point where a relatively high burden of taxation meets a relatively generous cushion of means-tested benefits. Since benefits are withdrawn as income rises, the tax and social security systems interact to create a new class of paupers who are better off living at the public expense than going out to work. Until the reform of the social security system in 1988, the implicit or marginal tax rates of those buried in the so-called 'poverty trap' were in some cases greater than 100 per cent. Even today a minority of benefit claimants are facing implicit or marginal tax rates of 70 per cent or more. The disincentive effects may extend to the wives of men whose earnings are relatively low, exacerbating the problem. In other cases, some people are better off unemployed than employed once the costs of working are taken into account. But these poverty and unemployment traps are difficult to eliminate because the obvious solution – cutting the marginal rate of tax – reduces the tax burden on everybody, and is therefore costly in terms of revenue forgone. There is no better measure of the perverse but intractable consequences of excessive public expenditure and taxation.

For the self-employed, progressive taxation undoubtedly blunts incentives. Unlike the employed, they are able to choose to work harder. But in a progressive system of taxation the marginal rate will always, by definition, exceed the average rate.[70] Progressive taxation also alters the pattern of relative incomes. A proportional tax, by contrast, ensures everybody has the same marginal tax rate and leaves the relationship between net incomes for different kinds of work unchanged. The perversities of progressive taxation are naturally more obvious to the self-employed than to the employed. Services which before taxation received the same reward may earn different amounts after progressive taxation and, in particular, the man or woman who earns a lot of money through brilliance or toil may end up with the same (or even less) than someone who earns relatively little through stupidity or idleness. This effect was lucidly explained by Hayek over thirty years ago:

> If, before taxation, a surgeon gets as much for an operation as an architect for planning a house, or a salesman gets as much for selling ten cars as a photographer for selling forty portraits, the same relation will still hold if proportional taxes are deducted from their receipts. But with progressive taxation of incomes this relation may be greatly changed. Not only may services which before taxation receive the same remuneration bring very different rewards; but a man who receives a relatively large payment for a service may in the end be left with less than another who receives a smaller payment. This means that progressive taxation necessarily offends against what is probably the only universally recognised principle of economic justice, that of 'equal pay for equal work'...A man who has worked very hard, or for some reason is in greater demand, may receive a smaller reward for further effort than one who has been idle or less lucky. Indeed, the more the consumers value a man's services, the less worthwhile will it be for him to exert himself further.[71]

In other words, progressive taxation alters the price signals for different (or even the same) kinds of labour. This may not matter much in the corporate, hierarchical economy, where people have no control over what they do or who they work for. But in the self-employed sector it means people either work less hard, or devote excessive time to tax planning, or are diverted into less useful or even untaxed forms of economic activity.

When he became Chancellor in 1853 Gladstone formulated a plan to abolish the income tax by 1859 because it pressed 'upon the whole too hard upon intelligence or skill, and not hard enough upon property as compared with intelligence or skill'.[72] He recognised that the progressive taxation of incomes reduces the propensity of people to make long-term and risky investments of their time, money or talents. Progressive taxation is particularly hard on the most enterprising individuals, who venture their talents or capital in the marketplace at the risk of huge personal loss rather than seek a secure and well-paid job. Some may invest in a specific project like a new product or technology, or even in a play, opera or book, whose value takes years to realise, and then pay tax at punitive rates in the few years when the money rolls in. Almost all self-employed people are affected by a tax system geared to the regular and predictable income of the employed earner on PAYE, when in reality their incomes may fluctuate wildly from year to year and they are forced to think not in terms of net monthly or weekly income over a forty-year career but of day-to-day cash flow and of large rewards in the form of capital at some uncertain point in the future.

A tax system which penalises such people is cutting off a vital source of innovation and investment. Most new economic, technological and even artistic developments must come from the individual entrepreneur, artist or small businessman most intimately acquainted with the opportunity, and who controls or is able to mobilise the human and material capital to exploit it. Yet progressive taxation inhibits the accumulation and investment of capital by such individuals, and denies them the incentive of the massive material rewards they need to compensate them for the possibility of the total loss of their investment. Progressive taxation crushes the most innovative, competitive, far-sighted and entrepreneurial spirits in an economy, and discourages those with ample personal resources they may be willing to place at the disposal of others who can use them productively. It prevents some individuals from amassing capital and others from investing it usefully. Instead, the tax system anoints the employed corporate time-server who can take full advantage of his mitigating tax allowances, beg his employer to pay him in tax-efficient share options or gold bars or life assurance policies, insist the company pays for his health insurance and his motor car and, if he reaches the top of the para-proprietary corporate hierarchy, exploit the lack of watchful owners by writing his own contract and paying as much of the corporate income into his own bank account as possible. The structure of the British tax system, and the structure of the British economy, are mirror-images of each other.

References

1   E. F. Jacob, The Fifteenth Century 1399-1485, OUP. 1988 Edition, page 78.
2   From the 1530s, when Henry VIII broke with Rome, the Crown also enjoyed the 'first fruits' and tenths previously paid to the Church. The revenues of the Royal Mail and the customs and excise were also captured by the Crown.
3   It was at the Restoration in 1660 that Parliament first gave the King a fixed annual income, when Charles II was voted £1.2 million a year in exchange for surrendering his feudal dues – wardships, tenures in capite, tenure by knight-service and so on. The sum never actually materialised. A more realistic arrangement was reached in 1698, when Parliament agreed to take over all military expenditure and guarantee William III an annual income of £700,000 a year by making up any shortfall in revenues the King received from the Crown Estates and the Customs and Excise. From that point the King was in theory a paid servant of Parliament, though the Hanoverians and their supporters in Parliament found many ingenious ways to maintain royal income and patronage.
4   Quoted in John Brewer, in The Sinews of Power: War, Money and the English State 1668–1783, Alfred A. Knopf, 1988, frontispiece.
5   Ferdinand Mount, The British Constitution Now, Mandarin, 1993, page 88.
6   Philip Hall, Royal Fortune: Tax, Money and the Monarchy, Bloomsbury, 1992, page 7.
7   Sir Arthur Bryant, Set in a Silver Sea, Collins, 1984, page 132.
8   R. B. Pugh, The Crown Estate: An Historical Essay, H.M.S.O., 1960, page 5.
9   Robert S. Hoyt, The Royal Demesne in English Constitutional History 1066–1272, Cornell University Press, Ithaca, New York, 1950, page 162.
10   The Hundred Years' War had exactly the opposite effect on the Valois monarchy in France, which emerged from the conflict with a standing army financed by arbitrary royal taxation. Royal despotism in France had finally to be ended by Revolution. England had a rather happier constitutional future ahead of it.
11   B. E. V. Sabine, A History of Income Tax, George Allen & Unwin Ltd, 1966, page 13.
12   Charles Wilson, England's Apprenticeship 1603–1673, Longman, 1975, page 90; D. M. Palliser, The Age of Elizabeth 1547–1603, Longman, 1992, pages 125-8.
13   Petition of Right, Clause 8, 1628. In Divine Right and Democracy: An Anthology of Political Writing in Stuart England, edited by David Wootton, Penguin Classics,

1986, page 170.

14   Godfrey Davies, The Early Stuarts 1603–1660, OUP, 1991, page 45.

15   Charles Wilson, England's Apprenticeship 1603-1673, Longman, 1975, page 100.

16   Walter Bagehot, The English Constitution, Introduction to the Second Edition, Fontana, 1973, pages 303–4.

17   John Brewer, The Sinews of Power: War, Money and the English State 1688–1783, Alfred A. Knopf, 1988, Table 3.2, page 66.

18   John Brewer, in The Sinews of Power: War, Money and the English State 1688–1783, page 73, puts fees at 2.4 per cent of income.

19   Sunday Times, 13 February 1994.

20   John Brewer, in The Sinews of Power: War, Money and the English State 1688–1783, Alfred A. Knopf, 1988, page 113.

21   Charles Adams, For Good and Evil: The Impact of Taxes on the Course of Civilization, Madison Books, 1993, page 260.

22   Patrick K. O'Brien, 'The Political Economy of British Taxation, 1660-1815', Economic History Review, 2nd ser. XLI, 1 (1988), page 26.

23   Observer, 16 October 1994.

24   The National Audit Office estimated the lost tax revenues in 1993 at £340 million of which all but £35 million was attributable to legitimate personal imports. Financial Times, 3 February 1995.

25   Financial Times, 9 June 1993.

26   Financial Times, 28 May 1994.

27   See Geoffrey Morley, The Smuggling War: The Government's Fight Against Smuggling in the 18th and 19th Centuries, Alan Sutton, 1994, pages 76-81.

28   Financial Times, 11 May 1994.

29   Quoted in B. E. V. Sabine, A History of Income Tax, George Allen & Unwin Ltd, 66, page 31.

30   A History of Income Tax, page 46.

31   A History of Income Tax, page 43.

32   Quoted in Wendy Hinde, Richard Cobden: A Victorian Outsider, Yale University Press, 1987, page 106.

33   Sunday Times, 20 February 1994.

34   Financial Times, 6 October 1994.

35   In 1976 a Conservative Opposition prided itself on diluting the sweeping powers the Labour Government was prepared to give to the Inland Revenue to raid premises and call for papers. Such are the corrupting effects of power.

36   Financial Times, 2 December 1994.

37   Paddy Hillyard and Janie Percy-Smith, The Coercive State: The Decline of Democracy in Britain, Fontana, 1988, pages 227 and 229.

38   Sunday Times, 26 April 1992.

39   Independent on Sunday, 24 October 1992.

40   Charles Adams, For Good and Evil: The Impact of Taxes on the Course of Civilization, Madison Books, 1993, page 457.

41   Hansard, 21 January 1994, Col. 846.

42   Financial Times, 13 April 1994.

43   Sunday Telegraph, 10 April 1994.

44 Financial Times, 24 May 1994.

40   Charles Adams, For Good and Evil: The Impact of Taxes on the Course of Civilization, Madison Books, 1993, page 457.

45   Quoted in Charles Adams, For Good and Evil: The Impact of Taxes on the Course of Civilization, Madison Books, 1993, page 278.

46   Patrick K. O'Brien, 'The Political Economy of British Taxation, 1660–1815', Economic History Review, 2nd ser. XLI, 1 (1988), pages 21–2.

47   'The Political Economy of British Taxation, 1660–1815', Table 4, page 9.

48   B. R. Mitchell, British Historical Statistics, CUP, 1988, Public Finance, Table 3, pages 581–6.

49   They peaked at 26 per cent of total gross revenue in 1856–57. See British Historical

Statistics, Table 3, pages 581–6.
50 B. R. Mitchell, British Historical Statistics, CUP, 1988, Public Finance, Table 3, pages 581–6.
51 Inland Revenue Statistics 1993, Table 1.1, page 9.
52 Inland Revenue Statistics 1993, Table 1.1, page 9.
53 The extension was scheduled to take place in two stages, an initial level of 8 per cent from April 1994 rising to 171/2 per cent in April 1995. The second stage of the increase was lost in Parliament in December 1994. See page 119.
54 Hansard, 1 November 1946, Cols 1000–4, Vol. 428.
55 James Callaghan, Time and Chance, Fontana, 1988, page 38.
56 J. A. Kay and M. A. King, The British Tax System, Fifth Edition, OUP, 1990, page 20.
57 See Nigel Lawson, The View From No. 11, Bantam, 1992, pages 364–71.
58 A third rate of income tax made no long-term political sense because it immediately excluded millions of voters from having any material interest in the government's declared target of a single basic rate of 20p in the pound.
59 Quoted in D. M. Palliser, The Age of Elizabeth England Under the Later Tudors 1547–1603, Longman, Second Edition, 1992, page 14.
60 Peter Mathias, The First Industrial Nation: An Economic History of Britain 1700–1914 Second Edition, 1983, pages 37-8.
61 See W. A. Thomas, The Finance of British Industry 1918–1976, Methuen, 1978.
62 Financial Times, 9 November 1994.
63 Letter, Financial Times, 18 November 1994.
64 Community Network Services estimate, reported in the Financial Times, 1 March 1994
65 See Charles Adams, For Good and Evil: The Impact of Taxes on the Course of Civilization, Madison Books, 1993, pages 470–1.
66 J. A. Kay and M. A. King, The British Tax System, Fifth Edition, OUP, 1990, page 53
67 Financial Times, 19 April 1994.
68 Inland Revenue Statistics 1993, Table 2.3, page 23.
69 Professor Cedric Sandford, sometime Director of the Centre for Fiscal Studies at Bath University, interviewed over 300 accountants in 1989 and 1990 and found the number who responded to the lower rates of direct taxation by working harder was much the same as the number who worked less for the same reason
70 The average tax rate is the proportion of income which is taken in tax; the marginal rate is the proportion of additional earnings which is taken in tax. Though it is perfectly possible for the average rate of taxation to rise without any increase in marginal rates, a tax system is properly described as progressive only if the marginal rate of taxation is higher than the average rate. This is certainly the case in Britain today. A single man earning £10,000 a year, for example, will pay an average rate of tax of 14.6 per cent in 1995–96 (assuming a personal allowance of £3,525, tax at 20 per cent on the first £3,200 of taxable income and tax at 25 per cent on the next £21,100 of taxable income) but if his incomerises to £15,000 he will pay tax at 25 per cent on the whole of the extra £5.000 of income.
71 F. A. Hayek, The Constitution of Liberty, Routledge, 1960, pages 316–17
72 Sir Llewellyn Woodward, The Age of Reform 1815–1870, OUP, Second Edition, 62, page 166.

PART TWO

The Loss of Prosperity

CHAPTER SIX

The Rights of Property

Who goeth a warfare at any time of his own cost? who planteth a vineyard, and eateth not of the fruit thereof? or who feedeth a flock, and eateth not of the milk of the flock?

I Corinthians 9:7

The seed ye sow, another reaps;
The Wealth ye find, another keeps;
The Robes ye weave, another wears;
The arms ye forge, another bears.

Sow seed – but let no tyrant reap;
Find wealth – let no impostor heap;
Weave robes – let not the idle wear;
Forge arms, in your defence to bear.

Shelley, *The Song to the Men of England*

'Great nations,' wrote Adam Smith, 'are never impoverished by private, though they sometimes are by public prodigality and misconduct.[1] It is the melancholy achievement of the collectivists who have dominated the political economy of the twentieth century to demonstrate beyond all reasonable doubt the truth of this observation. The economic history of the last one hundred years has shown that the elixir of growth is not the State itself but the Individual, pursuing his diverse and self-interested goals as best he can within a framework of personal liberties guaranteed by the State. Growth depends not on politicians or officials, or even on an abstraction called the free market, but upon the confidence of individual men and women to work and to invest. That no man will sow where another will reap is as good a summary as any of the economic case for private property. It was the opinion of no less an authority than John Maynard Keynes that 'the weakness of the inducement to invest has been at all times the key to the economic problem', and it is self-evident that individuals will not invest capital, invent new products or provide services if they cannot expect to reap the rewards of doing so.[2]

The decision to invest depends as much upon individual spirit as rational calculation, for it carries the risk of the total loss of the investment. It is for this reason that entrepreneurs must be confident that they will be allowed to keep most of the earnings which accrue from an investment and that they will be allowed to keep or to sell to others any assets which it creates. These rights to buy, own, sell, lend or mortgage are precisely those 'property rights' – in philosophical jargon, the right to possess, use, alienate and consume – which the primitive State was established to maintain, and which are numbered along with equality before the law and freedom of labour, speech and movement in any litany of the classical liberties. Their entrenchment and enforcement is the *sine qua non* of a successful capitalist economy. Where property rights are not safeguarded by the State but eroded by expropriation, taxation or inflation, property-owners lose not only what is taken from them but also the incentive to produce any more goods and services for exchange with others. There will be, in other words, less work, less trade, less saving, less investment and less economic growth. And that is the story of the British economy in the twentieth century.

The Importance of Property Rights to Prosperity

The importance of well-defined and enforceable property rights in creating a climate of investment and growth is no longer disputed. The whole of the developing world – in east and central Europe, east Asia, Latin America and even Africa – has recognised that market economies generate growth only because property rights permit extensive and efficient exchange of goods and services between millions of people and thousands of companies. They alone foster the specialisation of labour and higher productivity on which growth depends.[3] The rediscovery of the economic virtue of property rights is also redefining the role of the State. At the end of the twentieth century man is finding once again what was obvious to previous generations raised in an atmosphere of perpetual physical insecurity. This is that the entrenchment and enforcement of property rights is the principal purpose and duty of the State.

Ever since nomads gave way to settled agricultural communities, property-owners have sought to protect their assets from marauders. It is purely because this defence is the classic 'public good' – a good whose benefits accrue to everyone, giving no one an incentive to pay for it – that it becomes necessary to establish the State, to raise the taxes to fund security of property. 'The great and chief end…of men's uniting into commonwealths and putting themselves under government,' wrote John Locke, in the classic pre-Marxist exposition of the role of the State, 'is the preservation of their property.'[4] It is the varying ability of States to uphold their side of this bargain, by defining and protecting the rights of property, which largely explains the varying performance of different economies. It explains why no nation was able to achieve sustained economic growth, in the sense of output rising faster than population, for thousands of years before Holland and England achieved it for the first time in seventeenth-century Europe. It illuminates why the various collectivist experiments, in truncating and even abolishing the rights of property, have failed and will continue to fail quite so disastrously, and helps to explain why the long-term rate of growth of the British economy has slowed down so dramatically over the last two decades.[5]

In a seminal book published over twenty years ago the Nobel Prize-winning economist Douglass North demonstrated how the development and refinement of the laws of private property explained the emergence of the first modern capitalist economy in England more completely than any technological or quantitative changes.[6] In the Dark and Middle Ages the rights of property were poorly defined and protected, and active markets in land and goods were difficult to develop. Payment in kind rather than cash, the absence of organised markets and Church-sanctioned concepts like the 'just wage', the ban on usury and the 'just price' suppressed the price signals on which successful economic activity depends. Profits from productivity-raising innovations like windmills or the three-field system were also too poorly protected by law and too easily copied for the profits to accrue to their inventors. This suppressed innovation.

Throughout the Middle Ages, corrupt officialdom, poor communications, periodic invasion and incessant aristocratic violence limited the power and duration of government and made property rights chronically insecure. Crown and aristocracy anyway saw property rights not as the key to growth but as a source of revenue. Monopolistic rights to set up markets, manufacture goods, exploit inventions and sell services were sold to the highest bidder, or controlled by urban guilds which regulated output, wages, working hours, prices and standards in pettifogging detail. These monopolies deterred investment, restricted competition and stifled innovation, but were of course far easier to tax. Rights of property were further truncated by a variety of tolls on trade. Because no property right was secure, ambitious people were driven out of productive pursuits into the Church, the law, and competition for office at Court. The medieval economy was essentially a predatory one, in which aristocrats, armies and powerful officials competed for a larger slice of a static amount of wealth.

Seventeenth-century England finally escaped this stultifying pattern by entrenching rights of property securely for the first time. After the Civil War the country was run by an acquisitive and tax-paying political class rather than an absolute and over-taxing monarchy. Private property rights in land and labour were well established by custom, bolstered by a Lockean political philosophy and protected securely in practice by the constitution and the courts. The restrictive practices of the guilds were broken, and those of the trade unions resisted. Markets – including capital markets to channel money efficiently from savers to entrepreneurs – flourished, and disseminated undistorted price signals to manufacturers and traders. Primitive securities were devised and traded, lowering the cost of capital relative to land and labour and allowing more capital-intensive businesses to develop.

Other useful inventions, like the joint-stock company, double- entry book-keeping, patent laws and commercial insurance, were also devised. The customs barriers to internal and external trade were gradually lifted during the eighteenth and nineteenth centuries. A stream of enabling legislation facilitated the reclamation and enclosure of land, the building of roads, the improvement of towns, the construction of harbours and the excavation of canals. Abroad, the Royal Navy protected the rights of private property from piracy and rival trading nations. The contrast between the English economy at this time and those controlled by the absolutist monarchs of France and Spain was striking. The French and Spanish kings continued to burden property-owners with excessive taxation and borrowing, and to hamper trade with internal customs barriers, price-fixing, and stifling regulations. In Spain the State, far from protecting the rights of private property, periodically ruined its creditors by declaring the Crown bankrupt.

How Inflation Expropriates Property-Owners

No modern British government has declared itself bankrupt. Instead, governments have preferred to ruin their creditors by the surreptitious device of inflation, which steadily erodes the real value of debt. Between 1946 and the end of 1993 the average real rate of return on British government bonds was minus o.1 per cent. But the economic effects of inflation have spread beyond holders of govern- ment debt. Since the first oil shock of 1973 the British economy – like that of every Western country – has failed to match the growth rates it achieved in the 1950s and 1960s. The main explanation is the puncturing of the 'money illusion', in which workers mistake nominal increases in their standard of living for real ones. The incomes policies of the 1960s and 1970s failed to provide an alternative solution, trapping the economy in a wearying battle to contain inflation. To keep prices under control the authorities have had to run the economy at a rate of growth below its true potential.

Inflation is certainly a formidable enemy of the property-owner. Amid rising prices, wrote Keynes in *The Economic Consequences of the Peace*, 'all permanent relations between debtors and creditors, which form the ultimate foundation of capitalism, become so utterly disordered as to be meaningless. Lenin was certainly right. There is no subtler, no surer means of overturning the existing bases of society than to debauch the currency. The process engages all the hidden forces of economic law on the side of destruction, and does it in a manner which not one man in a million is able to diagnose.' If capital-owners have no protection from the ravages of inflation there is no incentive to save or to invest, except in inflation hedges like property or precious metals or Old Masters. And inflation is pre-eminently the responsibility of the State. Rising prices favour only the borrower, and the State is not only the greatest borrower of all but the one institution with the power to inflate away the real value of its debts by the simple device of printing money.

But inflation, like growth, is not solely an economic phenomenon. The immense powers of the State to spend, tax and borrow reflect a change in the nature of its role, from guarantor of the rights of property to arbitrator of the distribution of property. Although the Industrial Revolution raised living standards to unprecedented levels, it distributed the benefits unequally. Despite the enormous rise in the national income, and of the standard of living of every inhabitant of the country, inequality was probably at its height in Britain between 1880 and 1914. During these years a fiftieth to a thirtieth of the population enjoyed well over a third of the national income. Three quarters to nine tenths of the population had to make do with two fifths to a half of it.[7] The fact that the submerged three quarters were far better off under capitalism than they would have been under any alternative system did not necessarily reconcile them to their lot.

Extremes of wealth and poverty endangered the security of property rights, leading to a series of political concessions which ended in the universal franchise. Democracy has redistributed wealth more equally through the political system rather than revolution, so leaving society unequal but stable. Just as the State once taxed the populace to pay soldiers to fight battles in defence of property rights, so the State now taxes property-holders to ease the lot of the less well-of with free public services and welfare payments in hard times. Welfare, to borrow a phrase from Joseph Chamberlain, is the ransom property pays for its security. But it gives the State enormous powers to direct the distribution of the national income. The government has never controlled less than a third of the total national income since 1939, and today rarely controls less than two fifths.[8] The numbers who gain from higher taxation and public expenditure – either because they are on welfare or work In the public sector – are gradually approaching parity with productive labour and capital. Because they also have the vote, potentially inflationary levels of public expenditure and taxation are now deeply embedded in the political life of the country.

The Socialist Attack on Property Rights

As de Tocqueville warned, this search for equality is the chief characteristic of democracy. It is not surprising that the advent of the universal franchise coincided with the electoral success of an ideology which prizes equality above all else, and which is based on the mistaken belief that private property is the obstacle rather than the solution to sustained economic growth. 'The theory of the Communists,' wrote Karl Marx and Friedrich Engels, 'may be summed up in the single sentence: Abolition of private property.' The labour theory of value, which Ricardo adapted from Locke and Marx refined, held that labour was the source of all value but that its owners received only subsistence wages. The task of Labour was therefore to expropriate the property of the Capitalists, probably in a bloody revolution. Socialism never took this extreme form in Britain but even a revisionist Socialist like Anthony Crosland – who thought the labour theory of value was rubbish – did not doubt that the egalitarian policy conclusions were valid.[9]

Socialist government in Britain was also heavily influenced by the work of the Oxford don and Labour Party saint, R. H. Tawney. For him, economic growth was simply a matter of secondary importance:

Though British socialism is by no means indifferent to economic considerations, its foundations are ethical. Even if the way of co-operation did not yield all the economic advantages expected from it, we should continue to choose it. Both the type of individual character and the style of social existence fostered by it are those we prefer...Civilisation is a matter, not of quantity of possessions, but of quality of life. It is to be judged, not by the output of goods and services per head, but by the use which is made of them.[10]

Production for use rather than exchange has an appealing electoral ring, but it meant in practice an unwavering hostility to private property. Tawney nurtured a curious belief in the 'social function' of property rather than its natural or legal rights, which lingers on in even the least recherché of modern Socialist circles. By 'social functions' he meant the performance of work or services not to acquire wealth or possessions but to supply what was necessary, useful or beautiful. Workin to acquire riches he considered morally disgusting, economically wasteful and socially divisive. Like the mercantilists, Tawney saw competition between individuals and firms as a form of industrial warfare, in which the protagonists could of the military analogy that he argued (following J. A. Hobson) that capitalistic competition led inevitably to nationalism, imperialism, militarism and war.[11] Economic activity to perform a social 'function', by contrast, was ennobling, efficient and harmonlous.

The Labour leader and godfather of British social democracy, Hugh Gaitskell, admitted that Tawney's two great works – *Equality* and *The Acquisitive Society* – 'made a tremendous impact upon my generation...I always think of him as *the* Democratic Socialist *par excellence.*[12] Tawney was still sufficiently influential among the Gaitskellites who abandoned the Labour Party to create the Social Democratic Party in 1981 for them to name the party think-tank after him.. The musings of the current Labour leader Tony Blair; on Society and the Individual are really no more than variations on this long-standing Socialist theme.

But euphemistic language cannot cloak its meaning. *The Acquisitive Society*, in which Tawney gave the fullest exposition of the idea of 'social function', was a sustained attack on the classical conception of private property:

> 'Private property' has been the central position against which the social movement of the last hundred years has directed its forces. The criticism of it has ranged from an imaginative communism in the most elementary and personal of necessaries, to prosaic and partially realised proposals to transfer certain kinds of property from private to public ownership, or to limit their exploitation by restrictions imposed by the State. But however varying in emphasis and method. the general note of what may conveniently be called the Socialist criticism of property is what the word Socialism implies. Its essence is the statement that the economic evils of society are primarily due to the unregulated operation, under modern conditions of industrial organisation, of the institution of private property.[13]

As Tawney recognised, all forms of socialism have favoured the truncation of the rights of property. This is the one idea in socialism which never changes, no matter what form 'real, existing socialism' might take. Socialists disagree only over the method and the degree of the expropriation.

The chosen weapons of the post-war socialist governments were economic planning, the nationalisation of 'strategic' industries and especially the confiscatory taxation of incomes. These policies added up to a formidable direct and indirect attack on private property, even though compensation was paid to the previous owners of nationalised industries and the planning and taxation policies ostensibly enjoyed democratic consent. Nationalisation was the purest Tawneyism. Though even Tawney himself doubted its efficacy, private ownership was clearly incompatible with the public purpose or 'social function' he had adumbrated. He had envisaged publicly owned industries run by a new class of 'professional' managers dedicated to the achievement of high standards rather than 'speculative' profit and answerable to the consumer through the political system rather than the marketplace. The nationalisation programme of the Attlee government was suffused with this kind of thinking. 'It is quite a false conception,' the Labour Chancellor Stafford Cripps argued in the House of Commons in May 1949, 'to consider that it is necessary to make a profit out of any industry, except under a capitalist system.'

Plenty of otherwise reasonable people – Hugh Gaitskell, Herbert Morrison, James Callaghan among them – were persuaded that nationalisation would not only be more efficient than privately owned industry but that the workers in nationalised industries would be charged with a new spirit of social functionalism as they laboured on behalf of abstractions like 'the benefit of the people', 'the good of society' or 'the community.'[14] 'The public corporation must be no mere capitalist business, the be-all and end-all of which is profits and dividends,' wrote Herbert Morrison as late as 1953. 'Its board and officers must regard themselves as the high custodians of the public interest.'[15] Douglas Jay argued in 1946 that 'in a world where men and women are becoming progressively more educated, and in which fear and greed are thus steadily giving way as human motive to public spirit and pride in creative work, the need for public ownership and democratic control becomes steadily greater. Such is the inevitable conclusion . . . from a real under- standing of the nature of human needs and their satisfaction, and of the trend of modern organisation and economic life.'[16]

Douglas Jay's *Socialist Case* was based on Keynesian ideas of demand-management as well as planning, redistributive taxation and nationalisation, or what he called 'the need for maintaining effective demand by way of consumption rather than the illusory road of what has come to be called "investment"'.[17] The socialist political settlement of the post-war period committed successive governments to the manipulation of fiscal policy solely to meet pre- ordained economic targets without any reference to political principle or natural right. The task was simply to increase taxes to restrain demand when it was expected to be excessive and to decrease them when it was expected to be deficient. It was an approach to economic policymaking that

ended in the stagflationary mire in which the economy, run always with more
regard to the rate of inflation than the rate of growth, performs consistently
below its full potential. Even now, the debate over whether to raise or lower
taxes is usually discussed in terms of whether or not it will stoke up inflation
or create employment or win the election and not over whether or not
taxpayers are entitled to keep the wealth they have earned or created.

Socialist Atavism: The Idealisation of the Middle Ages

All collectivist philosophies are atavistic. They are rooted in a yearning for the
purer, more harmonious, way of life which is thought to have obtained in tribal
and pre-industrial eras. British socialism was no different. Its original believers
were drenched in nostalgia, rather than the economic principles or hard
realities of Marxism. They yearned to go back to the vanished England of the
Middle Ages. 'I just long to see a start made on the job of reclaiming, recreating
rural England,' wrote the leader of the Labour Party, George Lansbury, in 1934.
'I can see the village greens with the maypoles once again erected and the boys
and girls, young men and maidens, all joining in the mirth and folly of May
Day.'[18] A yearning for the harmonious social hierarchy of the Middle Ages was
common to early socialists like Ruskin, William Morris and Tawney. Their
detestation of capitalist civilisation was as much an aesthetic as a rational
judgment. It harked back to a mythical Merrie England, in which baron, knight,
blacksmith and plowman blended into an harmonious social whole as they
performed their separate economic and social 'functions'; the natural avarice of
men was tempered by the fear of hell, the just price and the usury laws; and the
well-defined and properly enforced property rights of possessive individualism
still lay centuries ahead. In 1894 one early Socialist, the journalist Robert
Blatchford, actually published a collection of his essays under the title *Merrie
England*.

In 1926 R. H. Tawney published an influential essay entitled *Religion and the
Rise of Capitalism*, in which he portrayed capitalism as an invention of the
Protestant ideologues and bourgeois revolutionists of the seventeenth century.[19]
The same view suffused his more overtly political writings. In *The Acquisitive
Society* he lamented the displacement of medieval harmony by the bourgeois
revolution of the seventeenth century:

> The rise of modern economic relations, which may be dated in England
> from the latter half of the seventeenth century, was coincident with the
> growth of a political theory which replaced the conception of purpose by
> that of mechanism. During a great part of history men had found the
> significance of their social order in its relation to the universal purposes
> of religion. It stood as one rung in a ladder which stretched from Hell to
> Paradise, and the classes who composed it were the hands, the feet, the
> head of a corporate body which was itself a microcosm imperfectly
> reflecting a larger universe...The essence of the change was the
> disappearance of the idea that social institutions and economic activities

were related to common ends, which gave them their significance and which served as their criterion.[20]

An influential Socialist philosopher of the post-war period, C. B. Macpherson, reinterpreted the writings of Thomas Hobbes, John Locke and other seventeenth-century philosophers and writers to show that they had invented a new socio-political theory which he called 'possessive individualism'.[21]

John Ruskin adored the flying buttresses, castle battlements and rude wooden cottages of medieval England and attempted at one stage a literal recreation of the medieval economy, funding a hand- made linen factory at Langdale. He influenced William Morris, who also opened his own business at Merton Abbey, the site of a medieval Augustinian priory. Morris once declared that 'the leading passion of my life has been and is hatred of modern civilisation'.[22] He meant, of course, industrial civilisation, though he was both a rentier and a capitalist himself. Even as an under- graduate at Oxford he had a private income of £700–800 a year (a sum worth £35–40,000 today), and he had enough spare capital to invest £15,000 (well over £600,000 today) of his own money in his business.[23] Like the champagne socialists of today, he did not let his private behaviour interfere with his political opinions. He ran the Merton workshops on conventional capitalist lines, arguing that 'you cannot have socialism in a corner'. By denying the workforce any share in the management or the profits he was saving them from becoming capitalists.[24] Medievalism informed all of Morris's work. It was the threat to the glories of Tewkesbury Abbey which led him to form the Society for the Protection of Ancient Buildings. He called on people to 'forget the snorting steam and piston stroke' and dream of a Merrie England of 'gaily-coloured tents arranged in orderly lanes' and 'London, small, and white, and clean'.

Morris's hypocrisy and meanness – Rossetti said of him that he would never give a penny to a beggar – were probably the only aspects of his character which medieval men and women would readily have understood.[25] For the medieval period was in reality an age of greed, violence, cruelty, ignorance, superstition, disease, filth and economic stagnation, in which the rich and powerful preyed mercilessly on the poor and vulnerable. 'Merrie England,' as Jim Dixon famously put it, 'was about the most un-Merrie period in our history.'[26] Yet the Socialist interpretation of medieval history was eventually translated directly into government policy, and especially into that of nationalisation. Socialists imagined that workers in publicly owned industries would be inspired by a sense of social duty, purpose and co-operation quite different from the alienation they experienced under the 'functionless property' of capitalism.

Their disappointment was predictable. Experience showed that the incentives to which the managers and workers in the nationalised industries responded were far removed from this ideal. Because they did not gain if costs were reduced or revenues increased, the managers who controlled the industries were interested primarily in empire-building rather than efficiency or profit. Without profitability as a gauge of success they developed an insatiable appetite for investment. The politicians responsible for funding the investment were unable to make hard commercial choices – say, to close a plant or sack a manager – without political embarrassment, so they tended to favour the short term over the long term and to use publicly owned industries to flatter interest groups, and especially the public sector trade unions. Market signals were muffled by soft loans or outright subsidies. The early British socialists failed to understand that ownership matters.

The Relevance of Ownership to Performance

As owner, the State is bound to botch the task of running a business. This is because its planners deliberately discard the information given by prices in free markets, suppress innovation and experimentation, and deny both managers and workers any sense of personal risk or success, and the sobering knowledge of failure. yet the revisionist socialists – since at least the time of Hugh Gaitskell and Anthony Crosland, who recognised as early as the mid-Igsos that nationalisation was both inefficient and electorally unpopular- still argue that the ownership of the means of production is irrelevant. 'The basic factor,' wrote Crosland, 'is not ownership, but large scale; and a collectivist economy, with no private owners, is no less characterised by the alienation of control than a capitalist economy. Indeed, even in the latter, ownership has less and less relevance to the question of control. The same trend towards large scale and complexity which alienates the workers from the means of production also alienates the owners. Capital requirements are so great that sole ownership gives way to fragmented shareholding; and many large companies today have more shareholders than workers.'[27]

Crosland concluded that the managerial problems facing private and public industry were much the same, and that modern workers could enjoy the fruits of their labour through a mixture of redistributive taxation, dividend controls and higher pay rather than public ownership. The Labour Party has never convincingly rid itself of its commitment to nationalisation, though its obeisance to the shibboleth probably owes more to the financial and electoral reliance of the party on the public sector trade unions than to any lingering confidence that nationalisation will prove efficacious. Even today, voters cannot be confident that a Labour government would not re-nationalise some of the privatised utilities Likewise the heirs of Crosland and Gaitskell, who ended up in the Liberal Democratic Party, argued during their time in the short-lived Social Democratic Party that 'the real industrial issues are those of efficiency and responsiveness to the consumer rather than ownership.'[28] Their Liberal allies – whose susceptibility to collectivist ideas has taken the party far from the great Liberal tradition of Gladstone, or even that of Beveridge, Keynes and Grimond – are infected with much the same thinking. The late David Penhaligon once described privatisation as 'a damaging irrelevance'.[29]

Collectivists of all kinds, having identified private property as the source of all economic and social ills, have always found it galling to admit the relevance of ownership to economic performance. 'Privatisation,' writes Cento Veljanovski, involves much more than the simple transfer of ownership. It involves the transfer and redefinition of a complex bundle of property rights which creates a whole new penalty-reward system which will alter the incentives in the firm and ultimately its performance.'[30] It was Aristotle who first argued that if an asset is to be used and maintained properly, it needs to be owned by somebody who has a personal stake in looking after it. Unlike Plato – who favoured, at least in *The Republic*, communistic forms of ownership – he understood that what belongs to everybody in practice belongs to nobody.

This is the central flaw in all schemes of public ownership, as the countries of east and central Europe have discovered since the Berlin Wall came down in 1989. Six years ago Mikhail Gorbachev's chief economic adviser, Professor Aganbegyan, wrote:

> Public ownership is the basic form of socialist ownership – of the land and its minerals, and of the state factories... The potential danger in this is that the property belongs to everyone but to no one in particular. The attitude to public property that may arise is that it is nobody's business, with many difficulties arising in consequence. Workers may use public resources uneconomically, they may work less well in a social economy than for themselves. The attitude to machinery in state factories is quite different from that, say, to personally-owned cars.[31]

But events east of the Elbe have merely demonstrated, in a particularly vivid way, a rare coincidence of economic theory and common sense.

Economic theory has long distinguished between the economic effects of property held in common and property held exclusively. In 1968 Garrett Hardin published a famous.paper entitled 'The Tragedy of the Commons', in which he demonstrated that an unowned asset or an asset from which others cannot be excluded, like common land, is bound to be over-exploited because nobody has an economic interest in managing it sensibly. Each individual using a piece of common land to graze his cows enjoys the full benefits of well-fed cows, but bears only a fraction of the costs. The effect is to encourage over-grazing and soil erosion. On privately owned land, by contrast, the cowherd avoids over-grazing because he collects the full cost of soil erosion as well as the rewards of well- fed cows. The same perverse incentives explain over-fishing of the unowned sea and pollution of the unowned atmosphere. They also explain why there is more litter in public parks than private gardens; why public sector employees are more likely to go on strike; and why council estates are so often dilapidated.

The Nature of Modern Property Rights: Bundles of Rights

The abuse of public property reflects a defective institutional mechanism. The inefficiency arises primarily because individual citizens cannot trade their ownership rights in a publicly owned business, and so have no incentive to ensure that its value is enhanced by the workers and managers who control it day-by-day. But tradable property rights are only a necessary and not a sufficient condition for economic efficiency. The costs of defining property rights in law, enforcing them in the courts and exchanging them in the marketplace must also be kept relatively low, or there will be a powerful disincentive to maintain an asset with a view to realising its value by selling it at some point in the future. Until the indexation of capital gains for tax purposes was introduced in 1982, for example, many owners of land and financial assets were unwilling to sell because they faced substantial tax penalties on purely inflationary gains.

An effective competition regime is also necessary to restrict the emergence of monopolies, whose owners enjoy the most private but the least efficient of property rights. All of the privatised utilities, for example, are subject to regulatory regimes which restrict their power to raise prices. Competition and proxy competition mechanisms of this kind are undeniably a truncation of the rights of private property but in reality no property right can ever be made absolute – possession of a knife does not entitle the owner to stab his neighbour with it – and every owner has duties as well as rights. An owner must certainly ensure that his property is not used for harmful purposes, and may be liable for damages if it is.[32] 'Unconscionable contracts', like those entered into by investors in Barlow Clowes or some personal pension contracts, are increasingly recognised as a limitation on the property rights of companies which use unscrupulous methods to sell their products.

In the event of a bankruptcy, or where an asset was used as security for a loan, private property is liable to distraint. Assets held in trust are not owned in the sense that they can be disposed of at will. Similarly, a patent or a copyright is unquestionably a form of private property, yet it is limited in scope and time. Many pieces of ostensibly private property, like Georgian houses, are subject to detailed listing requirements governing their appearance and alteration. In addition to these limitations of the rights of private property, there is also an extensive range of things which can be owned and many different kinds of ownership. Freehold title to land is easily comprehensible as a form of private property, and leasehold only slightly less so, but financial assets like shares, bonds, options and futures rest on complex legal relationships which are much harder to understand as private property.

These are among the reasons why it is more common today to refer to private property as a 'bundle of rights' – the right to possess, the right to use, the right to consume, the right to manage, the right to lend, the right to income, the right to capital, the right to security, the right to transfer, the right to bequeath, the right to destroy and so on – which can be unbundled and reassembled in a variety of combinations. Financial securities, for example, often assign the rights to the capital and the income from the same underlying asset to different owners. Private property is, as R. H. Tawney rightly recognised, a protean concept:

> Property is the most ambiguous of categories. It covers a multitude of rights which have nothing in common except that they are exercised by persons and enforced by the State. Apart from these formal characteristics, they vary indefinitely in economic character, in social

effect, and in moral justification. They may be conditional like the grant of patent rights, or absolute like the ownership of ground rents, terminable like copyright, or permanent like a freehold, as comprehensive as sovereignty or as restricted as an easement, as intimate and personal as the ownership of clothes and books, or as remote and intangible as shares in a gold mine or rubber plantation. It is idle, therefore, to present a case for or against private property without specifying the particular forms of property to which reference is made, and the journalist who says that 'private property is the foundation of civilisation' agrees with Proudhon, who said that it was theft, in this respect at least, that without further definition, the words of both are meaningless.[33]

But an over-fastidious approach to property rights can only cloud the importance of their establishment and enforcement. It was not a journalist but the great English jurist, Sir Henry Maine (1822–1888), who said that 'nobody is at liberty to attack several property and to say that he values civilisation. The history of the two cannot be disentangled.'[34] He was in the mainstream of an English legal and philosophical tradition which takes a robustly commonsensical view of the institution of private property, which seeks only to establish good title, takes it as read that private ownership increases general well-being and abjures the metaphysical questions which obsess collectivists, like 'How does a thing become mine?'

The commonsensical view has the princely advantage that it does not provoke endless discussion over the proper distribution of property between individuals. But it has the weakness of resting the case for the single most important capitalist institution – private property – on purely utilitarian foundations: it works better than any other economic system yet devised by man. The utilitarian case for capitalism is not enough to ensure the permanent defeat of collectivism. Liberty and property are less secure to the extent that they rely on arguments of expediency rather than of philosophical principle or natural right. The manifest material power of the Invisible Hand of Adam Smith and the successful reform of political institutions according to their Utility have already proved in- sufficient defences against an ideology which is never content to rest its case upon what Douglas Jay once called 'the facts of the real world'.[35] Collectivists, as Mrs Margaret Beckett reminded her electorate in the Labour Party leadership contest of 1994, like to keep their heads in the clouds as well as their feet on the ground.

Private Property as the Moral Basis of Capitalism

Above all, collectivists have always claimed for their creed an inherent moral superiority over possessive individualism. In 1948 Francis Williams, sometime public relations adviser to the Labour Prime Minister Clement Attlee, published a book entitled *The Triple Challenge: The Future of Socialist Britain*. In its early pages he wrote:

Here at last there is taking place a practical test of two vast and so far unproven assumptions. The first is that a planned socialist system is economically more efficient than a private enterprise capitalist system, the second is that within democratic socialist planning the individual can be given a larger social justice, a greater security and a more complete freedom than under capitalism. These are the basic assumptions on which the case for socialism rests. They are so far neither proven nor unproven...If the experiment succeeds the rewards will be enormous in terms of human well-being and national power. If it fails the consequences may be measureless.[36]

It follows that, if these two 'basic assumptions' can be comprehensively disproved, socialism will be finished. It has failed already the test of economic efficiency, but its adherents refuse to concede the second 'basic assumption': that socialism is more civilised, more humane – in a word, more moral – than economic individualism. Throughout its revisionist period the Labour Party has attempted to capitalise electorally on the widespread perception that collectivist 'values' are in some way morally superior. This is not surprising. 'Capitalism,' as Nigel Lawson has put it, 'has sought to rest its case on its practical success...Socialism, by contrast, has been forced by practical failure on to the high ground of morality.'[37]

Most people are reluctant to give moral endorsement to the truth that private vices like greed and self-interest can produce public goods like faster economic growth and a higher standard of living.[38] The unequal distribution of incomes and rewards which results from capitalism is also felt to be morally repugnant.[39] The first of these arguments is based partly on an illusion. Most people are primarily self-interested. Although self-interest is not synonymous with selfishness – it is far from self-interested, but utterly selfish, for a man to make himself destitute by giving away all his possessions – there is co point in devising an economic system which is based on some ideal conception of the nature of man, and then comparing its moral credentials with a system which makes use of self-interest. The proper comparison is between the property-based market economy and a politically determined distribution of income and wealth, and experience shows that a material dispensation decided by politicians and bureaucrats is far more objectionable. The Communist tyrannies of east and central Europe have provided ample evidence that the principal beneficiaries of a political distribution of wealth are politicians and bureaucrats.

The 'spontaneous order' of the marketplace, in which millions of competing firms and individuals unknown to each other discover how to satisfy each other's wants through the price mechanism, is infinitely preferable to a system in which property is allocated by politicians and of ficials according to their assessments of individual merit. The exchange of private property in the marketplace is morally pleasing precisely because it requires no central direction of this kind, and respects the dignity and individuality of each person. In the marketplace, no questions are asked about income and wealth, or marital status, or sexual orientation or place of birth or colour of skin. In the property-based market economy the individual as consumer, not the bureaucrat, is sovereign of all he surveys. As Hayek argued:

The institution of several property is not selfish, nor was it, nor could it have been, 'invented' to impose the will of property-owners upon the rest. Rather, it is generally beneficial in that it transfers the guidance of production from the hands of a few individuals who, whatever they may pretend, have limited knowledge, to a process, the extended order, that makes maximum use of the knowledge of all, thereby benefiting those who do not own property nearly as much as those who do.[40]

In other words, the property-based market economy enlarges human freedom because it creates social order without the need of the State. Indeed, the success of the market economy relies upon millions of free individuals scattered across the globe taking different, even contradictory, views of the value to themselves of a particular commodity, manufacture, service or snippet of knowledge. Property is therefore an important contributor to human diversity and freedom as well as to material prosperity.

The moral disrepute in which the property-based market economy is held also rests on a peculiarly literal interpretation of Adam Smith's famous aphorism that 'it is not from the benevolence of the butcher, the brewer, or the baker that we expect our dinner, but from their regard to their own interest'. Individuals enter a business career for a variety of reasons which stretch far beyond the need to earn a living by buying cheap and selling dear. It may be a family business they are determined to continue, a source of personal pride and fulfilment, or simply a kind of work they are good at or enjoy. Likewise, many people resist redundancy or retirement even where it makes no economic sense for them to continue working. The most menial and debased kinds of work are a form of human creativity. Even making money by trading currencies, if it is the only thing that some people can do well, has a rough nobility.

Every balanced individual has a life at work as well as at home, and few would regard them as entirely separate moral universes. In fact, most people work in order to acquire the means of life and opportunity for themselves and their families. While they are at work, they also know that they have enormous scope to use their intelligence and freedom to make suitable moral choices. An individual may work carelessly or conscientiously. A proprietor may humiliate and abuse his employees, or nurture, reward, train and motivate them. A difficult business decision, like closing a factory, will need the classical virtue of courage. And all lasting business relationships in a capitalist economy are necessarily rooted in honesty and trust, or they would not succeed. It is in the nature of a successful market transaction that both parties benefit from it: they would not enter into it if they did not. It is the collectivist economies, in which bureaucrats decide who gets what, which penalise truth, trustworthiness and hard work and reward corruption, cheating and theft. Few people in east and central Europe are surprised that it is the *apparatchiks* and the secret policemen who have found the transition to a life of crime so effortless.

Much of the collectivist attack on the 'immorality' of capitalism is anyway directed at Aunt Sallies. No English apologist for capitalism has ever argued that private property is an absolute value which absolves an owner from any responsibility to others. Karl Marx was quite wrong to argue, as he did in the 1840s, that 'the right of property is the right to enjoy one's fortune and to dispose of it as one will, without regard for other men and independently of society...the right of self-interest...[of] the egoistic man...an individual separated from the community, withdrawn into himself, wholly preoccupied with his private interest and acting in accordance with his private caprice'.[41] The whole of the Judaeo-Christian tradition emphasises the responsibility of the rich to share their wealth with others less fortunate. 'Private property is not entirely private. That is, it is not something to be grasped entirely for itself, or for oneself. Ownership can be *legally* free and clear, but it is not *morally* free and clear,' as one Catholic theologian has put it.[42]

The Whig tradition was always informed by the Christian teaching that the earth ws the common inheritance of men, and that nobody should be excluded from extracting the necessities of life. In the British imagination property has long carried duties which were not, as socialists have alleged, mere political cant or paternalism. They were a coherent and properly articulated facet of the Whig intellectual tradition. John Locke himself argued that the rich man had an obligation to afford relief to the poor out of his 'plenty'. This charitable obligation is quite different from voting for other people to pay taxes, which many collectivists mistake for a moral choice. Freedom is the condition of any moral choice, and the taxpayer forced into sharing his wealth with others is not making a moral choice but being coerced. In fact, excessive taxation is likely to de-moralise individuals by leaving them less of their own money to spend on charitable causes. 'No one,' wrote Aristotle, 'when men have all things in common, will any longer set an example of liberality or do any liberal action, for liberality consists in the use which is made of property.'[43] For the same reason, critics of capitalism cannot enjoy the luxury of criticising rampant materialism and consumerism as the products of an impersonal 'system' over which people have no control. Those who criticise the consumer society are criticising not the capitalist system, but the moral nature of the individuals who make it up.

The second moral objection to capitalism – that it results in insupportable inequalities – is simply incoherent. No modern collectivist advocates absolute equality, but equality is an absolute concept or it is nothing. Two individuals are still unequal even if the difference in their respective wealth is narrowed to vanishing point. Egalitarians who favour 'more' equality rather than absolute equality are merely expressing an opinion, not a principle, and one based on the envy which John Stuart Mill described as 'the most anti-social and evil of all passions'. It stems from an intuitive but mistaken belief that economic activity is essentially predatory. The wealth of one man, it is thought, is the cause of the poverty of another. It is a conversational commonplace in Britain today, for example, to believe that 'market economics' or 'Thatcherite economics' equates with a world in which 'the rich get richer and the poor get poorer'. In fact, predation of this kind is true only of the medieval economy from which so much of socialist economics takes its cue. A modern capitalist economy is not a zero-sum game in which one man's gain is another's loss.

Nor is free competition merely a euphemism for an unrestrained economic warfare in which the antagonists compete for a larger share of a fixed and unchanging national income.[44] In the free market only those exchanges of property which benefit both parties will actually take place. The property bought and sold in a capitalist economy is not theft, as Proudhon thought, but an exchange for mutual benefit. It is a dynamic process, in which the constant discovery of new or previously unmet wants enlarges the size of the national income. The wealth of everyone rises, but that of some rises faster than others. If absolute equality was ever achieved, this process of growth would cease. If those who work, save and invest receive the same rewards as those who do not, no work, saving or investment will take place.

But absolute equality is not merely inefficient. It is inequitable to guarantee the idle the same reward as the industrious. To achieve it would also require the creation of a terrifying State machine to assess how much each individual earned, what savings he had, how much of both he or she was entitled to keep and how much he or she was worth to 'society'. Yet egalitarians do not shrink from making such judgments. Professor John Broome wrote recently in the *Financial Times*:

> What egalitarians complain about is not inequality itself, but undeserved inequality. They believe pay should be in proportion to desert. When a labourer finds a director earning ten times as much as him, he knows the director does not work ten times as hard. So how does he or she deserve the pay? By talents and ability, perhaps? Capitalism rewards some talents, but not others. It rewards good accountants, persuasive salesmen, people who are quick to take a money-making opportunity, artists who produce popular ephemera. It does not reward modest, skilful and hardworking craftsmen, doctors who practice where they are most needed rather than where they are paid the most, poets and pure scientists who permanently enrich our culture. Why should the possessors of the capitalist talents be the ones who deserve reward, and not these others? Just because capitalism rewards a talent, it does not follow that this talent deserves reward more than others.[45]

It is impossible to avoid the suspicion that Professor Broome felt he too was over-worked, under-appreciated and poorly rewarded. To feel that way is part of the human condition.

'What is merit?' asked Lord Palmerston. 'The opinion one man entertains of another.' In any State-imposed condition of absolute equality the petty prejudices entertained by the official equivalents of Professor Broome would be imbued with the full majesty of the law. As Hayek pointed out, the relative incomes prevailing in different professions rarely accord with what people think they deserve, but they reflect faithfully the value which buyers of their services place on their talents.[46] It is one of the chief glories of a property-based market economy that the differences in individual income and wealth which result do not correspond to the assessment by paid State officials of the intrinsic moral worth or value to Society of particular individuals. In a market economy individuals place their knowledge, skill or technology at the disposal of others, satisfying the human instinct to 'truck, barter and exchange' and increasing the stock of wealth through the specialisation of labour without any element of coercion. The consequent distribution of rewards, as Lord Melbourne said of the Garter, has 'no damned merit in it'. It is rightly so. Most people would prefer to take their chances in the marketplace than to entrust their remuneration to some celestial Professor Broome and his calculus of personal merit.

References

1   Adam Smith, *The Wealth of Nations*, Penguin Classics Edition, 1986, page 442.
2   Quoted in Robert Skidelsky, *John Maynard Keynes: The Economist As Saviour 1920–1937*, Macmillan, 1992, page 607.
3   See 'Arguments for Private Ownership', in *Economic Review*, European Bank for Reconstruction and Development, September 1993, pages 113 to 132,and Hernando de Soto, 'The Missing Ingredient', *The Economist*, 11 September 1993.
4   From *Two Treatises*, II, section 124. Quoted in John W. Yolton, *The Locke Reader*, CUP, 1977, page 285
5   It is primarily the ability or inability of governments in the Third World to protect private property from nationalisation, political or random violence, theft and official corruption or to establish a corpus of commercial law enforceable by an independent judiciary which explains the varying pace and extent of economic development among the emerging nations.
6   Douglass C. North and Robert Paul Thomas, *The Rise of the Western World: A New Economic History*, CUP, 1973.
7   Harold Perkin, *The Rise of Professional Society*, Routledge, 1989, pages 28–31.
8   See Table 1, page 36.
9   C. A. R. Crosland, *The Future of Socialism*, Jonathan Cape, 1956, page 88.
10 Essay entitled 'Social Democracy in Britain', 1949, reproduced in R. H. Tawney *The Radical Tradition*, Pelican, 1966, page 174.
11 See R. H. Tawney, *The Acquisitive Society*, G. Bell & Sons, 1922, pages 43-4.
12 From an address by Hugh Gaitskell at a Memorial Service for Tawney, 8 February 1962. Quoted in R. H. Tawney, *The Radical Tradition*, Pelican, 1966, page 221.
13 R. H. Tawney, *The Acquisitive Society*, G. Bell & Sons, 1922, page 56.
14 One Labour MP described nationalisation as follows: 'When nationalisation is criticised people should bear in mind that it certainly is not the function of a nationalised industry to make a profit; its function is merely to contribute to a whole economic system which will ultimately make a profit, and it depends on arrangements at various stages as to what loss or profit should be taken on the steel or coal, or whatever it may be. The nationalised industry is a public service forming part of the whole system of the nation's production.' R. T. Paget, Hansard, 16 September 1948, Cols 292-3, Vol. 456.
15 Quoted in Anthony Sampson, *The Anatomy of Britain*, Hodder and Stoughton, 1962, page 534.
16 Douglas Jay, *The Socialist Case*, Faber & Faber, 1946, pages xiv-xv.
17 *The Socialist Case*, page xiii.
18 Quoted in T. E. B. Howarth, *Prospect and Reality*, Collins, 1985, page 114.
19 R. H. Tawney, *Religion and the Rise of Capitalism*, Penguin, Iggo.
20 R. H. Tawney, *The Acquisitive Society*, G. Bell & Sons, 1922, pages 10–12.
21 C, B. Macpherson, *The Political Theory of Possessive Individualism*, OUP, 1990. The book was first published in 1962.
22 From *How I Became a Socialist*. Quoted in Raymond Williams, *Culture and Society 1780–1950*, Penguin, 1975, page 154.

23 Fiona MacCarthy, *William Morris: A Life for Our Time*, Faber & Faber, 1994, page 65.

24 *William Morris: A Life for Our Time*, pages 455–6.

25 *William Morris: A Life for Our Time*, page 455.

26 Kingsley Amis, *Lucky Jim*, Penguin, 1961, page 227.

27 C. A. R. Crosland, *The Future of Socialism*, Jonathan Cape, 1956, page 70.

28 Liberal-SDP Alliance policy document, *The Time Has Come*, 1986, page 56.

29 *Liberal News*, 16 September 1986.

30 Cento Veljanovski, *Selling the State: Privatisation in Britain*, Weidenfild & Nicholson, 1987, pages 77–8.

31 Abel Aganbegyan, *The Challenge: Economics of Perestroika*, Hutchinson 1988.

32 The environmental enthusiasm of recent decades has given a new twist to this argument. Economists have long recognised that there are some spill-over costs or 'neighbourhood effects' on third parties when people are enjoying the use of private property for which it is not at present possible to charge the owner or recompense the third party. Pollution is a classic instance. In the past governments have preferred to pass regulations limiting smoke and chemical emissions, but ecologists have revived interest in taxing polluters (to make them bear the cost) or selling them licences to pollute (which those opposed to pollution may buy to prevent pollution occurring). But it is still not clear how discriminatory taxation or the sale of licences differs from thoroughly politicised decision-making, which is of course open to manipulation by vested interests. Experience suggests that no government can ever have a greater interest in managing resources sensibly than private owners. Pollution taxes and licences also depend on an ability to pay which poorer countries may not enjoy, and they will always find it cheaper to pollute.

33 R. H. Tawney, *The Acquisitive Society*, G. Bell & Sons, 1922, pages 56–7.

34 Quoted in F. A. Hayek, *The Fatal Conceit: The Errors of Socialism*, Routledge, 1988, page 29.

35 Douglas Jay, *The Socialist Case*, Faber & Faber, 1946, pages xiv–xv.

36 Francis Williams, *The Triple Challenge: The Future of Socialist Britain*, Heinemann, 1948, pages 5 and 7.

37 Speech to the British Association annual dinner, reproduced in *Financial Times*, 6 September 1993.

38 This is as much a High Tory as a Socialist criticism of capitalism. Carlyle disparaged 'epochs when cash payment has become the sole nexus of man to man'.

39 See, for example, the outcome of a MORI poll on collective versus individual values, reproduced in Dennis Kavanagh, *Thatcherism and British Politics: The End of Consensus?*, Oxford University Press, 1990, Table 10.2, page 299. In this poll 62 per cent of all respondents preferred a publicly managed economy to a free market one; 54 per cent preferred collective provision and a welfare state to individual provision; and 43 per cent preferred greater equality of incomes and wealth to private accumulation.

40 F. A. Hayek, *The Fatal Conceit: The Errors of Socialism*, Routledge, 1988, pages 77–8.

41 Quoted in Thomas A. Horne, *Propery Rights and Poverty: Political Argument in Britain 1l605–1834*, University of North Carolina Press, 1990, page 7.

42 Richard John Neuhaus, *Doing Well and Doing Good: The Challenge to the Christian Capitalist*, Doubleday, 199, page 187.

43 Quoted in Richard Schlatter, *Private Property: The History of an Idea*, Allen & Unwin, , page 17.

44 Unfortunately, companies often unwittingly endorse economic illiteracy of this kind. By making charitable donations, usually described as 'giving something back to the community', companies imply that they have taken something from people, when in reality they have given jobs, personal fulfilment and material sustenance to employees and their families.

45 *Financial Times*, 12 September 1993.

46 See F. A. Hayek, *The Constitution of Liberty*, Routledge, 1960, pages 85–102.

CHAPTER SEVEN

The Corporate Economy

The proper definition of the word capitalism is a society with the essential social, economic and ideological characteristics of Great Britain from the 1830s to the 1930s; and this, assuredly, the Britain of 1956 is not. And so, to the question, 'Is this still Capitalism?,' I would answer 'No.'

Anthony Crosland, *The Future of Socialism*

Society cannot become industrial unless industry is socialised. This is how industrialism logically ends in socialism.

Emile Durkheim

The collectivist critique of capitalism is anachronistic. It was formulated a century and a half ago, and addressed itself to forms of private property and economic organisation which even then were disappearing and which effectively ceased to exist altogether at least fifty years ago. During the course of the twentieth century the owner-managed enterprises of socialist demonology have been transformed into the multinational corporate behemoths of today. In 1880 the largest hundred firms accounted for perhaps a tenth of manufacturing output. By 1919 they commanded nearly a fifth; by 1930 a quarter; and by 1970 two fifths.[1] Although the increasing size of industrial firms reflected technical economies of scale from larger plants, vertical integration, central purchasing and national distribution, the main reason for the increasing size of firms was amalgamation. Companies merged into a smaller number of large industrial enterprises in a series of so-called 'merger waves' which took place in the 1880s, 1900s, 1920s, 1960s and 1980s. Similar amalgamations took place in the banking, insurance, shipping and property industries.

These developments led to the concentration of industrial production and financial and other services in the hands of a small number of giant firms controlling vast amounts of capital and labour. The top twenty firms listed on the London Stock Exchange in 1994 all had market capitalisations exceeding $10 billion, and an average payroll of nearly 80,000 people.[2] Businesses of this scale are unmanageable without specialised professional managers organised in vast bureaucratic hierarchies, directing the efforts of thousands of others according to a succession of 'scientific' theories of management. Their enormous appetite for capital also necessitated the emergence of a new breed of institutional investor capable of mobilising the sums required from millions of individual savers. The modern economy, in which a relatively small number of publicly quoted companies arc owned by an even smaller number of giant insurance companies and occupational pension funds, eventually emerged. Its chief characteristic is the separation of ownership and control. The investment institutions ultimately own the companies but delegate their day-to-day control to a cadre of professional, salaried managers. By the 1960s there were fewer small manufacturing firms in England than in any other advanced country, and it was unusual for any single individual or family to own a majority of the shares of any sizeable company. In the early 1990s both of the two biggest pension funds, the British Coal and British Telecom funds, owned financial assets worth over £12 billion. But the entire management of British industry probably owns less than a fortieth of the value of the companies they run. The heroic age of entrepreneurial capitalism, in which owner-managers financed their own companies, ploughed the profits of success back into the business and eventually reaped all of the rewards, has given way to what Leslie Hannah has called the Corporate Economy.

The Divorce Between Ownership and Control

The rise of the Corporate Economy marked a fundamental change in the nature of capitalism in England. A 'divorce between responsibility and ownership' was first noted by the Liberal Industrial Inquiry of 1928. Four years later two American academics, A. A. Berle and G. C. Means, published a classic work entitled *The Modern Corporation and Private Property*. It first highlighted the consequences of the growing separation between ownership by institutions and control by professional managers in modern, large-scale industrial capitalism:

> It has been assumed that, if the individual is protected in the right both to use his property as he sees fit and to receive the full fruits of its use, his desire for personal gain, for profits, can be relied upon as an effective incentive to his efficient use of any industrial property he may possess. In the quasi-public corporation, such an assumption no longer holds...it is no longer the individual himself who uses his wealth. Those in control of that wealth, and therefore in a position to secure industrial efficiency and produce profits, are no longer, as owners, entitled to the bulk of such profits. Those who control the destinies of the typical modern corporation own so insignificant a fraction of the company's stock that the returns from running the corporation profitably accrue to them in only a very minor degree. The stockholders, on the other hand, to whom the profits of the corporation go, cannot be motivated by those profits to a more efficient use of the property, since they have surrendered all disposition of it to those in control of the enterprise.[3]

The owner-managers of the early stages of industrialisation, which kept all the rewards of higher profits and incurred all of the penalties of increased losses, had a clear incentive to minimise costs and maximise earnings through investment and innovation. Today, the companies are owned by a variety of large financial institutions which delegate day-to-day control to professional managers. They usually own too little of a company to monitor its management effectively, and depend primarily on short-term share price performance to tell them how well the managers are doing. If a company fails to deliver returns, it is easier to sell the shares than attempt to revitalise the company. The managers, meanwhile, are free to pursue a self-interested agenda of their own. The inherent difficulty of getting salaried managers to run a company in the interests of its owners, rather than their own interests, when the shareholders are absentee rentiers, is arguably the biggest single issue in industrial capitalism today. Modern analysts have graced it with the title of 'the principal-agent problem', but it is essentially a problem of property rights: the owners of the property do not control it. The European Bank for Reconstruction and Development, which has grappled with precisely this problem in advising on privatisations in east and central Europe, has described the consequences:

Any private owner...of a large enterprise will be keen that all steps are taken to reduce costs, improve marketing etc.; the ownership will have a strong interest in diligent maintenance, purchase of inputs at the lowest prices, sale of output at the best prices, and in all cost-effective steps towards profit in the future. But the high capitalisation of the typical large enterprise creates...an agency problem...not altogether unlike that affecting state ownership of enterprises, and what may be called a free rider problem among the shareowners...A manager's independence from the owners of a private enterprise raises the same serious problems as independence from the owners of a state enterprise – for its cost management and for its direction – and of the economy in which it allocates resources. These problems...are abuse of privileges and dereliction of duties. There is also a subtle difference in the time perspective of shareowners and that of the manager. The shareowners have in common the proximate objective of achieving the highest possible price for their shares...their preference is always for the policy bringing the highest share price. The manager has a natural interest in the share price insofar as a higher share price will help him stay in the job, but he will also have an interest in other factors – the size of his responsibilities, the chance that the enterprise will be closed, and so forth – that will affect his earnings prospects. These other interests motivate the manager to run the enterprise differently from the way that would be best for the share price – and best for society's allocation of scarce resources. *The root of the conflict is that the property rights conferred by ownership of shares in an enterprise are transferable, or alienable, while the rights conferred by a manager's employment contract are not.* Since the manager will not be able to sell his managerial post to anyone, he does not have the same long-term horizon that an owner of the enterprise has; the latter would willingly sacrifice profits in the present for very far-off profits if the rate of return he expects to earn when he sells his interest to another buyer is attractive. Hence managers suffer from what is called short-termism, owners less so if at all.[4]

One constraint on the management is the market in corporate control, or the threat of takeover or capital starvation if the company under-performs relative to similar enterprises the shareholders can buy. Another constraint is official regulation through competition policy and the like, which prevents managers exploiting the consumer, and so using resources inefficiently.

But the evidence on whether takeovers actually lead to improved performance, or whether consumer protection is effective, is incon-exclusive. Both disciplines are at best crude and unpredictable proxies for an owner-manager taking all the risks and earning all the rewards. Their unsatisfactory nature has sparked a debate about the need for more effective 'corporate governance'. A committee of British businessmen chaired by Sir Adrian Cadbury has recommended the appointment of non-executive directors to company boards to represent the interests of the absentee shareholders. Ostensibly disinterested non-executive directors are now being injected into large company boards, with a brief to represent the shareholders rather than the management, but they are in most cases merely the pawns of the executive directors. Their calibre is widely believed to be low, and they are often embarrassed by an unexpected turn of events. Only occasionally need a director or manager fear that he or she will be sacked directly or indirectly by the shareholders as a result of the intervention of the non-executive directors.

Hope was once invested in exposing corporate managers to the perils of ownership through share and share option schemes and performance-related bonuses. But these incentives, because they are awarded by managers to themselves, have degenerated into little more than a tax-efficient form of executive remuneration. Managerial pay packages and employment contracts have become scandalously generous to men and women who have rarely if ever risked their own capital in the success of the enterprise they manage. Fortunately, institutional investors are increasingly alive to this abuse.

Some critics look to the French and German economies as an alternative solution to the principal-agent problem. In both of those countries fewer companies are publicly listed, and corporate governance has traditionally rested on a mixture of state ownership and tight control by a group of core investors (often big banks) represented on the board. A variant of this system has emerged in Japan. But a number of recent commercial disasters and financial scandals suggest that the so-called Rhine Model is no more successful than other methods of mimicking the disciplines of owner-management. The divorce between ownership and control is ultimately unbridgeable. But the problem it creates – an economy which is hostile to innovation, disinclined to invest for the long term, and which grows more slowly – is too important to ignore.

The Institutionalised Sclerosis of the Economy

The poor performance of the economy over the last half-century or so is conventionally attributed to the obsession of managers and shareholders with their short-term economic interests. But the problem is much more pervasive, and more heavily institutionalised, than that. Mancur Olsen has described the 'sclerotic society', in which the accretion of powerful vested interests gradually robs an economy of vitality. Economic growth is a dynamic phenomenon. Companies must adapt constantly to the changing circumstances, tastes, needs and requirements of the marketplace. The larger the scale of economic organisation, and the older and more institutionalised an economy becomes, the more difficult it is to do this. There is an accumulation of institutional rigidities which sap the dynamism of the young economy, with its thousands of individual entrepreneurs and small competing firms. Maynard Keynes came eventually to believe that the richer a society became, the reater its propensity to hoard rather than to invest. He underestimated the extent of human wants – and the ingenuity which even a sclerotic capitalism can apply to satisfying them – but he was right to identify the accumulation of experience, ideas, interests and institutions as the main brake on economic dynamism.

It is a serious moral as well as economic weakness of the modern capitalist economy that it has largely dispensed with the private owner risking his own money, energy and ideas on inspired hunches and replaced him with a passive and calculating institutional investor. Such figures command far less respect than the individualistic adventurers of the early days of capitalism. Indeed, it was a large part of the socialist case against capitalism that private property was anachronistic in the age of public companies, large industrial combinations, joint-stock banks and giant insurance companies. Property rights became so ill-defined that Tony Crosland was able to argue in the 1950s that capitalism, in the nineteenth-century sense at least, had effectively disappeared in England. Thirty years earlier R. H. Tawney had described the increasingly institutional and impersonal nature of property:

> In modern industrial societies the great mass of property consists, as the annual review of wealth passing at death reveals, neither of personal acquisitions such as household furniture, nor of the owner's stock-in-trade, but of rights of various kinds, such as royalties, ground-rents, and, above all, of course, shares in industrial undertakings, which yield an income irrespective of any personal service rendered by their owners. Ownership and use are normally divorced. The greater part of modern property has been attenuated to a pecuniary lien or bond on the product of industry, which carries with it a right to payment, but which is normally valued precisely because it relieves the owner from any obligation to perform a positive or constructive function. Such property may be called Passive Property, or Property for Acquisition, for Exploitation, or for Power, to distinguish it from the property which is actively used by its owner for the conduct of his profession or the upkeep of his household. To the lawyer the first is, of

course, as fully property as the second. It is questionable, however, whether economists should call it 'Property' at all, and not rather...'Improperly', since it is not identical with the rights which secure the owner the produce of his toil, but is the opposite of them.[5]

Tawney had uncovered a new class of *rentiers* for collectivists to attack, an institutionalised finance-capital which bore no relation to traditional forms of property and which appropriated the fruits of the labour of others through ground-rents or securities or royalties. He called it 'functionless property' and urged the State to restore purpose and function to it.

A form of property owned by a variety of impersonal institutions, but controlled by autonomous managers, was difficult to defend in the traditional Lockean terms of natural rights. It meant, in theory, that private ownership was no better than public ownership. Socialist thinkers like Tawney were not slow to see the implications. The managers of a company, to which institutional shareholders delegated the task of running the enterprise on a day-to-day basis, were not unlike the disinterested 'professional' managers he advocated as the sensible alternative to the Gradgrinds of the socialist imagination. The transformation of capitalist forms of ownership into the impersonal and institutionalised ownership of today so impressed Tony Crosland that he used it in 1956 to declare an end to the class war and most forms of nationalisation in favour of a planned, tightly regulated and heavily taxed corporate economy which would pay effortlessly for schemes of social egalitarianism like comprehensive schools, increased welfare payments, better housing, public art galleries and the heritage industry.

The Rise of the Corporate Economy

Crosland was the theorist of the 'mixed economy' which revisionist socialism selected as the alternative to class war and revolution. Part privately owned and part publicly owned, it was an economy in which the State undertook to maintain aggregate demand and to intervene and subsidise at the micro-economic level wherever necessary. Companies, for their part, employed people, collected taxes and paid pensions. The public and the private sectors worked in harmony with each other. 'On the academic level,' Crosland wrote, 'few serious economists now believe that a free price-mechanism leads in practice to a maximisation of economic welfare...The business world has also lost much of its ideological attachment to *laissez-faire*, and certainly has no desire to go back to the 1930s. Much as it dislikes detailed controls and high taxation, it now concedes that the government has a clear responsibility to intervene to whatever extent is required to maintain full employment (and hence high profits). In many industries an even wider governmental responsibility is accepted. It is not thought curious that the state should concern itself with the capacity of the steel industry, or be asked to aid industries which find themselves in export difficulties – cotton textile employers, for example, think it a scandal that the government declines to accept full responsibility for the level of their output.

Generally...private business now finds it quite natural that Whitehall should intervene in the economy to a degree which would have been thought outrageous a generation ago.'[6]

As Crosland rightly discerned, by 1956 the Democratic State and Big Business were openly living together in sin. What he described was the flowering of a romance which has occupied both parties for most of the twentieth century and in which the occasional violent row – like that over the nationalisation of the steel industry – has served only to camouflage a constant exchange of gifts and endearments. Through its economic, regulatory, fiscal, monetary and even foreign policies, the State has nourished and cherished the Corporate Economy, while businessmen, or their part, have flattered the State with their petitions for orders, subsidies and tax breaks. Between them, they have accomplished the euthanasia of the individual entrepreneur and the private family business; the domination of the economy by large and lumbering public corporations; the abdication of the rights and responsibilities of ownership to remote, impersonal and ineffective institutional investors; and the entrenchment of the State not only in the economy, but in the private life of the individual as well.

The Corporate Economy has left capitalism – the vital, free, moral, propertied, innovative and daring economic individualism of the heroic age of capitalism – dependent solely upon its own practical success, whilst at the same time making that success ever-harder to achieve. 'Welfare-state capitalism,' writes one analyst of the modern theory of property, 'can call on a limited loyalty, but capitalism is not, in spite of some heroic recent attempts, morally very engaging...If welfare capitalism falters badly or for long, it will not be able to rely on our loyalty to save it since we feel very little.'[7] This was foreseen by the Austrian economist, Joseph Schumpeter, who was convinced that capitalism was bound to destroy itself by evolving gradually into socialism. In *Capitalism, Socialism, and Democracy* – a book first published as long ago as 1942, but imbued with a powerful sense of the self-destructive nature of capitalism in a democracy whose voters are immune to rational arguments for a market economy- he mourned the passing of entrepreneurial capitalism. 'The capitalist process,' he wrote, 'by substituting a mere parcel of shares for the walls of and the machines in a factory, takes the life out of the idea of property...The holder of the title loses the will to fight, economically, physically, politically, for "his" factory and his control over it, to die if necessary on its steps...Dematerialised, defunctionalised, and absentee ownership does not impress and call forth moral allegiance. Eventually there will be nobody left who really cares to stand up for it – nobody within and nobody without the precincts of the big concerns.'[8]

The rise of the Corporate Economy began in the 1880s, at the beginning of the collectivist era. Until then, the useful role of the State in the economy was regarded as minimal. Its task was to maintain free trade and the gold standard and prevent combinations (of trade unions or businessmen) disrupting the beneficent processes of competition. Even the modified classical economics of Alfred Marshall – who was sufficiently alive to the changing political environment to see the case for a measure of State control of the economy – retained an innate faith in the potential of free individuals competing in free markets to raise the moral and material standard of living. Since the repeal of the Corn Laws freewheeling capitalism had created the richest and most dynamic economy the world had ever seen and, through the increasingly close integration of world markets, had spread its benefits beyond Europe to North America. The world economy in the few decades before the First World War was increasingly integrated, with people, goods, services, money and knowledge flowing more freely between markets than at any time either before or since.

John Maynard Keynes later looked back nostalgically on the pre-war economy as an 'economic Eldorado'. In a justly famous passage in *The Economic Consequences of the Peace*, published in 1919, he wrote:

> The inhabitant of London could order by telephone, sipping his morning tea in bed, the various products of the whole earth, in such quantity as he might see fit, and reasonably expect their early delivery on his doorstep; he could at the same moment and by the same means adventure his wealth in the natural resources and new enterprises of any quarter of the world, and share without exertion or even trouble, in their prospective fruits and advantages; or he could decide to couple the security of his fortunes with the good faith of the townspeople of any substantial municipality in any continent that fancy or information might recommend. He could secure forthwith, if he wished it, cheap and comfortable means of transit to any country and climate without passport or other formality, could dispatch his servant to the neighbouring office of a bank for such supply of the precious metals as might seem convenient, and could then proceed abroad to foreign quarters, without knowledge of their religion, language or customs, bearing coined wealth upon his person, and would consider himself greatly aggrieved and much surprised at the least interference. But, most important of all, he regarded the state of affairs as normal, certain and permanent, except in the direction of further improvement, and any deviation from it as aberrant, scandalous and avoidable.

But in the changing institutional and intellectual climate of the late nineteenth and early twentieth centuries, doubts were already being raised about the validity and efficaciousness of *laissez-faire*.

As the franchise was widened, politicians became increasingly convinced that the inequitable distribution of incomes by the invisible hand of the free market was threatening social harmony. The intellectual climate was changing too. The self-confident assumptions of the High Victorian age – that a man could do what he liked with his own property, and that the fulfilment of private ambitions was in complete harmony with the public good – were undermined by the collectivist ideas of a new generation of university dons, opinion-formers and *bien pensants*. Harold Perkin has described the emergence of a new class of 'professional experts', which included imperialists and eugenicists as well as socialists, during the late Victorian and Edwardian era. They worried about declining national physical prowess and economic efficiency, and thought the solution was for the

State to provide the education, social services and health programmes which would make 'society' more robust, productive and efficient. 'Britain in 1914,' writes Perkin, 'was still undoubtedly, and would long remain, a funda- mentally capitalist society. But the influence of the professional expert, with his belief in contingent property justified by service to society and in social efficiency for the benefit of the whole nation, had already begun to permeate the consciousness of the other classes and the policies and administration of the government.'[9] In *Wealth and Welfare*, first published in 1910, it was the neo-classical economist and successor to Alfred Marshall, A. C. Pigou, who first argued that it was possible in principle to redistribute income from rich to poor without undermining the productivity of the economy. The rise of collectivist ideas in the 1880s also coincided with what contemporaries believed to be a great economic depression, a 'crisis' of capitalism which persuaded many people that economic freedom was no longer working.

But it was a familiar culprit, the First World War, which ultimately destroyed the economic El Dorado. The conflict disrupted trade, diverted investment into purely destructive uses, strengthened some economies (notably the United States) at the expense of others and left a legacy of crippling international reparations and indebtedness which destroyed the global financial system and sparked a succession of beggar-my-neighbour trade policies which ended in mass unemployment and political violence. Capitalism lost its reputation for practical success. It was also during the First World War that the government, and especially the Ministry of Munitions, first began to plan, finance and direct the operations of major industrial enterprises. The paraphernalia of the modern managed economy, from export licences and production subsidies to price and exchange controls, and the sheer weight of public expenditure and taxation, rapidly transformed the expectations of decision-makers in the public and the private sectors of the economy. Certain key industries, notably the railways and the mines, were effectively nationalised.

The war led to a massive transfer of real resources from the private economy to the State. A peacetime economy geared to the satisfaction of consumer wants was comprehensively redesigned to produce the armaments needed to defeat the enemy. All other claims on the economy were simply swept aside. The State assumed the power to requisition any private or commercial assets it considered essential to the war effort. The supply and price of all commodities was controlled by the State. Price-fixing in agriculture – a melancholy innovation which has now reached its *reduction ad absurdism* in the European Common Agricultural Policy – was introduced for the first time. Rent controls were imposed on private landlords, also for the first time. In essential industries strikes and lock-outs were simply declared illegal. Wages, manning levels and working plactices were fixed by government diktat. Key workers were not allowed to change jobs. Deals were struck between the trade unions, the employers and the government, presaging the corporatist approach to industrial questions which bedevilled the productivity of the British economy for the next seventy years.

Growing interference in the economy necessitated a colossal augmentation of the bureaucracy. Five new departments of State were created to control shipping, labour, food, agriculture and conscription, with concomitant increases in the number of bureaucrats dilecting businessmen in matters of production, trade, technology, pay and employment. Companies were obliged to share previously secret technology and knowledge for the national good, and many businessmen and politicians became convinced for the first time of a national industrial inferiority to Germany and the United States. Leading businessmen began to doubt the virtues of competition and to endorse for the first time the idea of large-scale industrial mergers and trade protection policies.[10] By the end of the war the State, in the shape of a new Ministry of Reconstruction, had even assumed responsibility for the transition to a peacetime economy. Socialists thought the war, and its ruthless exposure of the shortcomings of British industry, provided comprehensive proof of the superiority of economic planning. 'The period of war economy,' enthused R. H. Tawney, 'accelerated the demise of the individualist, competitive phase of British capitalism. It stimulated organisation and combination among manufacturers; advertised rationalisation; strengthened the demand for tariffs; and encouraged, in another sphere, the settlement of wages and working conditions by national rather than by local agreements.'[11]

This judgment was premature. After the First World War, the principal political urge was to return the economy to normality. The burden of taxation was relieved and public expenditure fell – albeit settling at a higher plateau than before the war – and economic controls were largely lifted. It was the destabilising effects of the conflict on the pre-war patterns of trade and international finance, and the mass unemployment they caused, which finally blackened the reputation of *laissez-faire* capitalism beyond restitution. During the inter-war years, the crisis of capitalism predicted by socialist thinkers appeared at hand. J. B. Priestley's *English Journey* of 1933 is imbued with a powerful sense of the wastefulness and ugliness of industrial capitalism, and the belief that economic life could be organised better by a beneficent State. Many influential political and economic commentators, including figures as different as Maynard Keynes, R. H. Tawney and Harold Macmillan, concluded that it was the proper role of the State to rescue capitalism from itself. The State, it was argued, could compensate for the failures of private initiative. It could restore economic growth not through manipulation of the monetary and fiscal framework alone, but also by directing a movement of amalgamations among private firms. This could prevent capitalism degenerating into either a timid reflection of a fearful economic climate or an exploitative, monopolistic system dominated by huge industrial empires.

It fell to Maynard Keynes to reinterpret economics for a changed political and institutional climate. In 1926 he published a pamphlet entitled *The End of Laissez-Faire*, in which he concluded that the definition of the proper boundary between the sphere of the Individual and the State could no longer be settled on grounds of principle:

> Perhaps the chief task of economists at this hour is to distinguish afresh the Agenda of government from the Non-Agenda; and the companion

task of politics is to devise forms of government within a democracy which shall be capable of accomplishing the Agenda...We must aim at separating those services which are technically social from those which are technically individual...[The Agenda is] not...those activities which private individuals are already fulfilling, but...those functions which fall outside the sphere of the individual...those decisions which are made by no one if the state does not make them.[12]

This proved to be a recipe for ever-increasing State intervention, because it failed to question what governments are capable of accomplishing successfully and abandoned the classical distinction between public and private goods. It was not Keynes's intention. He was convinced that contemporary businessmen were too traumatised psychologically to invest (and consumers too fearful to encourage them by spending), and that capitalism therefore needed to call in a benign State to borrow and spend on public works to counteract the timidity and hoarding of the private sector. In its fully worked-out theoretical form, the *General Theory of Employment, Interest and Money*, (1936) the Keynesian approach argued that the government should conduct fiscal and monetary policy with the deliberate objective of managing aggregate demand to keep the labour force fully occupied. The Second World War, in which the effects of printed money were offset by massively increased rates of tax, seemed to provide a vivid practical demonstration of how this could be done successfully. The socialist economist, Douglas Jay, published the first edition of his blueprint for the Corporate Economy, *The Socialist Case*, in 1938. By the time the second edition was published eight years later he was able to write:

Five years' practical acquaintance with the Government's efforts to organise industry, first for the war effort and then for reconstruction, has convinced me that the case for Socialism, and in particular for conscious collective planning of the economic system, is stronger than it appeared to me writing in a more philosophic, or academic, spirit nine years ago. Then I knew it to be desirable, and believed it to be practicable. Now I knew it is both practicable and necessary and to judge by the result of the General Election of 1945, many others in Great Britain have learnt the same lesson.[13]

Seen from a perspective longer than nine years, the effects of the war on the economy are rather different. It made nationalisation and State direction of industry respectable; it accustomed businessmen to excessive rates of taxation; and it drove industry still further down the ruinous path of corporatism. It wiped out national financial resources, damaged or destroyed much of the national infrastructure, and directed labour and capital into industrial sectors – like shipbuilding, iron and steel and coal – which were better left to decline.

Post-war socialism, nationalisation and planning postponed still further an economic adjustment which was already overdue and lumbered the faltering post-war economy with excessive taxation. The extreme conditions of wartime had also imbued subsidised agriculture, science and technology with mythical powers of transformation, leading governments to suppose that they could initiate spectacular economic growth and innovation as well as preside over it. Perhaps the finest memorial to that conceit is the nuclear power industry, which has absorbed prodigious quantities of public money but never fulfilled its promise to produce electricity more cheaply than conventional power stations.

Businessmen initially welcomed the advent of the age of demand management and economic planning. Like most contemporary policymakers, they believed that State manipulation of the macro-economic levers could moderate the amplitude of the business cycle, by steadying investment, growth, employment, prices and the balance of payments. They had long recognised that the expansion of public expenditure and State regulation of the economy also created valuable business opportunities. War has always encouraged businessmen to seek favours from the State. The first lobbyists began to swarm around the public finances during the heavy expenditure occasioned by the incessant wars of the eighteenth century. Stanley Baldwin noticed that after the First World War Parliament was full of 'hard-faced men who look as if they had done very well out of the war'. The State had begun to dispense cash subsidies and fiscal favours on a large scale during the inter-war years, but the arrival of the Keynesian, planned economy of the 1940s lent a new respectability to their age-old arguments for tax breaks, subsidies and public contracts. These were later embellished with tales of well-picked winners and indicative planning drawn from France, Germany and the miracle economies of the Orient.

The Interdependence of Big Business and Big Government

As the role of the State in the economy expanded, it naturally became more sensitive to producer lobbying of this kind. Even before the First World War the government tolerated anti- competitive mergers between companies, arguing that they were essential to preserve international market share and jobs at home. The various committees on trusts which met between 1918 and 1921 actually endorsed large-scale mergers even if they resulted in monopoly, primarily because German and American competition was considered so threatening. The arguments which businessmen adduced for government acquiescence in takeovers – foreign competition, division of labour, economies of scale, protection of jobs, 'strategic' necessity and so on – merely camouflaged the base reality that the easiest way to enhance profits was to eliminate the competition. Anti-trust legislation was not passed until the Monopolies and Restrictive Practices Commission was established by the Labour government in 1948. It took so long because successive governments were persuaded by the arguments for 'rationalisation' of the big business lobbyists. Nor was there any well-organised consumers' lobby to argue against them.

'It was but a short step from this,' writes Leslie Hannah, 'to direct pressure on the government to intervene more positively to promote industrial change both by legislation and by providing finance for mergers and rationalisation.'[14] During the inter-war years ministers privately encouraged industrialists to merge with their competitors; public sector orders were given only to 'efficient' firms; stamp duty on mergers was lifted; the Bank of England was instructed to mobilise finance for them through the Bankers' Industrial development Company; and discriminatory subsidies and tariffs were used to persuade companies to merge. Regional policy was introduced to bribe companies to invest in particular localities, and it was during these years that a number of 'strategic' industries – electricity, railways, oil, mining and agriculture – first became accustomed to the meretricious pleasures of living off public money. When Neville Chamberlain finally reversed nearly a century of complete Free Trade by introducing a protective tariff in 1932, he explained it was not merely to raise revenue but to encourage import substitution, raise productivity and encourage industrial reorganisation.

Paradoxically, the lower tariff protection and tighter anti-trust policies pursued by post-war governments were also used by firms as an excuse to 'rationalise' through merger in order to compete. One side-effect of the 1948 Companies' Act, which obliged many enterprises to reveal information about their assets and income for the first time, was to facilitate mergers. But governments became openly involved in the promotion of mergers for the first time too. The Macmillan government created the British Aircraft Corporation in 1960 by persuading Vickers-Armstrong, English Electric and Bristol Aeroplane to merge. The Labour Government of 1964–70 set up a Ministry of Technology and a Department of Economic Affairs with a subsidiary, the Industrial Reorganisation Corporation (IRC), designed specifically to 'promote or assist the reorganisation or development of any industry' where this was felt to be in the 'national interest'. The IRC promoted large-scale mergers in computers (ICL), electrical engineering (GEC), motor-cars (British Leyland), ball bearings (Ransome & Marles) and scientific instruments (George Kent). The fourteen largest steel companies were renationalised, and private shipbuilders encouraged to merge.

Any merger sponsored by the IRC was released from review by the Monopolies and Mergers Commission, and the recalcitrant were threatened with the prospect of the Government buying a stake in the company. Taxpayers' money was used to influence and (in one case) settle the outcome of ostensibly private takeover bids. Merging competitors and steering government contracts towards favoured companies in this way was a form of intervention not unlike the Corporate State pioneered by fascist Italy, but businessmen were naturally delighted to be paid to merge. Ronald Grierson, the banker appointed IRC chief executive, stated his vision of the IRC was 'a forum where directors of large companies could discuss their ideas for mergers and reorganisation without feeling that they were talking to the government, but knowing that public money would be forthcoming'.[15]

As 'money illusion' evaporated in the 1960s and the Keynesian prescription began to break down, the State attempted to prolong its life with ever more detailed micro-economic interventions. A succession of national pay policies, in which the State attempted to dictate even what people were paid, were tried in a vain attempt to dictate even what people were paid, were tried in a vain attempt to contain the effects of the new consciousness of what inflation was doing to the standard of living. Prime Ministers entertained trade union leaders in Downing Street in the hope of persuading them to advise then members to endorse limitations on pay. Inevitably, the trade unions exacted a price in higher public expenditure, dividend controls and the like. A panoply of controls over pay, prices, dividends, credit and other aspects of economic life gradually accumulated as the State tried to steer the Corporate Economy. The Heath government, despite coming into office on a free market programme, made no serious attempt to reverse this corporatist approach to the management of the economy. Instead, it created a massive Department of Trade and Industry to intervene even more in private business, passed omnibus legislation to make the trade unions a more responsible arm of the Corporate Economy and eventually attempted to limit pay increases by statute. The government even nationalised two bankrupt enterprises, Rolls-Royce and Upper Clyde shipbuilders.

The Capture of the State by Business Lobbyists

Since 1979 the government has rightly emphasised deregulation, reduced public subsidies, disengagement from the private sector and increased competition. But in reality corporate business and the State are still closely intertwined. Even in the narrow sphere of mergers and acquisitions, where the government has until recently confined its intervention solely to checking whether or not a merger diminishes competition, the process is in practice highly politicised. Expensive lobbying machines trawl Parliament with arguments for and against a particular transaction. The various political lobbying firms which swarm around the Palace of Westminster today are thought to enjoy a collective turnover of around £20 million a year. Businessmen know that, in the end, the decision whether to refer a merger to the Monopolies and Mergers Commission (MMC) is the political decision of the President of the Board of Trade (albeit one taken on the advice of the Office of Fair Trading) and they are prepared to pay handsomely to influence his or her thinking.

In some instances, it is possible for a bidder to renegotiate the terms of a bid in order to make it more acceptable to the competition authorities. This is what happened, for example, when Guinness bid for Distillers in 1986. In the case of a bid for a privatised company, like the BP takeover of Britoil in 1988, the government had reserved the power to control the outcome directly through its ownership of a so-called 'golden share'. A great many State-owned companies were privatised with their freedom of action circumscribed in this way, and all of the privatised utilities are subject to price constraints laid down by official regulators. Future governments are at liberty to add a host of other factors – employment, regional policy, research and development expenditure and so on – to the criteria for judging the merits of a merger, and can be expected to do so. The MMC is already obliged to consider the impact of a merger on the distribution of industry and employment in Britain, and there is a clause in the 1973 Fair Trading Act enjoining it to take account of 'all matters which appear to them in the particular circumstances to be relevant'.

But business lobbying of government for favours is not confined to the takeover arena. The State is under constant pressure from businessmen to lower the burden of company taxation, reduce charges for power and water, grant tax breaks for particular types of investment, cut regulation, subsidise exports, training and investment and even change macro-economic policy in ways which business thinks will be helpful to their turnover and profits. Every conceivable business lobbying group expects its submissions in advance of the annual Budget to be taken seriously by the Chancellor. The Confederation of British Industry and the Institute of Directors may be said to exist for no other purpose than to lobby the government for favours. No Budget would be complete without the Freight Transport Association and the Automobile Association demanding a standstill on car taxes and fuel duty; the National Federation of Housing Associations calling for increased subsidies to housing and rents; and the Brewers and Licensed Retailers Association, the Tobacco Manufacturers Association and the Scotch Whisky Association warning of the exports and jobs which will be lost if the excise duties on alcohol and cigarettes are revalorised.

When a businessmen calls on the government to create 'a level playing field' through tax or regulatory changes, it is a sure sign that he is looking to the State to castrate his competitors. Throughout 1994 the major brewers, concerned by the impact on their business of cheaper imports from continental Europe, waged a concerted lobbying campaign for a reduction in the duty levied on beer. One theme was the increased revenue which would accrue to the Exchequer as beer sales soared in the wake of the cut. 'Cheap imports of beer from the Continent are damaging the industry at a substantial cost to the Treasury,' said the chairman of one brewing company, Greene King.[16] The argument has so far failed to impress Treasury ministers. in January 1995 the Ford Motor Company, a hugely profitable business and the second largest car manufacturer in the world, applied to the government for up to £100 million of taxpayers' money to support the production of a new range of Jaguar cars in Britain. It was accompanied by an explicit threat to move production abroad if the subsidy was not forthcoming.[17] High street retailers, to take another example, recently waged a successful campaign to change planning policy. By limiting edge-of-town shopping centre developments, they protected their own business.

Like any political decision, the outcome of a lobbying campaign is not determined by the power of the arguments for and against a particular course of action, or inaction. David Puttnam, a film-maker, wrote recently to a national newspaper:

> We film-makers are incurable optimists. Every year we await the Budget with bated breath – surely this must be the year in which the Treasury finally takes the plunge and does something to help our industry. We think about the taxbreaks that help the offshore oil industry offset its

huge risks (the self-same problem that dogs film investment); or the multi-million-pound cash grants to Japanese car companies and Korean electronics companies to persuade them to invest in Britain. But there are no such incentives for a company coming to Britain to make a movie. Why not?[10]

One reason why not is Puttnam's enthusiastic support for the government's political opponents. The political dividends accruing to the ruling party from subsidising wealthy film-makers are unlikely to be as high as those from subsidising the environment, or the disabled, or even small businessmen. Over the last fifteen years, for example, a government highly sympathetic to the small business lobby has conceded to it a stream of exemptions from tax, regulatory and reporting requirements. Political decisions are based on the politics of a case, not its merits.

In 1993–94 the Department of Trade and Industry had a total budget of £3.6 billion with which to fulfil its goal of helping 'UK business compete successfully at home, in the rest of Europe, and throughout the world'. It is spent on export promotion, subsidies to investment, research and development, design, training and re- training schemes, business advice networks, education, regenera- tion projects and especially inward investment. British taxpayers spend around £300 million a year subsidising inward investment from abroad. Last year, for example, Samsung of Korea received £58 million in grants and subsidised loans to open a manufacturing plant in Cleveland. A few months earlier, a Taiwanese textile company called Hualon was offered a £61 million inducement to build a factory in Belfast. Once established here, foreign companies are entitled to tap another £1½ billion of regional and employment subsidies too. The various regions of the country, organised in enterprise groups and development boards, now lobby against each other to secure the official status and cash hand-outs which will enable them to secure prestige foreign investments.

The State is now what Richard Titmuss called a 'pressure group State', in which the taxpayer is the patron not just of brewers and shopkeepers but of construction firms and armaments manufac- turers at home and motor and television manufacturers from all over the world. It is also a State which creates new business opportunities through its tax and regulatory policies. The capital allowances phased out in the 1984 Budget, for example, created a highly profitable leasing market for City merchant banks. The tax incentives to purchase personal equity plans (PEPs) and personal pensions created vast new commission-earning markets for life offices, banks and other fund managers. Likewise, dozens of waste disposal companies have profited directly from greater government regulation of the environment by offering 'environmentally sound' products and services which would not be economically viable in the absence of official intervention. The 'contracting out' of various central and local government services has created a bonanza for cleaning, computing and other service companies.

Governments are under constant pressure to intervene, protect or subsidise businesses, though the special pleading is usually dressed up as a 'national priority' of some kind. Many businessmen refer habitually to 'Great Britain plc', as if the government was at the head of a conglomerate of businesses dedicated to the promotion of national economic interests against foreign competitors. Politicians encourage this self-image, by referring habitually to 'competitiveness', as if individual people and companies were engaged not in peaceable and mutually beneficial trade but conscripts in an army waging war against the 'industrial policies' of other nations. Complaints that foreign governments are subsidising competitors, and that if the government does not subsidise its national champions to the same extent, exports and jobs will be lost, are now the common currency of political life. The celebrated Pergau Dam affair, portrayed in some newspapers as a seedy pay-off to an Oriental despot and his supporters, was in reality an entirely routine instance of taxpayers subsidising private sector exporters.

'Where the State controls so large a proportion of society's resources and the environment in which they are deployed,' writes Harold Perkin, 'self-interest impels almost every group to organise collectively to lobby the State for a larger share of what it has to hand out.'[19] The effect is to corrupt both statesmen and business- men. The widely perceived increase in the 'sleaziness' of govern- ment- MPs taking payments for asking questions, or receiving stipends from lobbying firms, or ministers accepting gifts from industrialists of dubious provenance – is the unavoidable consequence of the increased patronage of the State. In an economy where the State controls over two fifths of the national income, and has at its disposal a host of other revenue-generating licences for sale, companies have naturally become more dependent on the conduct of public policy in general and of public purchasing contracts in particular. This is obvious in the case of arms-suppliers, but pleas from the construction industry to invest in the infrastructure, save capital projects from retrenchment or subsidise infrastructural projects in the developing world (where subsidies can be camouflaged as 'aid') are a recurrent feature of the annual public expenditure round. The privatisation of various government services, usually presented as part of a drive to public efficiency, is further exacerbating the growing problem of the private sector dependency culture.

In many cases the government is called upon to rectify through subsidy a weakness which its own intrusiveness has created. A good example is the regular plea from industry for public subsidies for training. Businessmen argue that, if they train an employee who subsequently defects to another employer, they have merely subsidised a competitor. They cannot exclude others from the value of the investment they have made. Employers also maintain that education and training delivers wider social and economic benefits, in terms of a larger, cheaper and more skilled, knowledgeable and flexible workforce. Training is therefore a public good which should be subsidised by taxpayers. This is a classic instance of the State creating a 'market failure' which it is then called upon to remedy by providing a subsidy. It is progressive income tax which, by reducing the return to investment in education and training by individuals themselves, obliges the State to intervene.

Few individuals see the lower salary or wages of a traineeship, or the cost of a loan to finance their studies, as a worthwhile investment. The government, of course, will usually seek to finance any State-directed training schemes through a payroll or other levy on employers. Needless to say, both the House of Commons Trade and Industry Select Committee, and the Labour Party, have already declared themselves in favour of a training levy on employers. This is how business defeats itself, adding to labour costs whose flexibility is already reduced by the growing burden of income tax and National Insurance contributions and making it even less likely that trainees will be taken on or employment increased. It is hard to see why this is regarded as a more sensible solution than lifting the burden of taxation on individuals (and their parents), enabling them to make their own choices about education, training and work.

How the Tax System Sustains the Corporate Economy

The fiscal policy of the State, which is ultimately shaped by the relative effectiveness of different lobbies, has tended to reinforce the rise of the Corporate Economy. The bias against the distribution of dividends in the system of Corporation Tax introduced in 1965, intended to raise the level of industrial investment, was in fact one of the main factors which encouraged companies to make corporate acquisitions in the subsequent years. A takeover was or tell the only way shareholders could extract value from their investment. Even today, the corporation tax rules oblige companies to 'impute' to shareholders tax at the standard rate on dividends and remit this to the Inland Revenue as advance corporation tax (ACT). ACT is deductible from mainstream corporation tax, but companies with insufficient domestic profits to absorb the charge have a tax incentive either to reduce the dividend, weakening the share price and exposing the company to a takeover, or to take over a British company themselves in order to acquire the taxable profits they need. When Trafalgar House bid for Northern Electric in December 1994, one of its main objectives was to acquire a steady stream of earnings to offset an estimated £223 million of ACT and other tax losses.[20]

Until capital allowances for investment were reformed in the 1984 Budget, companies with large investment programmes but insufficient profits to offset against them were encouraged to buy retailers, financial services companies and other businesses which were profitable but not capital-intensive. In other words, acquisitions could increase profits by enabling a company to buy tax allowances. The ability to carry forward tax losses owned by Rover Group played a major part in the decision by British Aerospace to acquire the company, in a takeover whose industrial logic was otherwise hard to discern. Likewise, the penal rates of personal taxation which prevailed until the 1980s made it attractive for owners of private companies to realise their investment without excessive tax costs by selling their businesses to large public companies.

The fact that the interest payable on borrowings is deductible for tax purposes, but dividends are not, has encouraged companies to mount takeovers with retained profits or borrowed money rather than invest in organic growth. The haphazard growth of the tax system has also generated other peculiarities and arbitrage opportunities which companies have exploited through mergers and acquisitions. The differential treatment of takeovers funded with shares rather than cash and the rate at which transferred assets can be depreciated have both influenced companies active in the takeover market. The fiscal system has even encouraged inefficient corporate behemoths to remain intact, by making the de-merger of large conglomerations of businesses relatively unattractive in tax terms.

But it is in helping to institutionalise the management of savings and the ownership of British industry that the tax system has had its most profound influence over the shape of the modern corporate economy. Institutional investors – the pension funds, life offices and insurance companies – are almost wholly the creation of a State policy to use the tax system to encourage private provision of life assurance and savings for retirement. Once granted, the tax privileges proved difficult to undo. They were created by well- organised institutional lobbyists like the Life Offices' Association and the Association of Superannuation Funds, and they are defended fiercely by their modern successors: the Association of British Insurers and the National Association of Pension Funds. Leslie Hannah, the historian of occupational pension schemes, has observed:

> By the 1970s, pension funds alone accounted for as much as a third of the savings of the personal sector of the British economy. This was significantly higher than, for example, the United States: Britain had clearly become a country in which an unusually high proportion of savings was being channelled through institutional investors such as pension funds, and personal capitalism was correspondingly on the decline. The tax incentives for saving in this form appear to be the major reason for this remarkable development.[21]

The pension contributions of both employers and employees are deductible for tax purposes, and the accumulated pension funds are effectively exempt from both income tax and capital gains tax. Until 1984 life assurance premiums were also eligible for tax relief. Savers who choose to invest directly enjoy no such tax privileges. Even Personal Equity Plans (PEPs), introduced in an effort to revive private share ownership, have in practice degenerated into commission-based, institutional-style tax-efficient vehicles with none of the true characteristics of the direct ownership of property.

According to one study, the transfer in the balance of ownership of listed companies from direct investment by individuals to collective investment vehicles managed by pension funds, insurance companies, life offices, unit trust managers and investment trusts has proceeded at a rate of 1 to 1½ per cent a year for the last 35 years. Institutions now own 85 per cent of the issued share capital of British business, and can be expected on present trends to increase this proportion to 95 per cent by the turn of the century.[22] As the authors of the study put it:

> For most people, an understanding of corporate wealth creation is limited to the money wages they receive; they have no direct or recognisable stake in corporate capital. The penetration of investment products and funds such as pensions, life insurance and endowment policies is many times higher than direct share ownership. The Government has collected in this process by continually interfering in the savings market to the point of manipulation to encourage particular types of investments over others, and most particularly over direct shareholdings. Tax privileges have been given to many collective funds (for example the effective elimination of capital gains tax within such funds) and to investors who place their money with them (of which tax relief at the top rate on personal pension contributions is the most obvious example). These selective privileges have sponsored the divorce of many individuals from the wealth creation process. It is our contention that this divorce represents a fundamental and structural threat to the objective of creating an internationally competitive and dynamic [social] market economy.[23]

Karl Popper once described modern civilisation as an 'abstract society', in which people had lost touch with concrete relation- ships.[24] The institutionalisation of savings has left the motor car and the family house and its contents as the only concrete forms of property in the lives of the vast majority of men and women. The unseen securities traded on television screens by young men in striped shirts and braces no longer correspond to intuitive suppositions about what private property actually is. At work few people are ever spending or investing their own money, or even deciding what it is that they will do that day. Even fewer see the taxes they pay out of their wages or salaries as an expropriation of their property. The occupational pension, which is the second biggest investment most people ever make, is seen not as a personal asset or even as deferred income but as a deduction from the wage or salary slip. People today are quite cut off from the perils and the exhilaration of owning sufficient property to declare their independence of the State. Nothing is more threatening to liberty.

References

1   Leslie Hannah, *The Rise of the Corporate Economy*, Methuen, 1983, Second Edition, Table A2, Appendix 2, page 180.
2   The FT 500, *Financial Times*, 20 January 1994.
3   Quoted in Cento Veljanovski, *Selling the State: Privatisation in Britain*, Weidenfeld & Nicolson, 1987, page 86.
4   'Arguments for Private Ownership', in *Economic Review*, European Bank for Reconstruction and Development, September 1993, pages 119–20.
5   R. H. Tawney, *The Acquisitive Society*, G. Bell & Sons, 1922, pages 66-71
6   C. A. R. Crosland, *The Future of Socialism*, Jonathan Cape, 1956, page 499.
7   Alan Ryan, *Property and Political Theory*, Blackwell, 1984, page 187.
8   Joseph Schumpeter, *Capitalism, Socialism, and Democracy*, George Allen & Unwin,

page 142.

9 See Harold Perkin, *The Rise of Professional Society: England Since 1880*, Routledge, 989, pages 155–70

10 See Leslie Hannah, *The Rise of the Corporate Economy*, Methuen, Second Edition 83, pages 28–9.

11 Quoted in Alan Milward, *The Economic Effects of Two World Wars on Britain*, Macmillan, 1973, pages 20–1.

12 Quoted in Robert Skidelsky, *John Maynard Keynes: The Economist As Saviour 1920–1937*, Macmlllan, 1992, page 226.

13 Douglas Jay, *The Socialist Case*, Faber 8 Faber, 1946, page xi.

14 Leslie Hannah, *The Rise of the Corporate Economy*, Methuen, Second Edition, 1983, page 48

15 William Davis, *Merger Mania*, Constable, 1970, pages 133–4.

16 *Financial Times*, 8 July 1994.

17 *Financial Times*, 11 and 13 January 1995.

18 *Sunday Times*, 27 November 1994.

19 Harold Perkin, *The Rise of Professional Society: England Since 1880*, Routledge, 1989, page 317.

20 *Financial Times*, 20 December 1994.

21 Leslie Hannah, *Inventing Retirement: The Development of Occupational Pensions in Britain*, CUP, 1986, page 51

22 Matthew Gaved and Anthony Goodman, *Deeper Share Ownership*, Social Market Foundation, 1992, pages 10, 25 and 39.

23 Matthew Gaved and Anthony Goodman, *Deeper Share Ownership*, Social Market Foundation, 1992, page 15.

24 Karl Popper, *The Open Society and Its Enemies*, Vol. 1: Plato, Routledge, 1984, pages 173-4.

CHAPTER EIGHT

The Enslavement of the Individual

The day of combination is here to stay. Individualism has gone, never to
return.

John D. Rockefeller, creator of Standard Oil[1]

For national governments and national corporations the only answer is a
strong framework of rules that align the exercise of corporate power with
the public purpose. This is not an exercise in hope and prayer. It is one
of the dominant trends of the times.

John Kenneth Galbraith, 1977[2]

Freedom has a thousand charms to show,
That slaves, howe'er contented, never know.

William Cowper, *Table Talk*

The rise of the Corporate Economy was an integral part of the enslavement of
the Individual by the State during the course of the twentieth century. By
trapping large numbers in predictable routines and unchanging locations, and
stripping them of the power to determine both the hours they worked and the
remuneration they earned, the Corporate Economy made it easier for the State
to coerce them, and especially to tax them. As Charles Handy has pointed out,
the entire paraphernalia of the Welfare State – payroll deductions, pay policies,
the centralised provision of health and social services, health and safety
regulation, environmental rules, trade and investment incentives, and even fiscal
and monetary policy- would be impossible to organise and conduct without the
bureaucratic model and data collection capabilities of the Corporate Economy.
He writes:

> For the past 100 years and more the work organisation has been of great
> use to governments of every political persuasion. The organisation has
> been the way in which wealth has been distributed to the population, in
> their wage packets or salary cheques. The organisation has been, therefore,
> the natural and convenient way to collect taxes and to implement
> economic policy and to plan resources. If everyone has a job in an
> organisation then the world is easier to control. At the very least we know

where most of them are, and where most of them will have to live.
Similarly, organisations have been the easiest route for spending
government money. It is easier to pay hospitals to help sick people than to
pay the sick to find the hospitals, easier to pay schools or universities en
bloc than to pay individuals to go to the schools, easier to run your own
railways, coal mines or postal services than to leave it to others. Of course,
there are ideological reasons for keeping vital services in government
control but it cannot be completely accidental that the enthusiasm for
governments to own and control so much coincided with the same fashion
in organisations everywhere. 'If you want to control it, own it,' was the
message in every business in the 1960s and 1970s. Integration was the
smart word – horizontal integration, vertical integration or both together.
Buy your suppliers, buy your customers, buy your competitors if you can.
That way your world is more yours. It was only natural that governments
should hear the same message.[3]

The modern economy is primarily an employed economy. Most of the wealth
of Britain is now controlled by men and women who have never, on their own
account or at their own risk, invested their own capital in their livelihood. This is
in marked contrast to the agricultural economy of the pre-industrial age, when
virtually everyone was effectively self-employed. It differs also from the early
industrial economy, in which the proletarianisation of the unskilled and the semi-
skilled was leavened by millions of independent owner-managers, engineers,
lawyers, accountants, farmers, shopkeepers, self-employed craftsmen and others.

The Rise of the Salariat

The disappearance of the economically independent individual is a remarkably
recent phenomenon, especially at the upper end of the earnings scale. 'The great
feature of the [post-war] period was the decline of the small owner-managing
business man and the rise of the salariat,' writes Harold Perkin.[4] The demise of
self-employment is heavily concentrated in the period between the end of the
last war and the 1970s – the golden age of the giant business corporation, as well
as of economic growth – but the gradual loss of independence within the
workforce has continued in most occupational categories throughout the
twentieth century. As Table 13 shows, between 1911 and 1971 the number of
employers and self-employed people fell from a tenth of the workforce to a
twentieth. The collapse of self-employment was especially marked in the higher
professions like law, accountancy, architecture, medicine and journalism, which
were simultaneously enlarging their share of the total workforce.
Many partnerships incorporated, and companies started to employ their own
lawyers, architects and accountants rather than purchase their services from
independent firms. Almost all doctors and nurses became paid employees of the
State with the formation of the National Health Service in 1948. As other State
bureaucracies expanded they, too, absorbed increasing numbers. The parallel
growth of a private employment hierarchy was reflected in the shrinkage of

employers and proprietors, including farmers, shopkeepers and hoteliers as well as owner-managing builders, manufacturers and distributors. They shrank from a fifteenth of the workforce to a twenty-fourth over the sixty years to 1971. There was a commensurate increase in the number of managers and administrators employed by companies, from a thirtieth of the workforce to a twelfth, in the same period. And the number of clerical workers shuffling paper from the in-tray to the out-tray in the gargantuan office buildings of the modern corporation nearly tripled between 1911 and 1971, to a seventh of the total workforce. The share of the net national income accounted for by wages and salaries increased from 50.5 per cent in 1900 to 68.6 per cent in 1970. In the same period, income from self-employment and private companies fell from 36.4 per cent to 20.3 per cent of the net national income.[5]

Table 13	Occupational Categories 1998 Q1		
Occupational	**Percentage**		
	Self-employed	Of number employed	Of total workforce
Higher professions	14.9%	85.1%	11.6%
Lower professions	12.3%	87.7%	20.3%
Employers and proprietors	na	na	na
Managers & administrators	19.5%	80.5%	18.1%
Clerical workers	4.4%	95.6%	16.7%
Foremen & supervisors	na	na	na
Skilled manual	27.9%	72.1%	13.8%
Semi-skilled manual	8.7%	91.3%	10.6%
Unskilled manual	9.3%	90.7%	8.9%

Source: Quantime Database (LFS)

People and partnerships with unlimited liability have lingered on in certain professions and institutions, like the law, accountancy and the 'names' which underwrite risks on the Lloyd's insurance market. But even these categories are now gradually disappearing. The increased threat of litigation by disgruntled clients, and the pressure from them for greater transparency in costs and remuneration, is encouraging large legal and accountancy partnerships to consider limiting their liability through incorporation. One of the biggest accountancy firms in Britain, KPMG Peat Marwick, already plans to incorporate. At Lloyd's multiplying risks, scandals and the threat of litigation are encouraging names with unlimited liability to give way to corporate risk-takers, just as partners in stock broking and jobbing firms disappeared from the London Stock Exchange once protection from foreign competition and fixed commissions disappeared in the famous Big Bang of October 1986. The willingness of men and women to back their skill, enterprise and reputation for probity with their entire personal fortune will probably disappear completely within the next decade or so.

The Invention of Retirement

Significantly, the word 'employee' did not enter the English language until the 1850s, and the term 'unemployment' was unknown until the 1880s. The modern concept of 'retirement' on an occupational pension was not properly invented until the twentieth century, when it was introduced in response to what the historian of the industry calls 'the evolving nature of the employment relation- ship in large bureaucratic enterprises'.[6] The rise of the occupational pension was the clearest possible symptom of the declining inde- pendence of the ordinary working man and woman. Significantly, it was the railways – the first Big Business in the country – which initiated occupational pensions for its employees. But as late as the turn of the century only a twentieth of employees were covered by occupational schemes. Wealthy people who survived into old age still preferred to manage their retirement investments directly, and long-serving managers relied on an *ex gratia* payment from their employer at retirement.

Occupational pensions first became widespread during the inter-war years, partly because employers saw them as part of the price of an acquiescent workforce and a means of industrial discipline, but mainly because absorption into vast, salaried and scientifically managed corporate bureaucracies had robbed employees of any sense of self-help or self-reliance. John Mitchell, a pioneer of occupational pensions reform, admitted as much in 1935:

> The need of pension provision for employees upon retirement extends as our system of commerce and industry tends to concentration, and men become more and more dependent upon an organisation and less and less able to influence their own destiny.[7]

Until the reforms of the 1980s, when they became portable for the first time, occupational pensions were the badge of corporate dependency. The so-called 'early leavers', who took up an oppor- tunity elsewhere faced dire financial penalties. Pensions were part of a structure of incentives intended to lock employees into a relationship with a single company for the whole of their working life. They helped to prevent employees defecting to competitors, going on strike or taking too many risks at work. In short, occupational pensions were part of the price a company paid for the docile, dependent and unquestioning workforce they thought they needed. For the same reason, they were part of an economy which grew increasingly sluggish and unadaptable as the twentieth century wore on.

The Myth of a Corporate Meritocracy

But the most important effect of employment in a large corporate hierarchy is to sever the connection between the value of a service and its remuneration, cutting buyers and sellers of labour off from the rice sinals which lead to the most efficient allocation of resources. The salary of an employee in a large corporation is generally determined not by results (a measure of his or her value to the company) but by the subjective assessment of his 'merit' by his or her superiors, or what they think he or she deserves. This can take extreme forms. The National Health Service hospital consultants, for example, are eligible for three classes of so-called 'merit awards'. These are straightforward increases in salary ranging from £9,935 a year for a 'C' merit award to £47,299 for an 'A' merit award. They are given by some doctors to others on a purely subjective basis, usually sufficiently late in the career of predominantly male doctors to ensure that they count towards the calculation of the earnings-related, index-linked pension. They cost the taxpayer around £100 million a year There are no formal criteria for awarding these sums, and the mysterious and secretive way in which the awards are made attracted criticism even from the doctors' and dentists' pay review body.[8]

Similar excesses occur in the private sector. Because the salaries of directors of large industrial corporations are set by remuneration committees made up of directors of other large companies, they are invariably handsome.[9] Lower down the ranks, the subjective assessment of merit by middle-ranking managers is naturally biased towards the conformist, the politically astute, the personally congenial and even, it seems, the physically attractive. In a paper prepared for the United States Bureau of Economic Research, two economists recently announced that their researches indicated that plain people earn 5 to 10 per cent less than people of average looks, and that those of average looks earn 5 per cent less than those who are good-looking.[10] 'Reward for merit,' as Hayek put it, 'is reward for obeying the wishes of others in what we do, not compensation for the benefits we have conferred upon them by doing what we thought best.'[11] The likeliest explanation of the extraordinarily long hours British executives now work is the desire to impress the superiors who have the power to increase their pay and improve their prospects. Yet the mark of the truly free individual is to be dependent for his standard of living not on what others think of him or her, but what value his or her services can command in the marketplace. Subjection to the opinion of others is a tyranny which the paid employee, even if he tests his market value by changing his job, can never entirely shake off.

The Reality of the Corporate Wage-Slave

The employed economy also led to a marked change in English economic expectations. 'Whereas the small businessman was always an individualist who thought of himself as a potential self made man,' writes Harold Perkin, 'the white-collar worker looked firstly for a secure income, secondly for a pension, and thirdly for promotion within a stable framework of employment.'[12] The watchword of the Corporate hierarchy is Security rather than Freedom or Enterprise. Employment in a large corporation brings security of tenure, a predictable career path, an assured income, a host of fringe benefits like free health care and motor cars, more or less automatic pay rises and promotions, and ample provision for retirement in old age. It relieves the individual of the burden of equipping an office, or hiring staff, and even of spending his own money.

The company car, which has withstood all attempts to tax it out of existence, is well known for encouraging people to buy more expensive models than they would choose if they were spending their own money. Cars are still mainly designed for a corporate fleet market indifferent to the purchase price and the costs of deprecia- tion, taxation, fuel and maintenance. The evidence suggests that cost-conscious private buyers prefer low-mileage used cars.[13] But the insensitivity to price of the corporate employee extends far beyond the garage forecourt. Hotels, restaurants, air travel, theatre tickets, taxis, office space and especially lawyers all have price schedules geared to people who are not spending their own money. The modern corporate employee is a new kind of aristocrat, enjoying the economic privileges which go with being Director of Bottlewashing at Acme plc. But he is also a slave, work and leisure dividing his life exactly into halves and the one intended only to purchase the other. 'That state is a state of slavery,' thought Eric Gill, 'in which a man does what he likes to do in his spare time and in his working time that which is required of him.'

Creativity, inventiveness, adaptability – in a word, entrepren- eurialism – are not the characteristic virtues of the corporate employee. He or she is conditioned to expect change to bring more and better of the same, not radical discontinuities. The employee does not expect, and is not expected, to do more than he is instructed to do. Charles Handy has illustrated, with an anecdote drawn from his own early career with a major multinational in Malaysia, what happens when an employee shows initiative or flair:

> I came across what seemed to me to be some gross inefficiencies. I worked out some better options, sent them to the Operations Manager and waited – for his thanks. He sent for me.
> 'How long have you been out here?' he asked.
> 'Six months,' I replied.
> 'And how long has this company been successfully doing business here?'
> 'About fifty years, I suppose.'
> 'Quite so, fifty-four in fact; and do you suppose that in six months you know better than the rest of us and our predecessors in fifty-four years?'
> I asked no more questions for the next three years, had no more ideas, made no more proposals. My social life prospered, I recall, but I stopped learning, and growing, and changing.[14]

In a large corporation, thinking of new ways of doing things, or conceiving of new products or services, will always seem disrespectful to the wisdom of the past and impertinent to the superiors of the present.

In the Big Corporation, pay and promotion hinge on avoiding mistakes, a pattern which discourages people from trying new methods or taking on more responsibility than is absolutely necessary. 'The most difficult thing we face,' explains the managing director of a company trying to persuade directors to use technology to expand their business, 'is mind-set: "I've got my car, my holidays

– I don't want the trouble."[15] In this environment, growth comes to be seen as part of an automatic process in which managers, workers, officials and politicians are merely pressing different buttons on the same machine. This is how an economy becomes sclerotic. Economic progress depends not on the Corporation or the State but upon constant experimentation with new methods and ideas by individuals. The Corporate hierarchy, by crushing individuality, naturally reduces the volume of experiments. To succeed economically today, individuals need exactly the skills and qualities – flexibility, intelligence, foresight, energy, discipline, initiative, and the ability to sacrifice present pleasures for future benefits – which Big Corporations tend to suppress. Many people, especially if they are poor, unskilled and dependent on a mixture of State hand-outs and corporate employment, naturally have difficulty organising their life and responding constructively to opportunities which present themselves. Redundancy can be a personal disaster. Without the support mechanisms of the large company they have difficulty in keeping appointments, marketing themselves or thinking beyond the task in hand.

The economically independent individual is not at all like his corporate counterpart. He is not merely earning a living. He has a completely different mentality to the employee, as Charles Handy himself has pointed out:

> Portfolio [in the sense of a portfolio of jobs rather than one full-time job] people think portfolio money not salary money. They learn that money comes in fits and starts from different sources. There may be a bit of a pension, some part-time work, some fees to charge or things to sell. They lead cash-flow lives not salary lives, planning always to have enough in-flows to cover out-flows when both can be, to some extent, varied. Invoices sent and paid promptly with bills paid late has helped to keep many a small business financed, and portfolio people too...Portfolio money is a way of thinking.[16]

This way of life is naturally less secure than a job. But a degree of financial insecurity and personal anxiety is an inescapable feature of economic independence. Existing clients must be nurtured, and new ones contacted. There is no clear distinction between work and play, life and labour, home and office. The rewards are entirely personal, and never the trimmings of the corporate manufacturing and marketing machine. Life and work are integrated, albeit imperfectly. It is an insecure way of life, but a free one, and those who fear it are the victims of the decades of collectivist institutionalisation which have sapped self-reliance and self-respect. These are a new kind of men and women, unknown in Britain until the twentieth century.

Traditional Individualism

The English were never peasants. Unlike most parts of Europe in the pre-industrial age, in England the ownership of property, the provision of labour and the production and consumption of food were never based on the household or the extended family. Instead, property was owned by individual men and women, and both labour and goods were bought and sold for cash in the marketplace. In *The Origins of English Individualism*, the social historian Alan Macfarlane described the ancestral English like this:

> The majority of ordinary people in England from at least the thirteenth century were rampant individualists, highly mobile both geographically and socially, economically 'rational', market-oriented and acquisitive, ego-centred in kinship and social life. Perhaps this is no surprise, for it would make them very like their descendants…three centuries later.[17]

Another historian, Susan Reynolds, has demonstrated how baseless the romantic Socialist conception of medieval society as a feudal hierarchy of lords and peasants bound together by reciprocal rights and obligations actually is.[18] She argues that people even in the lower orders of society inherited, owned and bought and sold property quite independently of their social duties. 'Nobles and free men,' she writes, 'normally held their land with as full, permanent, and independent rights as their society knew, and they owed whatever service they owed, not because they were vassals of a lord, but because they were subjects of a ruler. They owed it as property- owners, normally in rough proportion to their status and wealth.'[19]

Medieval England was not feudal but individualistic. There was as much personal liberty, private property and free trade – in a word, individualism – within the rule of law as the crude political institutions of the age could afford. These virtues were not invented by the settled government of the country, but nurtured by it. By the time of the Civil War a class of individual owner-occupying farmers owned land absolutely, using it to produce cereals, meat and dairy products not for the use of the family but to exchange for cash in the marketplace. The towns were packed not only with consumers, but with self-employed bakers, brewers, butchers, tailors and others. The farmer relied not on his children to till the land – as likely as not, they were already married and living and working elsewhere – but on landless labourers hired for cash. Parents rarely lived with their children and grandchildren in the extended families characteristic of peasant societies, for children were expected not to till the family smallholding but to earn a living wage.

Cash and contractual relationships were far more common in England than the reciprocal relationships of a fictitious feudal society. The Poll Tax data of 1380–81 suggest that between a half and two thirds of adult males in England were wage-earning labourers or servants, four centuries before the Industrial Revolution drew the rural landless into the towns to work in the factories. There was even an active market in land from the fifteenth century, which was fully supported in English law by the middle of the sixteenth century. In matters of inheritance it was primogeniture, rather than joint ownership by all members of a family or clan, which predominated from the top of the social scale to the bottom. Macfarlane believes that true ownership – in the sense that a parent could sell land without interference from his or her children – was vested in the individual in England as early as the twelfth century. Almost all foreign observers, from Montesquieu and de Tocqueville to Marc Bloch, believed that this history of individualism was peculiar to England. Only the collectivists have refused to believe it. Macfarlane himself dates the origins of English individualism to the absolute rights of individual property enjoyed by the Saxon people even before they began to cross the sea to England fifteen hundred years ago. 'Within the recorded period covered by our documents,' he writes, 'it is not possible to find a time when an Englishman did not stand alone.'[20]

That the English were never peasants is probably the most important fact about the history of this country. Unlike many other agrarian economies in Europe, the English ignored the classic social progression of Marxist historiography, from feudalism to capitalism. Yet virtually the whole tradition of collectivist thinking is based upon the assumption that economic individualism is peculiar to modern industrial capitalism, which overthrew the earlier and more just society to which socialism promises a speedy return. To Karl Marx – who was convinced that property relations are everywhere and always merely an expression of the point on the spectrum between feudalism and communism which an economy has reached – it was inconceivable that individual property rights could exist before the Industrial Revolution. At the beginning of this century the German sociologist Max Weber added to the Marxist analysis the compelling idea that the adoption of the ascetic and secular morality of Calvinism in sixteenth- and seventeenth-century England favoured the emergence of capitalism. It lives on in popular argot as 'the Protestant work ethic', and rests entirely upon the supposition that the Catholic ethic which it displaced was reciprocal, just and distributive.

R. H. Tawney disparaged Puritanism for glorifying 'individual responsibility, not social obligation'.[21] For him, the 'bourgeois' revolution of the seventeenth century displaced the Merrie England of his imagination with the dark, satanic mills of the industrial age. The economic life of the Middle Ages – with its just price, and its ban on usury, price-fixing and market-rigging- was prized by all the early English socialists precisely because it valued social norms and ethical values over the impersonal market economy. It subjugated economic efficiency to political and social relations, allocating wealth according to status, and valuing the stability of the social hierarchy too highly to accommodate the immoderate returns and rampant individualism of capitalism. Tawney's successor, the Marxist historian Christopher Hill, has never doubted that the bourgeois revolution of the seventeenth century set English history on a new course towards industrialisation. In a highly influential book published thirty years ago, C. B. Macpherson argued that a new theory of individual ownership was formulated in the seventeenth century by thinkers like Harrington, Hobbes and Locke.[22] This belief that capitalistic notions of individual and exclusive ownership were somehow 'invented' in the seventeenth century, and super-imposed on an older and more just tradition of communal, limited and conditional ownership by a gang of greedy bourgeois revolutionaries, is an essential part of the collectivist myth.

The Myth of the Collectivist Economy

The invented memory of the reciprocal economy of the past – based on co-operation rather than competition, in which possessions are held in common rather than severally, and men and women are not shackled by bourgeois institutions like property and the family – is among the most powerful strands in collectivist thinking. Even Hayek was forced to concede that mankind developed not as sovereign individuals but as members of clans and tribes driven to altruism and reciprocity by the shortage of food and shelter, and merely argued that reciprocity was inappropriate to more developed societies. But he recognised the power of social atavism. 'I believe,' he wrote, 'that an atavistic longing after the life of the noble savage is the main source of the collectivist tradition.'[23] His fellow-exile Karl Popper has detected in all collectivist thinking a yearning for a simpler, more harmonious way of life. In exile in New Zealand during the Second World War he wrote a two-volume destruction of the totalitarian philosophers and politicians who sought a return to the 'closed society' of the tribe or medieval village.[24]

Popper argued that, to succeed, collectivism must suppress the power of men to improve their material conditions by the application of reason and return human existence to the brute ignorance and cruelty of the most primitive tribes. Human reason probably originated in the discussions between primitive men and women over the allocation of food and shelter. Its application to a wider range of economic problems eventually created the division of labour and useful abstract rules like freedom and respect for private property. Reason also displaced the medieval inhibitions on economic growth like the just price and the usury laws. The powerful intellect of Adam Smith destroyed mercantilism – typified in England by the Navigation Acts – almost single-handedly. The collectivist longing to go back to a simpler and more harmonious state is a revolt against that history of intellectual and practical economic achievement. It is a revolt against the use of reason in human affairs.

The Myth of Private Property as the Origin of Alienation

Unsurprisingly, it was the most important of the political ro- mantics, Jean-Jacques Rousseau, who initiated the search for the authentic human personality which has dominated collectivist analysis of the human consequences of capitalist economics. He did so by overturning the Lockean universe which then prevailed. For John Locke private property was the essential means of self-expression. Every man had what he called 'a property in his own person' and it was by the use of part of that property – the labour of the mind or the body – that the individual acquired the right to own the things with which he had 'mixed' a portion of himself:

> Though the earth, and all inferior creatures, be common to all men, yet every man has a property in his own person: this nobody has any right to but himself. The labour of his body, and the work of his hands, we may say, are

properly his. Whatsoever then he removes out of the state that nature has provided, and left it in, he hath mixed his labour with, and joined it to something that is his own, and thereby makes it his property. It being by him removed from the common state nature hath placed it in, it hath by this labour something annexed to it that excludes the common right of other men. For this labour being the unquestionable property of the labourer, no man but he can have a right to what that is once joined to, at least where there is enough, and as good, left in common for others.[25]

The philosophical weaknesses of this argument for private property were obvious immediately. Does the milliner retain property rights in the hats she makes and sells, or do labourers acquire rights of property in the soil they till? Are individuals entitled to own property which they merely inherit?

But its seminal value and polemical powers were enormous. Ricardo adapted it to develop the labour theory of value, which was further modified by Marx to explain how the capitalist exploits the labour of the proletarian. Perhaps inadvertently, the Lockean conception of property as a natural right also initiated the process by which property ceased to be a static or conventional element in the social and political hierarchy and became an economic asset freely exchangeable among individuals in a market economy. By untying Property from Society, he sparked a whole tradition of collectivist thought dedicated to putting them back together again. The 'mixing' of the subjective personality with the objective matter of Nature also set up a second line of argument which Hegel, Marx and their successors in sociology and social psychology explored in order to explain the *alienation* of the individual from his 'true' or 'authentic' self in the capitalist economy.

John Locke argued that the State was invented to protect the life, private property and liberties of men (their 'propriety') against the natural violence and greed of other men in the State of Nature.[26] Rousseau inverted this argument. In his *Discourse on Inequality* he portrayed the lives of men in the State of Nature not as Hobbes had seen them – 'solitary, poor, nasty, brutish and short' – but as healthy, happy, good and free. Natural man wandered through the jungle, living off its fruits, berries and streams, making love with passers-by and concerned only with his own sustenance and survival and not with dehumanising and bourgeois considerations like private property and his family. The State, far from tempering the natural aggression, competitiveness and greed of men, actually created these undesirable characteristics by alienating men from their true self.

Part II of the *Discourse* opens with one of Rousseau's most celebrated passages of rhetoric:

The first man who, having enclosed a piece of land, thought of saying 'This is mine', and found people simple enough to believe him, was the true founder of civil society. How many crimes, wars, murders; how much misery and horror the human race would have been spared if someone had pulled up the stakes and filled in the ditch and cried out to his fellow men: 'Beware of listening to this impostor. You are lost if you forget that

the fruits of the earth belong to everyone and that the earth itself belongs
to no one!'[27]

In Rousseau's State of Nature people are not appropriating Nature as property
by mixing their labour with it but taking from it only what they need for some
useful purpose. Property was for use, not exchange. In the developing capitalist
society of the day men were alienated because they were beholden to false
wants, constantly comparing their own possessions with those of other people,
working incessantly to acquire more, and wracked by feelings of shame,
inadequacy, resentment, anxiety, insecurity and vanity as they contemplated the
wealth of their contemporaries. It is easy to see where R. H. Tawney got his
ideas of 'functional' and 'functionless' property.

Rousseau had furnished an anthropological argument. It was a useful
touchstone for all subsequent critics of the low morals of capitalism, and of the
psychological distress competition and acquisitiveness cause to individuals.
The work of generations of social anthropologists in comparing the happiness
of primitive societies with the alienation of the industrial civilisations was really
no more than an elaboration of Rousseau's intuitions about the 'noble savage'.
Citing primitive but happy tribes which know nothing of private property, like
the Busl ell or the Maoris of New Zealand, remains a standard argument among
those opposed to capitalism.[28] An influential anthropological study published in
1974 argued that hunter-gatherers, far from subsisting perpetually on the edge
of oblivion, are actually members of the 'original affluent society'. All their
material needs are met, and their daily life is not the relentless and hectic grind
of getting and spending which characterises industrial society but a round of
sleep and leisure interrupted only periodically by the 'work' of searching for
food. Ownership, even of food, is unknown because there is no point in stealing
or storing what is freely available in the lakes and forests. Individuals also know
that they have to share their catch with others to make others share their catch
with them in future, creating a reciprocal rather than a possessive culture.

Furthermore, since possessions are an encumbrance rather than a luxury to
people constantly on the move there is not much point in material
aggrandisement. The political authority needed to enforce property rights is
unnecessary and therefore unknown. 'This matter of presents gave us many an
anxious moment,' wrote Laurens Van der Post of his dealings with the hunter-
gatherers of the Kalahari desert. 'We were humiliated by the realisation of how
little there was we could give to the Bushmen. Almost everything seemed likely
to make life more difficult for them by adding to the litter and weight of their
daily round. They themselves had practically no possessions: a loin strap, a skin
blanket and a leather satchel. There was nothing that they could not assemble
in one minute, wrap up in their blankets and carry on their shoulders for a
journey of a thousand miles. They had no sense of possession.'[29]

In anthropological economics, the change from a hunter-gathering to a pastoral
economy is conventionally seen not as the first step towards self-sustaining growth,
but as a defeat inflicted on a contented humanity by demographic pressure.
Archaeological evidence certainly suggests that the decisive step in the creation of

property rights in the British Isles was the development of settled agriculture, and in particular the invention of the two-oxen plough.[30]

Forest-clearance for pasture began in Mesolithic times (around 8000 BC), but people were still insufficiently settled to own land. Although farmsteads and fortified hilltops like Earn Brea in Cornwall are dated to the Neolithic Age (5000–2500 BC), recognisable 'fields' did not appear in England until the Early and Middle Bronze Ages (2500-1600 BC). These irregular plots of land, associated with adjacent hut-circles, suggest ownership was not unknown even before the age of hunter-gathering was properly over.

Thousands of new settlements, from hut circles in small enclosures to fortified hilltop villages like Mam Tor in Derbyshire, appear in the Later Bronze Age (1600-800 BC). This era also saw the creation of the first properly planned agricultural landscapes. The extensive field system at Horridge Common on Dartmoor, for example, covers 2,000 acres. The establishment of settled agriculture demanded the establishment of fixed property in land. Building huts meant acquiring property. Ploughing and reaping implied a division of labour and the provision and ownership of tools. It became obvious, in ways not apparent in the chase, who was most skilful or worked hardest. Without security of title, tenure would have remained precarious, the incentive to labour limited and productivity minimal. Settled agriculture necessitated the development of relatively complex systems of political authority and law to enforce rules which were unnecessary in more primitive societies. To that extent, Rousseau was right to see the origins of civil society and private property in the actions of the first man who claimed a patch of land as his own.

Alienation and the Origins of State-Worship

In the *Social Contract*, which opens with the famous words 'men are born free, but they are everywhere in chains', Rousseau appeared to argue that individuals could overcome their alienation from their true and natural selves only by allowing themselves to be subsumed into the sovereign collective of the State. Hegel, the first of the German State-worshippers, was heavily influenced by this idea. He aimed to reconstitute the Nation-State as an extended Tribe whose values and laws are the 'true' morality to which all individuals must aspire. The appropriation of private property through labour was a crucial aspect of his theory of 'self-realisation', by which individuals pass through lesser collectivities like the family and civil society en route to the perfect freedom of complete submission to the State. By fashioning pieces of property from the bounty of nature men free themselves from nature, transforming it into compliant images and artefacts which can then be given, exchanged and accumulated. This facilitates the development of the family and civil society, by enabling men to provide for other people and exchange goods and services with them.

In the Hegelian perspective, the appropriation of property is also the dialectical mechanism by which man brings his reason to bear upon the inert material of the world. It is the means, in other words, by which mind triumphs over matter.[31] The individual expresses himself – or realises himself – by what he creates and owns, just as the mind and skill of the artist turn the inert material of oil and canvas into a finished work of art.[32] For Hegel, property is the embodiment of mind, a concrete expression of the achievements and culture of the society in which a man lives and the State to which he aspires. It anchors him in a world which outlives him, and gives his work an objective life beyond his own. The things he makes and owns enable him to leave traces which remain after his death, the mark he leaves on the world to signify that once he existed. The acquisition of property through labour was therefore a key part of the process by which individuals gain in self-knowledge and freedom, and so gradually overcome their alienation from the ideal, or Absolute Idea, towards which they are striving. But the gap between the ideal and the real self is an inescapable imperfection of life, leading to the 'unhappy consciousness' posterity knows as alienation.

Hegel's metaphysical analysis of property had one crucial implication. It meant that the rights of property were bound to be infringed whenever the creator had no control over the ultimate destination of his work. Marx turned this into a persuasive new secular theory of alienation. He described capitalism as a system in which individuals became alienated from their 'essence' (or 'species-being') because the product of their labour, the principal means of self-expression of the human species, is appropriated as private property by the capitalist. He saw this alienated condition as the direct result of the institution of private property, which necessitates a division of labour in which people produce goods for their own use but solely for exchange with others. Because workers in a capitalist society are not producing for their own needs and enjoyment, the goods they make are no longer a source of satisfaction to their maker. In producing them, a man sees himself as a means to an end which is not his own. He becomes an object to himself, and looks on other human beings merely as objects as well. Only with the abolition of private property can men and women re-connect themselves to their 'species-being'.

The Marxist analysis of alienation was relevant to a particular type of capitalism in mid-Victorian Manchester, where the existing technology necessitated a cruel existence for the majority of industrial workers. But it rightly seems parochial today. Even as Marx wrote, the legislation of 1856 and 1862 which permitted the formation of joint-stock companies was encouraging the owner-managing capitalists he detested to incorporate and limit their personal liability The legislation initiated the long process by which the ownership of industry in England was gradually divorced from its control, and the modern Corporate Economy came into being. The limitation of liability was the decisive change. It was argued that the risks of investment had become too large not to limit the risk of each shareholder to the value of the stock he or she bought in the company.

Arthur Bryant, the last of the Whig historians, understood the significance of the change:

The historic justification of private property had been that it fostered responsibility and acted as a bulwark against tyranny. It was now unwittingly being used by the individual to purchase freedom from responsibility. It was putting despotic powers in the hands of mechanical corporations without personal conscience or sense of obligation...The later Victorians, for all the probity of their private and domestic lives, allowed the economic initiative of their posterity to pass to the soulless corporations which gave them their wealth and income...In the late 'fifties and early 'sixties, to suit the convenience of the commercial community Liberal Governments passed legislation conferring on joint-stock companies the privilege of limited liability. Henceforward fictitious bodies, enjoying the legal rights of individuals, could incur unlimited financial obligations without their individual shareholders becoming fully responsible for them. Up to this time a man's power to make money by transferring his credit and freedom of commercial action to others was restrained by his liability for the obligations they might incur. This check on irresponsible delegation was now removed. A man could grow and remain rich in security and even innocence from business practices which would have outraged his conscience as an individual. He could avoid both the risks and stigma of transactions done by others in pursuit of profits in which he shared...Ownership and enjoyment of the nation's wealth was thus increasingly separated from its control. And the conscience of the individual ceased to regulate its use directly.[33]

This was an economy which orthodox Marxism did not recognise, but one to which the metaphysics of Hegel seem far more relevant than the natural rights of Locke. Few institutional shareholders have acquired stock in a company by mixing their labour with its assets. Ownership of shares depends on an elaborate structure of legal relationships by which the holder can lay claim to a share of the profits (and the assets in the case of a winding-up) which in no way depends upon the mixing of labour. The fact that the Courts will recognise title on the basis of a name on a register or a piece of paper is the ultimate triumph of mind over matter: an affirmation of will in the world, as Hegel might have put it.

The new kind of capitalist enterprise which dominates the English economy today has breathed new life into the idea of alienation. Freud described the 'repression' of the personality which stems from conforming constantly to social roles and expectations laid down by others, evident in the pathetic urge of bank clerk Smith to keep up with sales clerk Jones. Emile Durkheim, in a sociological echo of the familiar collectivist tribalism, argued that the rational, employed, consuming individuals of modern economics were quite cut off from the consolations offered by traditional standards, values and rules. They suffer from a form of alienation he called 'anomy'. Neo-Marxists like Herbert Marcuse attempted to synthesise the economic, sociological and psychological aspects of alienation into a coherent explanation of the feelings of estrangement, powerlessness and depersonalisation people undoubtedly experience in large and predominantly bureaucratic economies and societies. 'The danger is that the bigger a company becomes,' wrote the banker Sir Siegmund Warburg of his own management responsibilities, 'the more difficult it is to deal with it on a personal basis, and the more you become slaves of a big bureaucratic machinery.'[34]

The employee in a Big Corporation is the alienated slave of a big bureaucratic machine because he is never the originator of his own activities but relies instead on instructions from his superiors. But the boss himself is completely unlike the owner-entrepreneur of Marxist demonology. Weber argued that the central villain in modern capitalism is not in fact the property-owning capitalist at all, but the manager, the bureaucrat and the administrator. The modern employee is faced not with subjugation to an owner, he thought, but with the choice of fitting into the bureaucratic hierarchy or not. In extreme versions of this outlook – of which John Kenneth Galbraith's *New Industrial State* is the best-known example – the differences between corporate hierarchies and government departments or public corporations start to disappear, and employees of all kinds become merely victims, as both producers and consumers, of monopolistic price- and wage-fixing corporations in both the private and the public sectors.

Latter-day English socialists were deeply impressed by this analysis. Generations of socialists had believed that all they had to do was supplant the owner-manager with the State, and the power of the capitalist to exploit the consumer and the wage-earning worker would be lanced. But the emergence of large corporate bureaucracies meant that the traditional capitalist enemy had ceased to exist. The complexity and scale of modern industrial operations had edged him off the stage of world history, to be replaced by vast and remote corporations owned either by passive and funtinless institutional shareholders, or by a State lacking the powers or knowledge to intervene and control a nationalised industry effectively. Revisionist socialists concluded, with Tony Crosland, that they did not need to do anything about capitalism any more because capitalism of the diabolical Victorian kind was no longer around to overthrow.

'If one of these paternal factories were taken over by the State tomorrow,' wrote the socialist writer J. B. Priestley after a visit to the Cadbury factory at Bournville in 1933, 'only one weakness of the system would disappear, the fact that the whole organisation is there for private profit; all the other weaknesses and dangers would remain, for the individual workman would still be compelled to look only in one direction for all the benefits of his life, would remain, for the individual workman would still be made for his factory and not his factory for him, could confuse and mislay all his values, even though the directors had now to report to a public ministry instead of to a body of shareholders.'[35] As early as the 1930s, if not before, the giant private corporations were becoming a part of the apparatus of the State of their own accord.

Big Business relied on the State to manipulate aggregate demand for its products, on the public education system for trained manpower, on public purchasing contracts for orders, on public subsidies for exports and research and development, and on incomes policies and trade union laws for industrial discipline. For its part, the State was pleased to have a captive institutional audience to simplify the collection and administration of taxes and the implementation of social and economic policies. The whole of political life was subsumed in a single project: to raise the standard of living of the voters by pulling a variety of fiscal, monetary and micro-economic levers. By adjusting various financial aggregates, and encouraging directly some forms of behaviour while discouraging others, it was possible to manipulate an integrated public and private corporate economic system into ever-higher investment, output and employment. The modern industrial system did not need to be socialised because it was socialising itself. 'From the standpoint of the employee,' wrote Arnold Toynbee in 1958, 'it is coming to make less and less practical difference to him what his country's official ideology is and whether he happens to be employed by a government or commercial corporation.'[36]

References

1   Quoted in Charles Handy, The Empty Raincoat: Making Sense of the Future, Hutchinson, 1994, page 41.
2   J. K. Galbraith, The Age of Uncertainty, Andre Deutsch, 1977.
3   Charles Handy, The Age of Unreason, Arrow, 1990, page 189.
4   Harold Perkin, The Rise of Professional Society: England Since 1880, Routledge, 1989, page 460.
5   David Butler and Gareth Butler, British Political Facts 1900–1985s, Sixth Edition Macmillan, 1988, page 392.
6   Leslie Hannah, Inventing Retirement: The Development of Occupational Pensions in Britain, CUP, 1986.
7   Quoted in Leslie Hannah, Inventing Retirement: The Development of Occupational Pensions in Britain, CUP, 1986, page 15.
8   Observer, 1 May 1994.
9   This, of course, is an aspect of the 'principal-agent' problem. See pages 160–5 above.
10   Financial Times, 18 April 1984.
11   F. A. Hayek, The Constitution of Liberty, Routledge, 1960, page 100.
12   Harold Perkin, The Rise of Professional Society: England Since 1880, Routledge, 1989, pages 97–8.
13   'Motor industry alarmed as private sales decline', Financial Times, December 1994.
14   Charles Handy, The Age of Unreason, Arrow, Iggo, pages 57–8.
15   Quoted in Financial Times, 8 December 1994.
16   Charles Handy, The Age of Unreason, Arrow, 1990, page 153.
17   Alan Macfarlane, The Origins of English Individualism, Basil Blackwell, 1979, page 63.
18   See Chapter 6, page 144.
19   Susan Reynolds, Fiefs and Vassals, OUP, 1994, page 477.
20   Alan Macfarlane, The Origins of English Individualism, Basil Blackwell, 1979, page 196.
21   R. H. Tavney, Religion and the Rise of Capitalism, Penguin Edition, 1990, page 270.
22   C. B. Macpherson The Political Theory of Possessive Individualism, OUP, 1962.
23   F. A. Hayek, The Fatal Conceit: The Errors of Socialism, Routledge, 1988, page 19.
24   See Introduction, page 12.
25   From Two Treatises, II, Sections 25–39, quoted in John W. Yolton, The Locke Reader: Selections From the Works of John Locke, CUP, 197, pages 289–90.
26   For an explanation of personality or propriety in this sense, see above, pages 29-30.
27   Jean-Jacques Rousseau, A Discourse on Inequality, Penguin Classics Edition, 1984, page 109.
28   See, for example, Marion Shoard, This Land is Our Land: The Struggle for Britain's

Countryside, Paladin, 1987, pages 18–19

29 Laurens van der Post, The Lost World of the Kalahari, Morrow, 1958, page 276 quoted in Marshall Sahlins, Stone Age Economics, Tavistock, 1974, page 12.

30 But private property was probably known to earlier generations. Even Van der Post's Kalahari Bushmen owned their own loin strap, blanket and satchel. Doubtless the earliest hunter-gatherers to settle in the British Isles owned their own bows and arrows, and their furs and spears. They probably fashioned their own tools, and so acquired ownership rights over them as well. The tools buried with the dead certainly suggest that they owned them, perhaps because they made them or worked with them. The flint, zinc and copper mines of the pre-agricultural age may well have been owned by those who worked them, and the nomadic pastoralists of the Mesolithic era probably owned their cows and sheep, since people would scarcely work to produce milk and wool unless they could keep it. Avebury and other fortified hilltops which survive from the Neolithic Age also suggest political organisation was sufficiently well-developed to enforce rights of property

31 Perhaps this explains the sense of personal defilement many people experience after the theft of their property.

32 Unlike Locke, Hegel did not regard 'liberties' and 'persons' (in the sense of bodies) as Property. Hegel saw 'alienability' as the mark of true property, which ruled out lives and liberties.

33 Arthur Bryant, The Search for Justice, Collins, 1990, pages 176–7.

34 Quoted in the Financial Times, 9 December 1994.

35 J. B. Priestley, English Journey, Penguin, 1979, page 97.

36 Quoted in John Kenneth Galbraith, The New Industrial State, Second Edition Pelican, 1978, page 111.

CHAPTER NINE

The Resurrection of the Rentier

Every function super added to those already exercised by the government, causes its influence over hopes and fears to be more widely diffused, and converts, more and more, the active and ambitious part of the public into hangers-on of the government, or of some party which aims at becoming the government. If the roads, the railways, the banks, the insurance offices, the great joint-stock companies, the universities, and the public charities, were all of them branches of the government; if, in addition, the municipal corporations and local boards, with all that now devolves on them, became departments of the central administration; if the employees of all these different enterprises were appointed and paid by government, and looked to the government for every rise in life; not all the freedom of the press and popular constitution of the legislature would make this or any other country free otherwise than in name.

John Stuart Mill, *On Liberty*[1]

There was never a socialist putsch in England because there did not need to be one. Between them, the State and the Corporate Hierarchy enslaved the country, reducing the vast majority of people to dependency on paternalistic employers and public services. The company provides a place to work, a regular wage or salary, a pension, perhaps a motor car as well or a loan to buy the season ticket. The State educates the workforce for a lifetime of of fice or factory work, and uses the taxes helpfully deducted by the employer to underwrite the stability of society with free health, unemployment and social security services. It is not hard to see why people find living and working in this kind of system deeply unsatisfactory. Most employees are alienated, in the sense that they derive minimal satisfaction from their job. They divide their life exactly between Work and Life, with the first providing merely the means to purchase more of the second. They see work as the means to a new house or car or a night out, rather than as an end in itself. They show little concern with the nature and quality of their work, and actively resist responsibility.

Although people undoubtedly do not work solely for money – self-esteem, the society of others and the support of their family are also important – financial considerations are clearly paramount. Even rich people are notoriously reluctant to give up money in return for more interesting work, no matter how hard management consultants like Charles Handy work to persuade them that time is as valuable as money. The system is unarguably demoralising. It is scarcely conducive to the happiness of individuals and their families if they concentrate on bread-winning to the exclusion of all else, and come home tired and bad-tempered and unable to understand why their husbands or wives or children are not satisfied with the pay cheque alone. Even where people are working shorter hours – and the of ficial working week, if not the actual one, is much shorter than it was a century ago – increased leisure is a poor consolation for a job which is boring. 'A firm,' writes Alan Ryan, 'is now a good device for providing one with a money income, and not a very good device for providing much else.'[2]

The Loss of Individual Autonomy

The combination of working for an impersonal bureaucracy and living in a Welfare State has shrunk the scope for self-determination to vanishing point. People are alienated precisely because they have so little control over their own life. Yet this inhuman system, and the dependency it spawns, is the culmination of a whole tradition of collectivist thinking in England whose overriding purpose was to reunite the real self and the ideal self, alienated from each other by property-based capitalism. At bottom, collectivists believed that all of the classical freedoms – freedom of speech, freedom of movement and so on, as well as private property – were quite useless to people without sufficient education, health and financial security to take advantage of them. Their solution was to invite the State to make sure that individuals were always amply endowed with each of these things, through the public provision of education, health and social security. Equality, they thought, would enable people to seize control of their personal destiny.

Collectivists subscribed to the 'positive' species of freedom identified by Isaiah Berlin, which stems directly from the belierof Rousseau, Hegel and other State-worshippers that true freedom lies not in being left alone to do what you like ('negative' freedom, or non-interference) but in somehow 'realising' the Self by merging it with the State. Berlin described it like this:

> I wish my life and decisions to depend on myself, not on external forces of whatever kind. I wish to be the instrument of my own, not of other men's, acts of will. I wish to be a subject, not an object; to be moved by reasons, by conscious purposes, which are my own, not by causes which affect me, as it were, from outside. I wish to be somebody, not nobody; a doer- deciding, not being decided for, self-directed and not acted upon by external nature or by other men as if I were a thing, or an animal, or a slave incapable of playing a human role, that is, of conceiving goals and policies of my own and realising them.[3]

Nothing could be less apt as a description of the reality of life and work in the Corporate Economy and the Welfare State. It is ironic that the historical role of this positive freedom – the desire to make individuals the master of their own fate – was, as Isaiah Berlin went on to point out, to act as a cloak for despotism in the name of a wider freedom.[4]

The conflict between the 'positive' and the 'negative' conceptions of freedom is where the battle for the future of Britain is still being fought today. 'Positive' freedom masquerades as 'autonomy', or what John Gray has called 'the condition in which a person can be at least part author of his life, in that he has before him a range of worthwhile options, in respect of which his choices are not fettered by coercion and with regard to which he possesses the capacities and resources presupposed by a reasonable measure of success in his self-chosen path among these options'.[5] Though its adherents differ on the precise dose to be administered, autonomy argues always for greater equality – or at least a more equal distribution of wealth – as the route to the enlargement of personal liberty and self- determination. 'The achievement of a more equal distribution of wealth and power, and the resultant increase in the sum of freedom for the community as a whole, is the principal goal of socialism,' wrote Roy Hattersley in *Choose Freedom*, the book in which he adumbrated the aims and values of a modern socialist party.[6]

Autonomy has achieved a number of popular formulations in collectivist circles, including 'empowerment', 'the enabling state', 'a hand-up not a hand-out' and the slogan currently favoured by the Liberal Democratic Party, which is promising to use oceans of taxpayers' money to make 'everybody a somebody'. It rests on the belief that all social problems, and not just the obvious ones like health and sanitation, are the products of a defective social organisation rather than individual inadequacy. There is therefore no limit to its capacity for interference with the freedom of individuals. With their specious promises of democratic 'account- ability' the collectivists argue that the consequent accumulation of power and property by the State can never be too great, since the experts will use their powers wisely and the people will periodically give their consent. 'The doctrine,' writes Isaiah Berlin, 'that accumulations of power can never be too great, provided that they are rationally controlled and used, ignores the central reason for pursuing liberty in the first place – that all paternalist governments, however benevolent, cautious, disinterested, and rational, have tended, in the end, to treat the majority of men as minors, or as being too often incurably foolish or irresponsible; or else as maturing so slowly as not to justify their liberation at any clearly foreseeable date (which, in practice, means at no definite time at all). This is a policy which degrades men, and seems to me to rest on no rational or scientific foundation, but, on the contrary, on a profoundly mistaken view of the deepest human needs.'[7]

Most people have an intuitive grasp of their deepest needs. It is to be free to choose, and not to be chosen for. The 'positive' liberty proffered by the State, however construed, cannot in the end supply this need. Its appetite for directing men is so great that the freedom to choose is what it eventually obstructs. By monopolising whole areas of human endeavour – education, health and social insurance, pensions, and so on – it gradually narrows the field of choice, and through taxation it erodes the material means which alone can bring freedom of choice to life. It was significant that William Beveridge, the architect of the Welfare State, retained in his blueprint for postwar social security the principle of insurance by the individual against poverty, unemployment and ill-health. He thought it was the key not only to an affordable Welfare State, but to the survival of the self-respecting economic individualist. But his kind of thinking was rapidly overtaken by the notion of citizenship', in which so called social rights to education, decent housing, unemployment benefit, health care, social security and even free contraceptives are granted parity of esteem with the classical freedoms of speech and movement and property.

Likewise, the exchange of labour for a regular wage or salary and a company car (and an occupational pension, if the redundancy payment does not intervene first) is scarcely compatible with individuals controlling their own destiny. The large private employers dictate what happens in most of the waking hours of their employees, and the basis on which they are remunerated. The system is also based, as Harold Perkin has explained, on a powerful intellectual and organisational hegemony:

> In post-industrial society, it is the professional bureaucrat, private and public, who increasingly seeks to impose his principle of social organisation – *la carrière ouverte aux talents*, the stable career hierarchy, and management by experts - and his social ideal – a functional society efficiently organised to distribute rewards according to personal merit professionally defined – upon old-fashioned individual capitalist and proletarian worker alike. Just as in industrial society' the capitalist saw no necessary function for the landlord, so in post-industrial society the professional bureaucrat, not least in corporate business, sees nonecessity for the individual capitalist, who is simply an irritant, a quixotic element, an unpredictable maverick in an otherwise stable system of bureaucratic imperialism. Likewise, the traditional, insecure, wage-earning proletarian, without career expectations, staff status or pension rights, is an evolutionary throwback, to be gradually transformed into a professional worker with statutory rights and responsibilities.[8]

It is hard to see how individuals can break free of their dependency on this system without revolutionary changes in both mental attitude and in the current pattern of property ownership.

The Crumbling of the Corporate Economy

Fortunately, some of these are occurring already. During the 1 g80s the century-long trend towards the bureaucratisation of the work- force was at last reversed. As Table 14 shows, the number of self- employed has increased from 8 per cent of the workforce to over a tenth. From just under 2 million in 1979 the number of self- employed people increased by two thirds to 3.3 million at the peak of the economic boom in Iggo. Despite the decline in the number of self-employed people during the recession which followed, the proportion of independents within the workforce is still higher than it was a decade ago. But the changes in the shape of the workforce were not confined to the self-employed. Perhaps only two thirds of the 21.3 million employees are in full-time employment, and only one third of them in conventional nine-to-five, five-day-week jobs. Most people expect to work weekends at least occasionally, and to have days off in the week. More people are working from home or on the road, using modern communications equipment to keep in touch with clients and colleagues. In extreme cases, companies have abandoned the traditional office altogether. Far more people are now working part-time or on temporary assignments. Some are semi-retired going back into the labour market as and when they choose. The changes in the labour market reflect the changing shape of the economy. The number of employees in manufacturing has shrunk from around a third of the workforce in 1979 to a fifth today. The proportion employed in services has climbed from well over half to getting on for three quarters in the same period. The number of women in employment has climbed from two fifths to a half, and the number working part-time from a third to nearly a half. Service industries find flexible staff cheaper and more useful, and they are able to recruit from a far wider spectrum of people than old-style manufacturing industries. An American analyst, William Bridges, has described the traditional job as a 'historical artefact' well adjusted to the methods of mass industrial production which developed in the nineteenth century but inappropriate to a modern, flexible and service-based economy.[9] In Britain, Charles Handy believes modern businesses are now changing from huge organisations which offer jobs for life to thousands in vast bureaucratic hierarchies into clusters of key executives and workers, who then recruit outsiders to help them complete particular tasks. Large companies are certainly employing fewer people. One recent report estimated that between 1981 and 1991 the number of companies employing more than 500 people shrank by a quarter, but that by the end of the period there were 300,000 more businesses employing fewer than roo people.[10] In other words, most people in work are still employees, but they are employed mainly by small companies. Both large and smaller companies tend to recruit people temporarily, transforming a significant proportion of career salarymen into self-employed 'entrepreneurs' who manage a sequence or portfolio of different careers, clients and full- and part-time jobs. '[This pattern] has grown,' writes Handy, 'because it is cheaper. Organisations have realised that while it may be convenient to have everyone around all the time, with their time at your command because you have bought all their time, it is a luxurious way of marshalling the necessary resources.'[11] Fewer people working harder to produce more is obviously cheaper. Outside contractors, and self-employed, part-time and temporary workers are less costly in terms of salary, office or factory space, superannuation benefits and especially in terms of tax and National Insurance.

Table 14   Structure of Employment in the UK

	Number (000s)	% of total workforce
		December 1997
Employees	23,082	82%
Self employed	3,312	12%
Unemployed	1,411	5%
Trainees	169	1%
HM forces	211	1%
Total	28,185	100%

Labour Market Trends, April 1998

It is easy to exaggerate the significance of this trend. As Table 14 shows, three quarters of the labour force are still employees. Nearly half of all male employees can still expect to work for the same company for at least twenty years, suggesting the 'job for life' is not yet dead.[12] But the hierarchy of employment is beginning to crumble, and the changes reflect more than mere economics. More women are working as well as rearing children and, as the economy has shifted away from manufacturing and towards services, the opportunities for them to do so have expanded commensurately. The balance of employment within the economy is shifting from large-scale and labour-intensive manufacturing employment towards small-scale and highly flexible service industries like finance, insurance, consultancy, advertising, journalism, television, films and publishing. These industries do not require legions of male employees performing repetitive tasks in large factories, but allow people to work from home or small offices and for a variety of different employers. Women, seeking to organise a working life around their family, can make good use of their flexibility.

The Reinvention of Human Capital

Charles Handy argues that a new mentality is needed to cope with the new way of working. He says people should ditch the old hierarchical and nine-to-fiveish ways of thinking, invest in themselves and their talents, take personal responsibility for their future and be willing to make and learn from mistakes and trade money for time, thereby becoming active rather than passive players in the drama of their own life.[13] The scope to take this advice is being enlarged by the changing locus of employment and wealth within the economy. In an increasingly service-based and knowledge-driven economy, writes Handy, 'focused intelligence, the ability to acquire and apply knowledge and know-how, is the new source of wealth...Intelligence is the new form of property'.[14] When wealth was concentrated primarily in agricultural land, real estate was naturally the dominant form of ownership. Industrial capitalism, and particularly the invention of the joint-stock company, necessi- tated the creation of tradable financial securities. But as an industrial economy develops, its demand for brute strength and clerical skills declines and its appetite for educated and technologically skilled people increases.

A narrow definition of property – one which excludes its many non-financial satisfactions – is the right to a flow of income. These may come from rents on land, company profits, or interest and dividends on securities. To the extent that educated intelligence equips a man or woman with the power to earn a stream of income from fees, it is also a form of property. By investing in education and knowledge, and then creating an artificial scarcity by erecting barriers to entry by others, professions like medicine, the law and accountancy have long managed to turn their expertise into a human capital capable of extracting an economic rent.[15] The social historian Harold Perkin has described this kind of intelligence-as- property:

> Since the essence of property is the right to (some portion of) the flow of income from the resource owned, this professional capital, which is manifestly more tangible than stocks and shares, less destructible than many forms of material property (buildings burn more readily than people), and capable of self-renewal by means of improvement in skills and expertise, is thus in the truest sense a species of property – albeit contingent property, contingent upon the performance of the service.[16]

Perkin perhaps presses his case too far by including all forms of white-collar employment – from dons, through journalists and bank managers, to industrial managers and barristers – in his classification of 'professionals', or owners of human capital capable of extracting an economic rent.

But the argument is nevertheless compelling. Just as the great landowners used freehold title, and owner-managers financial capital, so the professional of the late twentieth century has turned human capital into the dominant form of wealth today. One historian reckons that human capital today accounts for 52 per cent of the national income, compared with only 15 per cent a century or so ago when rents profits and wages were the dominant form of wealth.[17] In 1992 the total net wealth of the personal sector was estimated at £2.3 billion, but the value of human capital was worth nearly ten times as much.[18] And, although it can be taxed where it is bought and sold (to an employer or client), human capital cannot in the end be monopolised by a single employer or expropriated by the State. It is free to join another company, emigrate to another country, or apply itself in another field. Nor does it necessitate employment in a bureaucratic hierarchy. Human capital can be sold to lots of different buyers.

The kind of economy Handy envisages is not unlike England before the rise of the Corporate Economy. Farmers, plumbers, bricklayers, carpenters, electricians, lawyers, accountants, journalists and many other kinds of self-employed people paid for their own education and training with their own time or money, sold their services for fees rather than salaries and usually worked for more than one employer. Unfortunately, the modern corporate employee is unlikely to metamorphose into the kind of enterprising individual Handy describes without a great deal of distress and dislocation. Trade union leaders, themselves largely the creation of the Corporate Economy, routinely describe the full-time workforce as anxious, insecure, stressed and cowed by a terror of losing their job rather than looking forward to life outside the stultifying embrace of the Big Corporation. The part-time and increasingly female workforce they see as a race of under-paid and over-worked hamburger-flippers who would in a sane and secure world be ensconced in 'proper' full-time jobs. The fact that otherwise reasonable people cannot conceive of a life outside the Big Corporation, and regard anything less than a full-time salaried job as demeaning, is one measure of the depth and intensity of the corporate dependency culture which has taken root in Britain over the last one hundred years. Even the famously flexible workforce at the Nissan plant in Sunderland, for example, preferred a 'normal' working week and redundancy for a minority to shorter working hours for everyone (and maybe alternative employment) during the recent economic downturn.

The Failure of the Property-Owning Democracy

Most people still conceive of themselves as employees, not employers of their own talents, and work as a place they go to rather than an activity they control or enjoy. It used to be thought that this divide between employers and employees could be overcome through a mixture of greater worker participation in managerial decisions and the 'property-owning democracy'. Schemes designed to give employees a greater sense of 'ownership' in the firm they work for are one of the longest running themes in politics. Even amid the rampant individualism of the early Victorian economy, John Stuart Mill doubted that 'the division of the human race into two hereditary classes, employers and employed, can be permanently maintained'. He predicted the emergence of a new partnership between the two, in which workers contracted to perform services for companies, managers and workers agreed to split profits and co-operatives of workers took over the management of some large enterprises.[19] A number of early industrialists – Robert Owen, Titus Salt, William Lever – tried various forms of co-operative, paternalistic and welfare ventures to bridge the gap between employer and employed.

The Webbs coined the phrase 'industrial democracy' at the end of the nineteenth century, and both world wars witnessed ventures into worker consultation. During the inter-war years the Liberal Party developed an interest in employee consultation and shareholding and it was in 1978, during its infamous cohabitation with the ruling Labour Party, that the Liberal supporters of the government were able to persuade their socialist partners to introduce incentives for profit-sharing. The Corporate State and the Corporate Economy were themselves based on the fiction that forms of ownership could be developed which fell short of full proprietary rights. The post-war nationalisations were seen at the time as a mechanism for creating a new spirit in industry. As late as 1975 a Labour Government appointed a Royal

Commission on Industrial Democracy to explore how the new spirit might be carried into the private sector as well. In the 1950s the Conservative Government countered with Anthony Eden's vision of a 'property-owning democracy'. The Conservative programmes of selling council houses and privatising the nationalised industries were animated by the prospect of creating a new class of owners and inheritors.

It cannot be said that these policies were a triumph. The odd success like the employee buy-out at National Freight Corporation (now compromised anyway by the expansion of the capital needs of the company) cannot conceal the fact that co-operatives, employee buy-outs, employee share schemes, worker-directors, privatisations and profit and performance-related pay structures have manifestly failed to shake the basic structure of corporate capitalism in Britain. A survey of one privatised company found nine tenths of managers and workforce denying that the ownership of shares in the company by employees had replaced the 'us and them' attitude with a sense of common purpose. Similar proportions denied that employees worked any harder or more carefully.[20] Equivalent results were obtained from a study of employee share ownership in a Midlands factory.[21] Save-As-You-Earn Share Options Schemes, Employee Share Ownership Plans and Profit-Related Pay Schemes seem to be adopted primarily because they are an advantageous way, in tax terms, of paying workers. Shareholdings are usually too small to convey a proper sense of ownership, and workers turn out to be just as interested in selling at a profit as the most cynical institutional shareholder.

Meaningful involvement in the management and direction of any company with more than twenty employees is unlikely to be achieved. Employees also rightly consider it inadvisable to tie all of their income-producing assets, including their job, their savings and their pensions, to the fortunes of a single enterprise. Most people opt to save through institutional vehicles like deposit accounts, personal equity plans, mutual funds and insurance companies. In the end, the biggest financial asset most people ever acquire – their occupational pension – is still supplied by a paternalistic company, and the pensioner has no say at all over how the scheme is run or where and how his savings are invested. Even after retirement, the pensioner is still locked into the company scheme and cannot take his capital and manage it himself. A great many people rely for their livelihood on State benefits or a State pension which is not backed by a pool of capital of any kind. Instead, the value of their income depends entirely on the balance of political advantage remaining in their favour.

An Unearned Income for All

It is impossible to give employed people or State dependants any real sense that they are the authors of their own lives without the widespread accumulation of personal capital. If income-producing assets were sufficiently widespread that each individual received a significant proportion of his total annual income from them, the conventional link between the standard of living and nominal salaries and wages or contributory or means-tested State benefits would be at least partially broken. This would not only begin to dissolve the rigidities of the Corporate Economy – particularly the manifest reluctance of employees, where they are reliant on their earnings to maintain their standard of living, to allow wages to fall to market-clearing levels – but it would also help to solve the problem of dependency on the State. Possession of personal capital would also facilitate the emergence of the 'portfolio' economy which Charles Handy has described, by giving people the financial confidence to vary their working habits and even to enlarge their familial, social and aesthetic activities. This will certainly necessitate changes in the relationship between companies and their employees. But, if Handy is right, many of the necessary changes are occurring already. The basic shape of the working week – eight hours a day, five days a week – approach which takes account of a more independent and intelligent (and more female) workforce. Direct employment is shrinking in favour of hiring individuals for specific tasks. One important change – giving individuals control of their own pension funds, and especially breaking the linkage of pension values to the final years at work – awaits a fundamental reconsideration of the whole structure and purpose of the company.

Handy believes just such a fundamental reconsideration is now imminent. 'I question,' he writes, 'whether the idea of a company as a piece of property which can be owned by anyone with enough money to pay for it, or bits of it, a property which can be bought and sold over the heads of all those who work and live there, is still a valid concept in an age where people not things are the real assets.'[22] He thinks the task of a business can no longer be simply to create value for impersonal institutional shareholders, when the real property of the company lies not in its plant, machinery and cash but in the intellects of its people. Rather, it is a 'community' or association of shareholders, a 'wealth-creating club' of workers, customers, suppliers and even pensioners (what he calls the 'stakeholders') in which the institutions are merely the stewards of the property rather than its owners. Handy touches on the great weakness of the modern corporation: its impersonality, its lack of any recognisably human purpose, its reliance on rewarding labour rather than capital and its divorce of ownership from control. Corporate capitalism has a depressingly utilitarian flavour to it. It is driven not by any moral but merely by what one writer calls 'increasingly efficient solutions to the problem of economic efficiency'.[23] Distant owners, self-interested managers and wage-slave workers all lack any real sense of 'ownership' in an enterprise.

Handy believes that sense of ownership can be restored because the traditional forms of capital – money, factories, machines, institutions – are yielding to human capital, and the owners of the human capital can own the company. 'We are hung up on ownership, on the idea of property,' he says, arguing that the joint-stock company must in future be seen as a club or association of producers, suppliers and customers rather than as an employer and profits-generator.[24] But it is difficult to see how different this would be from the status quo. Handy himself admits that 'outwardly, little would look different, but inside it would feel very different'.[25] He then lapses into a form of

Christian Socialism which R. H. Tawney would probably recognise. 'The principal purpose of a company,' he writes, 'is not to make a profit, full stop. It is to make a profit in order to continue to do things or make things, and to do so ever better and more abundantly. To say that profit is a means to other ends and not an end in itself is not a semantic quibble, it is a serious moral point. A requirement is not a purpose.'[26] This does not seem very different from Tawney's 'social function' of capital in the socialist Nirvana. Another conclusion is that the State should raise the value of human capital by investing more heavily in education and training, perhaps through payroll levies. This would ensure that everybody gets their fair share of the new kind of human capital, or 'intellectual property', which he has described. It is dispiriting to find it is the State, yet again, which would be responsible for the distribution even of the new kind of intellectual wealth.

Table 15   Investment Income in 1990–91

Lower Limit	Number of People (000s)	Amount (£ mn)	Average Total Income	Per Cent of Total Income
£3,005	3,200	£1,910	£600	4%
£5,000	7,450	£6,900	£930	16%
£10,000	5,750	£7,220	£1,300	17%
£15,000	3,530	£5,810	£1,600	13%
£20,000	2,560	£7,600	£3,000	18%
£30,000	974	£5,550	£5,700	13%
£50,000	364	£8,050	£22,000	19%
Total	23,800	£43,000	£1,800	100%

Source: *Inland Revenue Statistics 1993*, Table 3.5.

It would be far more appealing to create the kind of economy Handy envisages by ensuring that individuals themselves have the purchasing power to buy the time, skills and knowledge they need to pursue flexible and rewarding careers and lead happy and fulfilled lives. In economic jargon, what is required is a shift in market rewards away from labour and towards capital. In practical terms, this means the possession by every individual of what the Georgians and Victorians would have called a 'sufficiency' or 'competence'. These terms were used to describe a private income sufficient to relieve a man or woman of the obligation to work, or at least to work full-time, at a job they would not, in an ideal world, have chosen. Samuel Brittan has resurrected the idea in liberal market economics as 'a modest competence'.

A modest competence is disagreeable only if the distribution of capital is so highly concentrated that the majority of people have little or no unearned income. At the moment 23.8 million people receive an investment income of some sort from rents, interest payments or dividends. As Table 15 shows, the total amount received was £43 billion in 1990–91. But the average annual payment is only £1,800, or just over half of the current personal tax allowance of £3,445. Only 1.34 million people, or just 3½ per cent of the total adult population, receive an average of more than £5,700. One third of the adult population has no investment income at all, or at least none that it declares to the Inland Revenue. In Iggo-gl investment income probably amounted to less than a tenth of total personal income before tax. The total measured investment income of £43 billion in 1990–91 is also trifling compared with earnings from employment that year of £275 billion, total transfers by the State to the private sector of £64 billion and total public expenditure of £223 billion.

Table 16   Personal Sector Balance Sheet 1982–92

£ billions	1982	% Total Assets	1992	% Total Assets
Residential Buildings	364.7	38.2	1,091.7	39.2
Other Tangible Assets	83.5	8.7	121.5	4.4
Life Assurance and Pension Funds	161.8	16.9	703.9	25.3
Gilts & National Savings	38.3	4.0	61.1	2.2
Bank Deposits	61	5.4	169.8	6.1
Building Society,v Deposits	67.0	7.0	186.3	6.7
Mutual Funds	4.6	0.5	23.4	0.8
Shares: Home & Overseas	48.8	5.1	144.3	5.2
Other Financial Assets	40.3	4.2	104.2	3.7
Other Intangible Assets	95.1	10.0	178.2	6.4
Total Assets	955.7	100.0	2,784.4	100.0
Financial Liabilities	(127.7)	13.4	(487.9)	17.5
Total Net Assets	828.0	86.6	2,296.5	82.5

Source: *Economic Trends*, Table 12.2.

The modesty and high concentration of investment income is not the only problem. Most people also exert minimal control over whatever savings they have. This is partly because they have neither the time nor the competence to manage their own investments, but it has also occurred because the tax system has tended to reinforce the institutionalisation of savings. Most of the popular institutional savings vehicles – occupational and personal pensions, life assurance, Personal Equity Plans (PEPs), Tax Exempt Special Savings Accounts (TESSAs) and so on – arc chosen because they have tax advantages. This granting of fiscal privileges to certain kinds of savings encourages institutionalisation because the Inland Revenue always manages to persuade the Treasury that restrictions and regulations are necessary to prevent abuse of the privilege or outright tax evasion. Rules and regulations are always easier to monitor and enforce if the management of personal assets is carried out mainly by institutions which the State can authorise and approve rather than individuals themselves. It is merely one of the many ways in which the

Corporate Economy and the Corporate State are self-reinforcing.

The two largest assets most people acquire over the course of their working lives are a house and a pension. As Table 16 shows, in 1982 residential houses, life assurance policies and pension funds accounted for 55 per cent of total personal sector assets. Ten years on, they account for 64.5 per cent. Both pensions and owner-occupied houses are essentially creations of the tax system. Interest payable on mortgages has long enjoyed a tax subsidy, though this is gradually being phased out, and residential houses continue uniquely to enjoy a complete exemption from Capital Gains Tax. Likewise, pension contributions and investments are subsidised by the tax system and the investments of the pension funds themselves receive income and capital gains free of tax. In short, the tax system still favours earnings from a job home ownership and collective forms of investment rather than the accumulation of significant personal capital.

The grant of tax privileges to certain kinds of saving is necessary mainly because overall levels o taxation are excessive. In the Corporate Economy and the Welfare State, tax structures are also seen as an arm of social policy. All other incentives given to savers are designed not only to compensate people for excessive levels of personal taxation, but to encourage what the State sees as desirable forms of behaviour. It is offensive on both of those rounds. It is also economically inefficient. The main effects of tax privileges are to distort the allocation of income and capital between various types of investments – apparent, most obviously, in the tendency of new fiscal privileges to divert money from one type of savings vehicle to another – and to provide jobs for Inland Revenue officials and tax accountants.

The Injustice of Tax Perks Only for the Rich

The system is also unjust, because the privileges are exploited mainly by the highest-paid employees, who naturally have more money to spare. The point at which income tax becomes payable for a married man with two young children fell from 101.2 per cent of average manual earnings in 1950 to 36.3 per cent in 1992-93.[27] In 1950 less than an eighth of average earnings was taken in income tax; today it is nearer a fifth. Despite all the reforms and so-called 'tax cuts' of the last fifteen years, a marginal rate of taxation of 44 per cent is still chargeable on the vast majority of incomes. A special absurdity of the system is that marginal rates may actually be lower at the higher rates of income, if the various tax breaks available are taken into account. It was calculated in 1 990 that, net of tax perks, a man on a nominal income of £150,000 paid a marginal rate of 26.7 per cent and an average rate of 11.4 per cent but a man on average earnings paid a marginal rate of 34 per cent and an average rate of 22.7 per cent.[28]

In other words, once savings incentives are taken into account the income tax system is highly regressive. It is not always appreciated how valuable tax privileges are to those who can afford to take advantage of them. Today, a well-paid executive can save perhaps £75,000 a year in tax-free form, with £20,000 in an Enterprise Investment Scheme, £18,000 in Personal Equity Plans (PEPs) for himself and his wife, £3,000 apiece in Tax Exempt Special Savings Accounts (TESSAs) and the rest in pension subsidies up to an earnings cap of £78,600. Similarly, a wealthy married couple might already have invested well over £100,000 in PEPs if they have used the maximum allowances every year since the scheme was introduced in 1986-87. Even if they never buy another PEP again, the total value of their tax-free portfolio at the end of twenty years will amount to roughly £500,000 if its value grows at the current long-term gilt rate of 8 per cent a year.

Table 17   The Cost of Various Tax Shelters in 19994

Tax Relief	Value (£000s)
Contracted-Out NIC Rebate for Pensions	7,500
Income Tax Relief for Pension Schemes	7,400
Mortgage Interest Relief	4,300
Contributions to Personal Pensions	1,600
Redundancy Payments to £30,000	1,000
Capital Gains Tax on Main Residence	1,000
NIC Incentive to Personal Pensions	750
Profit-Related Pay	300
Tax-Exempt Special Savings Accounts	300
National Savings Certificates	240
Life Assurance Premiums	230
Various Capital Gains Tax Reliefs	190
Business Expansion Scheme	180
Personal Equity Plans	150
Profit-Sharing Schemes	95
Savings-Linked Share Option Schemes	95
Private Medical Insurance for the Over-60s	70
Share Option Schemes	55
Total	25,455

Source: *H.M. Treasury, Tax Ready Reckoner and Tax Reliefs.*

A tax-free half-million-pound endowment is gratifying for wealthy taxpayers, but it will mean somebody else's taxes will have to go up if public expenditure remains unchanged. 'One man's tax privilege is another man's tax burden,' as Nigel Vinson has put it. The savings of poorer households, which tend to be concentrated in interest-bearing bank and building society accounts, are among the assets which are more heavily taxed as a result. It is those who are already relatively rich who are the main beneficiaries of the current system of tax reliefs for saving, and it is the relatively poor who cannot accumulate personal capital because they have to pay for those reliefs. As Table 17 shows, the Treasury estimates the cost of the major tax privileges for saving at £25.5 billion, or 44 per cent of the total yield from income tax in 1993-94. If the privileges were abolished it would be possible to charge a single flat rate of income tax of 15 per cent. That would be the most valuable step towards the creation of a tax system which lifts the fiscal inhibitions on the wider ownership of wealth, because it would allow people to keep enough of what they earn to save more than they do at present.

Fortunately, the Inland Revenue is already being forced to alter its methods. PAYE was devised and organised around the static, salaried employee who could be relied upon to think of his salary in gross terms for political purposes and in net terms for spending purposes. Even today, 21.8 million of the 25.4 million income tax payers are taxed before they have even received the money they earned. The self-employed, who actually enjoy the use of tax revenues for a few months before paying them to the Customs and Excise, are naturally the traditional enemy of the tax collector.[29] But there are now more of them than at any time since the 1920s, and their numbers are expected to increase as the shape of the labour market continues to change.[30] The self-employed rightly have greater scope to offset their expenses against their income tax liability, and tend to pay less in income tax than employees with the same earnings. They also have a more generous National Insurance regime than the employed. Even the public sector will eventually be forced to offer more work to people who are self-employed.

Similarly, the increase in part-time work is reducing income tax revenues. The main reason part-timers pay less than their full-time equivalents is because employers can use them to arbitrage the system of tax allowances. An individual can earn £3,525 a year before paying income tax in 1995–96, and pays a rate of 20 per cent on the next £3,200 of income before the basic rate of 25 per cent cuts in. The effect of this pattern of allowances on income tax receipts is substantial. One full-time employee earning £12,000 a year will pay £2,040 in income tax, but two part-time people earning £6,000 a year each will pay only £1,120 between them. Similarly, National Insurance contributions are not payable until a worker earns at least £59 a week, and the rate is levied at only 2 per cent on the next £59 and 10 per cent on the next £322 of earnings. The full-time individual on £12,000 a year pays £647.76 in National Insurance contributions, but two part-time workers on £6,000 a year pay only £117.28 between them. There are employers' National Insurance contributions on top, but these are not payable on behalf of anybody working less than 15 hours a week.

The main enemy of the individual accumulation of capital is the direct taxation of personal incomes, but inherited wealth is also under attack by the State. The current Inheritance Tax is popularly supposed to be a voluntary tax. In 1989–90 it was not paid by twelve times as many estates as paid it and it raised the relatively modest sum of £1.2 billion, making it a prime case for immediate abolition.[31] The spread of home ownership and the rise in house prices means that the current threshold of £154,000 is far too low. The tax also picks and chooses between beneficiaries (exempting not just the spouse, but State bodies, charities and even political parties) in a thoroughly reprehensible way. Individuals who seek to avoid the tax by disposing of assets are still required to live for at least seven years and, if they die too soon, they often face double taxation for Capital Gains as well as Inheritance Tax. The Inheritance

Tax, despite its modest incidence, is still the best instance anywhere in the tax system of the malign and debilitating effect the arbitrary use of State power can have on private and family life.

Until Harcourt introduced modern Estate Duty at rates of 1 to 8 per cent in 1894 a progressive tax on inheritance was unthinkable in Britain. Of course, the 1694 Stamp Act had taxed wills, and Lord North taxed legacies during a wartime emergency, but even in its last days at the end of the nineteenth century estates were being taxed at an exceptionally modest 3 per cent. By breaching a principle, Harcourt offered a hostage to fortune which the Labour Government of 1974–79 was the first to take. The Capital Transfer Tax it introduced in March 1975 was once described as 'the first direct attack in English law against the institution of private property'.[32] This was a far from hyperbolic description of a tax which effectively sought to extend the old Estate Duty to lifetime gifts, making it a comprehensive tax on all transmissions of personal wealth. The burden naturally fell particularly heavily on family businesses and farms. A particularly vicious twist affecting lifetime gifts was the taxation of the amount the Revenue thought the donor would have given in a tax-free environment. In theory, that meant that Capital Transfer Tax on large gifts could exceed the value of the gift itself.

The Cultural Importance of Inherited Wealth

The effects of capital taxation spread far beyond the economic. 'The power of perpetuating our property in our families,' thought Burke, 'is one of the most valuable and interesting circumstances belonging to it, and that which tends the most to the perpetuation of society itself. It makes our weakness subservient to our virtue; it grafts benevolence even upon avarice.'[33] Children naturally expect to enjoy the property of their parents, and parents generally wish to demonstrate their affection for their children (and their property) by transmitting it to them. Disinheritance by the State therefore disrupts the natural expectations of society. The attachment to family and personal possessions is in most cases so intense that the law neglects at its peril the desire to inherit. As Alan Ryan has put it:

> [A child] has lived with the owners and, surrounded by their possessions, gets into the habit of seeing his own future bound up with them. The parents, too, project their present concern for the child into the future and, if nothing disturbs them, expect him to enjoy their goods in due course. So the law has raw material in the form of expectations to work on.[34]

Few sentiments are more bathetic than the desire expressed by so many of the self-made men of the 1980s to leave nothing to their children, on the grounds that they will become lazy or indulgent. It robs their accumulation of a large part of its moral purpose, and what some might see as its only moral purpose.[35]

Men and women of independent means are also an essential source of funding and innovation in those fields – charity, the fine arts, education and research, the preservation of the natural and architectural heritage, some sports, and the development and propagation of new ideas in politics, morals and religion – where the market has a limited capacity to contribute. It is not necessary to look to Venice, Florence and The Netherlands for evidence of the unarguable connection between private wealth and great art or social achievement. William Caxton, who brought the printing press to England, made enough money in his early life to devote his later years to translating and publishing French romances. The housing reformer, Octavia Hill, was supported in her work by an endowment given to her by her friends. The wartime literary magazine, *Horizon*, was supported by the margarine heir, Peter Watson. A modern successor, *The Literary Review*, is supported by Naim Attallah. William Morris, the Victorian socialist, used his private fortune to subsidise a variety of left-wing political groupings and journals.

The textile heir, Samuel Courtauld, used over £300,000 of his private wealth to assemble for the nation the fine collection of Impressionist paintings now on display to the public in Somerset House. Vivien Duffield – who inherited a fortune from her father, Charles Clore, the creator of the Sears group of retailers – has given away £90 million to a variety of charities, medical foundations and arts organisations. On a more prosaic level, dozens of football clubs in England are maintained by their besotted owners. There are countless other examples. It is a formidable criticism of the egalitarian tradition that it prizes the preservation of high and popular culture in this way so lightly. There are civilised and desirable objects which capitalism is not merely incapable of supplying, but which its perfectly rational bias in favour of mass-production for mass-consumption may actually undermine. Paradoxically, high culture survived in the well-educated but impoverished societies of east and central Europe precisely because there was no marketplace in which to buy the easier consolations of pulp fiction, mass sport, television and journalism.

Hayek himself thought that the cultural function of the discerning rich was so important that, if wealthy people did not exist, it would be necessary to invent them.[36] Maynard Keynes was once reproved by his friend Marcel Labordere for advocating in the General Theory the 'euthanasia of the rentier', as part of his generalised attack on excessive saving. Labordere's argument was one Keynes immediately conceded was right:

> The rentier is useful in his way not only, or even principally, on account of his propensity to save but for deeper reasons. Stable fortunes, the hereditary permanency of families, and sets of families of various social standings are an invisible social asset on which every kind of culture is more or less dependent. To entirely overlook the interests of the rentier class which includes benevolent, humanitarian, scientific, literary institutions and groups of worldly interests (salons) may, viewed in a historical perspective, turn out to have been a short-sighted policy. Financial security for ones livelihood is a necessary condition of organised leisure and thought. Organised leisure and thought is a necessary condition of a true, not purely mechanical, civilisation.[37]

Hayek later recalled that Keynes himself had once expatiated to him on the 'indispensable role that the man of independent means plays in any decent society'.[38] After all, the great Cambridge economist himself had determined to become financially indepen- dent precisely because he felt that he needed a sufficiency to buy the time to impart the many important things he had to say and accumulate the money to support the authors and artists he valued. By 1936 Keynes's stock market speculations had amassed a fortune worth £500,000, or about £13 million in modern prices. Among the projects he spent it on was the design and construction of the Arts Theatre in Cambridge, in which he invested £20,000 of his own money (about £500,000 today).[39]

The State Official and the Corporate Employee are naturally hostile to inherited wealth. They believe that everybody should work for their living, and have the self-discipline to put aside sufficient to keep themselves when they are no longer willing or able to work. The early socialists and opinion-formers who invented the Welfare State, appalled by the conspicuous waste of the Idle Rich, gave this essentially envious opinion rudimentary ideological support. The 'champagne socialists' of the Driberg-Maxwell-Lever-Hollick school were a much later invention, though the first Labour Prime Minister, Ramsay MacDonald, took £40,000 in cash and securities (over £1 million in modern prices) and a Daimler from his friend Alexander Grant 'so that I may not require, whilst absorbed in public duties, to worry about income'.[40]

Tony Crosland, the leading philosopher of champagne socialism, later mocked the Socialist saints Sidney and Beatrice Webb for their austere vision of the good life. In *The Future of Socialism*, he quoted with evident distaste Beatrice Webb's admission in *Our Partnership* that 'owing to our concentration on research, municipal administration and Fabian propaganda, we had neither the time nor the energy, *nor yet the means*, to listen to music and the drama, to brood over classic literature, to visit picture galleries, or to view with an informed intelligence the wonders of architecture'. It was charac- teristic of Crosland's own muddled thinking that he felt able to combine, within six pages of each other, a call for 'greater emphasis on private life, on freedom and dissent, on culture, beauty, leisure, and even frivolity' with a demand for swingeing taxes on gifts, death duties and capital gains.[41]

Even today, heavy taxes on inheritance are thought by many collectivists to be essential to the egalitarian-cum-meritocratic society they favour. But a wealthy family may take several generations to develop the requisite sensitivities, and denying them a chance to flourish cuts off one further avenue of social experi- mentation. If everybody has to devote all of their time and energies to earning a living, the finer aspects of civilisation will naturally wither. And the State is a poor substitute as patron, its efforts being as susceptible in this sphere as in any other to being captured by the bureaucrats which administer the funds or the well-organised lobbyists which flatter them. The State-subsidised culture which already exists tends to be hostile to genuine innovation, over-priced and to act as a form of regressive taxation.[42] The displacement of the private patron by the State is undoubtedly a large part of the explanation of the deplorable condition of the cultural life of Britain today.

This coarsening of cultural life was foreseen by Oscar Wilde, in his last and brilliant essay, *The Soul of Man Under Socialism*, published in 1891. 'If the Socialism is Authoritarian; if there are Governments armed with economic power as they are now with political power;' he warned, 'if, in a word, we are to have Industrial Tyrannies, then the last state of man will be worse than the first...It is to be regretted that a portion of our community should be practically in slavery, but to propose to solve the problem by enslaving the entire community is childish.'[43] Wilde was inspired to write the essay after listening to a speech by Bernard Shaw, who said afterwards that it was witty and entertaining but had nothing to do with socialism. In fact, Wilde had pinpointed the essence of socialism. He saw that the most powerful argument for private property was precisely what socialists believed it lacked: its freedom-preserving and freedom- enhancing qualities.

'In consequence of the existence of private property,' continued Wilde, 'a great many people are enabled to develop a certain very limited amount of Individualism. They are either under no necessity to work for their living, or are enabled to choose the sphere of activity that is really congenial to them, and gives them pleasure. These are the poets, the philosophers, the men of science, the men of culture – in a word, the real men, the men who have realised themselves.'[44] Ironically, some of the most influential figures in the development of Socialism in Britain – Ruskin, Engels, Morris and Hyndman among them – fell into exactly this class. Their writings and activities prove that access to private property is not merely a safeguard against coercion, but the means to the expression of personal values and ideals even where these are antipathetic to the system which gives them life. It also nourishes freedom by buying time and broadening the options open to the individual. Private wealth is the main source of cultural, social and political innovation, providing the financial support for 'experiments in living' and the social 'dissidence' which is at the heart of the free and dynamic society.

The acquisition by everybody of an adequate personal endow- ment is therefore not merely about the liberation of the individual from the constrictive grasp of the Welfare State and the Corporate Economy. It is also about the means of access to the Good Life. On the flyleaf to his essay On Liberty, John Stuart Mill reproduced a passage from Wilhelm von Humboldt's *Sphere and Duties of Government*. The Prussian philologist and educational reformer advocated a minimal State dedicated to nothing but the liberty of the individual. 'The grand, leading principle, towards which every argument unfolded in these pages directly converges,' it read, 'is the absolute and essential importance of human development in its richest diversity.' As long as the vast majority of people are almost wholly dependent on a paternalistic State and an equally pater- nalistic Employer, the scope for individuals to realise their own true talents and personalities – to become at least part-authors of their own lives – will remain severely circumscribed.

The dream of a country in which every individual is an owner, an investor, an inheritor and a rentier is obviously some way off. To ensure that each of the 37½ million adults in the country enjoyed an unearned income amounting to just a third or so of average earnings, or £5,000 a year, would require personal capital of between £120,000 and £150,000 a head.[45] That would amount to a total capital requirement of between £4½ and £5½ trillion, or roughly twice the measured total national net wealth in 1992. But that is no reason not to dream of it, or not to start working towards a wider distribution of capital today. It is arguable that one great opportunity- a privatisation programme which redistributed State assets worth £55.2 billion, or £1,472 a head, between 1979 and 1993 – has been missed already. The comprehensive reform of the public expenditure, tax, education and social security systems outlined in the final chapter of this book is one way to make up for lost time.

References

1   John Stuart Mill, *On Liberty and Other Essays*, OUP, 1991, pages 122–3.
2   Alan Ryan, *Property and Political Theory*, Blackwell, 1984, page 183.
3   Isaiah Berlin, *Four Essays on Liberty*, OUP, 1992 paperback edition, page 131.
4   Isaiah Berlin, Introduction to *Four Essays on Liberty*, OUP, 1992 paperback edition, page xlvii.
5   In fact, Gray argues that negative liberty is a facet of 'autonomy'. See John Gray, The Moral Foundations of Market Institutions, IEA Health and Welfare Unit, 1992, page22.
6   Hattersley argued that 'socialism exists to provide – for the largest possible number of people – the ability to exercise effective liberty'.
7   Isaiah Berlin, *Introduction to Four Essays on Liberty*, OUP, 1992 paperback edition, page lxii.
8   Harold Perkin, *The Rise of Professional Society: England Since 1880*, Routledge, 1989, pages 288–9.
9   *Financial Times*, 23 December 199
10   *Financial Times*, 12 September 1994.
11   Charles Handy, *The Age of Unreason*, Arrow, 1990, page 25.
12   Simon Burgess and Hedley Rees, 'Jobs for Life Still Available to Many', *Financial Times*, 9 December 1994.
13   See Charles Handy, *The Age of Unreason*, Arrow, 1990, pages 44–63.
14   Charles Handy, *The Empty Raincoat: Making Sense of the Future*, Hutchinson, 1994, page 23.
15   In economics, a rent is the sum a man or woman can earn by their skill or expertise in excess of its next best use. Placido Domingo, for example, may earn £100,000 a year as an opera singer, but the job for which he is next best suited may be a roadsweeper at £5,000 a year. He is therefore exacting an economic rent of £95,000 a year. An economic rent is a measure of scarcity value, which can be created artificially by the erection of barriers to entry in the form of strict training requirements and qualifications, security of tenury and monopolistic control of particular types of expertise. Barristers excluding solicitors from the higher courts is a classic instance of a professional monopoly. University dons and medical consultants, to take another example, have used a mixture of laborious qualification periods, examinations and security of tenure to create an artificial scarcity from which they can extract an economic rent.
16   See Harold Perkin, *The Rise of Professional Society: England Since 1880*, Routledge, 1990, page 8. This conception of property can be misconstrued. If property is a right to an income, in the shape of selling a skill to an employer (people with jobs), going on welfare (for unemployed, sick or retired) or selling a skill to a variety of buyers in the marketplace (self-employed people), guaranteed access to an income can be seen as a property right. Socialists have argued that workers

'own' their jobs, and the introduction of statutory redundancy payments was arguably based on that belief. In extreme socialist experiments – like that which took place in the Soviet Union between 1917 and 1989 – rights to an income become politically distributed rather than stemming from the ownership or sale of a skill. This rightly seems thoroughly suspect. It must be doubtful if the employed and those on welfare do 'own' their jobs or non-jobs in this way: they are not transferable or alienable in any meaningful sense of the term, and certainly do not give the owner exclusive rights of use.

17   Peter H. Lindert, 'Unequal English Wealth Since 1670' Journal of Political Economy, Vol. 94 1986, page 1131.

18   The value of human capital can be estimated by calculating the difference between total personal income and unskilled incomes. Capitalised at a dividend yield of 3–4 per cent, this was equal to about £200 billion in 1992.

19   John Stuart Mill, Principles of Political Economy, Book IV, Chapter 7, 'Probable Future of the Labouring Classes', Penguin, 1985, pages 126–9.

20   'It's Still Us and Them', Theo Nichols and Julia O'Connell Davidson, Financial Times, 7 March 1991.

21   'The Impact of Employee Share Ownership on Work er Attitudes', Human Resource Management Journal, April 1991.

22   Charles Handy, The Empty Raincoat: Making Sense of the Future, Hutchinson, 1994, page 131.

23   Alan Ryan, Property, Open University Press, 1987, page 103.

24   Charles Handy, The Empty Raincoat: Making Sense of the Future, Hutchinson, 1994, page 163.

25   The Empty Raincoat: Making Sense of the Future, page 153.

26   The Empty Raincoat: Making Sense of the Future, page 136.

27   See Table 11, page 100. See also Inland Revenue Statistics 1992, Appendix C.

28   Philip Chappell, 'The Assault on Fiscal Privilege', in Which Road to Fiscal Neutrality?, Institute of Economic Affairs, September 1990, Table 1, page 31.

29   See Chapter 5, page 115.

30   See above, Table 14, page 214.

31   Inland Revenue Statistics 1993, Table 12.5.

32   Roger Scruton, The Meaning of Conservatism, Penguin, 1980, page 108.

33   Edmund Burke, Reflections on the Revolution in France, Penguin, 1973, page 140.

34   Alan Ryan, Property and Political Theory, Blackwell, 1984, page 99.

35   Capitalism is conventionally seen as purely utilitarian. But all forms of work, investment and accumulation offer scope for the fulfilment of moral purposes. A successful business provides work, as well as goods and services, for others; it creates wealth which did not exist before, which can be used for good or bad purposes; it offers great scope for the creative use of talents, skills, knowledge and intellect, and for the education and training of the young. It can also enable people to take personal responsibility, express their own creativity and acquire self-respect. The so-called 'Protestant work ethic' always recognised this, and Catholic theology is now catching up. see Michael Novak, The Catholic Ethic and the Spirit of Capitalism, Free Press, 1993, especially page xv.

36   F. A. Hayek, The Constitution of Liberty, Routledge, 1960, page 126.

37   Quoted in Robert Skidelsky, John Maynard Keynes: The Economist As Saviour 1920–1937, page 584.

35   F. A. Hayek, The Constitution of Liberty, Routledge, 1960, note 7, page 447.

39   John Maynard Keynes: The Economist As Saviour 1921–1937, pages 524 and 528.

40   David Cannadine, The Decline and Fall of the British Aristocracy, Yale University Press, 1990, page 322.

41   C. A. R. Crosland, The Future of Socialism, Jonathan Cape, 1956, pages 518 and 523–4

42   See David Sawers, Should the Taxpayer Support the Arts?, Institute of Economic Affairs, 1993.

43   'The Soul of Man Under Socialism', reproduced in Oscar Wilde, *De Profundis and Other Writings*, edited by Hesketh Pearson, Penguin Classics, 1986, page 21.

44   'The Soul of Man Under Socialism', reproduced in Oscar Wilde, *De Profundis and Other Writings*, page 21.

45   Assuming a dividend yield of $3^{1}/_{2}$–$4^{1}/_{2}$ per cent.

PART THREE

The Loss of Virtue

CHAPTER TEN

The Destruction of the Moral Order

Lord have mercy upon us, and incline our hearts to keep this law.
Rehearsal of the Ten Commandments,
Book of Common Prayer, 1662

Liberty is the highest political end of man. No country can be free without
religion. It creates and strengthens the notion of duty. If men are not kept
straight by duty, they must be by fear. The more they are kept by fear, the
less they arc free. The greater the strength of duty, the greater the liberty.
Lord Acton

What we have become – and we're afraid to admit it- is a pagan society.
We're no longer a Christian country.
Father Michael Conaty, Tyneside parish priest[1]

'England's not a bad country,' wrote the novelist Margaret Drabble in 1989. 'It's
just a mean, cold, ugly, divided, tired, clapped-out, post-imperial, post-
industrial slag-heap covered in hamburger cartons.'[2] Most would add drug-and
crime-ridden, and some depraved, to this unflattering portrait of the condition
of England now. Though the Prime Minister himself has warned against
nostalgia for Golden Ages that never were, few would disagree that England
today is far removed from the one whose shores Rupert Brooke left behind some
eighty years ago: the one land he knew where men with Splendid Hearts may
go. Since the poet died from the bite of a mosquito, the health and well-being
and the material circumstances of life of the vast majority of British men and
women have improved immeasurably. But almost nobody believes the moral
condition of Britain has moved in any direction save that of deterioration. The
country is in the grip of a profound moral crisis.

The Attack on Individualism

The standard collectivist explanation of the catastrophe is to blame it on
rampant economic individualism. At the 1988 Labour Party conference the

then leader of the Labour Party, Neil Kinnock, made a celebrated attack on the recent admission by Margaret Thatcher that she thought there was 'no such thing as society'. To rapturous applause, Kinnock orated:

> 'There is no such thing as society,' she says. No sister, no brotherhood. No neighbourhood. No honouring other people's little children. 'No such thing as society.' No number other than one. No person other than me. No time other than now. No such thing as society, just 'me' and 'now'. This is Margaret Thatcher's society.[3]

Of all the fallacies to which the collectivists of the twentieth century have subscribed, the old lie that the freedom of the individual is enlarged and protected by membership of a group is the most lamentable of all. It stems directly from the thinking of continental State-worshippers like Rousseau, Hegel and Marx, and has no place in the affairs of a people rightly suspicious of abstract ideas and arbitrary power.

The belief that the individual can 'realise' himself only through metaphysical union with a greater whole – *Der Mensch im Grossen*, as Germans like to put it – is a Teutonic idea of the kind to which the British are traditionally immune. Yet no belief is more widespread among the opinion-formers of today, at every point along the political spectrum. The leader of the Labour Party, Tony Blair, believes that 'the central message of the modern Labour party is to reunite notions of individual aspiration with notions of a strong cohesive society so that the process of social improvement leads to self-improvement...Its values and principles...stem from an essential belief in the role of society and its relationship to the individual.'[4] Likewise, the Liberal Democratic Party leader, Paddy Ashdown, disclosed recently in a book entitled Beyond Westminster that 'this country will not solve its problems unless we can unleash the power and imagination of Britain's communities'. His followers preface almost all of their activities with the word 'community', as if it were a magic talisman.

The newspapers are filled with laments for esteemed national institutions and traditional 'communities' brought low by the unforgiving pursuit of economic self-interest. 'If for 14 years you preach disrespect for everything save the profit and loss account, the result is the 1990s,' thunders Joe Rogaly of the *Financial Times*.[5] The crime wave, fractured families and sexual depravity, mused the Dean of Salisbury in the same newspaper, are 'the direct consequence of policies and attitudes which have exalted personal choice over community responsibility, personal gain over the common weal, competition over co-operation. Those are the basics of the Thatcher years.'[6] The Bishop of Birmingham lambasted the National Health Service reforms for reducing patients 'to the status of a unit of consumption and exchange'.[7] David Cannadine, an American-based historian tempted occasionally to expatiate on the lost world of the Welfare State, opined recently that the 'confrontational, acerbic and destabilising' policies of Thatcherism had undermined deference, tolerance, decency, fair-mindedness, public-spiritedness and all established institutions, including the Conservative Party.[8] He obviously talks to his wife, Linda Colley, since she had expressed exactly the same opinion in *The Times* some months earlier.[9] Peter Hennessy, another journalist-cum-historian of the same school, is composing a multi-volume personal monument to 'those brave, semi-collectivist years of mid-century Britain...of hope and public purpose'.[10]

An increasing number of Conservatives are also persuaded that 'the community' is an appropriate slogan for post-Thatcherite politics. This is less surprising than it seems. High Toryism, since at least the time of Carlyle, has had a fondness for Germanic ideas of 'nation' and 'community'. It was a nineteenth-century German sociologist, Tonnies, who first employed the terms *Gemeinschaft* ('community') and *Gesellschaft* ('society') to distinguish between groups of people bound by ties of affection and groups of people associated with each other only by the division of labour and the law of contract. *Gemeinschaft* has always appealed to a certain kind of Conservative. The so-called 'One Nation' Conservatives, who trace their intellectual origins to the Disraeli of the Young England period, have a natural affinity with German sociological ideals. It is a bond they share with Christian Socialism.[11] The thinking of the so-called 'Wets' of the first Thatcher administration, who argued that their party had been captured by an alien creed of Manchester liberalism, owed more to German philosophy and its ideas of 'organic' community than they cared to admit. In *The Politics of Consent*, published a year after he left the government in 1983, Francis Pym argued that individualism had to be balanced by a sense of interdependence:

> The unrestrained exercise of individual will has produced the worst excesses of history, because it precludes relationship with others. The harmony of the world depends on its countless human relationships. A balanced individuality is the rock on which most secure relationships are built. ampant individualism is the rock on which they founder...However strong and self-reliant any of us may be, we are all dependent on others...Life is a partnership. Each individual is dependent on other individuals for both material and emotional needs, whether we choose to acknowledge this or not. Within any nation, all members of society must see themselves as interdependent, or society cannot function.[12]

Ian Gilmour's gravest charge against the Thatcherites, in a book published in 1992, was that they were 'blind to the existence of collectives'.[13] The book, which is an extended treatment of the view that the Conservative Party was captured by alien ideologues, is entitled *Dancing With Dogma*.

Ironically, the notion of community' has enabled Conservative politicians drawn from another wing of the party to make common cause with the former 'Wets'. The Home Secretary, Michael Howard, opined recently that 'man is a social as well as a political animal. He needs more than freedom to make sense of his life. Above all, he needs to belong as well as simply to be.'[14] John Patten, the former Education Secretary, has argued in the House of Commons that a 'new civic and community agenda...may dominate British politics for the next fifteen years just as surely as privatisation and other issues have dominated it for the past fifteen years'.[15] Dr John Gray argues that 'if the threat to a liberal form of life came in the Seventies from an invasive and overly ambitious State, in the Nineties it comes from the desolation and collapse of communities and the excesses of individualism, which have in fact been compounded by policies which conceive of marketisation as an all-purpose cure-all for economic and social ills. If, in the Seventies, the principal danger to liberal civilisation came from the hubris of government, in the Eighties and Nineties it has come from hubristic liberal ideology, in which a fetish is made of individual choice and the needs of solidarity and common life go unrecognised or spurned.'

Dr Gray writes, in an argument whose premises are virtually indistinguishable from those of Ian Gilmour, that liberalism has destroyed conservatism from within. He writes of the social effects of the free market policies of the last fifteen years:

> Communities are scattered to the winds by the gale of creative destruction. Endless 'downsizing' and 'flattening' of enterprises fosters ubiquitous insecurity and makes loyalty to the company a cruel joke. The celebration of consumer choice, as the only undisputed value in market societies, devalues commitment and stability in personal relationships and encourages the view of marriage and the family as vehicles of self-realisation. The dynamism of market processes dissolves social hierarchies and overturns established expectations. Status is ephemeral, trust frail and contract sovereign. The dissolution of communities promoted by market-driven labour mobility weakens where it does not entirely destroy, the informal social monitoring of behaviour which is the most effective preventive measure against crime.[16]

It is an astonishing catalogue of crimes – unemployment, inner-city deprivation, anomy, the dissolution of the family, the rising divorce rate, crime and more – to attribute to a recent, partially achieved and relatively short-lived episode in the political history of Britain. Gray is correspondingly pessimistic. Paradoxically, he forecasts class war and a reversion to nationalistic or even fascistic government unless orthodox politicians adopt the kind of policies - protectionism, environmentalism and a kind of Tawneyism, in which economic growth is subordinated to its social function – which would be much admired by nationalistic socialist or proto-fascist politicians. A programme of this kind is currently being popularised by Sir James Goldsmith.

The Snobbery of Collectivism

There is nothing new in the indictment of the false values of the materialistic consumer society. Plato and Aristotle both despised the commercial classes. The Bible is full of admonitions against the vain pursuit of riches. In medieval England the accumulative tendencies of trade and industry were blunted by the demands of the social hierarchy, and money-lending, subject to the usury laws, was left to Italians and Jews. Rousseau saw man in commercial society as a slave to the opinion of others, endlessly keeping up with the Joneses and consoling himself with material fripperies. The virtuousness of the farmer ('a stake in the country') and the wickedness of the trader is one of the longest running themes in Western thought and civilisation, but the mass-production of the industrial age gave it a new edge. Capitalism was thought to have necessitated a shift in the nature of material things, from the means of life to the end of life, because the allocation of resources was determined by market forces responsive only to the urge to consume. John Stuart Mill derided America as a country in which 'they have the six points of Chartism, and they have no poverty, and all that these advantages do for them is that the life of the whole of one sex is devoted to dollar-hunting and of the other to breeding dollar-hunters'.[17]

Karl Marx was expressing a commonplace view in Victorian England when he castigated a 'fetishism of commodities' which made people slaves to their own possessions.[18] Oscar Wilde despised the capitalist because he 'thought that the important thing was to have, and did not know that the important thing is to be'.[19] John Ruskin and William Morris became socialists primarily because capitalism littered the urban world with unbeautiful things and covered the countryside with towns. Even the apostle of Manchester Liberalism, Richard Cobden, counted it a great disappointment that he failed to moralise the entrepreneurial and industrial culture of the Victorian era. 'The perpetual chagrin of his life,' wrote his first biographer, 'was the obstinate refusal of those on whom he had helped to shower wealth and plenty to hear what he had to say on the social ideals to which their wealth should lead.'[20] In *The Acquisitive Society*, R. H. Tawney denounced the disposal of property by individuals under capitalism as lacking any 'social justification'.[21] Maynard Keynes, an acquisitive man fallen among Freudians, called the love of money 'a somewhat disgusting morbidity, one of the semi-criminal, semi-pathological propensities which one hands over with a shudder to specialists in mental disease'.[22] In the 1960S thousands of otherwise sensible people subscribed to a so-called 'counter-culture' which rejected consumerism despite the obvious dependence even of its own insignia – long-playing records, psychedelic T-shirts, flared trousers and joss-sticks – on mass-production techniques. Thirty years on, it is still fashionable to disparage materialism whilst enjoying its benefits.

The simultaneous worship and disparagement of material plenty is a modern paradox. It reflects a mixture of artificial disdain for material success, the bogus cultural resistance of the chattering classes, and the feelings of embarrassment and guilt that an unfulfilled longing for the nobility of poverty can produce. The production of material goods is arguably the single most important objective of the entire political and economic superstructure, yet politicians can still find a ready audience for their attacks on the consumerism on which it depends. Man is praised as producer, but reviled as consumer. The inverted snobbery of intellectuals, actors, novelists, film-makers, advertising executives, television journalists and some wealthy barristers and businessmen is amply chronicled. But perhaps, as Schumpeter predicted, capitalism is also a victim of its own success:

> Capitalism creates a critical frame of mind which, after having destroyed the moral authority of so many other institutions, in the end turns against

its own; the bourgeois finds to his amazement that the rationalist attack does not stop at the credentials of kings and popes, but goes on to attack private property and the whole scheme of bourgeois values. The bourgeois fortress thus becomes politically defenceless.[23]

The relentless search of the capitalist for cheaper and better ways of doing things is easily contrasted with the 'meaningful' nature of life and work in pre-capitalist society, and it is a comparison intellectual collectivists of all kinds are still subconsciously inclined to make.

There is also a certain amount of mental laziness at work. Understanding the law of comparative advantage, or the allocative function of the price mechanism, or the infinite amount of work there is to be done, or the fact that growth in a capitalist economy is literally without limit, takes a modest amount of intellectual effort. It is difficult to grasp that the global marketplace of today is in fact an extended order of co-operation between people who live thousands of miles from each other and have absolutely nothing in common.[24]

Likewise, almost everybody believes that personal greed is the sole motivating force of capitalism. In fact, entrepreneurs and investors are driven by an infinite variety of motives – including benevolence and altruism – which the mechanism of the market- place helps them to fulfil. The Body Shop, to take an obvious instance, is a firm which successfully combines both consumer capitalism and environmentalism: two ways of life widely thought to contradict each other absolutely. Free markets do depend on competition between different ways of running businesses, including working conditions, job security and means of remuneration, which collectivists believe should be uniform. But they also reward co-operative behaviour, in the shape of joint ventures, long-term business relationships and teamwork between managers and workers. Many critics also disregard the role played by the falling cost of technology – like water meters, road-pricing and telephone networks – in drawing into the market economy activities previously considered outside its scope.

At bottom, most people believe intuitively that capitalism is a zero-sum game, in which the winners take from the losers and multinational companies with huge advertising budgets manipulate people into buying what they do not need. Consumers undoubtedly do acquire material goods they want rather than need, and the shops are awash with culturally insignificant objects which require minimal effort to use, understand or operate. But, unlike the political choices made on behalf of the voters, the choices made by consumers are in no sense obligatory. It is part of the genius of capitalism to offer people a vast array of material and other possibilities which they are then free to accept or reject. People often prefer the baser options, but material plenty alone gives them the choice. They could just as easily choose to raise their moral, intellectual, artistic and cultural condition, because capitalism has lifted them out of dehumanising poverty and incessant labour and provided means enough to educate them, keep them healthy and purchase time for leisure. Indeed, the whole purpose of wealth and property, as John Locke saw it, was to enable 'all mankind to flourish as much as may be'.[25] People often spurn the best opportunities in favour of the worst. But, if the Good Life consists of the free enjoyment of the full development of the potentiality of each individual human being, more Good Lives are likely to be realised in a rich society than in a poor one. Unlike the starving millions of the agrarian economies of collectivist romance, or the hungry masses of the undeveloped world today, British men and women are free to choose what to do with the time and money release from the struggle for survival has given them.

Politicians and commentators are equally free to make propaganda against the choices which people make, but it is both pointless and objectionable to attempt to force people to be free of their baser self. Besides, a country in which, following Marx, it is possible to 'hunt in the morning, fish in the afternoon, rear cattle in the evening and criticise after dinner' is more likely to be realised under capitalism than any other system. Keynes pictured a future for capitalism in which all material wants were satiated and 'we shall honour those who can teach us how to pluck the hour and the day virtually and well, the delightful people who are capable of taking direct enjoyment in things, the lilies of the field, who toil not, neither do they spin'.[26] The higher productivity of the capitalist economy is already allowing people more leisure to enjoy its fruits. And its fruits, as Ferdinand Mount has pointed out, can have moral as well as material content:

> The car-worker refuses to accept that he is 'spiritually stunted'...simply because he works 46 hours a week on an assembly line. Nor would he dream of denying that the work is very boring. But he would and does strongly assert that he makes a deliberate choice, fully conscious of what he is sacrificing, in order to *provide a better life for his family*. That last phrase, hurried over with impatience by the intellectual obsessed with self-realisation, constitutes the heart of the argument. For working men do not tamely register contentment with their car, their washing-machine, their extra weeks of holiday and their warm, dry houses. And they do not passively accept these consumer durables in the way that a hard-worked carthorse munches its oats. They will argue, if strongly pressed, that these are, simply, good things because they make life easier *for one another*; wives are not worn out at the age of thirty-five, children are educated, husbands pay more attention to their wives, go out to pubs together. What is strongly contested by the working class is the definition of these goods as *materialist*; on the contrary, they are aggressively defined as of potential social and spiritual value and capable of altruistic uses. Seen from outside and above, from some Olympian spectators' stand, these goods may seem to be greedily devoured by materialist families; seen from ground level and from inside the family, the goods are seen as gifts and transfers between one member and another, charitable gifts which express affection and repay filial, parental and marital debts, thus blessing both the giver and the receiver.[27]

An earlier and more realistic generation of English socialists did not doubt that their primary task was to spread the goods things of life, not to lecture consumers about false values. In his memoirs, published in 1971, George Brown argued that post-war affluence- television sets, Mediterranean holidays, motor cars and so on – was the principal achievement of the Labour Party (he also thought, presciently, that it would make it more difficult for socialists to win elections). He did not like it – 'society in Britain nowadays is largely a selfish society,' he wrote – and forecast the rise of a new generation of socialists, who would have known motor cars and television all their life, and wanted ideals rather than more goods to consume.[28] Tony Blair, who was at school then, is living proof that he was right. Capitalism has to prove itself afresh to each new generation of collectivists.

A belief in the moral superiority of collectivism, like a decision to join the Unification Church or the Hare Krishnas, undoubtedly meets a psychological need. That yearning for a purer, better, more spiritual and 'less selfish' self, which has fuelled totalitarianism throughout the twentieth century, is now the last redoubt of a creed which is, by every objective test of its utility, an abject failure. Its adherents can be forgiven their nostalgia, but the sentimentality of collectivism is clouding a proper appreciation by the elite of the origins of our present catastrophe. The beginnings of the moral dissolution of the British way of life lie not in the selfishness unleashed by Margaret Thatcher during her relatively brief period in office during the 1980s but in the soul-destroying machinations of the collectivist State over the last one hundred years.

The Amoral State Against the Moral Individual

Moral behaviour is the result of individuals adhering to a code of conduct enforced not by the civil or criminal law, but by the private sanctions of praise or blame. Morality is not, by its nature, a province in which the State can hope to succeed. On those occasions where the State has attempted to redress specifically moral problems in recent years, like single parenthood, absent fathers and the age of homosexual consent, it has rightly looked ridiculous or arbitrary or both. Where the State is tempted to use the welfare system to discriminate between worthy and unworthy individuals, on the grounds that those who receive taxes must also pay them, an unattractive moral authoritarianism discloses itself. David Willetts provides a good example:

> The use of the welfare state as a powerful instrument to reinforce some of the elementary rules of behaviour is to give it an explicitly civic function. If it is recognised that the welfare state is a powerful civic institution then we are entitled to try to use it to reinforce the shared values of the community...We may perfectly legitimately want to identify certain categories of people for whom we wish to pay more than others. We may want to say that a war widow should receive more than an unemployed single man. We may be willing to see students taken out of social security on the grounds that this is the wrong way of starting their adult careers – whereas the same argument does not apply for, say, pensioners. These are not judgments about the moral worth of individuals, but they are

judgments about relevant differences between circumstances of different groups. There is a logic to focusing on categories of claimants rather than entirely on the incomes of individuals.[29]

There is certainly a logic to reducing benefits for some classes of claimant on the basis that some people are more deserving or needy than others. It is also logical to set up the Child Support Agency to pursue aberrant fathers for relying on the taxpayer to support their progeny. But it is precisely because they blur the fine distinction which separates exclusively political actions from moral decisions that policies of this kind are proving so troublesome to implement. Whether political decisions and moral judgments inhabit different spheres, or whether politically motivated actions have no moral content, or whether personal moral responsibility for political decisions is diluted or even suspended by virtue of holding political office, are questions best left to philosophers. It is clear only that no political action can be entirely independent of moral considerations. Those people who abuse politicians personally for implementing policies with which they disagree – as in 'Hey, hey, LBJ, how many kids did you kill today?' or 'Virginia Bottomley killed my daughter' – assume that they are personally and morally responsible for prosecuting wars, tolerating unemployment and homelessness, closing hospitals and schools and so on. Others argue that government, particularly in basic areas like law and order and the defence of the realm, would become impossible if politics was subordinated to morality. Politics is a mechanism by which moral choices are made. It is because it is such an inefficient and arbitrary mechanism that its role in moral arbitration should be circumscribed as far as possible.

Authentic moral choices, in which one person weighs the consequences of his actions on the lives of others, are pre-eminently the sphere of the individual conscience. They are made not under the threat of punishment by the State but on the basis of a personal capacity for indulgence or self-restraint. But that capacity is not an intuition planted by Nature. It is inculcated by the ethical ideas, beliefs, mores and habits of Western civilisation, rooted in the history of all but the most modern men and women and transmitted to successive generations by the variety of spontaneous, self- generating institutions through which they traditionally passed on their journey from the cradle to the grave. And it is because the State has narrowed the scope of individual conscience, and displaced and pulverised those institutions which were responsible for the transmission and enforcement of an informal moral code, that it is the main author of the current predicament.

The Bifurcation of Natural Law and Civil Law

The most important of the historic mechanisms for the transmission of moral codes of behaviour was the Christian Church, and it was for centuries part of the purpose of the State to uphold Christian institutions and values. This was not because morality and religion are interchangeable – manifestly, they are not

– or because pre-modern Britain was a theocracy. It is because morality and religion, and Church and State, were historically intertwined, and moral obedience was thought to depend on supernatural authority. For 1500 years morality was regarded as a part of the natural law, an unwritten code which had a higher moral claim on man than any law which was merely conventional in origin. Natural law and civil or conventional law overlapped, as in the classification of murder as a crime, but the motivation for obeying a moral law differed completely from the fear of detection and punishment in a case of murder. In Britain – where for hundreds of years not just the State, but the whole of intellectual and institutional life was suffused with the Christian faith – the legal code naturally reflected the values of Christianity

The laws of the land and the laws of heaven were mutually comprehensible and mutually supportive. The moral law under- pinned the ability of men and women to control their baser appetites, and the civil and criminal law was invoked only where people failed to do so. The Book of Common Prayer of the Church of England, for example, has never doubted that the political authorities are engaged in upholding Christian civilisation as well as civil society:

> We beseech thee also to save and defend all Christian Kings, Princes and Governors; and specially thy servant Elizabeth our Queen; that under her we may be godly and quietly governed: And grant unto her whole Council, and to all that are put in authority under her, that they may truly and indifferently minister justice, to the punishment of wickedness and vice, and to the maintenance of thy true religion, and virtue.[30]

In the Middle Ages men did not think of legislators and judges making law: God made it, and the authorities merely discovered it. It was not open to mere mortals to tinker with it or to change it. Until lawmaking became fully politicised in the nineteenth century, the laws of Church and State were seen as part of the same organic whole. It was expected that the values of Christian civilisation would be reflected in the laws and institutions of the State, and those who transgressed those values were punished as much by the opinion of their fellow Christians as they were by the majesty of the civil and criminal law.

Church and State began to separate at the time of the Reformation, but did not divorce completely until the nineteenth century. Political liberty originated in religious liberty – the gradual lifting of the civil disabilities of Dissenters, Jews and Catholics prefigured the achievement of civil liberties – and was, to that extent, the second step towards the secularisation of the State. Religious freedom undoubtedly complicated the task of maintaining a moral consensus on a religious basis, by fostering a scepticism about the claims of the supernatural. This undermined the Christian moral consensus. Morals are not philosophical opinions, susceptible of proof or disproof in reasoned argument, but commonplaces to which people are accustomed. Once religious truth became a matter of public debate, people naturally began to question the validity of its moral teaching. But the expectation that religion would become purely a matter of individual choice and cease to be a part of the political domain after the Toleration Act of 1689 failed to materialise in the eighteenth century. The Georgian era closed with a powerful evangelical religious revival, which persisted into the Victorian age. Organised religion remained a potent force in English politics until at least the First World War. Gladstone was able to mobilise popular religious opinion at the time of Italian unification in the 1860s, and again at the time of the Bulgarian massacres of the late 1870s. One of the obstacles the early English socialists encountered to acceptance of their creed was its association with atheistic doctrines. The Church of England was foremost among the established institutions of the State. Imperceptibly, it charged individuals with fundamental moral principles. It was a symbol of the continuity of the Christian moral consensus. It taught Property its duties to the poor, the destitute and the sick. It was rooted in the institution of the family, and hallowed the family life on which the transmission of moral values depended.

The early and mid-Victorians struck a difficult balance between the demands of the liberal State, the preservation of an established Church, the claims of reason and the evangelical conscience. They managed, in short, to secularise the State without secularising Society. It was only the advent of democracy which finally turned the State into the enemy of organised religion. The democratic State is by its nature wholly secular. A democratically elected government which tolerates several different religions cannot be seen to uphold or exert pressure on behalf of only one if it is to remain representative. Gladstone told Henry Manning at the beginning of his career that 'politics would be an utter blank to me were I to make the discovery that we were mistaken in maintaining their association with religion'.[31] But by the time he died in 1898 democracy had prised apart State and Church, freedom and morality, politics and theology. Moreover, as the State moved into its democratic-collectivist phase it ceased to be concerned only with the enlargement of the freedom of the individual. Politics itself became a moral project, in which the restriction of freedom and the expropriation of property were the instruments of the eradication of the moral evil of poverty. During the twentieth century collectivist politics replaced religion for many people as the chief vehicle of zeal and commitment. Politics became, for the first time in the history of Britain, a moral activity. The government of the country ceased to be imbued with Christian principles, precepts and values and became instead the plaything of what John Stuart Mill called the 'tyranny of opinion'.

It was part of the price of the nationalisation of education, for example, that it should be accompanied by its secularisation. For the Victorians, the purpose of all education was to teach morality, and in particular a morality based on Christianity. This was not a task which a representative democratic State was in a position to perform. When R. A. Butler included in the 1944 Education Act a requirement on State schools to conduct a daily act of worship and to include regular religious instruction in the curriculum, he relied on all the main religious denominations to agree an appropriate syllabus. By doing so, he was not so much honouring this long-standing function of the educational system as burying it. As Harold Laski pointed out at the time, by endorsing compulsory religious education the churches were 'announcing that they have exhausted their religious vitality and desire to be no more than an arm of the State's police power'.[32] Today, of course, the State cannot risk offending ethnic minorities by teaching Christianity alone. The best the government can manage is compulsory religious education weighted in favour of Christianity. Most teachers are no longer practising Christians anyway. They are primarily public sector employees, imbued with all the political correctness of their caste and answerable to local and national State officials whose political masters cannot afford to offend non-Christian voters. The modern religious syllabus is obliged to incorporate the other three major religions of the world-Judaism, Islam and Buddhism – as well as Christianity, and religious matters are more likely to be explained in factual than in moral terms.

The nationalisation and secularisation of education was one of the many ways in which democracy shattered the shared religious opinions – the moral consensus – on which the government of the country had been based since the Dark Ages. Cardinal Manning had expressed his fear of the consequences in a letter to his friend, the Prime Minister, William Gladstone, as early as November 1871:

> Of this I am sure as of the motion of the earth. My belief is that faith is gone from society as such; morals are going; and politics will end in the paralysis of the governing power. The end of this must be anarchy or despotism. How soon I do not know. France is there already: Italy will be: and England will not stand for ever. I have been a fearless Radical all my life; and am not afraid of popular legislation, but legislation without principles is in strict sense anarchy. I see no principle now but the will of the majority; the will of the majority is not either reason or right. My belief is that Society without Christianity is the Commune...What hope can you give me?[33]

Zealous collectivists detested religion because it commanded a loyalty higher than loyalty to the State. Many of the early English socialists, like George Bernard Shaw, were for this reason fiercely atheistic. In its extreme forms, collectivism itself became a substitute religion. Hegel made the State, not the Church, the objective truth and perfect morality towards which the individual was striving. In Marxism, religion was not merely socially undesirable - a part of the 'false consciousness' of the proletarian in bourgeois society, a symptom of social division or a reflection of a particular mode of production – but an actual moral evil, which kept men in a state of servility by reconciling them to their alienated condition. In the dominant State ideology of the twentieth century, all moralities were merely instruments of social control or tools of class oppression. 'Communists,' wrote Marx in 1845, 'preach no morality at all.'[34]

The Impossibility of Deriving Ethics From Reason Alone

The secularisation of the democratic State is not yet complete. The Church of England remains established, its prelates endure in the House of Lords and the sovereign is still Defender of the Faith. But the disestablishment of the Church is openly discussed by journalists, politicians, bishops and even princes. The Archbishop of Canterbury himself is too afraid of being accused of ethnocentricity or even racialism to resist the State edict that religious instruction in its schools encompass five or six major world religions rather than Christianity alone. Liberals everywhere argue without serious fear of contradiction that the blasphemy laws are ripe for abolition, or at least for extension to other creeds. The Church, in intellectual retreat since the Enlightenment, lacks the confidence and the numbers to preach a faith undiluted by contemporary democratic concerns and has itself become merely the supernatural branch of the collectivist moral project. It is often forgotten how recent this is. The membership of the Church of England has been in relative decline ever since it failed to capture the urban proletariat during the second half of the nineteenth century, but its loss of power as a social institution is heavily concentrated into the last seventy-five years or so. The First World War marked the beginning of a steep and absolute decline in Church membership, though it did not reach its present derisory levels until after the Second World War. The Church of England now claims a membership of 1.81 million, less than a twentieth of the adult population and a smaller number of adherents than the Church of Rome. But the total membership of all the main denominations in the United Kingdom in 1992 was 6.72 million people, or just 15 per cent of the adult population. This is one fifth less than the total as recently as 1975.[35] Although various forms of religious enthusiasm – Mormons, Jehovah's Witnesses and the like – are growing, as are Oriental affiliations like Islam and Hinduism, organised religion has less social influence today than at any time since Augustine landed in Kent in 597. One survey showed that the United Kingdom had the lowest level of active Church membership among adults in Europe.

The secularisation of a country is a prolonged and complicated process, with sociological as well as intellectual origins. As recently as 1905 it was thought scandalous for the Prime Minister, Arthur Balfour, to have played golf on a Sunday, but the twentieth century has since given rise to a host of competing attractions to going to Church. One survey found that most young people preferred to lie in bed with the *Sunday Times*, pausing between the supplements only to fornicate. Shops, restaurants, country houses, sports events and car boot sales are all now an integral part of the post-coital British Sunday. Modern transport and communications have also made people more mobile, broadening the range of leisure activities and dissolving the social unacceptability of not going to Church. The urban life of the city, and its utilitarian ethic, seem soulless and mechanical, and the Church lacked a physical presence in the poorer quarters of the new industrial towns until the modern economy was far advanced.

But science is a more formidable enemy of religion than sociology. Reason has mounted a variety of attacks on religion since at least the seventeenth century, and the highly influential writings of Voltaire and Rousseau derived from the eighteenth. But it was the powerful scientific ideas of the industrial age – especially those of evolution – which were ultimately most destructive of Christianity. Intellectual doubt did not penetrate popular consciousness immediately. For most Victorians and Edwardians, morality was still objectively ascertainable. 'Opinions alter, manners change, creeds rise and fall,' the Roman Catholic Lord Acton declared in his inaugural lecture at Cambridge in 1895, 'but the moral law is written on the tablets of eternity.'[36]

Victorian intellectuals, alarmed by the moral implications of popular release from the fear of the supernatural, made strenuous efforts to prove that Christian doctrine and Christian ethics were completely separable. But this, as Owen Chadwick has pointed out, was a task in which it was impossible to succeed except in the narrowest terms:

> At the beginning of the [nineteenth] century nearly everyone was persuaded that religion and morality were inseparable; so inseparable that moral education must be religious education, and that no sense of absolute obligation in conscience could be found apart from religion. That moral philosophers taught the contrary made no difference. Except in the case of a small number of exceptional groups or people, morality never had been separated from religion in the entire history of the human race; and therefore those who undertook to provide a system of morality which should have no links with religion, because they were convinced that the prevailing religion was in ruins, had a task of exceptional difficulty, a task which was perhaps beyond their power if they wished to make their system of morality no mere theory but a system which would touch the conscience of a large number of ordinary men and women... There is all the difference between a philosophical theory of ethics, which is always likely to be the property of a small group of specially equipped thinkers, and a system of ethics which has the potency to be acceptable in society.[37]

John Stuart Mill's essay, *Utilitarianism*, reflects the difficulty of trying to base Christian morals on the principle of utility. 'In the golden rule of Jesus of Nazareth,' he writes at one point, 'we read the complete spirit of the ethics of utility. To do as one would be done by, and to love one's neighbour as oneself, constitute the ideal perfection of utilitarian morality.'[38]

Mill and the utilitarians were driven eventually to rely on a mixture of education, habit, memory (of the pleasure of right actions, and the pain of wrong ones) and mutual convenience to heave the moral imperative into line with th greatest happiness of the greatest number. Henry Sidgwick, the professor of moral philosophy at Cambridge at the time Acton spoke, laboured mightily but without success to devise a more coherent system of utilitarian ethics. Leslie Stephen tried to base a new system of ethics on evolution. Auguste Comte, who accepted that religion was one of the foundations of moral life, resorted to the desperate expedient of founding a new religion of science. The early John Stuart Mill was much impressed by Comte's scheme to use education and social discipline to replace 'egoism' with 'altruism', and even argued that the new Religion of Humanity should incorporate some aspects of conventional religion, such as belief in a deity.[39] Like Comte, he recognised the utility of religion, as 'the strong and earnest direction of the emotions and desires towards an ideal object, recognised as of the highest excellence, and as rightfully paramount over all selfish objects of desire'.[40] It was significant that not one of these thinkers doubted that, if it was at all possible to have morality without Christianity, the morality would still be Christian. The intellectuals who thought otherwise or even hated Christian ethics, like Marx, Nietzsche, Kierkegaard, Ibsen and Lawrence, came later. A practical moral sense was almost universal in Victorian and Edwardian England, but the theoretical foundations destroyed by science were never properly rebuilt. The moral injunctions Victorians and Edwardians intuitively grasped as a result of their education, habits and collective memory lacked intellectual authority, once the supernatural sanction was withdrawn.

Living in a highly moralised age also made Victorian and Edwardian thinkers unduly optimistic about the moral capacity of modern, liberal man. High-mindedly – naively, even – they expected men and women to follow their highest and best interests and instincts without the sanction of divine authority, moral consensus or religious dogma. 'Liberty as a principle,' argued the later Mill, 'has no application to any state of things anterior to the time when mankind have become capable of being improved by free and equal discussion. Until then, there is nothing for them but implicit obedience to an Akbar or a Charlemagne, if they are so fortunate as to find one.'[41] Some of those brought up in this intellectual milieu eventually realised how much they had taken Christian ethics for granted, and the contribution organised religion made to the enforcement of moral rules which were useful for reasons quite unconnected with the supernatural. In 1934 John Maynard Keynes, whose beliefs were formed in the pagan and sensual intellectual climate of Edwardian Cambridge, wrote a letter to Virginia Woolf: 'I begin to see that our generation – yours and mine...owed a great deal to our fathers' religion. And the young...who are brought up without it, will never get so much out of life. They're trivial: like dogs in their lusts. We had the best of both worlds. We destroyed Christianity, yet had its benefits.'[42]

Keynes's intellectual mentor was G. E. Moore, the Cambridge philosopher best remembered for coining the term Naturalistic Fallacy, to describe the difficulty Reason has in identifying the natural properties of goodness, or in making the awkward passage David Hume identified from facts ('is') to values ('ought'). This finally detached morality from any belief in Natural Law, apparently making it impossible to describe moral goodness in normal terms and giving rise to modern expressions like 'value judgment' and 'value-free' to distinguish between factual description and moral judgment. It made all moral judgments seem purely subjective, more like bigotries or prejudices than the results of rational moral discourse. The Naturalistic Fallacy left morality dependent on a form of intuitionism, or the belief that fundamental moral truths are apprehended not by empirical observation, but through some autonomous moral faculty. Moore could still assume, as Mill and the Victorians had before him, that people had both the moral faculty and the will and intelligence to use it. In a paper delivered in 1938, entitled My Early Beliefs, Keynes regretted the naivety of this brand of thinking:

We repudiated all versions of the doctrine of original sin...We were not aware that civilisation was a thin and precarious crust erected by the personality and will of a very few, and only maintained by rules and conventions skilfully put across and guilefully preserved. We had no respect for traditional wisdom or the restraints of custom. We lacked reverence...[We believed] the human race already consists of reliable, rational, decent people, influenced by truth and objective standards, who can be safely released from the outward restraints of convention and traditional standards and inflexible rules of conduct, and left, from now onwards, to their own sensible devices, pure motives and reliable institutions of the good...We entirely repudiated a personal responsibility on us to obey general rules...We repudiated entirely customary morals, conventions and traditional wisdom.[43]

Keynes was deeply conscious, in retrospect, of how much his optimistic view of human nature owed to the network of rules, conventions and institutions he and his generation inherited from the Victorians.

The Destructive Effects of the Great War

That network was pulverised by the First World War. To an age saturated with sex, journalism and soap opera the hundreds of thousands of men who flooded the recruiting stations on the outbreak of war in 1914 seem at best naive and at worst the willing dupes of the Old Lie: *Dulce et Decorum Est Pro Patria Mori*. In fact, they were impelled by neither naivety nor by a saccharine patriotism concocted by unscrupulous politicians and the popular press. They were private family men whose public lives rarely extended beyond the vast multitude of entirely private organisations and institutions which filled the free hours of ordinary people in an age not yet acquainted with the Welfare State and television. Their primary motive was their anxiety not to let down their family, friends and colleagues. The military historian John Keegan has characterised that pre-lapsarian England as an age 'of vigorous and buoyant urban life, rich in differences and in a sense of belonging – to workplaces, to factories, to unions, to churches, chapels, charitable organisations, benefit clubs, Boy Scouts, Boys' Brigades, Sunday Schools, cricket, football, rugby, skittle clubs, old boys' societies, city of fices, municipal departments, craft guilds – to any one of those hundreds of bodies from which the Edwardian Briton drew his security and sense of indentify'.[44]

Joe Hoyles, a former rifleman at the Battle of the Somme, told Lyn Macdonald why he had joined up:

There were five of us joined up together, Archie Nicholson, Fred Lyons, Frank Bell, Sid Birkett and myself. We all worked at W. H. Smith's in Nottingham. I'd absolutely made up my mind and, when we went up to the barracks to join up, I said, 'We're going into the finest regiment in the British Army.' And they said, 'What's that?' And I said, 'The Rifle Brigade.

Left of the Line and pride of the British Army.' I was only seventeen, but it was a unique regiment to me. In my own little town of Oakham, there were two officers of the Rifle Brigade who used to come home on leave and they looked so smartly dressed in the green and black and always with a black sash around their shoulders. It caught my eye.[45]

The names of the regiments, brigades and divisions all testified to a local rather than a national patriotism. In the Pals Battalions the recruits were often from a single town, village, factory, street, shop or sports club, and they rarely referred to themselves as parts of an Army Corps, Division or Battalion. They were the 'Sheffield Pals' or the 'Hull Mob'. This was true of officers as much as men. Lionel Sotheby, an officer drawn from quite the opposite end of the social spectrum1 to Joe Hoyles, wrote that 'Eton will be to the last, the same as my Parents and dear Friends are to me now... To die for one's school is an honour.'[46]

The England of 1914 enjoyed a strong moral order as well as a vital civic culture. On the outbreak of the conflict the Secretary of State for War, Lord Kitchener, was able without fear of ridicule to issue the following written advice to the men of the British Expeditionary Force as they left for France:

Be invariably courteous, considerate and kind. Never do anything likely to injure or destroy property and always look upon looting as a disgraceful act. You are sure to meet with a welcome and be trusted; your conduct must justify that welcome and that trust. Your duty cannot be done unless your health is sound. So keep constantly on your guard against any excesses. In this new experience you may find temptations both in wine and women. You must entirely resist both temptations, and, while treating all women with perfect courtesy, you should avoid any intimacy. Do your duty bravely, Fear God, Honour the King.[47]

The message seems absurdly prim today. But in those far-off days liberty was popularly perceived not as permissiveness or the right to do as one pleased, but as the opportunity to do as one ought. 'The liberty,' as Acton expressed it, 'to do not what we like but what we ought.'[48] The historian E. L. Woodward wrote after the war that he had joined up not to resist German barbarism, but because he felt it was morally wrong to resist the laws of his country merely because they no longer suited his individual preferences. An identity between individual wishes and the public good still seemed eminently possible, provided people worked hard, did their duty and exercised self-restraint. Liberty was then a doctrine not of rights but of duties. Most of the men did not know it, but they were living proof of John Stuart Mill's expectant belief that morality could survive the death of God, at least temporarily, because it had attained a new and objective reality in the social and voluntary institutions of the country and was validated by both law and public opinion. 'Hence it is said with truth,' wrote Mill in *A system of Logic*, that none but a person of confirmed virtue is completely free.'[49]

The conception of liberty as duty struggled to survive the horrors and slaughter of the trenches. The imminent threat of death is a solvent of all virtue, and the war had a coarsening effect on every kind of personal behaviour. By the end of the conflict Kitchener's Army was not so much preventing intimacy between men and women, as organising official brothels. The war machine counted 416,891 cases of venereal disease among British servicemen between 1914 and 1948. Morals loosened on the Home Front too. Fornication and adultery became widespread, as the trenches reminded men of the transience of human life. (The fear of death is a famously prolific author of venery, Mass Observation finding in the Second World War that the Blitz led to a vast increase in unpremeditated and sexual intercourse.) The war also gave many men the novel experience of travelling abroad, and work in the factories took women away from home for the first time. Almost all young adults had more money, and less parental control, than before the war. Contraceptive sheaths became universally available for the first time during the war though this did not prevent an increase of a third in the number of illegitimate births. On Armistice Day total strangers copulated in public in Trafalgar Square.[50] Marriages and divorces increased. Skirts became shorter, and brassieres and cosmetics more popular.

At the front, swearing and obscene songs became commonplace. It is hard to imagine respectable Victorians enjoying the bawdy songs of the kind the men sang on their way to the front:

> Do your balls hang low?
> Do they dangle to and fro?
> Can you tie them in a knot?
> Can you tie them in a bow?
> Do they itch when it's hot?
> Do you rest them in a pot?
> Do you get them in a tangle?
> Do you catch them in the mangle?
> Do they swing in stormy weather?
> Do they tickle with a feather?
> Do they rattle when you walk?
> Do they jingle when you talk?
> Can you sling them on your shoulder,
> Like a lousy fucking soldier?

Lyn Macdonald recounts a story of Haig reproving a Colonel for allowing his battalion to sing this song on the march as late as 1916.[51] But it was during the First World War that the word 'fuck' achieved conversational respectability for the first time. After the Somme and Passchendaele, the pre-war faith in virtues like duty, honour, character, integrity, service and sacrifice seemed absurdly naive. Cynicism, derision and disenchantment took their place. It may be hard to believe it, but the football hooligans who wrecked the Heysel Stadium are the spiritual heirs of the men who fought and died in the trenches.

Faith in the integrity and competence of the political and military leadership of the country also failed to survive the First World War, diminishing faith in statesmen and opening a gulf between the generations. The wilting faith of the young in the authority of their seniors was captured by Siegfried Sassoon in his poem *The General*:

> 'Good morning; good morning!' the General said
> When we met him last week on our way to the line.
> Now the soldiers he smiled at are most of 'em dead.
> And we're cursing his staff for incompetent swine.
> 'He's a cheery old card,' grunted Harry to Jack
> As they sloggged up to Arras with rifle and pack.
> But he did for them both by his plan of attack.

In another poem Wilfred Owen rewrote the ending of the story of Abraham and Isaac, to make the old man kill his son rather than the ram.

Religious leaders were completely discredited, partly by their willingness to play the role of recruiting sergeant for the State and partly because they failed to find any convincing theology of war. Most clergymen were swept up in the patriotic fervour, decking churches in flags and standards and bombarding their congregations with jingoistic sermons. The Bishop of London himself, Dr Arthur Winnington-Inram, told one congregation that:

> To save Liberty's own self, to save the honour of women and the innocence of children, everything that is noblest in Europe, everything that loves freedom and honour, everyone that puts principle above ease, and life itself beyond mere living, are banded in the great crusade – we cannot deny it – to kill Germans: to kill them not for the sake of killing, but to save the world; to kill the good as well as the bad, to kill the young men as well as the old, to kill those who have shown kindness to our wounded as well as those fiends who crucified the Canadian sergeant, who superintended the Armenian massacres; who sank the *Lusitania* and who turned the machine-guns on the civilians of Aerschott and Louvain – and to kill them lest the civilisation of the world should itself be killed.[32]

Like Auschwitz for a later generation, the horrors of the trenches made it impossible for many to believe any longer in a benevolent God. The experience opened up a great gulf between God and human experience. Any faith in religion I ever had is most frightfully shaken by the things I've seen,' wrote one Englishman killed in the war.[33] A famous Army padre, Geoffrey Studdert-Kennedy (Woodbine Willie), was driven by this experience of the Western Front to the heretical conclusion that God Himself suffered in the trenches with the soldiers. 'I was crucified in Cambrai, And again outside Bapaume; I was scourged for miles along the Albert Road, I was driven, pierced and bleeding, With a million maggots feeding, On the body that I carried as my load,' as he put it in one of his rough rhymes.[34] But his argument that all Christian ethics was a call to suffer with God did not convince. Either God did not exist or, if He was prepared to preside over such horrors, He was monstrous.

The Age of Moral Relativity

Post-war intellectual enthusiasms were also hostile to the survival of traditional morality. Marxism, which became popular in England for the first time between the wars, saw all moralities as relative to the economic and social structure and traditional morality as a bourgeois construct without independent stature, which was doomed to expire with the bourgeoisie in the holocaust of revolution. 'The Ruling Ideas of each age,' argued the *Communist Manifesto*, 'have ever been the ideas of its ruling class.' Men and women who appeared to be making moral choices were in reality just pathetic reflections of vast and impersonal economic forces whose workings they could barely understand, let alone defy. All subsequent sociological thinking was merely a succession of variants on this original Marxian relativity. Emile Durkheim, the inventor of modern sociology, argued that law has authority only when underpinned by the moral authority of social norms, and that as the norms change so can the law. Max Weber, whose argument that scientific sociology must deal in facts alone drew inspiration directly from G. E. Moore and the Naturalistic Fallacy, longed for a 'value-free' analysis of the human condition, and explained submission to authority in purely sociological terms.

'But what good do morals do us?' asked Friedrich Nietzsche, who argued that Christian morality was no more than a plot to restrain exceptional talents and that people should make up their own moralities. He believed that in cruelty rather than pity lay the glory of mankind. Sigmund Freud, like Nietzsche, portrayed man as a being in the grip of dark forces which cannot be properly understood. In his view, the impulses underlying moral (and even rational) behaviour were fraudulent. By encouraging people to shed their 'repressed' natures, he discredited the whole notion of self-control. His ideas achieved popular currency in England after the First World War, where a vogue for psychology was stimulated by the experience of 'shell shock' during the conflict. *The Interpretation of Dreams* was published as long ago as 1900, but the 'unconscious', the 'ego', and the 'inferiority' and 'Oedipus complexes' did not pass into everyday usage until the 1920s. Freudianism not only provided a rational underpinning for the liberation of 'repressed' sexual appetites, but undermined public confidence in the view that criminals were invariably bad. Freud made it respectable to think that people were acting out of unconscious motivation. It was in 1923 that the British Medical Association first recommended the appointment of psychiatric experts to assess the mental condition of criminals, and psychiatric evidence gradually became admissible in court. If even criminals were not bad but sick, there was little hope of choosing between right and wrong in any sphere of human activity. 'Man was now left to himself, yet he was not even master of his own intelligence and will,' was how the historian Llewellyn Woodward found the post-war world. 'It would appear that he was free only to laugh, and the echo of this laughter down the corridors of time was not a pleasant sound.'[55]

Sexual morality, already undermined by the war, was further tilted in a permissive direction by the purely behavioural approach of anthropologists like

Malinowski. Cultural anthropology taught relativity in its most trivial form, indicating that what was good and true in one culture was not necessarily so in another. This made it very difficult for people to criticise the behaviour of others, for fear that they were judging them by inappropriate standards. Philosophical anthropologists added historicism to the relativistic brew of their cultural colleagues, or the belief that an age can be understood only by reference to its own beliefs and principles. This further damaged confidence in universal human values by making it impossible to reach definitive judgments even about the past, for fear of applying inappropriate concepts and standards. Historians are routinely castigated for judging the past by the standards of the present. This is in many ways admirable, but it can make it difficult to condemn even such obvious evils as the extermination of European Jews. The American academic James Wilson recalls a discussion about the Holocaust with one of his students. 'It all depends on your perspective,' the student said. 'I'd first have to see those events through the eyes of the people affected by them.'[56]

In the field of philosophy, Wittgenstein denied that there is any universal truth and argued that thought and conduct were merely word-games. Language imposed its own vision on the world. People could not hope to know anything about the inner experiences of another when they could not share those experiences, and merely inferred them from the way they behaved. Logic was relative. Asking why people did things became logically improper. It is now thought that Wittgenstein was clinically insane, but in their time his obscure ideas did much to destroy confidence in philosophy as a guide to right actions. The existentialism invented by Kierkegaard and developed by Heidegger and Sartre attracted few followers in a still relatively commonsensical Britain, but its emphasis on self-development could not but deny the existence of an objective morality. Its adherents urged people to make up their own moral codes. Even the new social sciences of economics and sociology were apt to examine people en masse, and treat them as rational calculators rather than as morally responsible individuals. And in the natural sciences Einstein's theories of relativity, devised and empirically proven between 1905 and 1923, buried the Newtonian universe of absolute time, length and motion forever. If even time and space were relative, men mistakenly but understandably concluded, there could be no absolute knowledge, objective truth, ascertainable value or right and wrong. 'Everything being now relative,' as John Galsworthy put it in *A Modern Comedy*, 'there is no longer absolute dependence to be placed on God, Free Trade, Marriage, Consols, Coal or Caste.'[57]

All of these novel ideas were characterised by determinism (the view that everything has a cause, or that there is no room for free will and so no room for praise or blame) or relativism (the view that beliefs and principles have no universal validity but are specific to the time, place and group in which they are held) or both. These two methods, common to science and perverted science alike, are the mortal enemies of morality. If all moralities are purely conventional, or relative to time and place, none can have universal validity. Likewise, if everything that happens is determined, moral choices simply cannot be made. 'Determinism,' writes Isaiah Berlin, 'clearly takes the life out of a whole range of moral expressions.'[58] If relativism was a novel threat, determinism was a problem of long standing. The medieval and early modern Church was a dedicated opponent of astrology precisely because it was incompatible with the Christian doctrines of human free will and moral autonomy. People were as quick then to attribute their moral failings to the influence of the planets as the patients of psychiatrists are today to blame personal weaknesses on child-abuse or sub-conscious memory.[59]

Shakespeare, who wrote at a time when astrology was still taken seriously, saw the truth clearly enough:

> This is the excellent foppery of the world, that when we are sick in fortune – often the surfeit of our own behaviour – we make guilty of our disasters the sun, the moon, and the stars: as if we were villains by necessity, fools by heavenly compulsion, knaves, thieves and treachers by spherical predominance; drunkards, liars and adulterers by an enforced obedience of planetary influence; and all that we are evil in, by a divine thrusting on: an admirable evasion of whoremaster man, to lay his goatish disposition to the charge of a star![60]

Astrology was the means medieval and early modern men and women chose to explain the inexplicable and to evade moral responsibility. In its capacity to provide excuses for even the most egregious behaviour, and to proffer explanations for events or behaviour for which no rational explanation can be adduced, sociology and psychiatry are merely the modern equivalents of astrology. rimlrials were riot slow to see the possibilities. A broken home, a forceps birth, a poor education, even 'the black rage' which stems from generations of racialism, are routinely advanced in mitigation of serious crimes.

The relentless determinism and materialism of modern science, though perfectly respectable and even beautiful in the laboratory, becomes in the wider context another bludgeon of the morally responsible individual. Chemicals can be used successfully to alter states of mind. Francis Crick, a Nobel laureate on account of his co-discovery of DNA, recently published a book which reduced human consciousness to what he called 'the behaviour of a vast assembly of nerve cells and their associated molecules'. Darwinian biology, the first science to dispense with the need for God, portrays a world of blind indifference in which the good are as likely to perish as the bad. 'Nature red tooth and claw', as Tennyson noted even before the publication of Origin of Species, mocks the humane and kindly feelings of moral individuals.[61] The genetic determinism of modern biology, if it leaves the individual free to make moral choices at all, reduces it to a self-interested strategy for survival.

Likewise, physicists, if they complete their search for a grand unifying theory, will possess a method of terrifying deterministic power. They will, as Stephen Hawking puts it, 'know enough to determine what happens in all but the most extreme situations'. But as Hawking himself asks:

> If we are all determined by grand unified theory, none of us can help what we do, so why should anyone be held responsible for what they do?[62]

He believes human beings retain free will because their behaviour is still unpredictable, partly on account of the uncertainty principle of quantum mechanics, but mainly because it is simply too difficult to perform the necessary mathematical calculations to make accurate predictions at the level of the human brain. The ability to predict the future accurately would also, of course, enable people to alter the outcome. He concludes that free will is an 'effective theory', perhaps untrue but chosen for us by natural selection and usable in everyday moral discourse and decisions. This is an exceptionally weak theoretical foundation for moral behaviour.

The Pervasive Influence of Bad Ideas

Hawking is satisfied by it because he believes that the study of human behaviour and the investigation of the fundamental laws of science can (and should) be kept entirely separate. Unfortunately, this is impossible. The ideas of the scientists and social scientists of the nineteenth and twentieth centuries may appear far removed from everyday life, but they have demonstrated a consistent ability to insinuate themselves into the private lives even of uneducated men and women. In the famous and oft-quoted concluding passage of the *General Theory of Employment, Interest and Money*, Keynes argued that 'the ideas of economists and political philosophers, both when they are right and when they are wrong, are more powerful than is commonly understood. Indeed the world is ruled by little else...I am sure that the power of vested interests is vastly exaggerated compared with the gradual encroachment of ideas...Soon or late, it is ideas, not vested interests, which are dangerous for good or evil.'[63]

Intellectuals dispute quite how this process occurs. Some think ideas cause social and moral change – as in the notion that Rousseau 'caused' the French Revolution – whilst others take the quasi-Marxist view that new ideas are the fruit of the efforts of men to make sense of changed economic and social conditions. There is a famous story that Voltaire refused to allow atheism to be discussed in front of the servants. 'I want my lawyer, my tailor, my servants, even my wife, to believe in God,' he said, 'then I shall be robbed and cuckolded less often.'[64] Likewise, John Stuart Mill thought that his atheism was so dangerous that it should be confined to 'really superior intellects and characters...in the case of all others I would much rather, as things now are, try to improve their religion than to destroy it'.[65] Before the age of mass communications, it was perhaps possible to think that atheism could be confined to the salon. But, in an age of travel, cheap newspapers and universal education, it is obvious, as T. S. Eliot once put it, that 'the ideas which flatter a current tendency or emotional attitude will go farthest; and some others will be distorted to fit in with what is already accepted'.[66]

Those individuals most likely to appropriate (and distort) ideas useful to their cause are what Hayek unflatteringly called 'second- hand dealers in ideas' – dons, teachers, journalists, clergymen, novelists, and so on – whose primary interest is to advance an argument by novelty rather than truth. The politician, if he is alive to his constituency, is then obliged to take them seriously. When the Bishop of Birmingham, for example, criticised the National Health Service reforms for reducing patients 'to the status of a unit of consumption and exchange' he was expressing the widespread, though mistaken, view that market economics is a zero-sum game, like a chain letter or the National Lottery, in which the winners gain at the expense of the losers. The criticism was not even relevant to the problem at hand. But it was quickly seized upon by journalists, who asked the then shadow Health Secretary, David Blunkett, to express a view. He, needless to say, saw the Bishop's comments as confirmation of his view that there is a 'contradiction…between commercial values and caring ones'.[67] This is the process by which bad ideas, as well as good ones, are turned into public opinion.

Relativistic and deterministic modes of thinking once confined to the laboratory or the library are transmitted by a host of unseen processes to a wider audience, gradually making them part of the common intellectual methodology of the unsophisticated majority. They have left moral behaviour and moral discourse in a thoroughly confused condition. Right and wrong are always relative. Discrimination between good and bad is moral authoritarianism. In a world of individual freedom and moral autonomy, people must work out their own moralities. Some want to save the rain-forests, others to cure poverty by exporting the trees. Some people think all vivisection is wrong, and others that it is justifiable for medical research. Isaiah Berlin believes that there is now such an incommensurable plurality of values, it is impossible to embed any moral convictions at all. A nationwide poll of people under thirty-five bears this judgment out. Two out of three could no longer tell right from wrong; few could recall more than three of the Ten Commandments and, when shown them, considered an average of only five to be important; two in five thought there were no absolute rights or wrongs; and nearly half thought moral questions should be decided by majority vote.[68]

Morality has become an intellectual leap of faith ungrounded in rational argument, or a matter for determination by the normal processes of majoritarian democracy. There is no single or absolute answer any more to the primal question: how shall we live? People are trapped in a solipsistic void, in which the promptings of the individual conscience are right and true precisely because they are the promptings of the individual conscience. Even a senior clergyman of the Church of England, who might be expected to see the moral life as a dialogue between man and God or Truth, argues instead that 'establishing truths of faith and morals is an ongoing task offering – usually – only provisional answers. There is only a continuing dialogue between scripture, tradition, reason and contemporary knowledge. Absolutes are not on offer.'[69] Perhaps only the Pope, and Evangelical Christian or Muslim fanatics, dare to believe that there are still absolute moral truths out there some- where awaiting apprehension by man.

The End of Moral Absolutism

Alasdair MacIntyre, in an influential book first published in 1981, argued that in the absence of morals justified by appeals either to tradition or to the supernatural, moral argument becomes merely interminable. Traditional moralities are specific to time and place, trapped in personal and social histories rather than universally true, and dominant in any particular culture only because one moral order was challenged successfully by another. ;ven moralities ostensibly based on Reason cannot escape this specificity. Each prevailing moral order, in other words, is merely the best so far. 'Morality which is no particular society's morality,' writes MacIntyre, 'is to be found nowhere. There was the-morality-of-fourth-century-Athens, there were the-moralities-of-thirteenth- century-Western Europe, there are numerous such moralities, but where ever was or is morality as such?'[70]

It follows that Reason alone is unable to devise a justifiable set of moral principles invulnerable to all objections. As MacIntyre puts it:

> We have all too many disparate and rival moral concepts...the moral resources of the culture allow us no way of settling the issue between them rationally. Moral philosophy, as it is dominantly understood, reflects the debates and disagreements of the culture so faithfully that its controversies turn out to be unsettleable in just the way that the political and moral debates themselves are. It follows that our society cannot hope to achieve moral consensus.[71]

Ultimately, he thinks, moral claims rest solely on assertion, or even personal opinion or preference, bolstered by selective mining of past moral orders and the implausible inventions of their modern successors. 1 ne moral characters which emerge, he says, are the Aesthete, who pursues sensual pleasures without limit, and the Manager, who manipulates life and society in the interests of stability rather than good. Often, these two types co-exist within the same personality. Moral responses differ in different aspects of life, or in different circumstances. A man may be a loyal employee at work and a wife-beater at home, or a vivisectionist by day and an anti-abortion campaigner by night. Unlike the Aristotelian 'virtuous man' – in which honour, courage, prudence, temperance and justice are merely different facets of a single integrated moral personality – modern man is morally fragmented.

Moral values are personalised and habitual virtues undermined. 'Whose body is this? Who owns my life?' was the repeated query of Sue Rodriguez, a terminally ill patient who fought a long court battle in Canada to claim what she saw as her constitutional right to a medically assisted suicide.[72] It was disclosed recently that the Crown Prosecution Service had decided not to prosecute a man who killed his wife, even though there was sufficient evidence to convict him, because it was a 'mercy killing'. This flatly contradicted the conviction for attempted murder of Dr Nigel Cox in 1992, after he kad agreed to administer a lethal injection to a terminally ill patient. 'Every case is looked at on its own merit,' explained a CPS spokeswoman. 'This one is exceptional.

Every case has unique factors.'[73] Moral judgments, even over a great moral issue like euthanasia have become rurely personal or circumstantial. They are therefore completely arbitrary. Even political discourse has shifted from the discussion of what is right and wrong to questions of managerial and technical competence, in which rational agreement can still be reached about what it is best to do. In the 1980s, for example, the balance of the social security budget was shifted from pensioners to families with large numbers of children and single parent families. 'My view,' argued the Social Services Secretary at the time, 'was that we should examine whether the money was reaching those that most needed it and whether the priorities of the system laid down in 1945 were still the same.'[74] There was no question of choosing, as the Victorians would have done, between the deserving and the undeserving poor.

All the great moral issues – abortion, sexuality, marriage and divorce, genetic engineering – are now resolved by the application by the State of reasonable age or time limits, or the publication of purely technical advice on the use of contraceptive sheaths and such like, rather than confronted directly and decided one way or the other. Dr Jim Howe, the physician who campaigned tirelessly for the death of Tony Bland, a victim of the Hillsborough football stadium disaster, was a characteristic exponent of this method. After Mr Bland's life-support machine was switched off, he told a journalist:

> Absolute dogmas do not work. If you have absolute dogmas, you will find people doing things that are morally dubious and trying to hide them, whereas if you have open and full discussion with people who have been trained to think clearly – like moral philosophers and lawyers – you'll be much more likely to get it right.[75]

It is possible, as the case of Dr Howe demonstrates, to use the power of reason to prove that there is, after all, something worse than death.[76] The growing numbers of elderly people, many of them chronically ill or incapable of looking after themselves, represent a growing temptation for the State to sanction and pay for the death of some of its citizens. There is every reason to expect the State to appoint a committee of experts to formulate guidelines on the practice of euthanasia within a few years. Such a committee has already met on the question of genetic engineering. A family unable to agree among themselves is already testing the ability of the courts to decide between life and death for a relative marooned in the so-called persistent vegetative state. The dominant urge in modern moral discourse is always to find the solution that reasonable men would hit upon, if only they could shed the moral precepts and prejudices of the whole of Judaeo-Christian culture. State-sanctioned and even State-funded killing will eventually overthrow that culture altogether.

The hope that profound moral problems can be solved by committees of experts, assembled specially for the purpose, is a tragic symptom of the loss of a common moral idiom. Dame Mary Warnock is an Oxbridge don – famous mainly for describing Margaret Thatcher as epitomising 'the worst of the lower middle class' and 'not exactly vulgar, just low' – who chaired the committee on genetic engineering.[77] Invited recently by the *Sunday Times* to discuss the 'rebirth of ethics', she confessed that the public was impatient of the inconclusive ramblings of secular philosophy and longed for 'some instant philosophy, like instant coffee'. Her solution was a new moral consensus capable of engaging the feelings of individuals. She wrote:

> We have, I believe, become frightened to recognise that morality must have an element of love and hatred in it, because we have been over-impressed with the need for tolerance of moral views (and therefore moral feelings) different from our own. We, and our children and grandchildren, are constantly told that we are members of a plural society, and that we must therefore accept other people's morality as equal with our own...But we have yet to learn how to say this (and believe it) while at the same time strongly and with full commitment holding to certain moral ideals ourselves.[78]

It is natural to hope that there is some set of universal moral values, which can be distilled from all the religions and philosophies of history and on which all men and women of intelligence and goodwill everywhere can agree, but it is hard to see how abstracted principles of this kind can ever fully engage the human feelings, passions and sentiments on which moral behaviour must ultimately depend. Although morality has never depended on religion alone, for centuries the moral vocabulary of the British people was set by the Christian church. That common moral idiom now lies prostrate at the feet of the natural and behavioural sciences. It cannot be reconstructed artificially.

References

1   Quoted in *Financial Times*, 27 February 1993.
2   From Margaret Drabble, *A Natural Curiosity*.
3   Quoted in Colin Hughes and Patrick Wintour, *Labour Rebuilt: The New Model Party*, Fourth Estate, 1990, page 96.
4   Interview, *Financial Times*, 11 June 1994.
5   *Financial Times*, 1 January 1994.
6   *Financial Times*, 15 January 1994.
7   Sermon to BMA annual conference, reported in *The Times*, 4 July 1994.
8   Spectator, 16 April 1994.
9   The Times, 31 January 1994.
10 Peter Hennessy, *Never Again: Britain 1945-1951*, Jonathan Cape, 1992, page 453.
11 See Chapter 11.
12 Francis Pym, *The Politics of Consent*, Hamish Hamilton, 1984, page 1889-9.
13 Ian Gilmour, *Dancing With Dogma: Britain Under Thatcherism*, Simon & Schuster, 1992, page 272.
14 Michael Howard, *Conservatives and Community*, the 1994 Disraeli Lecture, 28 February 1994, *Conservative Political Centre*, June 1994, page 10.
15 *Hansard*, 17 November 1994, Col. 155.
16 John Gray, *The Undoing of Conservatism*, The Social Market Foundation, June 1994, page 11 and page 22.
17 Quoted in Alan Ryan, *Property*, Open University Press, 1987, page 41.
18 Asa Briggs, *Victorian Things*, Penguin, 1988, page 15.
19 'The Soul of Man Under Socialism', reproduced in *Oscar Wilde, De Profundis and*

   Other Writings, edited by Hesketh Pearson, Penguin Classics Edition, 1986, page 25.

20   John Morley, *The Life of Richard Cobden*, T. Fisher Unwin, Fourteenth Edition, 1920
     pages 945–7.

21   R. H. Tawney, *The Acquisitive Society*, G. Bell & Sons, 1922, page 27.

22   From a vision of the future entitled 'Economic Possibilities for Our Grandchildren'.
     Quoted in Robert Skidelsky, *John Maynard Keynes: The Economist As Saviour
     1920–1937*, Macmillan, 1992, page 236.

23   From Joseph Schumpeter, *Capitalism, Socialism and Democracy*, George Allen &
     Unwin Ltd, 1957, page 143.

24   The anonymity of trade has not prevented communitarian thinkers from describing
     the global economy as a new form of 'community'. Computer networks such as the
     Internet, are often described in this way. It is of course fallacious to believe that a
     temporary and impersonal coincidence of interests, as in the exchange of goods or
     information, creates a 'community' of shared values or personal sympathies.

25   Quoted in Alan Ryan, *Propery and Political Theory*, Blackwell, 1984, page 5.

26   From a vision of the future entitled 'Economic Possibilities for Our Grandchildren'.
     Quoted in Robert Skidelsky, *John Maynard Keynes: The Economist As Saviour
     1920–1937*, Macmillan, 1992, page 236.

27   Ferdinand Mount, *The Subversive Family: An Alternative History of Love and
     Marriage*, Unwin Paperbacks, 1982, pages 163–4.

28   George Brown, *In My Way*, Penguin, 1972, pages 261–9.

29   David Willetts, *Civic Conservatism*, The Social Market Foundation, June 1994, pages
     43–5

30   From the Communion Service, Book of Common Prayer of the Church of England,
     1662.

31   5 April 1835. Quoted in Philip Magnus, *Gladstone*, John Murray, 1963, page 35.

32   Paul Welsby, *A History of the Church of England 1945–1980*, OUP, 1984, page 20.

33   Quoted in Owen Chadwick, *The Secularization of the European Mind in the
     Nineteenth Century*, CUP, 1975, page 125.

34   Quoted in *The Secularization of the European Mind in the Nineteenth Century*, page 67

35   Central Statistical Office, *Social Trends, 1994 Edition*, Table 11.8, page 145.

36   Quoted in Modris Eksteins, *Rites of Spring: The Great War and the Birth of the Modern
     Age*, Bantam, 1989, page 118.

37   Owen Chadwick, *The Secularization of the European Mind in the Nineteenth Century*,
     CUP, 1975, pages 229–30.

38   John Stuart Mill, *Utilitarianism, in On Liberty and Other Essays*, paperback edition
     OUP, 1991, page 148.

39   Gertrude Himmelfarb, *On Liberty and Liberalism: The Case of John Stuart Mill*,
     Institute for Contemporary Studies, 1990, page 89.

40   *On Liberty and Liberalism: The Case of John Stuart Mill*, page 88.

41   From *On Liberty*, in John Stuart Mill, *On Liberty and Other Essays*, OUP, 1991, page
     15. Gertrude Himmelfarb has pointed out that the early Mill was more pessimistic
     about human nature than the Mill of On Liberty. In an earlier essay he had argued
     that 'the acquisition of virtue has in all ages been accounted a work of labour and
     difficulty, while the decensus Averni on the contrary is of proverbial facility; and it
     assuredly reuires in most persons a greater conquest over a greater number of
     natural inclinations to become eminently virtuous than transcendentally vicious'.
     See Gertrude Himmelfarb, On Liberty and Liberalism: The Case of John Stuart Mill,
     Institute for Contemporary Studies, 1990, page 87.

42   Quoted in Robert Skidelsky, *John Maynard Keynes: The Economist As Saviour
     1920–1937*, Macmillan, 1992, page 517.

43   Quoted in Robert Skidelsky, *John Maynard Keynes: The Economist As Saviour
     1920–1937*, Macmillan, 1992, page 408.

44   Quoted in John Stevenson, *British Society 1914–45*, Penguin, 1984, page 50.

45   Lyn Macdonald, *Somme*, Macmillan, 1984, page 25.

46   Peter Parker, *The Old Lie: The Great War and the Public School Ethos*, Constable,

1987, page 96.

47   Quoted in Lyn Macdonald, 1914, Penguin, 1987, pages 61–2.

48   Quoted in Richard Harries, *Is There a Gospel for the Rich?*, Mowbray, 1992, page 99.

49   Quoted in Gertrude Himmelfarb, *On Liberty and Liberalism: The Case of John Stuart Mill*, Institute for Contemporary Studies, 190, page 108.

50   A.J. P. Taylor, *The First World War*, Penguin, 1987, page 251.

51   Quoted in Lyn Macdonald, *Somme*, Macmillan, 1983, pages 201–2.

52   Quoted in M. Winter, *The Experience of World War I*, Equinox, 1988, Page 169.

53   Quoted in Arthur Marwick, *The Deluge: British Society and the First World War*, Second Edition. Macmillan. 1991, page 28

54   William Purcell, *Woodbine Willie*, Mowbray, paperback edition, 1983, page 152.

55   Quoted in Arthur Marwick, *The Deluge*, Second Edition, Macmillan, 1991, page 277.

56   Interview, *Financial Times*, 25 October 1993.

57   Quoted in Arthur Marwick, *The Deluge*, Second Edition, Macmillan, 1991, page 277.

58   Isaiah Berlin, *Introduction to Four Essays on Liberty*, OUP, paperback, 1969, page xii.

59   Keith Thomas, *Religion and the Decline of Magic*, Penguin, 1991, pages 428–9.

60   King Lear, I, ii.

61   Popular appreciations of Darwinism in late Victorian England helped to discredit individualism as a moral creed. The 'survival of the fittest' seemed to imply that the weakest and most vulnerable must perish. Some contemporary businessmen, influenced by the writings of Herbert Spencer, certainly proclaimed Competition, Capitalism and even Monopoly as examples of the 'survival of the fittest'.

62   Stephen Hawking, 'Is Everything Determined?', in *Black Holes and Baby Universes*, Bantam, 1994, page 117

63   Quoted in Robert Skidelsky, *John Maynard Keynes: The Economist As Saviour*, Macmillan, 1992, page 570.

64   Quoted in James Q. Wilson, *The Moral Sense*, The Free Press, 1993, page 219.

65   Gertrude Himmelfarb, *On Liberty and Liberalism: The Case of John Stuart Mill*, Institute for Contemporary Studies, 1990, page 52.

66   T. S. Eliot, *Notes Towards the Definition of Culture*, Faber & Faber, 1962, page 87.

67   *The Times*, 4 July 1994

68   Mori poll for *The Big Holy One*, a Radio 1 religious programme. Reported in the *Observer*, 9 October 1994.

69   Hugh Dickinson, Dean of Salisbury, *Financial Times*, 12 February 1994.

70   Alasdair MacIntyre, *After Virtue: A Study in Moral Theory*. Second Edition. Duckworth, 1985, pages 265–6.

71   *After Virtue: A Study in Moral Theory*, page 252.

72   *Observer*, 20 February 1994.

73   *Observer*. December 1994.

74   Norman Fowler, *Ministers Decide*, Chapmans, 1991, page 209.

75   *Sunday Telegraph*, 7 March 1993.

76   It is perhaps not surprising that a doctor should voice such opinions. As Simon Wiesenthal has pointed out, there seem to be powerful psychological affinities between the authority and desire to save life and the authority and wish to inflict pain and death Doctors were among the most enthusiastic participants in the Nazi death machine 'Physicians,' he writes, 'played a considerable role in the death machinery of the Third Reich... No other profession (with the exception of teachers, who, of course, were under pressure and wished to keep their jobs in state schools) was quite so addicted to Nazism: nearly 50 per cent of all physicians in Germany after 1933, and in Austria after 1938, were members of the Nazi Party.' See *Simon Wiesenthal, Justice Not Vengeance*, Mandarin, 1990, page 139.

77   According to the *Sunday Telegraph*, in October last year Dame Mary preached a sermon in the chapel of Sidney Sussex College which queried whether 'the principle of the sanctity of human life does indeed constitute an absolute value, giving rise to moral imperatives'. She concluded that it did not. See *Sunday Telegraph*, 2 January 1994.

78   *Sunday Times*, 10 April 1994.

CHAPTER ELEVEN

The Delusion of Christian Socialism

The instructions of a secular morality that is not based on religious doctrines are exactly like what a person ignorant of music might do, if he were made a conductor and started to wave his hands in front of musicians well-rehearsed in what they are performing. By virtue of its own momentum, and from what previous conductors had taught the musicians, the music might continue for a while, but obviously the gesticulations made with a stick by a person who knows nothing about music would be useless and eventually confuse the musicians and throw the orchestra off course. This sort of confusion is beginning to take place in the minds of people today.

Leo Tolstoy, 1893[1]

It is not by the State that man can be regenerated, and the terrible woes of this darkened world effectually dealt with.

W. E. Gladstone, 1894[2]

What, gentlemen, is Conservatism? It is the application of Christianity to civil government. And what is English Conservatism? It is the adoption of the principles of the Church of England as the groundwork of legislation. Gentlemen, I say it with reverence, the most Conservative book in the world is the Bible, and the next most Conservative book in the world is the Book of Common Prayer.

Archdeacon Christopher Wadsworth, February 1865[3]

Christianity was the dominant force in the creation of the common moral, intellectual and artistic culture of Western civilisation. T. S. Eliot was so convinced of this fact that he thought Europe could not survive the loss of the Christian faith:

> I do not believe that the culture of Europe could survive the complete disappearance of the Christian Faith. And I am convinced of that, not merely because I am a Christian myself, but as a student of social biology. If

Christianity goes, the whole of our culture goes. Then you must start painfully again, and you cannot put on a new culture ready made. You must wait for the grass to grow to feed the sheep to give the wool out of which your coat will be made. You must pass through many centuries of barbarism. We should not live to see the new culture, nor would our great-great-great grandchildren: and if we did, not one of us would be happy in it.[4]

The collectivists disagreed. They thought it was adequate to replace the worship of God with the worship of the State. The Fabians and New Liberals of late Victorian and Edwardian England were heavily influenced by the leading English Hegelian, T. H. Green, who provided them with a theory of the State as a moral agent redressing the injustices of private property.[5] Collectivism gradually filled the moral vacuum left by the demise of Christianity. By 1945 Church leaders were as convinced as Socialist politicians that the Welfare State was a profound moral departure, a new kind of civilisation. The nationalisations of the 1940s were seen at the time as a spiritual project. 'In planned production for community consumption,' wrote Beatrice Webb in a book published in 1940, 'the secular and the religious are one.'[6] Significantly, the book was entitled *I Believe*.

Atavism Revisited: Christian Socialism

Many of the earliest State-worshippers were agnostics, rationalists or atheists but over the last century and a half the most important group of English collectivists were the so-called Christian Socialists. Both the current leader of the Labour Party, Tony Blair, and his predecessor have described themselves as Christian Socialists. According to a recent survey by the *New Statesman and Society* magazine, ethical or Christian Socialism dominates the thinking of a majority of modern Labour MPs, who rank the Bible and the writings of R. H. Tawney above *Das Kapital*.[7] Some Christian Socialists idealise the 'apostolic communism' of the early Church, or cite the fundamental Christian belief that everything belongs to God ('the earth is the Lord's'). Tom Driberg, the libidinous Labour MP who revived Christian Socialism in the 1950s, argued that the common ownership of the means of production was a form of koinonia, or Christian fellowship.[8] But Christian Socialism was really the invention of mid-Victorian High Toryism. John Wesley – whose Methodism had a greater influence over the Labour Party than Marxism, as Harold Wilson was fond of saying – was High Church and High Tory, and his creed of resignation, obedience and subordination undoubtedly helped to inoculate eighteenth- and nineteenth-century British men and women against socialistic sentiments. Another High Tory, Thomas Carlyle, detested democracy, free market economics and individualism, and longed for Germanic hegemony in Europe as the means of realising his ideal of an 'organic community' ruled over by supermen. He denounced economics as 'the Dismal Science' and lambasted 'the Gospel of Mammon' for subordinating all human relations to contract and exchange:

We call it a Society; and go about professing openly the totalest separation, isolation. Our life is not a mutual helpfulness; but rather, cloaked under due laws-of-war, named 'fair competition' and so forth, it is a mutual hostility. We have profoundly forgotten everywhere that Cash-payment is not the sole relation of human beings.[9]

When the journalist W. T. Stead asked the first Labour MPs in 1906 which authors had most influenced their thinking, Thomas Carlyle ranked fifth behind John Ruskin, the Bible, Charles Dickens and Henry George, the author of Process and Poverty.[10] In the 1870s and 1880s Christian Socialism was strongly associated with High Church Anglicans, whose Catholic sympathies led them to value the corporate over the individual and to dismiss troublesome questions of authority. The founding father of Christian Socialism was J. M. Ludlow (1821–1911), a layman familiar with the teaching of the Social Catholics in France. Its main propagator in the mid-to-late Victorian period was the High Church Guild of St Matthew founded by the Reverend Stewart Headlam (1847–1924). Bishop Brooke Westcott, a Cambridge theologian whose opinions were imbued with the twin influences of Cambridge Idealism and the Oxford Movement, was the first president of the Christian Social Union founded in 1899. He warned in 1890 that individualism saw humanity as 'disconnected and warring atoms' while socialism regarded it as an 'organic whole'.[11] Two years later, as Bishop of Durham, he played a decisive role as mediator in the Durham coal strike.

Westcott's views were often compared in his lifetime to those of Frederick Denison Maurice (1805–1872), the intellectual clergy- man and scourge of the selfish doctrine of competition whom modern Christian Socialists prefer to identify as the founder of their creed. His thinking was popularised in the novels of Charles Kingsley (1819–1875), who was much influenced by Carlyle, and who in turn influenced early socialists like William Morris. Both Maurice and Kingsley came from the liberal rather than the catholic wing of the Church of England, and formulated Christian Socialism as a non-revolutionary movement of social reform in the aftermath of Chartism. Abortive attempts were made to start co- operative workshops and evening classes to persuade the working classes of the virtues of the 'science of partnership'. The main fruits of Christian Socialism were the Working Men's College in Red Lion Square, the Charity Organisation Society, the housing projects of Octavia Hill and the dissemination of the notion that Christianity had a role to play in the world as well as the mind. But these attempts to remind Property of its 'duties' were still far removed from apostolic communism. At bottom, Christian Socialism was based on the familiar medieval romanticism of the socialist imagination. Its inspiration was the paternalistic landed aristocrat of the Middle Ages employing, housing and feeding his tenants, with Victorian middle-class experts playing the role of the absent squire amid the squalor of the East End.[12]

Leading late Victorian Socialists like Ruskin and William Morris were essentially atavists, seeking to recreate the *communitas communitatum* of the pre-Reformation Middle Ages, in which Church and State were parts of an organic and hierarchical whole which discouraged 'avarice' through usury laws, the just price and terrifying parables of greedy economic individualists being licked by the flames of Hell. It was Ruskin, Morris and Octavia Hill who invented the modern heritage industry – an essentially collectivist enterprise, in its capacity to truncate or even override the rights of property – to save the medieval buildings and unspoiled landscapes which filled the Merrie England of their imaginations. Octavia Hill was convinced of the restorative properties of light and air, so rarely found in the slums of the industrial age, and became a powerful patron of the Kyrle Society, the Commons Preservation Society and the National Trust. The Trust was once aptly described as a peculiarly English form of nationalisation, though the ability of its drab but perfect presentations to drain the life from great private houses is characteristic of collectivist historicism everywhere.

Christian Socialism, as originally conceived, was virtually in- distinguishable from the organic society idealised by Carlyle or the alliance of aristocrats and proletarians favoured by Disraeli during his High Tory or Young England phase or even, for that matter, the One Nation Toryism of today. Medieval romanticism was a common reaction to industrial squalor and the stress of economic individualism and, to that extent, Christian Socialism and One Nation Toryism share a common paternalistic and backward- looking origin. This atavism is a feature common to all forms of collectivism, none of which fails to idealise some retrievable form of 'community'.

The leading theorist of modern Christian Socialism, R. H. Tawney, looked back to a time when the Church was not the handmaiden of Capitalism, and considered his 'functional' society to be not only a recreation of the organic society of the past but primarily religious in conception. In 1922 Tawney complained that the Church of England had, at some point after the Reformation, abandoned its proper role as the organ of collective thought and will and become 'the moral police' of a capitalist State.[13] As science, war and industrialisation undermined the traditional role and thinking of the Church in the twentieth century, and congregations shrank, leading Anglicans were inclined to agree. They sought a new role as propagandists for a redistributive Welfare State. It was during the inter-war years, when economic depression persuaded many people that capitalism was on the brink of collapse, that many of the post-war generation of leading Anglicans came to share Lewis Donaldson's claim that 'Christianity is the religion of which socialism is the practice'.

Hewlett Johnson (1874–1966), the celebrated 'Red Dean' of Canterbury, was for many years the most prominent convert to this point of view. He was initially attracted in the 1930s to the Social Credit scheme of Major Clifford Douglas, a crackpot plan to dispense with the supposed evils of the price mechanism by subsidising producers and consumers to sell and buy goods and services at below cost price. But after a visit to Soviet Russia in 1937 he became a convinced Communist and public apologist for Stalin, who awarded him a 'peace prize' in 1951. Mervyn Stockwood, no reactionary himself, wrote of Johnson after his death:

He went [to the Soviet Union], he saw, and was conquered...No matter what adverse reports reached him – of secret trials, terrorism, concentration camps, the atrocities of Stalin, the invasion of Hungary – he was unmoved. His loyalty to the official line of the Russian Communist Party was unflinching. He held fast to what he wanted to believe and dismissed from his mind anything which might shatter his illusions... Having decided that Soviet Communism was helping the cause of human betterment, he refused to criticise... He was as enthuasistic for the Peking, as he had been for the Moscow, regime, although it was said that the criticism and counter-criticism of the two expressions of Communist rule were a cause of embarrassment to him, had he been capable by then of embarrassment.[14]

The significance of Johnson's best-seller on the Soviet Socialist achievement, *The Socialist Sixth of the World*, lay in what it ignored rather than what it mentioned. After the war he was a regular visitor to Communist China and Cuba, and became an active propagandist on behalf of both regimes. He ended his days engaged in psychical research, convinced that proof of corporeal resurrection would facilitate a reconciliation between Christianity and dialectical materialism.

But the capture of the Church of England by Socialism owes more to William Temple than to cranks like Hewlett Johnson. Temple (1881–1944) was easily the most influential churchman of his age. As early as 1908 he had concluded that 'socialism... is the economic realisation of the Christian gospel', but it was not until the Second World War that his opinions became a decisive influence in national affairs.'[15] This was partly because they were no longer peculiar to the Anglican Church, but had become organised Christian orthodoxy. When *The Times* of 20 December 1940 carried a letter from senior churchmen calling for the abolition of extreme inequality it was signed by the Archbishops of York and Canterbury, the Roman Catholic Archbishop of Westminster and the Moderator of the Free Church Council.[16] In early 1941 a conference of the Anglican Industrial Christian Fellowship at Malvern College resolved that private ownership of capital was an obstacle to the Christian life. Pamphlets popularising such views sold over a million copies. Temple was then Archbishop of York, but in 1942 he ascended to the see of Canterbury. That year he published a best-selling Penguin entitled Christianity and the Social Order. In it, he declared that Karl Marx was 'not far wrong' in scourging capitalism for reducing human relations to 'naked self-interest and callous cash payment' and advocated nationalisation of the joint stock banks, dividend controls and economic planning. He thought that Christians should aim not at 'the salvation of individuals one by one, but at that perfect individual and social welfare, which is called the Kingdom of God or the Holy City'.

Temple was sufficiently sympathetic to socialism to have joined the Labour Party in 1918. For many years it was supposed that Temple himself devised the term 'welfare state', as a deliberate contrast with the 'warfare state' or 'power state' of the Nazis and, by implication, with the war of all against all under capitalism. It now seems that it was actually coined by an obscure professor of international relations at Oxford in 1934, but Temple was certainly responsible for popularising it.[17] He must have seemed thoroughly up-to-date in the mid-1940s but his values, like those of his friend and mentor Tawney, really belonged to the romantic past of his imagination. He believed, like his medieval predecessors, that nobody should ask for more than a 'just' reward for their labour or a 'just price' for their goods. He was opposed to banks making a profit from lending money, just as the medieval Church had upheld the usury laws. Medieval economics, as Tawney pointed out in *Religion and the Rise of Capitalism*, was a branch of theology. Temple's views were far from the lies and wilful blindness of Anglican clergymen like Hewlett Johnson, but he and his successors were still extraordinarily tolerant of political extremism. Johnson, disowned by his fellow-canons as early as 1940 and denounced by the Archbishop of Canterbury in 1947, was not asked to resign his post until 1963. Another Socialist cleric, Canon Stanley Evans, wrote an obituary of Stalin – the greatest genocidal maniac in history – which lauded him as the leader of the historic struggle for emancipation of the working class and the colonial peoples and an 'outstanding leader in the struggle for world peace'.

Few were prepared to go as far as Johnson and Evans. But except for those clergymen who have succumbed to the sinister charms of liberation theology – a mainly, though not exclusively, Marxist interpretation of Christianity as a struggle against oppression and oppressive ideologies, which is more interested in 'realising' religious truth than in apprehending it – Christian Socialism of one sort or another has been the Anglican orthodoxy throughout the twentieth century. As early as 1908 Lord William Cecil told the pan-Anglican Congress that he felt 'almost out of place speaking as a person with no belief in socialism'.[18] The curious ideas of William Temple continue to exert a powerful influence over Anglicans of all political persuasions. In a Parliamentary debate on the disestablish- ment of the Church of England in February 1989, both Conservative and Labour MPs felt comfortable calling in support of their arguments the writings of Willim Temple. One Conservative member even argued that Temple had 'redeemed' Christian Socialism.[19]

The former Bishop of Durham, David Jenkins, is probably the best-known modern exponent of Christian Socialism in the Church of England. In his Hibbert lecture of April 1985 he gave a textbook account of the historicist-collectivist delusions on which it is based:

> To return to the ethics of the 19th century entrepreneurial individualism is either nostalgic nonsense or else a firm declaration that individual selfishness and organised greed are the only motivations for human behaviour... To promote a materialistic market-orientated individualism as the key to human social progress is to make an equally destructive mistake about the possibilities and the needs of men and women and to turn one's back on real political and social progress which has been made. Realism about sin should not lead to cynicism about altruism or pessimism about the possibilities of collective organisation and communal care.[20]

Jenkins was not above calling the Conservative government 'wicked' (in a sermon at Easter 1988) and thought even bus deregulation was worthy of analysis in terms of his Christian values. Just as many Christian Socialists in Parliament doubt whether it is possible to be a Christian and a Conservative at the same time, few mainstream Anglican clergymen today believe that economic individualism is compatible with leading a Christian life. The publication by the Church of England in 1985 of its infamous report entitled Faith in the City – which explicitly identified 'Thatcherite' individualism, rather than post-war collectivism, as the cause of inner-city deprivation – did not mark a radical ideological departure for the leadership of the Anglican Church. Its argument that 'the excessive individualism of much Christian thinking in the nine- teenth century' proved 'Marx's perception that evil is to be found, not just in the human heart, but in the very structures of economic and social relationships' was by then an entirely orthodox piece of Christian Socialism.

The Irrelevance of Christian Socialism Today

That orthodox Christian Socialist tradition, despite its continuing popularity in the Church of England and the modern Labour Party, is now exhausted. In Christianity and the Social Order Temple argued flatly that 'the Christian conception of men as members in the family of God forbids the notion that freedom may be used for self- interest'. Theological reasoning of this kind, which skates blithely over the difficulties of achieving a transcendent heavenly bliss through socio-political action in a real world where even the worker-heroes are motivated by self-interest, was always unsound. Its equation of self-interest with selfishness is embarrassing, and its blindness to the inherent conflict between the spiritual and the natural aspects of humanity is an unexpectedly large lacuna in the predominant Anglican intellectual orthodoxy of the twentieth century. But the most damaging residue of Christian Socialism today is a continuing antipathy to market economics which is quite out of joint with reality. Christian Socialism originated at a time when the actual workings of capitalism could be contrasted unfavourably with the theoretical workings of socialism. Seventy-odd years on, socialist economic planning is a palpable failure; modern welfare capitalism bears little resemblance to the devil-take-the-hindmost economy Christian Socialism was invented to oppose; and the success of the market economy in raising the standard of living and broadening the sphere of individual choice is a spontaneous human achievement about which the old ways of thinking have nothing of value to say. 'The hardest thing required of the Christian Socialist committed to helping the poor obtain justice,' as one thoughtful Christian Socialist has already admitted, 'will be saying "I made mistakes".'[21]

It is not enough to say, as the Bishop of Southwark recently did, that 'the social and political expression of neighbour love is justice - and that relates as much to social systems as to personal values'.[22] Christian Socialism desperately needs new doctrines of creation, sin, forgiveness and hope which can take account of its long-standing intellectual shortcomings and its denial by experience. One bishop, Richard Harries of Oxford, has at last detected a basic congruity between Christian faith and a free market. 'The market economy is both congruous with and expressive of the high Christian evaluation of human freedom,' he writes. 'It allows people to share in the creativity of God, using their initiative and willingness to take risks for the common good.'[23] But he fails in the end to escape the straitjacket of a stale collectivism, recommending State intervention to make the market economy work for the 'common good'. Harries also seems convinced, like Roy Hattersley, that equality is synonymous with freedom. Intellectual incoherence of this kind is in many ways the hallmark of the Church of England, which has a well-deserved reputation for being able to see both sides of every issue. The last Archbishop of Canterbury was criticised from within

his own Church for habitually 'nailing his colours to the fence'. But it would be a mistake to assume that most Anglican clergymen are simply unable to choose between conflicting political ideologies. The overwhelming majority of them opted many years ago, at theological college if not before, for Christian Socialism. They did so because they had lost confidence in the traditional mission of the Church.

Christian Socialism: The Refuge of the Uncontent

The Reverend Alan Billings, a former deputy leader of Sheffield City Council and one of the influences behind *Faith in the City*, believes that Christian Socialism is primarily a reflection of the declining confidence of the Church in its traditional teachings and role:

> Throughout the present century, the churches (the largely clerical leadership, that is) has persuaded themselves that theology could yield political wisdom and that that wisdom was left of centre – or at any rate 'collectivist' – in character. The social ethic of the churches had become centred on the concept of social justice (understood as a 'bias to the poor' or promoting greater equality) to be achieved through State inter-vention...For much of the 1970s and 1980s we have seen clergy much more politically-minded and much more left of centre than their congregations: what one correspondent in the *Yorkshire Post* called *Guardian* readers talking to *Telegraph* readers. How did the clergy become so politicised? Is it some measure due to a crisis of confidence on the part of the ordained ministry – a consequence of the steady decline in church membership and influence during the whole of this century. In a society which increasingly finds little place for organised religion, the role of the ordained minister outside the Christian community is problematical. Some clergy have sought to relieve this tension...by re-defining their role in ways which a more secular society does value – or so the clergy believe...By the time of Faith in the City...a politicised Church had come to embrace both collectivist policies and the consensual or corporatist approach to government.[24]

It is this which explains the strictures of the former bishop of Durham on the conduct of the miners' strike, or the Bishop of Birmingham on the management of the National Health Service. Far from directing the attention of their congregations to the next world, clergymen are desperate to seem *relevant* in this one. Whilst Christianity is not just about directing attention to the next world but rightly concerned with this one – when Jesus said 'my kingdom is not of this world', he was talking about its origin, not its location – the result of repeated and detailed criticism of public policymakers is to reduce popular perception of religious truth to the status of political opinion.

The former Bishop of Durham, who questioned in public the reality of the Virgin Birth, the Resurrection and the Ascension, also provided a striking example of how hard many modern clergymen find it to articulate Christian dogma, let alone believe it. His language and ideas are famously convoluted, as if the new formulations he tries to explain are too incoherent to be capable of comprehensible expression. But he is in a long tradition of doubting prelates. A Bishop of Birmingham raised doubts about the literal truth of Christian doctrines as early as 1947. In 1963 the then Bishop of Woolwich, John Robinson, announced the 'death of God' in his best-selling but difficult and confused book, *Honest to God*. 'I do not fully understand myself all that I am trying to say,' he said afterwards.[25] It contained the notorious claim that 'nothing can of itself always be labelled "wrong"'. He had earlier given a stout defence of pornography in the *Lady Chatterley* trial, likening sexual intercourse to Holy Communion ('lower case, of course,' he added). *Honest to God* launched the hopeless project of a demythologised, religionless Christianity or anthropomorphic life-force, by arguing that God was not above the world in heaven but 'in, with and under the conditional relationships of this life'. There was plenty of characteristically Anglican bathos in the book – prayer was described by Robinson as 'seeing the diary in depth and preparing on the telephone to meet our God' – but it was not hard to predict where such reasoning would end up. By the early 1970s Robinson was arguing frankly, in *The Human Face of God*, that Jesus was not the Son of God but merely a human being in whom divinity was made manifest.

The Church of England was not immune to the spirit of the 1960s, and Robinson's assertion that 'nothing of itself could be labelled wrong' was a gift to a decade in which young people yearned for a spirituality devoid not only of God but of morality. Many turned to Oriental mysticism or mind-bending narcotics, or the shrill banalities of the Jesus Movement, in search of refuge from the supposed evils of Western materialism. The response of the Church of England was not to reaffirm traditional ethics, but to rewrite its liturgy, worship and theology in the hope of keeping up with secular developments of this kind. By the 1970s Anglican scholarship seemed to be engaged in a sustained attempt to 'demythologise' Christianity altogether. Don Cupitt, the Dean of Emmanuel College, Cambridge, declared that the Incarnation was both unintelligible and unsupported by scripture. The Dean and his fellow-travellers in the Sea of Faith network – named after a television series and book Cupitt produced – have ceased to believe in God as an objective reality and, borrowing heavily from logical positivism, have come to see the deity as an entirely self-referring idealisation of human aspirations. They are atheistic humanists rather than Christians, and it is hard to see why they wish to remain part of the Church.

Atheistic humanism is a direct contradiction of Christian truth. The humanists are able to stay in the Church only because the larger group of thinkers who remained religious have adopted wholesale the humanistic moral and intellectual agenda. Edward Norman described in his 1978 Reith lectures how the churches and churchmen had lost confidence in the traditional claims of Christianity, and reinterpreted the faith as a programme of social and political action which invoked the State to resolve collective sins like inequality and racialism. Christian values became indistinguishable from the morals and ideals of a transient political viewpoint. It is a characteristic of secular and political values that their perceived virtue depends not on whether they are true but upon the ideas and circumstances to which they are applied.[26] The eternal, unchanging, timeless values of Christianity were subsumed in human and secular values which are unvarying only in their relativity. The primary concern of the faith – personal spirituality, the relationship of the individual soul to eternity – was subordinated to the claims of collective political action. It has left the Church, stripped of its supernatural pretensions, as little more than the Social Democratic Party at prayer.

Although every religious faith has succumbed to some extent to worldly influence, no religious denomination is more thoroughly politicised and secularised than the Church of England. Important sections of the Jewish, Roman Catholic and Islamic faiths have taken a firm stand on moral principles. They have endured ridicule and opprobrium as a result, but are confident in the belief that truth will prevail eventually. An Archbishop of Canterbury, by contrast, asked himself in 1978: 'Do we want to indoctrinate children into our own beliefs?' He then answered himself as well: 'God forbid.'[27] It was an apt measure of the religious confidence which the Church of England forfeited during its mistaken bid to keep up with the world rather than to transcend it. 'No one who really believes in his values,' as Edward Norman wrote at the time, 'leaves their acceptance to chance, particularly when it comes to children.'[28] The Church of England has become a weak Church preaching a weak faith, and in no sphere is its lack of confidence more obvious than in the one field which it might have expected to make its own: morality.

The Secularisation of Christian Morality

On all the great moral issues – adultery, fornication, divorce, abortion, euthanasia – the Church of England is confused. On the question of divorce it is unable to decide about second marriages at all, leaving it up to the discretion and conscience of local clergymen to decide whether they are prepared to marry divorcees. One awkwardness is that clergymen themselves are getting divorced in record numbers, principally because of adultery by male priests. A Norfolk clergyman was not asked by his bishop to resign until he wanted to get married for the third time, to a woman who was reputedly already living with him in the vicarage. 'As a church we must face the realities of contemporary life,' the dismissed vicar told his congregation, 'or else we cause people to suffer a lot of guilt, and look ridiculous in the process.'[29] His sermon was a good illustration of how the virtue of ideas like 'tolerance', 'flexibility', and 'understanding' is entirely dependent on the problem to which they are applied. What makes the Church look ridiculous is not clinging to its traditional teaching in all circumstances, but abandoning it in all circumstances. Unlike abortion and euthanasia, the Christian position on divorce and adultery is quite unambiguous. Adultery is specifically forbidden by the seventh Commandment, and the tenth forbids a man to covet his neighbour's wife. Adultery and marriage are also one of the few areas in which Jesus himself laid down a rigorous rule. He taught that it was a grave sin even to think about committing adultery, that divorce was a violation of divine will unless there was evidence of sexual misdemeanour, and that divorce and remarriage is itself a form of adultery.[30]

Any institution enslaved by the climate of opinion and behaviour in a secular society will struggle to give clear moral leadership, and the Church of England is bound eventually to abandon the task of moral instruction altogether. A Methodist minister recently proposed exactly this. He argues that, since Christian moral values are so far out of step with contemporary mores, people should no longer look to the Church for moral guidance but develop a new public ethic of responsible hedonism':

> It is time to recognise that the Church is enmeshed in a moral tradition which is ascetic and altruistic, and which has been shaped by the centuries in which celibacy was celebrated as a high virtue. By contrast, contemporary society is modelled by a desire to fulfill its appetites and to further its interests, accepting more or less responsible constraints on its self-seeking behaviour. Its values are essentially hedonistic. There has been a tendency to pretend that our society suffers from a failure of an ascetic ethic, whereas in fact we suffer from the failure to recognise, develop and practise a proper hedonism...It seems about time for us to come clean, to seek to develop a thoroughgoing hedonism, to replace a half-hearted and failed ascetic-altruistic morality. This attempt may sound simply self-indulgent and self-serving, easily caricatured as 'fun with sex and money'. But there is much more at stake than this...It soon becomes necessary to talk about serious fun with sex and money.[31]

Churches are apt to measure their social influence only by the numbers who go to church, when their values are actually treasured among a far wider audience than their dwindling congregations. More than two thirds of the population express some form of religious affiliation, and the Church of England alone encounters many times its active membership through baptisms, weddings and funerals.

It is a pity that the Church refuses so many opportunities to reinforce its undoubted moral authority by making a distinctively religious, rather than secular and political, contribution to public debate. Leading churchmen are no longer what both John Stuart Mill and R. H. Tawney referred to (disparagingly) as the 'moral police'. Instead, they have become like other democratic politicians, seeking out the opinions of others only in order to flatter them. Alan

Billings has wisely concluded:

> We have to heed the warning that for many lay people the church has
> become more and more politicised. There are times, too many times, when
> it looks less like a church, meeting people's religious needs, and more like
> a political pressure group. As such it becomes increasingly marginal in the
> life of the nation since people look to the church to say something about
> God and the gospel not about housing policy or defence. Or rather, they
> used to look to the churches for spiritual and religious guidance but do so
> with less confidence since the church appears preoccupied with other
> matters. If this situation is to be put right, the clergy will need to recover
> confidence in their religious role…that of evangelist and teacher
> concerned with the patient preaching and teaching of the Christian faith
> to a generation of Christian people who are becoming more and more
> distanced from their tradition. Present in churches now are the
> generations who neither went to Sunday school nor had Christian
> education in the RE lesson. There can be no revival of Christianity, no
> permeation of this culture with Christian values, without an educated laity,
> grounded in the Christian tradition. Mrs Thatcher knew that and the
> failure of the church to hear what she was saying was a lost opportunity.[32]

This is not as pious a hope as it might seem. Between 1830 and 1850 – the
heyday of the 'entrepreneurial individualism' Bishop Jenkins reproved so sternly
– the Church of England was transformed from a corrupt, scandalous and
inward-looking corporation into one of the most vital public institutions in
British life. Clerical poverty was attacked. Pluralism was ended. The wealth of
the cathedrals was redeployed in the industrial cities. The Church founded one
university – ironically, in Jenkins's former seat at Durham – and countless
schools and hospitals. A great age of missionary work at home and abroad was
begun.

The Failure to Develop a New Ethic of Capitalism

The Church has scarcely embarked on the intellectual revolution which it must
undergo if it is to recreate a Christian culture. Like their colleagues in the pulpit,
the Christian Socialists in Parliament have also made few fundamental changes
to their view of the world. For all their talk of policy reviews, and interest in
'market failure' rather than the command economy, the collectivist mind is by its
nature irredeemably Statist, anti-market and resistant to a proper understanding
of the dynamic nature of the capitalist economy. Armed with a methodology
rooted in the Middle Ages, they cannot free themselves of the instinct that in a
capitalist economy the rich get richer because the poor are getting poorer.
'Capitalism,' writes Richard Harries, 'like all forms of organised self-interest, will
if left to itself further the interests of the wealthy and powerful at the expense of
the relatively poor and powerless. The poor and the powerless may participate
in the prosperity created by capitalism, but never enough; and others will be

simply used or, still in some places today, exploited.' He calls for 'affirmative action, positive discrimination, in order to help the most vulnerable human beings attain their potential'.[33] He means, of course, coercion by the State.

For all the lip-service collectivists like Bishop Harries pay the market economy today, the role of property rights in providing the incentive to work and to invest, and in the facilitation of trade and exchange, is lost on them. The centrality of the price mechanism, in continually uncovering new and unsatisfied wants and allocating goods, services and labour to satisfying them in the most efficient way, is a mystery to them. The fact that exchanges between individuals, companies and countries would not take place unless they were mutually rewarding cannot dislodge in them an instinctive dislike of free markets and free trade. Technological progress and rising productivity, the sources of expanding wealth and work, appear to them merely as the harbingers of unemployment. And the higher economic importance of man as consumer rather than producer – the truth, as Adam Smith put it, that 'consumption is the sole end and purpose of production' – is counter-intuitive to minds reared on a mixture of medieval romance and Marxist theories of alienation. Collectivists cannot rid themselves of the suspicion that all economic relationships are ultimately exploitative, and that production is more important than consumption. Only the belief that there are fixed amounts of work and wealth to go round can explain the ineradicable collectivist urge to license the State to decide the distribution of income, wealth and work, through progressive taxation, social transfers, minimum wages, incentives to invest, work-sharing schemes, industrial subsidies, price controls and import bans.

Tawney portrayed capitalism as the economic equivalent of warfare, and modern Christian Socialism is still trapped in that kind of thinking.[34] He wrote at a time when the socialist experiment was still untried. But the persistence of the Christian Socialist immunity to market economics decades after the experiment has failed is not difficult to explain. It stems not from stupidity, nostalgia or obstinacy. It reflects the fact that the Christian Socialist critique of capitalism is not a technical one at all. It is a form of moral repugnance. Collectivists are repelled by the basic insight of the market economy: that the self-interest of one individual can further the welfare of others. In the collectivist imagination, self-interest is co-terminous with selfishness. 'There is no doubt,' writes Richard Harries, 'that many people, including a good number of Christians, remain uneasy about a market economy for a number of reasons, first and foremost because it seems to be based on and to encourage self-interest, both in a personal and in an organised form. Or, to put it more harshly, its driving force is sheer greed.'[35] But unlike selfish acts, which are undertaken exclusively for personal profit or pleasure, self-interest does not exclude the possibility that individuals can still be doing what they want to do even though the main beneficiaries of their actions are individuals other than themselves. The individual who seeks promotion or a higher salary is usually doing so not for his own sake, but in order to acquire a better life for his family. Altruism, even philanthropy, may be self-interested.

Psychological experiments and game theory tend to confirm that Homo

Economicus is in fact governed by a sense of fairness and reciprocity rather than just maximum gain. Most businessmen seek reasonable rather than excessive profits on deals, confident that if they treat a customer fairly they will be able to trade with him or her again. No legitimate businessman would regard it as acceptable to shoot his business rivals. Success in commercial life depends on a reputation for integrity and trustworthiness. Market transactions, as Arthur Okun once put it, are governed by an 'invisible handshake' as well as an invisible hand.[36] Individuals often sacrifice material advantage to their sense of sympathy or duty or fairness or self-control. Undoubtedly some businessmen are greedy for gain, but there are also a great many virtues to be found in a business career. Material success requires labour, patience, diligence and perseverance. It needs creativity, inventiveness and initiative. It provides opportunities to give work to others, and to train, educate and nurture them.[37] People also want to possess things not for the sake of aggrandisement, or trading for gain, but because they are beautiful or useful or because they want to give them away. Possessions can be used to increase the amount of friendliness and goodwill in the world. This was obvious to Aristotle, who argued that 'it is a very pleasant thing to help or do favours for friends'.

Nor can people help their fellow men and women unless they have first acquired the material means to do so. George Peabody, the American financier who founded the Peabody housing estates, gave £650,000 (about £30 million in modern prices) to house poor Londoners between 1862 and 1868. 'I found,' he wrote at the time, 'that there were men in life just as anxious to help the poor and destitute as I was to make money...For the first time I felt a higher pleasure and a greater happiness than making money – that of giving it away for good purposes.' Octavia Hill, another housing reformer, was able to complete her work only because a group of friends had clubbed together to provide her with a capital endowment. The work of dozens of charitable trusts set up by other rich individuals and families – Guinness, Wellcome, Sainsbury, Levehulme, Rowntree, Nuffield, Wolfson, Weston, Moores and so on – is evident in cities, schools, universities and hospitals all over the country.

Of course, collectivists are apt to think that the Welfare State is a moral enterprise of a similar kind to private charity. 'If the Christian message without God is to love one's neighbour as oneself,' writes the social historian Harold Perkin, 'then the twentieth-century welfare state could claim to be more Christian and certainly more moral than Victorian England, since it had expanded the concept of neighbour beyond the parish and poor law union to the whole nation.'[38] This is pure Christian Socialism. But it is based on a misconception. Forcing other people to pay higher taxes has no discernible moral component. As Bishop Harries has said:

> One basic, underlying principle emerges for anyone who is concerned with Christian liberation and transformation. It is the necessity of somehow keeping in touch with, and allowing oneself to be affected by, those who are losing out in the struggles of this world. Pictures on television are not enough, books are not enough. There needs to be

personal contact and experience of some kind.[39]

Paying taxes is not enough. Taxation is expropriation, not altruism. 'He that soweth little shall reap little,' as Saint Paul put it, 'and he that soweth plenteously shall reap plenteously. Let every man do according as he is disposed in his heart, not grudging, or of necessity; for God loveth a cheerful giver.'[40] There are no cheerful taxpayers.

The principal weakness of Christian Socialism is its glorification of the collective over the individual. This is rooted in a theology which stresses the *koinonia*, fellowship and corporate life of the Church over the uniqueness and dignity of each individual human being in the sight of God. It feeds on the nostalgia for the reciprocal social hierarchy and 'just' economy of the Middle Ages which is common to all forms of socialistic thought. It is based on a misdiagnosis of capitalism, in which competitive economic individualism shatters the organic community of the past into millions of atomised individuals, driven by selfish greed and bound only by the cash nexus. The consequent illiteracy of the alternative economic programme advanced by major Christian Socialist thinkers like F. D. Maurice and R. H. Tawney – co-operation not competition, production for use not profit, and altruism rather than self-interest – was merely the result of identifying the opposite of what they believed to be the chief characteristics of *laissez-faire* capitalism. The final step was to conclude that organic community can be rebuilt only by employing political methods, since no institution but the State was powerful enough to control market forces and redistribute wealth and property from the rich to the poor. These are the kind of ideas which continue to inspire Christian Socialists like Tony Blair, who was exposed to Christian communitarianism at Oxford.

The Church of England provides a comfortable spiritual home for socialist politicians. By investing the material world with moralworth, Christian Socialism overcame the awkward antagonism between spirit and matter and obliged faithful Christians to set about realising their faith in the daily life of the world through social and political action. This was a symptom of the decay of Christianity as an authentic religion, concerned not with social justice but convinced of the vanity of all earthly endeavours and obsessed with the salvation of the individual soul. As atheistic science and philosophy undermined the confidence of the church that its moral claims were true at all times and in all places, the reinterpretation of Christianity as a programme of social and political action offered its leaders an alternative role. But the Church has paid a high price for its continuing 'relevance'. Its values are thoroughly politicised and secularised, unleashing them from the claims of eternity and tying them instead to the passing political enthusiasms of men. Christian Socialism also drew the Church away from its traditional social role of building the self-governing institutions – churches, schools, hospitals, monasteries - which not only made a reality of its own obedience to the Golden Rule ('love thy neighbour as thyself') but gave it a concrete role in the lives of ordinary men and women. No amount of political activity could ever replace that palpable evidence of the Christian faith in action.

Like all former socialist institutions, the intellectual and empirical collapse of Christian Socialism has marooned the Church in a collectivist past which it cannot as yet bring itself to make any serious effort to escape. The new-found enthusiasm of all the major political parties for various brands of communitarianism has even encouraged some Christian Socialist churchmen to believe that the intellectual climate is not as hostile to their beliefs as they had once assumed. 'To be free as a human being,' writes Bishop Harries, in the most comprehensive attempt yet to devise an Anglican theology of capitalism, 'is to be part of a community, part of a network of relationships in which one is valued, relationships that are characterised by mutual giving and receiving. This includes personal responsibility but it also sees the self as essentially related to other selves, not as a self-reliant, autonomous being, who dips in and out of relationships when he or she chooses.'[41] This marks little advance on the Christian Socialist view, stretching back to at least Thomas Carlyle, that the individual self lives only in relation to others and is fulfilled only as a person-in-community. It smacks, as it always did, of the reactionary conceptions of organic, integral and seamless community which infest German metaphysics as well as socialist communitarianism.

The Outlines of a New Theology of Capitalism

Yet the Church has to hand a powerful theological tradition on which it could draw to devise a new doctrine capable of imbuing a triumphant capitalism with immense moral power. When Jesus warned that 'inasmuch as ye have done it unto one of the least of these my brethren, ye have done it unto me', he was celebrating the uniqueness of every individual soul.[42] 'Are not two sparrows sold for a farthing?' he asked his disciples. 'And one of them shall not fall on the ground without your Father. But the very hairs of your head are all numbered.'[43] There is more joy in heaven over one sinner who repents, or one lost sheep which is found, than any number of people who have no need of repentance.[44] The parables of Jesus were not tales of great collective achievements but the stories of individuals like the Good Samaritan or the Prodigal Son. The Sermon on the Mount is not a call to collective social action, but an impossible ethical challenge to each individual to overthrow all normal forms of thinking and behaviour. Like Socrates, Jesus was a radical and disruptive individualist, challenging all the norms of what the modern Church or State would doubtless call 'the Judaean community'. It is not surprising that he died alone, on a Cross, at the hand of the State.

In the Protestant tradition of Christianity in Britain each individual is called by God and is ultimately responsible to God for his or her actions, which are intended to include working honestly and hard to acquire the material means to help other people. Shirley Letwin has contrasted the 'vigorous virtues' of this tradition – uprightness, energy, adventurousness, independence and so on – with the 'softer virtues' of kindness, humility, gentleness, sympathy and cheerfulness favoured by the collectivists. The robust or muscular tradition of

Protestantism blossomed in the Victorian age of confidence about religious, economic, political and moral progress, and wilted in the century of war, taxation, doubt and socialism. The weak, vulnerable and crucified God of the modern Church of England – once a potent symbol of the strangeness and paradox of a divine power, which did not punish men for their wickedness and vice but instead elected to bear the consequences of their sin on a cross – is now no more than the pale religious reflection of the collectivist search in politics, not for the flourishing, vibrant and adult individuality of Humboldt or Mill, but for the timid and child-like dependence of social security. The Psalms of the Book of Common Prayer are steeped in highly individualistic and personal reflections, but *Hymns for Today* is packed with sentimental pap.

In the Christian individualist tradition, personal moral responsibility means free men and women choosing to do not what they would like to do or what they are forced to do by others but what their conscience dictates that they ought to do. No creed rooted in German metaphysics and its violent repugnance at individualism, like Christian Socialism, can possibly accommodate this powerful idea: that only the uncoerced individual is capable of a moral action. It is the commonest fallacy of collectivist thinking to assume that collectivities like the State can exhibit human characteristics like kindness or charity. Ruskin himself identified the tendency to attribute human feelings to nature as the Pathetic Fallacy. A willingness to advocate the redistribution of the income and wealth of others, and even to vote for it, is neither moral nor kind nor altruistic nor charitable. Where people do not choose to help their neighbours but are forced to do so by the State, no moral transaction takes place. It is merely the coercion and expropriation of one section of the population by another.

Tony Blair says, following orthodox Christian Socialism, that 'the basic principle that distinguishes the Labour Party from the Conservatives is that we are prepared both economically and socially to use the power of society in order to advance the individual'.[45] But, once this idea is translated into practice, it will involve taking the income and wealth of some people in order to give it to others in the form of public charity, public services, public subsidies and public housing. Christian Socialists might delude themselves that this shows that they 'care' and that 'the community' recognises its obligations to other members of the 'community', but it does not feel like that to those who are coerced into surrendering a portion of their property to the State. Nor does it feel like that to those who receive from the State, since they are long since accustomed to think of welfare payments as a political right. Individualist social welfare, by contrast, teaches that the authentic moral choices are those which men and women make with their own time and money and not those which they are compelled to make by the State. The obverse of moral action is moral risk. The virtuous do not merely abide by the law, but exercise their moral faculties and personal judgment. 'The letter killeth, but the spirit giveth life.'[46]

But Christianity does not just teach that all improvements in social and economic arrangements are worthless without courageous, kind and selfless individuals to put the new systems into practice. It also teaches that the individual is the only proper moral end and object of all human thought and action, including politics. In Christian ethics, each individual is made in the image of God. This makes each individual inviolable, but also unique. 'Each of us has a distinctive contribution to make, one that can be made by no other,' writes the Catholic theologian and political economist, Michael Novak. 'It is part of a very real adventure of life for each of us to find that spark of originality and uniqueness that the Creator placed in us, and to strike from it the fires that no other individual can bring into the world.'[47] The uniqueness and centrality of the individual human personality is reinforced by Christian eschatology, which teaches each man and woman that their sin, judgment and redemption are intensely personal. Importantly, it also teaches that every individual human being is going to live forever. 'If individuals live only seventy years,' as C. S. Lewis once put it, 'then a state, or a nation, or a civilisation, which may last for a thousand years, is more important than an individual. But if Christianity is true, then the individual is not only more important but incomparably more important, for he is everlasting and the life of a state or a civilisation, compared with his, is only a moment.[41]

This idea is unique to Christianity. There is nothing like it in classical thought, the other main influence on the moral values of Western civilisation. Both the Romans and the Greeks tolerated slavery, Aristotle and Plato were notoriously disparaging about the lower orders, and the Greeks even put Socrates to death when he refused to yield to the popular will. The instinctive collectivism of the ancient world was neatly encapsulated by an Oxford classics don, who disclosed recently in his memoirs that he had planned to cause the death by suicide of a troublesome colleague. It seems his immersion in Hellenism had prepared him for just such a task, as he told a journalist afterwards:

> The Greeks would always worry more about harm or injustice to the community in general than about the individual. They would execute just to be on the safe side.[49]

Unsurprisingly, Western thinking about politics and the State originated in the classical rather than the Biblical texts. The Bible is at best ambiguous about the role of the State. In the New Testament, conscience and politics are portrayed as inhabiting different spheres. In Revelation the predominant political power of the time, the Roman Empire, is depicted as idolatrous in its demands that people worship the Emperor rather than God. Saint Paul calls on Christians to obey the divine rather than the temporal power. Since at least the Reformation, and arguably since Roman times, Christian theology has also sanctioned the idea of a just rebellion against State tyranny.

Community: The Mask of Despotism

History shows that all of the worst things which a State can inflict upon individual human beings – conscription, apartheid, expro- priation, compulsory contraception, genocide – are characteristic- ally masked by some collective abstraction like 'the State', 'society', 'nation', 'race', 'proletariat', 'community', or 'spaceship Earth' whose interests are said to override those of the individual, and so justify the coercive or repressive activities of the State. The Nazi regime justified the extermination of the mentally ill, the physically deformed, the alcoholic and the chronically ill long before it turned to the extermination of the Jews, because it believed that the lives of individuals were less important than the strength and purity of the race. Today, the Indonesian foreign minister defends the repressive policies of his government on the grounds that 'our human rights concept is not individualistic, but relies more on the interests of the community, the nation and the state, which cannot be overlooked'.[50] It is significant that warfare, which demonstrates the power of the State over the individual at its most elemental, has spawned a whole dictionary of euphemisms to help people kill each other by reducing individual human beings to ciphers. In *Bravo Two Zero*, the best-selling count of an SAS patrol behind the lines in Iraq, Officers are called 'Ruperts' an Arabs 'ragheads'. Even friendly soldiers lose their names to mere tags like 'Geordie' or 'Legs' or 'Dinger'. People are not killed but 'slotted'. Likewise, the generals conducting the air raids on Iraq referred not to bombing people but to 'servicing a target' or 'visiting a site'.

The Gulf War was an instance of *realpolitik*. But the origins and conduct of the Falklands War, which was a victory for great principles and a just cause, made no difference to the individuals killed and maimed. The painfully reconstructed face of Simon Weston is a constant reminder of the price that one individual paid for victory in the South Atlantic. It is the survival of his individuality – his personal courage and selflessness – that has enabled him to translate the bitter experience into the charitable work of the Weston Spirit. For 255 other people from these islands and their dependencies who fought and died in the same conflict, there was no survival of individuality, or victory for high principle, or resurrection of personal hopes. Their loss of life, liberty, individuality and potentiality was total. But politicians do not find collective abstractions necessary only when they are sending people to their death. They use them at all times when they cannot bear the reality of what they are doing: coercing individual human beings. The casualties of the humdrum wars against inflation or the battle for exports cannot expect the State to take account of their personal misery, except perhaps by coercing others into giving them money to compensate for their loss. 'The ogre strolls with hands on hips,' Wrote W. H. Auden as the Soviet tanks rolled into Czechoslovakia in 1968 to the accompaniment of a cacophony of collectivist euphemisms, 'while drivel gushes from his lips.'

State worshipping collectivists are doomed by theory as well as practice to treat individuals as means, and not as ends. The categorical imperative of Immanuel Kant entreats mankind to 'act so as to treat every rational being, whether in yourself or in another, never as a means only but always also as an end'. In Kant's view, this moral law of the absolute value of every individual human being was objectively binding on all beings, including God. It is only the State – the State of Kafka's 'K' or Schindler's 'list' or Blair's 'community' – which erases the individuality of man, and which ceases to treat each human being as an end in himself or herself. It is the morality of the criminal, who can live with his crimes only by ceasing to think of them as offences against individuals and their possessions. The sanctity of the individual, his uniqueness and infinite value to his Creator, is the one true universal human value which transcends all collectivist and criminal endeavours. It is the great gift of Judaeo-Christian civilisation to the world.

The value of that gift is well understood by Pierre Sane, the Senegalese secretary general of Amnesty International, an organisation which deals with the consequences for individual human beings of the State-worship of the twentieth century. 'Even if it is Western, it is the bearer of universal values,' he told a journalist recently. 'The issue is whether a collective has the right to torture people in their own collective. If you had a culture which practised anthropophagy [cannibalism] and argued "this is our culture" we will tell them "even if it's your culture it's not acceptable. So stop it!"... [liberty] is not just a yardstick. It is the minimum that makes an individual a real human being.'[51] Collectivists always value the group, even the group of cannibals, more highly than the individual. They value it more highly even than the individual who is eaten for lunch by his fellow-citizens. It is highly significant that the near-universal interest of Western politicians in human rights is such a recent moral development. The concept, of course, was of far less importance in other centuries, when the State was neither omni-present nor omnipotent and its tools of repression were so much less effective.

It is because of the historic disrespect of all collectivities for the life of the individual that the current enthusiasm, in every political party, for a return to 'community' has such a sinister ring to it. The 'community' to which politicians and commentators refer is a fiction. It is a weasel word which sucks all meaning out of the words which follow. The release of the former inmates of State-run mental hospitals into 'the community' to be cared for provides a perfect instance of its treacherous qualities. In reality, they were condemned to spend their nights in State-financed hostels, and their days wandering the streets. The headline above a story in *The Times* in April 1994 read: 'Mentally Ill Left to Fend for Themselves in the Community.' The community that was going to care for them did not exist. Young people taken into 'community care' in London have made the same discovery. Where the State is not acting *in loco parent is*, nobody else does, and they end up back on the streets. Susan Andrews, a London woman who looks after her aged mother and two elderly aunts, has had the same disarming experience. 'My mother had to go into hospital earlier this year and after she came out, a social worker called for a while,' she told the *Observer* recently. 'But the visits suddenly stopped. When I asked about it, the social services department said that after six weeks they pass cases on to "the community" – what they meant was me.'[52] In the autumn of 1994 Gloucestershire County Council announced that it had stopped providing 'community care' to the elderly altogether. It seems the Department of Social Security had failed to supply sufficient funds. The 'community' in this instance turned out to be millions of anonymous taxpayers all over the country, not the good and kindly burghers of Gloucester and Cheltenham. Central government now spends £1.8 billion a year on 'community care', but Susan Andrews reckons she 'saves the State up to £1,500 a week, but she doesn't get so much as a thank-you from anyone'.

Dick Atkinson, who has made the boldest and best attempt to connect the language of 'community' to social readily, ended up describing networks or clusters of self-governing institutions – schools, family centres, residents' associations, youth and sports clubs, housing associations and voluntary groups – whose success or failure ultimately depended on the individual initiative and self- reliance of the responsible 'active citizen' and not, despite his best efforts to identify communal goals and values, on some noumenal 'common sense of community'.[53] The 'community' is a figment of the collectivist and bureaucratic imagination. There are only individuals, and those who preface their ideas and policies with the word 'community' are usually interested only in its potential to conceal the reality of what they are doing. Calling the poll tax a 'community charge' could not in the end conceal the fact that it was paid by individuals. Nor can journalistic references to 'the black community' or 'the Asian community' or the 'medical community' or the 'psychological community' bear any interpretation which is not demeaning to the individuals which fall into any of these categories. 'A nation,' David Hume rightly observed, 'is nothing but a collection of individuals.'

The Sanctity of the Individual

There are living in Britain today nearly sixty million individual human beings, and each one of them is unique. They are unique not just in theological or philosophical terms, but in biological terms as well, as Matt Ridley has pointed out:

> Human beings are individuals. All individuals are slightly different. Societies that treat their constituent members as identical pawns soon run into trouble. Economists and sociologists who believe that individuals will usually act in their collective rather than their particular interests ('From each according to his abilities, to each according to his needs' versus 'Devil take the hindmost') are soon confounded. Society is composed of competing individuals as surely as markets are composed of competing merchants; the focus of economic and social theory is, and must be, the individual... It is one of the remarkable things about the human race that no two people are identical. No father is exactly recast in his son; no daughter is exactly like her mother; no man is his brother's double and no woman a carbon copy of her sister – unless they are that rarity, a pair of identical twins. Every idiot can be father or mother to a genius – and vice versa. Every face and set of fingerprints is effectively unique. Indeed, this uniqueness goes further in human beings than in any other animal. Whereas every deer, or every sparrow, is self-reliant and does everything every other deer or sparrow does, the same is never true of a man or a woman and has not been for thousands of years. Every individual is a specialist of some sort, whether he or she is a welder, a housewife, a playwright or a prostitute. In behaviour. as in appearance, every human individual is unique.[54]

In fact, each human personality develops and changes continuously, as a result of new knowledge and experiences. Several different personalities can co-exist within the same brain over the same same lifespan, vastly expanding the range of individuals whose lives the collectivist planners of the ideal 'community' or 'society' are impatient to direct.

It is impossible for anyone to know what each of these sixty million unique and evolving individual personalities seeks from life. No external agency can ever know enough about them or their aspirations to be certain that it is acting in their best interests. There is no 'community' of interests or values to which each and every individual subscribes, and which overrides the interests and values of any one individual. It follows that the interests of some can be advanced only at the expense of others, making all collectivist projects by definition coercive. There is no better illustration of this than the miners' strike of 1984–85. 'Collectivism,' wrote the historians of that strike, 'can only work through unity of action: its enemy is self-evidently individualism, where the collective's units – people – follow their own rather than the collective's interests, where the two conflict. Strike action is the supreme example of collective activity in the labour movement, and thus the strike-breaker, or 'scab', is the acme of individualism.'[55]

To suppress the individualism of miners who wanted to work, striking miners did not hesitate to resort to physical violence. Working miners were spat at or sprayed with paint and brake fluid. Bales of hay were dragged into the roads and set on fire to prevent men getting to work. Pickets noted the registration numbers of miners driving to work, and visited them at home later to slash their tyres. Bricks were thrown through the windows of working miners' homes. They and their wives were ostracised and threatened by their fellow-villagers, and banned even from the shops. Their houses were daubed, or even set on fire, and their children abused and bullied at school. The names of 'scabs' were posted in shop windows, and instructions given to the shopkeeper that they were not to be served. Shopkeepers who refused to help striking miners were threatened. One man was killed on his way to work by a slab of concrete thrown from a motorway bridge. A young Durham miner hanged himself after being taunted continuously about being a 'scab'. A Warwickshire miner received an anonymous note threatening to break the kidney dialysis machine which kept his son alive. The pregnant wife of a Staffordshire miner was nearly struck by a piece of concrete thrown through the window of their house. It landed on the baby's cot. Even if working miners moved to live elsewhere, they were often followed and attacked in their new home by unforgiving strikers.

The miners' strike was a cruel exposition of the true spirit of collectivism, and of the fictitious reciprocity and communitarianism of the much-lauded pit villages. 'Even in the most embattled "us versus them" situations,' writes Samuel Brittan, 'it is individuals, not collectives who feel, exult, triumph or despair.'[56] The essential task of a humane political creed is, as John Stuart Mill pointed out, to delineate the areas of individual human life which are free of coercion by others, whether or not they are organised as the State:

Whatever theory we adopt respecting the foundation of the social union, and under whatever political institutions we live, there is a circle around every individual human being, which no government, be it that of one, of a few? or of the many, ought to be permitted to overstep: there is a part of the life of every person who has come to years of discretion, within which the individuality of that person ought to reign uncontrolled either by any other individual or by the public collectively. That there is, or ought to be, some space in human existence thus entrenched around, and sacred from authoritative intrusion, no one who professes the smallest reard to human freedom or dignity will call in question: the point to be determined is, where the limit should be placed; how large a province of human life this reserved territory should include.[57]

Mill thought he had discovered a golden rule which would enable statesmen to know where the boundary of the State ended and that of the Individual began. 'The sole end for which mankind are warranted, individually or collectively, in interfering with the liberty of action of any of their number,' he wrote in On Liberty, 'is self-protection.'[58]

This attempt to base the liberty and sanctity of the individual on a principled footing proved doubly tragic. Because no action is ever entirely self-regarding, it proved to be a constantly renewable licence for the State to interfere. 'Wherever the self-interest of one person was incompatible with the self-interest of another, wherever (the contemporary play on words had it) the rights of property became the wrongs of the poor, there was a case for intervention to create the very conditions in which mutual self-help and competition could freely operate,' writes one historian of the rise of the Welfare State.[59] Mill was alive to this difficulty, and struggled to arrive at a strict definition of other-regarding or injurious actions which the State was at liberty to restrict or prevent. He was concerned that governments would be driven by public opinion to interfere with liberty whenever individuals deviated from the standards of behaviour of the majority, and feared an expansion of 'the bounds of the moral police, until it encroaches on the most unquestionably legitimate liberty of the individual'.[60]

Mill thought the greatest threats to his principle of liberty were drunkenness and religious bigotry. Writing at the height of the minimal State of Victorian England, he could not have foreseen the relentless pressure on the governments of today to intervene even in such minutiae of private life as the drinking habits of cross-channel motorists and the bowel movements of dogs. He was confident he could rely on the traditional virtues of his fellow countrymen – their sense of duty, prudence and self-respect – to limit the number of occasions on which the State would be required to reconcile a clash of individual interests. This was why he argued that 'none but a person of confirmed virtue is completely free'. But he could not have foreseen that, as the State intervened ever more widely and on a larger scale, the individual capacity for self-respect, self-restraint, self-development and self-government would diminish so rapidly. 'The term duty to oneself, when it means anything more than prudence,' he wrote, in a passage now rich in pathos, 'means self-respect or self-development; and for none of these is any one accountable to his fellow creatures, because for none of them is it for the good of mankind that he be held accountable to them.'

References

1   From his essay 'Religion and Morality', reproduced in Leo Tolstoy, A Confession and Other Religious Writings, Penguin Classics, 1987, page 150.

2   Quoted in John Morley, The Life of W. E. Gladstone, Macmillan, 1903, Vol. I, page 375.

3   Quoted in Owen Chadwick, The Secularization of the European Mind in the Nineteenth Century, CUP, 1990, page 108.

4   T. S. Eliot, Notes Towards the Definition of Culture, Faber & Faber, 1962, page 122.

5   See Harold Perkin, The Rise of Professional Society: England Since 1880, Routledge, 89, pages 125–7.

6   Quoted in T. E. B. Howarth, Prospect and Reality: Great Britain 1945–1955, Collins, 85, page 21.

7   Reported in the Independent on Sunday, 25 September 1994.

8   Francis Wheen, Tom Driberg: His Life and Indiscretions, Chatto & Windus, Iggo, pages 320-1.

9   Quoted in The Oxford Book of Money, Kevin Jackson (ed.), OUP, 1995, page 268.

10   Reported in the Independent on Sunday, 25 September 1994.

11   Quoted in Alan Billings, Christian Socialism: the death of a tradition?, Southwell and Oxford Papers on Contemporary Society, February 1992, page 3.

12   See Chapter 6, pages 144-6.

13   R. H. Tawney, The Acquisitive Society, G. Bell & Sons, pages 227–42 and especially page 228.

14   Dictionary of National Biography, 1961–70, OUP, 1981, page 592.

15   Quoted in Alan Billings, 'Christian Socialism: the death of a tradition?', Southwell and Oxford Papers on Contemporary Society, February 1992, page 3.

16   John Stevenson, British Society 1914–45, Penguin, 1984, page 452.

17   Peter Hennessy attributes the term to Alfred Zimmern, Professor of International Relations at Oxford in the 1930s. See Never Again: Britain 1914–45, Jonathan Cape, 1992, page 121.

18   Quoted in Alan Billings, Christian Socialism: the death of a tradition?, Southwell and Oxford Papers on Contemporary Society, February 1992, page 3.

19   Hansard, 13 February 1989, Col. 25.

20   Quoted in Cento Veljanovski, Selling the State: Privatisation in Britain, Weidenfeld & Nicolson, 1988, page 43.

21   Alan Billings, Christian Socialism: the death of a tradition?, Southwell and Oxford Papers on Contemporary Society, February 1992, page 8.

22   Presidential address to Southwark Diocesan Synod, 5 November 1994.

23   Richard Harries, Is There a Gospel for the Rich?, Mowbray, 1992, page 102.

24   Alan Billings, Mrs Thatcher and the Churches – Reflections on Lost Opportunities, Milton Keynes & Malvern Papers, September 1993.

25   Quoted in Paul A. Welsby, A History of the Church of England 1945–80, OUP, 1986, page 111

26   'The political Christ', in Edward Norman, Christianity and the World Order, OUP, , pages 1–14.

27   Quoted in Christianity and the World Order, page 8.

28   Christianity and the World Order, page 9.

29   The Times, 28 November 1994.

30   Matthew 19:3; Mark 10:2–12.

31   Reverend John Kennedy, 'Why is the Church So Bad At Making Us Good?', in Teaching Right and Wrong: Have the Churches Failed?, IEA Health and Welfare Unit, November 1994, pages 19–20 and 22.

32   Alan Billings, Mrs Thatcher and the Churches – Reflections on Lost Opportunities, Milton Keynes & Malvern Papers, September 1993.

33   Richard Harries, Is There a Gospel for the Rich?, Mowbray, 1992, page 111.

34   He was quite sure that the only alternative to the 'socially functional' society he

envisaged was actual 'war...continuous war'. See R. H. Tawney, The Acquisitive Society, G. Bell & Sons, page 224.

35   Richard Harries, Is There a Gospel for the Rich?, Mowbray, 1992, page 91.

36   James Q. Wilson, The Moral Sense, The Free Press, 1993, page 64.

37   To be fair, Richard Harries is alive to these possibilities but concludes, bleakly, that capitalism tends in practice to be exploitative. See Richard Harries, Is There a Gospel for the Rich?, Mowbray, 1992, pages 94–5.

38   Harold Perkin, The Rise of Professional Society: England Since 1989, Routledge, 1989, pages 435–6.

39   Richard Harries, Is There a Gospel for the Rich?, Mowbray, 1992, page 71.

40   2 Corinthians 9:7.

41   Richard Harries, Is There a Cospel for the Rich?, Mowbray, 1992, page 101.

42   Matthew 25:40

43   Matthew 10:29–30.

44 Luke 15:4–10

45   Financial Times, 11 June 1994.

46   2 Corinthians 3:5.

47   Michael Novak, 'The Person in Community', in Christian Capitalism or Christian Socialism?, IEA, April 1994, page 70.

48   C. S. Lewis, Mere Christianity, Fontana, 1979, page 70.

49   Sir Kenneth Dover, president of Corpus Christi College, Oxford, quoted in The Times, 28 November 1994.

50   Quoted in Sunday Telegraph, 13 November 1994.

51   Financial Times, 19 June 1993.

52   Observer, 18 December 1994.

53   Dick Atkinson, The Common Sense of Community, Demos, 1994.

54   Matt Ridley, The Red Queen: Sex and the Evolution of Human Nature, Viking,1993, page 11.

55   Martin Adeney and John Lloyd, The Miners' Strike 1984–5: Loss Without Limit, Routledge & Kegan Paul, 1988, page 257.

56   Samuel Brittan, 'There Is No Such Thing as Society', J. C. Rees Memorial Lecture, University College of Swansea, 9 November 1992, page 24.

57   John Stuart Mill, Principles of Political Economy, Books IV and V, Penguin Classics Edition, 1985, page 306.

58   John Stuart Mill, On Liberty, paperback edition, OUP, 1991, page 14: 'The sole end for which mankind are warranted, individually or collectively, in interfering with the liberty of action of any of their number, is self-protection...The only purpose for which power can be rightfully exercised over any member of a civilised community not a sufficient warrant. He cannot rightfully be compelled to do or forbear because it will be better for him to do so, because it will make him happier, because, in the opinions of others, to do so would be wise, or even right. There are good reasons for remonstrating with him, or reasoning with him, or persuading him, or entreating him but not for compelling him, or visiting him with any evil in case he do otherwise. To justify that, the conduct from which it is desired to deter him, must be calculated to produce evil to someone else. The only part of the conduct of any one, for which he is amenable to society, is that which concerns others. In the part which merely concerns himself, his independence is, of right, absolute. Over himself, over his own body and mind, the individual is sovereign.'

59   Derek Fraser, The Evolution of the British Welfare State, Second Edition, Macmillan 84, page 122.

60   See Gertrude Himmelfarb, On Liberty and Liberalism: The Case of John Stuart Mill, ICS Press, 1990, pages 96–108.

61   John Stuart Mill, On Liberty, paperback edition, OUP, 1991, page 87.

CHAPTER TWELVE

The Destruction of the Family by the State

The proletarian is without property; his relation to his wife and children has no longer anything in common with the bourgeois family relations...Law, morality, religion, are to him so many bourgeois prejudices, behind which lurk in ambush just as many bourgeois interests...On what foundation is the present family, the bourgeois family, based? On capital, on private gain...The bourgeois family will vanish as a matter of course when its complement vanishes, and both will vanish with the vanishing of capital.

Karl Marx and Friedrich Engels, *The Communist Manifesto*

In fact the single marriage family, which is called by anthropologists and sociologists the nuclear family, is possibly the shortest lived familial system ever developed.

Germaine Greer, *The Female Eunuch*

The family is a subversive organisation. In fact, it is the ultimate and only consistently subversive organisation. Only the family has continued throughout history and still continues to undermine the State.

Ferdinand Mount, *The Subversive Family*

It is customary to argue today that the destroyer of the traditional moral and social restraints on individuals in England was the possessive individualism unleashed by the successive Conservative governments of the 1980s. In fact, philosophers of liberal capitalism from Hume to Hayek have always recognised that the pursuit of self-interest must in practice be limited by an unwritten code of moral constraints. Hume thought that the peace and security of society depended on universal observance of three fundamental laws of nature, *that of the stability of possession, of its transference by consent,*[1] and of the performance of promises' . ' These essential rules were not invented, but the legacy of the past. 'The rules of morality are not the conclusions of our reason,' he wrote. Adam Smith – famous for his assertion that 'it is not from the benevolence of the butcher, the brewer, or the baker, that we expect our dinner, but from their regard to their own interest' – agreed that economic self-interest was naturally and properly fettered by a sense of duty and established rules of behaviour. 'Every man,' he wrote in *Wealth of Nations*, 'so long as he does not violate the laws of justice, is left perfectly free to pursue his own interest in his own way.'

De Tocqueville believed that freedom could not survive the disappearance of a framework of moral rules. Only Jeremy Bentham, the inventor of the cost/benefit analysis school of ethics, could possibly believe that 'money is the instrument of measuring the quantity of pain and pleasure. Those who are not satisfied with the accuracy of this instrument must find out some other that shall be more accurate, or bid adieu to politics and morals.'[2] He naturally thought that it was possible to design the ideal society through the use of Reason alone. Hayek considered that an informal moral framework was an indispensable condition of freedom. The alternative, in his judgment, was not simply coercion by the State but social and and economic stagnation. It is precisely because an informal code of behaviour is flexible that it leaves room for the spontaneity, and experimental changes, modifications and improvements on which the progress of the species depends. The State, whose laws are rigid, narrowed the scope for constructive change.

In *The Constitution of Liberty*, Hayek described the kind of moral framework he had in mind:

> We understand one another and are able to act successfully on our plans, because, most of the time, members of our civilisation conform to unconscious patterns of conduct, show a regularity in their actions that is not the result of commands or coercion, often not even of any conscious adherence to known rules, but of firmly established habits and traditions. The general observence of these conventions is a necessary condition of the orderliness of the world in which we live, of our being able to find our way in it, though we do not know their significance and may not even be consciously aware of their existence. In some instances it would be necessary, for the smooth

running of society, to secure a similar uniformity by coercion, if such conventions or rules were not observed often enough. Coercion, then, may sometimes be avoidable only because a high degree of voluntary conformity exists, which means that voluntary conformity may be a condition of a beneficial working of freedom. It is indeed a truth, which all the great apostles of freedom outside the rationalistic school have never tired of emphasising, that freedom has never worked without deeply ingrained moral beliefs and that coercion can be reduced to a minimum only where individuals can be expected as a rule to conform voluntarily to certain principles.[3]

The collectivists have never shared Hayek's distaste for State power. They also learnt from Karl Marx and other sociologists that any moral framework was merely an expression of class or sectarian interests, and therefore an obstacle to the achievement of Utopia. The collectivist is never content to accept any social institution as the undesigned but evolved prescription of the past, seeking always to 'revolutionise', 'reform', 'renew' or 'reinvent' whatever structures he encounters. The enemy of the virtuous society, of stability, decency, altruism, generosity, tolerance and self-restraint, is not the greedy individualist of the

1980S but the collectivist State of the twentieth century. It has not only called into question the validity and usefulness of traditional morality, but systematically attacked all of the social institutions responsible for its existence and transmission from one generation to the next.

The Historical Reality of the 'Bourgeois' Family

'If individuals have no space protecting them from the State,' writes Michael Novak, 'they have no "self" for self-government.'[4] The State is an implacable opponent of all of the individual spaces in which the individual learns self-respect, self-restraint and the value of self-development. The most important of these is the family. In the collectivist imagination, the family is associated with sexual repression, bourgeois values, Poujadism and other morbid symptoms of psychological ill-health. Rousseau, who but his children in an orphanage, was pleased to be able to devise a philosophical explanation for his behaviour. Socialists railed against the inequality produced by family inheritance and education. Marx thought the links between parent and child and families and education for life were 'bourgeois clap-trap'.[5] Collectivists denigrate the family relentlessly, by talking of 'relationships' rather than families and 'partners' rather than husbands or wives. But traces of the repressive interpretation of the family can be found in Hobbes and Locke, and it was in the course of a plea for easier divorce laws that John Milton issued his celebrated call to 'let not England forget her precedence of teaching nations how to live'.[6] Even John Stuart Mill, an early feminist, thought the family was the main instrument of the subjection of women. Modern opponents of the family are more likely to be influenced by the warped inventions of sociology and its brothers in intellectual infamy, anthropology and psychology. The 'bourgeois' and sexually repressive family is a useful myth with which to discredit individualistic capitalism.

Thinkers like Locke were concerned – mistakenly – that the family was an obstacle to individual freedom. This has not prevented many collectivists continuing to believe that the nuclear family was a 'bourgeois' invention, devised in the seventeenth century by Protestant thinkers and theologians like Locke and a new breed of capitalistic individualists at the expense of the impersonal, extended and economically integrated family of peasant society.[7] Anna Coote of the Institute for Public Policy Research told a journalist as recently as 1990 that 'the traditional nuclear family was never a universal model but rather reflected the economic needs and social values of Victorian society...Rather than attempting to promote the Victorian family, policies should be designed to make the most of a range of family types, including one-parent families and reconstituted two-parent families.'[8] In fact, modern scholarship recognises that the family creates individualistic capitalism rather than capitalism the family. In *Origins of English Individualism*, Alan Macfarlane traced the nuclear family in England back at least as far as 1250. He considered the 'bourgeois family' an essential cultural pre-condition of the first industrial economy. Supportive evidence is now accumulating that the nuclear family was a crucial ingredient in the astonishing success of the East Asian economies in the 1980s.[9]

The 'bourgeois family' probably goes back to the earliest human societies. By contrast with the mendacious efforts of early anthropologists and psychologists – who were apt to draw unfavourable contrasts between the sexual liberation of primitive peoples and the supposedly repressed condition of their counterparts in modern industrial civilisation – modern biologists and anthropologists have recently rediscovered the fact that marriage and the nuclear family make reproductive and economic sense. In most societies, female adultery is treated more seriously than male adultery precisely because it threatens to bring alien children into the family. Similarly, the sexual division of labour is common to all known human cultures because a single woman with a small child is not a viable economic unit. Even hunter-gathering societies rely on men to hunt for distant but protein-rich meat and women to gather nearby vegetables and fruit, so that she can simultaneously look after dependent children and guard against starvation if the hunting expedition is fruitless. Mankind is also unusual among primates in the amount of help fathers give to their children, if only in the shape of physical protection, food or money. The sexual division of labour is an economic system which cannot work unless the two sexes enter into a monogamous relationship to share the rewards of each other's labours. It is significant that the most notorious attempt to eliminate these gender-roles – the Israeli *kibbutzim* – succeeded only in resurrecting them in more virulent form.[10]

Modern biology explains why the 'bourgeois family' is so persistent. Matt Ridley believes that the aboriginal woman sought a monogamous relationship in order to prevent men dividing their child-rearing activities among several families:

> No hunter-gatherer society supports more than occasional polygamy; and the institution of marriage is virtually universal. People live in larger bands than they used to, but within those bands the kernel of human life is the nuclear family: a man, his wife and children. Marriage is a child-rearing institution: wherever it occurs the father takes at least some part in rearing the child even if only by the provision of food. In most societies, men strive to be polygamists; but few of them succeed. Even in the polygamous societies of pastoralists, the great majority of marriages are monogamous ones. It is our usual monogamy, not our occasional polygamy, that sets us apart from other mammals, including apes. Of the four other apes (gibbons, orange-utans, gorillas and chimpanzees), only the gibbon practises anything like marriage.[11]

Historically, human beings have preferred adultery to polygamy precisely because it is less threatening to the family. Attempts to override a genetically determined preference for monogamy (as in any free-love commune) invariably fail. Sex roles reassert them- selves, and free love is crushed by the continuing pressures of sexual jealousy and possessiveness. Despite the best efforts of anthropologists, sociologists and psychologists to prove that monogamous marriage and the nuclear family are diseases of modern civilisation, the nuclear family is clearly not a mere social convention. It is written into the genetic coding of man. It is, as previous generations might have said, a part of the natural law.

The Family as the Nursery of Morality

Even in advanced industrial societies, the usefulness of the institu- tions of monogamous marriage and the nuclear family is un- questionable. If liberty is not to degenerate into licence, and destroy itself by making massive State coercion unavoidable, the freedom of the individual needs to be combined with strong but informal social controls and an effective code of personal morals. The family is where these informal and personal rules – voluntary restraint, respect for others, moral responsibility and so on – are learnt, and where the quality of the free citizen is determined. It teaches individuals the virtues of prudence, sympathy and generosity. As two recent analysts have put it:

The studies show, and sociological and psychological theory explain, that unless a child is brought up in the constant atmosphere of human beings negotiating the business of getting on with one another, co-operating, controlling their anger, affecting reconciliations, he cannot learn what it is to be an effective member of a social group. He can only Learn this as he learns his native tongue, by experiencing the phenomenon, in this case social interaction, taking place outside of himself, yet his being part of it densely and continuously.[12]

Family life nurtures men and women fit and able to work, and sufficiently in control of themselves to abjure a life of crime. This is as true of parents as it is of children. 'He that hath wife and children,' wrote Francis Bacon, 'hath given hostages to fortune; for they are impediments to great enterprises, either of virtue or mischief.'

The efforts of sociologists to prove or disprove the role of family breakdown in the increase of criminal activity in the post-war world are of little interest to those not party to the petty squabbles of academia. Most people rightly regard it as beyond dispute that a child brought up by two loving parents is more likely to be well- adjusted, hard-working and happy than a child from a broken or irregular home.[13] 'The family,' adds Michael Novak, 'is the major carrier of culture, transmitting ancient values and lessons in ways that escape completely rational articulation, carrying forward motivations and standards of judgement and shaping the distribution of energy and emotion, preferences and inclinations.'[14]

The family plays the crucial role in the transmission of the values which make a country a safe and flourishing one in which to live and work. This is common ground across all political parties. Although the extent of family breakdown can be exaggerated – as David Willetts has pointed out, the proportion of the population living in a household headed by a married couple has fallen by well under ten per cent over the last thirty years – there is also widespread agreement that the family is under unprecedented pressure.[15] Where opinions differ is on the origins of that pressure, and what can be done to relieve it. The conventional explanation is that a mixture of declining religious faith, personal and sexual libertarianism and market-driven economic change has undermined the institutional, social and economic foundations of family life. John Gray has concluded that the crisis is so advanced that remedial treatment is impossible.[16]

Others believe the family can be propped up by a mixture of exhortation and increased State expenditure and intervention. But both the conventional diagnosis and the conventional prescription are wrong. It is the State that is attacking the legal and intellectual foundations of the family, and which is steadily eroding its economic security. Until it is stopped, the family cannot recover.

Permissive Legislation

The breakdown of a tradition of law and opinion which supported the family can be dated fairly precisely to the 1960s, when contraception, abortion, co-habitation, pre-marital sex, divorce, pornography, single parenthood, venereal disease, and an agrees- sive and ideological feminism first became socially acceptable. The Abortion Bill, which allowed a pregnancy to be terminated on demand provided two doctors were satisfied it was necessary on medical or psychological grounds, was passed in 1967. The Family Planning Act, which authorised local authorities to dispense contraceptives and contraceptive advice for the first time, was passed the same year. The oral contraceptive pill, invented in the mid-1950s, began to be used widely in Britain from the late 1960s. It enabled young people to experiment sexually without the fear of conceiving an unwanted child. Not entirely antipathetically, the emergence of a distinctive feminist movement led to a general coarsening of relations between men and women. The key feminist text of the era, Germaine Greer's *Female Eunuch*, was published in 1970.

A superficial 'cult of youth', characterised by rock music, drugs, outlandish clothes and sexual licence, took shallow root. The philosopher of the age was a Californian-based Freudian-cum- Marxist called Herbert Marcuse who, despite the obscurity of his texts, persuaded many young people that revolution would come from overthrowing the prevailing morality. 'Once a specific morality is firmly established as a norm of social behaviour,' he wrote, 'it is not only introjected – it also operates as a norm of "organic" behaviour; the organism receives and reacts to certain stimuli and "ignores" and repels others in accord with the introjected morality, which is thus promoting or impeding the function of the organism as a living cell in the respective society.'[17] This was thought to mean that industrial civilisations forced people to conform, and that it was the task of students, blacks, terrorists and bohemians to overthrow the repressive conformity of the 'system' by demonstrating, taking LSD and saying 'fuck' to people who might be shocked by it. Marcuse's new theory of alienation' transformed freedom from Acton's opportunity to 'do as one ought' into mere self-expression.

The Family Law Reform Act and the Representation of the People Act, both passed in 1968, lowered the age of heterosexual consent and the voting age to 18. The Divorce Reform Act, which introduced the concept of 'irretrievable breakdown' for the first time in place of the previously required 'matrimonial offence' followed in 1969. The breakthrough in the publication of pornography came in 1960, when Penguin Books defended successfully in the courts their decision to republish *Lady Chatterley's Lover*. Theatrical censorship was abolished in 1968, paving the way for a series of dramas notable mainly for nudity and foul language. The censorship of cinema films was also relaxed, leading eventually to an unceasing diet of sexual intercourse and violence on the big screen. It was in 1964 that Mrs Whitehouse felt obliged to set up her 'Clean Up TV' campaign. On a television programme in late 1965 Kenneth Tynan expressed the view on a live television programme that he would like to see two thespians 'fuck' on stage. His own production of *Oh, Calcutta!*, aptly described by the *New York Times* as 'the kind of show that gets pornography a dirty name', came close to realising this dream. By the end of the 1960s 'fuck', 'shit' and 'crap' had all appeared in national newspapers.

In the schools, traditional teaching methods were ditched and the newly comprehensivised schools were forced to adopt trendy teaching methods devised by the Nuffield Foundation and others. In 1971 Anthony Sampson described a visit to an avant-garde comprehensive called Countesthorpe College near Leicester:

> Countesthorpe College rises from a sea of mud in the midst of a middle-class housing estate, and two miles from a working-class estate: the two form the main catchment area. Local adults can use the school's facilities, and their community association is part of the buildings. The school is built in the shape of a big circle, of one storey only; the grey brick and stained woods, the curved walls, and the skylights dispersing soft light give a background of peaceful relaxation, and the windows look out on to greenhouses and fishponds. The school is made up not of rooms but of spaces and recesses – essential for the 'project' work on which the teaching is based. There are dramatic gyms, a huge art space, a black-cube shaped theatre workshop, and a stage. The lessons are equally unconventional: the courses have elaborate titles like 'Creative Expression in Two and Three Dimensions' or 'The Individual and the Group', reflecting the inter-disciplinary approach as in new universities. The children are only streamed for learning languages; the rest of the learning is through project work. There are special sessions for 'non-involved' children who go into a remedial group to work on motorbikes to satisfy their aggression. The children are encouraged to express themselves by using tape recorders: 'The spoken word is more important for most than the written word.' There is no headmaster at Countesthorpe, only a 'warden' called Tim: he has no proper office, but moves around, in a springy and speculative walk, from recess to recess. Tim McMullen is a genuine 'anti-head': he is a slim, complex man, whose own shape and style seem experimental. He came from a public school and hates the public school system... Experiments can't do worse than the existing schools, he maintains.[18]

The grammar schools were destroyed or driven into the private sector, knocking down a ladder of opportunity for ambitious children and their parents.

In the universities, social sciences like sociology and anthropology and the half-baked ideas of Continental intellectuals were never taken so seriously. Sussex University, which pioneered 'inter-disciplinary studies', ditched examinations in favour of continuous assessment, installed condom machines in the lavatories and provided psychiatric counselling for students, was the most notorious of a stream of third-rate State-sponsored universities set up in the 1960s to peddle degrees to the middle classes.

Outside the Groves of Academe, all traditional forms of authority were ridiculed in magazines like *Private Eye*, television shows like *That Was The Week That Was* and books like *The Establishment: A Symposium*, edited by Hugh Thomas, and Anthony Sampson's successive *Anatomies of Britain*. One progressive social historian, surveying the moral changes of these years in an approving chapter entitled 'The End of Victorianism', writes: 'All the reforms of the late fifties and sixties marked a retreat from the social controls imposed in the Victorian era by evangelicalism.'[19]

The Rise of the Divorcing Society

But the biggest single change in family law and opinion sponsored by the State was the easier dissolution of marriage. 'All the historian can say with confidence,' writes the chronicler of family life in England, 'is that the metamorphosis of a largely non-separating and non-divorcing society, such as England from the Middle Ages to the mid-nineteenth century, into a separating and divorcing one in the late twentieth, is perhaps the most profound and far-reaching social change to have occurred in the last five hundred years.'[20] Today, between a third and two fifths of all marriages fail. People have always wanted to divorce, and the Church had to struggle for centuries before it wrested control of the institution of marriage from the civil authorities, but divorce on the current scale is almost exclusively a post-war phenomenon. In Scotland, where divorce was permitted from the mid-sixteenth century, the rate remained negligible until the twentieth century. The pattern was the same in England in the years following the first liberalisation of the divorce laws in 1857. The number of successful divorces increased from 141 in 1861 to just 580 in 1911, barely twice as fast as the population increased in the same period.

As Table 18 shows, the rate of divorce has increased dramatically since the Second World War. In the first half of the twentieth century almost all petitions were submitted by upper- and middle-class men seeking a legitimate second marriage, or unhappy wives seeking permission to remarry. The high cost of divorce meant dissolution was still closed to most of the poorer classes. Lawrence Stone reckons that the increase in the number of divorces between 1858 and 1914 was 'no more than a shift of legal categories, and does not signify much, if any, increase in marital breakdowns...As long as there were under a thousand divorces a year in a population of about forty Million, England still remained basically a non- divorcing society.'[21] Even the apparent surge in the early 1920s did not signify any serious increase in marital breakdowns, most of the divorces being attributable to wartime strain and hurried mistakes repented at leisure.[22] Stone argues that until 1960 the increase in the divorce rate was to a large extent a shift of legal categories among marriages which had already broken down, as more of the separated found it legally possible and affordable to get divorced.[23]

Table 18   Divorce: Numbers and Incidence

Year	Divorce Decrees	Divorce Rate Per 1,000 Married Couples
1851	4	0.0001
1861	141	0.04
1871	161	0.04
1881	311	0.07
1891	369	0.07
1901	477	0.08
1911	580	0.09
1921	3,500	0.46
1931	3,800	0.44
1941	6,400	0.63
1951	29,000	2.6
1961	27,000	2.1
1971	79,200	5.9
1981	155,600	11.9
1991	171,100	13.4
1992	172,900	13.5
1993	177,800	13.7
1994	171,300	13.3
1995	167,700	12.9

Sources: Lawrence Stone, The Road to Divorce; Social Trends, 1994.
Annual Abstract of Statistics, 1998

The massive surge in marriage breakdowns since the war, and especially since the 1960s, is certainly due at least in part to wider social forces over which the State has limited control or influence. The increase in the number of working women has greatly enlarged the number of separated and divorced wives able to support themselves. In the past, a separated wife faced exceptionally severe penalties. Her private income was retained by her husband; her private property was at his mercy; she could not enter into legal contracts, borrow money or buy or sell property; and her children were controlled by their father. The greater involvement of women in the labour market is mirrored by the declining participation of some men, especially the unskilled and middle-aged. Many males now have little to contribute to a marriage economically, and women prefer to do without a husband rather than marry one who is unemployed or engaged in crime. This effect will increase in the early twenty-first century, when for the first time there will be a demographic shortage of women rather than men.

As the economic interdependence which sustained many marriages in the past – man at work, with wife cooking, cleaning and child-minding at home – dissolves, the strain on marriages is undoubtedly increasing. People are also getting married earlier, which multiplies the risk of a mistake being made in a mood of ephemeral passion or inexperience. Between 1931 and 1971 the age at first marriage fell by three years, and marriages by teenagers rose from just under a seventh of all marriages to over a quarter.[24] Divorce may also be replacing death as the way marriages end. It is generally reckoned that divorce has merely cut the average duration of marriage back to the level achieved by the earlier age of death in the nineteenth century, or about fifteen years.

Antibiotics and effective contraception have reduced the risks of marital infidelity, in terms of venereal disease and unwanted pregnancies, and fundamentally altered the nature of sex from a means of procreation into a means of personal communication or pleasure. The waning of the Christian faith, and the declining confidence of the established Church, have also undermined the religious sanctions against divorce. The Church of England maintained total opposition to divorce until the 1920s, when radical churchmen began to argue for the first time that the grounds of legitimate divorce be widened beyond adultery alone.

It is also unclear how far the State can be blamed for changing expectations of marriage. Matrimony is now regarded not as a vital social institution, intended to civilise sexual appetites and provide a stable environment for raising children. It has become what one analyst calls 'the great romantic act: everything is ventured on one great gesture of individualism, with no attention at all being paid to the wider kin, very little...to close kin; and not very much to anything other than the most formal of religious or societal obligations...Spousal and parental obligations [are] increasingly regarded as matters of taste and fashion rather than of permanent social commitment.'[25] Marriage is now little more than another vehicle of individual satisfaction, whereas in earlier centuries family, friends, neighbours, all the major social institutions, and Church, State and Judiciary worked together to uphold the institution. Today, only the happiness of the individual counts, and there are no social or institutional pressures on struggling couples to stay together. 'The problem of divorce and remarriage,' writes Lawrence Stone, 'began to be seen in purely secular terms, and the interests of the happiness of the individual to take priority over the alleged stability of society and the interests of the state...Perhaps...the most important influence of all in driving up the divorce rate...[is] the idealisation of the individual pursuit of self-gratification and personal pleasure at the expense of a sense of reciprocal obligations and duties towards helpless dependants, such as children, and/or to society as a whole.'[26]

Two sociologists agreed recently that it is the changed attitude towards marriage which has had the most devastating impact on the family:

After a period of long and slow transformation, the sacred family quite suddenly lost most of its credibility, and (in a process that is, of course, far from complete) its place was taken by rational exchange...In terms of belief about what is morally objectionable or practically unwise the approved pattern is one of individual entrepreneurs, each free to strike a bargain as producer of sexual gratification with any willing consumer.[27]

As late as 1971 it was orthodox to believe that mothers living in sin were not entitled to the same public support as married mothers.[28] Yet today unmarried, abandoned or divorced mothers are so much a feature of everyday life that it is *de rigueur* to portray them in radio and television soap operas. In this climate, those who do not condone adultery or divorce find it difficult, embarrassing or even absurd to condemn them.

It is accepted opinion in political, official and ecclesiastical circles that the declining stability of the institution of marriage is a social phenomenon over which the State has little control or influence. A consultation paper issued recently by the Lord Chancellor's Department included on its first page the following statement:

> The Government is committed to marriage and the family. Many of its policies have at their root a desire to maintain and support family life. But it is pointless, and harmful, not to recognise that many marriages break down. The causes for this lie deep in the fabric of society. Even if it were thought desirable, the ability of the Government to influence family relationships at this level is limited. Certainly, changing the divorce law cannot save irretrievable marriages. But the law and procedures can have a major effect on the way in which divorces are conducted, and on the impact of a divorce on those concerned.[29]

It is an astonishing statement, disclaiming any responsibility for the demise of marriage and restricting the obligation of the State to facilitating the arrangement of divorce and looking after the best interests of any children.

Liberal Divorce Laws

The truth is that the State has reinforced, and in many cases actually underwritten, the unravelling of the social institution of marriage. Matrimony, contrary to popular opinion, is not just a religious sacrament like Baptism or Holy Communion. Marriage has, according to Article XXV of the Thirty-Nine Articles, 'grown partly of the corrupt following of the Apostles, partly [from]…states of life allowed in the Scriptures…[but] not any visible sign or ceremony ordained of God'. It is a civil contract which the Church for many centuries has carried out on behalf of the State, even to the extent of keeping the registers of marriages (the civil registration of marriages was not introduced until 1836). Marriage is therefore undeniably the responsibility of the State. It is because the Church of England is an established church that the State is able to place it under a legal obligation to wed anyone who wishes to get married in a church.

The Church of England is increasingly uncomfortable with the dilemmas this imposes upon it. The Church has a high doctrine of marriage – 'What God has put together, let no man put as under' – which is at odds with the view of the State that marriage is soluble where it has 'broken down irretrievably'. Many divorcees resent the fact that the Church will not always remarry them in church, precisely because they see the Anglican establishment as part of the structure of the State. It is for these reasons that some clergymen believe the Church of England should now abandon its role in solemnising a civil contract and confine itself to services of blessing.

Since 1857 the State has gradually loosened the formal con- straints on the marriage contract to the point where it is now possible for either party to get divorced more or less on request, with the courts taking a serious interest only in the custody and welfare of any children of the marriage. Yet few spectacles are more affecting than the efforts of the courts to determine by which of its parents a child should be brought up. As any 'tug-of-love' case vividly demonstrates, one parent will always feel that the court has reached the wrong decision. And a child unfortunate enough to fall into the hands of the social services can expect to find his or her future determined more by the ideological preoccupations of of ficials than by any reasonable assessment of his or her best interests. Political correctness usually dictates, for example, that it is better for a black or Asian orphan to languish in care or a foster-home than it is for him or her to be adopted by a white couple who might undermine or confuse their ethnic identity. Only the State could possibly decide that ethnic identity is more important than parental attachment. It is ironic that the 1853 Royal Commission on Divorce should have maintained that one of the chief reasons for retaining the legal obstacles to divorce was to 'protect children from the inconstancy of parents' .

Divorce was nevertheless officially recognised for the first time in 1857, but on grounds of adultery alone. Adultery was well-chosen, and not solely because of the betrayal of trust which men and women would recognise today. It was because marriage was and is the most important vehicle for the transmission of family property, and even a single act of adultery by a wife could raise questions about paternity which threatened its orderly descent down the generations. The Divorce Reform Act of 1937 added to adultery two new grounds for divorce – desertion for three years and cruelty – but was not intended fundamentally to undermine the social institution of marriage. Sir Alan Herbert, the prime mover behind the Act, was concerned mainly to be rid of the morally degrading effects of fabricated encounters in seaside hotel bedrooms. 'We are rapidly reaching a situation,' he thought, 'in which no stigma whatever will attach to a public confession of adultery.' In the preamble to the Act, which he wrote himself, Herbert stated the objects of the legislation were true support for marriage, protection of children, the reduction of illicit unions and the restoration of respect for the law. The ending of the hardship of the unhappily married was only one objective among many.[30]

It was the Divorce Reform Act of 1969 which marked a funda- mental change in the attitude of the State towards marriage. The crucial first clause of the Act (prefigured by the majority report of the 1956 Royal Commission on Marriage and Divorce) abandoned any attempt to place divorce in a broader social or moral context at all:

After the commencement of this Act the sole ground on which a petition for divorce may be presented to the court by either party to a marriage shall be that the marriage has broken down irretrievably.[31]

Husbands and wives could separate after two years by consent, or five years if one partner wished to remain married. The widening of the grounds for divorce to include unreasonable behaviour mirrored the unrealistic expectations people now had of marriage and created, in effect, divorce on demand.

The veteran Labour politician and feminist, Dr Edith Summerskill, was regarded as a figure of fun when she denounced the 1969 Act as a 'Casanova's Charter'. It was the last gasp of the Victorian feminist tradition, which had sought always to improve the position of women within marriage rather than give them a means of escape from it, and echoed Gladstone's resistance to the 1857 legislation on the grounds that it would 'lead to the degrada- tion of women'. But to most people, says Arthur Marwick, the 1969 legislation 'offered freedom to both sexes from an irksome and unjust social control'.[32] It seems hard to believe it now but Leo Abse, the main architect of the Act, forecast that there would be more not fewer stable, legitimate and happy households.[33] It was then believed that children were better off if unhappy parents separated amicably than if they stayed together, a theory now flatly contradicted by new research carried out at Exeter University. The Exeter researchers found that children of single or step parents were twice as likely to have psychological, educational and behavioural problems and that these were multiplied significantly where a child experienced a series of divorces.[34] Illegitimacy was also expected to fall in the wake of the 1969 Act as people were freed to divorce and remarry. In fact, declining respect for the institution of marriage meant it actually increased substantially.

The churches acquiesced in the sociological orthodoxies which underpinned the 1969 Divorce Reform Act with scarcely a murmur of complaint. An Anglican report prefigured the legislation in 1966, and the bishops scarcely criticised the legislation at all as it passed through Parliament. The Methodists and the Presbyterians supported it too. In the 1970s the Anglican Church was one of the prime movers behind the 'Special Procedure' of 1973, which enabled couples without children to get divorced even more quickly. The process by which Church and State have abandoned any responsible role in upholding the institution of marriage is now complete. The Church of England leaves it up to the discretion of individual clergymen to decide whether or not to agree to remarry divorcees in Church. The traditional discussions between clergymen and couples wishing to marry in Church are regarded by an increasing number of clergymen as a waste of time. The view that the Church should abjure any formal role in the marriage contract is gathering ground.

The Church feels itself to be powerless before unstoppable social trends which make a mockery of its traditional teaching on the subject of marriage. Likewise, the State continues to see its role as merely that of henchman to behavioural forces it is powerless to deny. The Matrimonial and Family Proceedings Act of 1984 created an absolute bar on divorce until one year after marriage, but this was only a recognition in statute of the fact that the courts routinely waived the previous three-year discretionary bar. Its stipulation that the courts give first consideration to the welfare of the children – by which was meant primarily a reduction of parental bitterness and hostility, and an appropriate division of the financial spoils – marked the final abandonment by the State of any serious attempt to reflect in law the centrality of the institution of marriage to the welfare of children.

Underwriting Divorce

There is now also considerable financial help from the State, as well as legislative support, for divorce. The rate of divorce was for centuries constrained by its enormous expense. In the middle ages divorce was confined to the rich, who alone could afford the best canon lawyers. Seventeenth- and eighteenth-century aristocrats could secure a divorce by a Private Act of Parliament, but it was still highly expensive. Legal aid for divorce was introduced in 1914 and widened in 1920, 1949 and 1960. Unsurprisingly, the proportion of divorce petitions supported by legal aid shot up from a fifth to a half in the 1950s, and legal aid to divorce cases is now running at £180–200 million a year. The Welfare State has further reduced the risks of divorce by providing a safety net for divorced individuals unable to support themselves. Legislation obliging husbands to support their estranged wives was introduced comparatively early. Maintenance of Wives Acts were introduced in 1878 and 1886 to enable battered and deserted wives to obtain maintenance orders against their errant husband. The Married Women's Property Acts of 1870, 1874 and 1882 gave women full control over their own property. The Matrimonial Property Act of 1970 established another new principle: that a divorced wife was entitled to half the family wealth.

The Child Support Agency, set up in April 1993 to trace errant husbands failing to support their ex-wives and children, has six offices, 5,400 staff and an annual budget of £184 million. Its target of saving £530 million in benefits currently being paid to victims of divorce was never likely to be achieved, but it is one measure of the costs to the taxpayer of the explosion of failed marriages.[35] The Agency was set up because divorced couples no longer assume full financial responsibility for their actions, let alone moral responsibility. The taxpayer is currently bearing such a large part of the burden of maintaining the children of errant fathers that there was sufficient political pressure for the government to be drawn into a hazardous campaign to relieve it by direct action. The cost to the taxpayer of supporting single parents has risen by 171 per cent in real terms since 1979, to a total of £6.6 billion in 1992–93. This accounts for more than half of all welfare spending on families.[36] The wider social costs are impossible to quantify accurately, but they include higher levels of unemployment, ill health and criminality and lower academic performance by the children of single parents. These all increase public expenditure on unemployment and other benefits, repairing damage to people and property, and on extra policing, court time and prison places. When a marriage guidance agency put the average cost to the taxpayer of a divorce at £10,000, it was probably a substantial underestimate.[37]

It is popularly supposed that the liberalisation of the divorce laws merely brought into the open the secret misery of thousands of couples. Certainly every liberalisation of the divorce laws was followed by an increase in the number of divorces. But it is possible to detect, from the passage of the 1969 legislation, a change in the trend. Divorce is no longer a reshuffling of people from the legal category of 'married' to the legal category of 'divorced'. It is the solution to the disappointed expectations of the self-expressive individual. The 1984 legislation in particular, by allowing couples to petition for divorce on their first wedding anniversary, led to a tremendous surge in failed marriages. In 1991 the number of divorces, at over 171,000, was the highest on record. For every two marriages in Great Britain that year, there was one divorce.[38]

The easier dissolution of marriage tends, as the Prince of Denmark found after the death of his father, to feed on itself 'Ere the salt of most unrighteous tears had left the flushing of her galled eyes, she married. O most wicked speed, to post with such dexterity to incestuous sheets.'[39] The sheer volume of divorces numbs the moral senses. A country where four senior members of the Royal Family get separated or divorced is naturally one in which family and neighbours are relatively indifferent to the failure of a marriage. The increased statistical likelihood of failure encourages more couples to co-habit rather than marry, but research both in the United States and by the General Household Survey suggests that marriages preceded by co-habitation are more likely to fail. This is mainly because both parties have, by definition, less respect for the institution of marriage.[40] The higher divorce rate also means more people remarry – remarriages have risen as a proportion of all marriages from 14 per cent in 1961 to 36 per cent in 1991 – but second marriages are even likelier to fail than first marriages.[41] Divorce, in the jargon, is 'sociologically reinforcing'. Widespread divorce increases the wariness of marriage; wariness of marriage increases the expectation of failure; failure induces a hasty remedy; the first divorce facilitates the second, and so on.

Taxation

By making divorce easier and cheaper, the State has hastened the destruction of the institution of marriage, and so helped to undermine the family. The consequences include an increase in poverty, which necessitates higher public expenditure. Higher public expenditure necessitates higher taxation, and the main victims of higher taxation are the families which manage to survive. A State spending machine which consumes nearly a half of the national income cannot avoid taxing people at relatively low levels of income – there are not enough 'rich' people for it ever to be otherwise – but it is a special absurdity of the current fiscal system that it punishes the nuclear family. Families which stay together demand less of the State in terms of subsidies and social services, and financially secure families are less likely to split than those which are under financial pressure, yet the tax system systematically discriminates against them. This is partly because they are simply easier to tax. They tend to be static, law-abiding and in work.

The most important way in which the State has used the tax system to attack the family is by increasing the burden of income tax and National Insurance contributions on married couples with children. In 1939 the income tax threshold was £225 a year, and average wages £180 a year. Because a married man had to earn one and a quarter times average earnings before becoming liable to income tax, a married couple on average earnings paid no income tax and, indeed, only a fifth of the working population paid any income tax at all. But after the war the real value of the personal allowance for income tax – the key to the progressivity of the system - was eroded steadily. As Table 11 showed, forty years ago a married man with four children did not start to pay income tax until he had earned nearly one and a half times average manual earnings. A married man with two children did not start to pay tax until he had earned at least four fifths of average earnings.[42] Today, a married man with any number of children starts to pay income tax when he has earned less than a third of average manual earnings.

This massive increase in the burden of taxation on families was almost entirely the effect of so-called 'fiscal drag', the process by which rising nominal incomes push taxpayers into the higher tax brackets (even though their real incomes may actually be declining) because the personal allowances are not adjusted to take account of the rise in prices. charitably, the State found it difficult to measure real incomes at times of rising prices. More realistically, the State used inflation as a cloak for reducing the tax thresholds. The effect of fiscal drag was not properly stabilised until the 1977 Budget, when an unlikely alliance of Nigel Lawson and two Labour MPs, Jeff Rooker and Audrey Wise, managed to secure an amendment to the Finance Bill obliging the Chancellor to seek explicit Parliamentary approval to override the indexation for inflation of the personal income tax allowances. But this has only slowed down the rate of deterioration in the tax position of the average family. Far from improving under successive Conservative governments ostensibly committed to low taxation and the support of the family, the burden of taxation borne by families has actually got worse. As Table 10 showed, married couples with children on average earnings, or even three quarters of average earnings, are paying more in income tax and National Insurance contributions in 1995-96 than they did in 1978–79.[43]

A married man with two children in Britain now starts to pay income tax after he has earned only £5,245. In the United States the comparable threshold is well over £10,000.[44] But the shrinking value of the married couple's allowance is only one aspect of the fiscal attack on the family by the State. 'The British tax and social security system,' joke John Kay and Mervyn King, 'has traditionally encouraged the poor to co-habit, those on average incomes to marry and the rich to get divorced.'[45] The steady erosion of the value of mortgage tax relief is a sensible long-term policy for a variety of reasons, but without any compensating reductions in income tax it merely raises the cost of maintaining a family home. The imposition of Value Added Tax on domestic fuel falls into the same category. An analysis by the Institute of Fiscal Studies of all the tax changes that took place between 1985 and 1994 found that nearly two thirds of traditional families – a one-earner couple with children – were worse off than they were ten years ago as a result, and that nearly half of two-earner couples with children were also worse off. But the overwhelming majority of single people in work, and two-earner couples without children, were better off.[46] The pattern continued in the November 1994 Budget, in which single and dual income families with children were those hit hardest by the tax changes.

Until 1977–78 the long-standing principle that the income tax regime should take account of the family responsibilities of the taxpayer was recognised by additional child tax allowances. The State eventually concluded that this was a wasteful subsidy to families which did not need it and replaced it with a tax-free cash benefit, Child Benefit. But, even in the case of a direct subsidy, the State has failed to live up to its obligation to at least maintain the real value of Child Benefit. Its value was frozen from 1987 to 1990. It was soon being argued by fiscal purists that Child Benefit is wasteful, and doubtless it will eventually be means-tested or limited in scope. Even the Labour Party is pondering whether or not to tax it. For some families, there will then be no recognition anywhere within the tax and social security system of the additional costs of bringing up children.

The main pressure within the fiscal system is already directed towards giving subsidies to lone working mothers for child care. This represents a further discrimination against the mother who stays at home to bring up her children. Tax relief for workplace nurseries was introduced in the March Iggo Budget, and in the November 1993 Budget the Chancellor announced a £28 a week child-care allowance payable to single mothers. This is not a new phenomenon, but part of a systematic discrimination against the family by the tax and benefits system. Patricia Morgan has shown that between 1980 and 1992 a lone parent was consistently better off – after tax, National Insurance, council taxes and benefits – at all income levels than a married couple with two children.[47] This is a classic instance of the perverse sequence of events which can occur when the State ceases to operate according to any set of principles. In theory, a child-care allowance will reduce the cost to the taxpayer of supporting single mothers through Family Credit by encouraging some of them to go back to work. Meanwhile, the reform of the taxation of husband and wife has made families with working wives worse off, despite the fact that one of the main reasons why the number of working wives has increased is the vastly increased burden of tax the family is being asked to bear and one of the main reasons why families are breaking up is the financial insecurity they face. It is bitterly ironic that the taxpayer is now subsidising mothers from broken marriages to go out to work.

The separate taxation of husband and wife, laudable enough in its aim of ensuring that the tax system recognises women as inde- pendent individuals, was accompanied by a further erosion of fiscal support for married couples. Until 1990 the income of a married woman was treated for tax purposes as belonging to her husband. Although married women had enjoyed the right to a separate assessment for income tax since 1914, their income was still taxed as if it was earned by their husband. An earning wife was granted an earned income allowance equivalent to the personal allowance, and the husband enjoyed a married man's allowance of one and a half times the personal allowance. But a non-earning wife was given no allowance at all. This system obviously gave a considerable tax advantage to a family where both parents worked, by giving dual earning households an allowance equivalent to two and a half times the personal allowance but a single earning household an allowance of only one and a half times the personal allowance. This was a form of discrimination against particular types of family: the one where the mother gives up work to look after the children, or where the wife gives up work to look after her husband (particularly after he reaches pensionable age).

The Chancellor at the time the separate taxation of husband and wife was devised, Nigel Lawson, wanted to give every man and woman a personal allowance, fully transferable between them and financed by phasing out the bonus given to dual earning couples. This proved impossible (not least because the Inland Revenue could not cope with transferable allowances). So the Treasury opted instead for independent taxation of husbands and wives without transferable allowances, leaving in place a married couple's allowance which Nigel Lawson says he hoped would 'wither on the vine'.[48] The rate of relief on the married couple's allowance was duly cut, first to 20 per cent and then to 15 per cent by the present Chancellor, who describes the married man's allowance as 'a bit of an anomaly'. When it disappears completely, married couples will be on exactly the same fiscal footing as the single, the widowed and the divorced. This is a depressing outcome in an economy where an increasing number of wives are being forced out to work, under the pressure of excessive taxation.

The Economic Vulnerability of the Modern Family

The clearest evidence of the fact that the family is now under unprecedented economic pressure is the falling birth rate. For a population to remain stable each woman must bear 2.1 children, but in Great Britain today the rate is only 1.8 children. This is partly because contraception has enabled people to forgo the inconvenience of reproduction, but it also reflects the undoubted fact that many people feel they simply cannot afford the size of family they would, in an ideal world, like to have. This not only means that the labour force is failing to reproduce itself, placing upon future generations an even higher burden of taxation as a smaller number of productive people struggle to support a larger number of pensioners. It also means that the family is failing to sustain itself, in terms of wealth and possessions, over several generations. The heavy burden of tax, and the failure of the tax and social security systems to discriminate in favour of the family, contradict the long-standing biological and historical fact that the family has proved the most viable economic unit and, as the main vehicle for the transmission of property and wealth down the generations, the primary source of social stability and achievement.

As Matt Ridley has pointed out, a mother living alone with children would not survive outside a Welfare State or a Corporate Economy in which women were able to survive on social security benefits or able to work. Marriage is an economic institution, especially for the raising of children. Child-rearing is the greatest expense most adults bear, and it can take more than twenty years before a child is capable of earning a living. A mother cannot work full-time and look after children at the same time, so an income has to be supplied by someone else. In exchange for the risk of forgoing the opportunity to work herself, a mother will seek a binding commitment from her husband to support her and her children. The acquisition of a reliable income to support mothers and their children – and the need to create a vehicle for the ownership and transmission of property down the generations – were the main economic reasons for the emergence of the monogamous Western family.

Alan Macfarlane has shown that in England, as far back as at least the thirteenth century, land was not owned communally, as in a peasant society, but held by individuals who were free to bequeath it to their children. Though fathers usually bequeathed it to their eldest son, land was also a commodity which could be bought and sold to acquire something better for future generations of the same family. Men and women acquired property in land in order to feed themselves and their family. Families also had to accumulate sufficient to give their daughters a marriage dowry (money brought by a wife to a husband to enable them to set up an independent household). Younger members of English families always tended to move out of the parental home to set up on their own, precisely because they and their parents had accumulated sufficient land or money to do so. It is not surprising that litigation over land transactions and wills was so commonplace within English families.[49]

It is partly because marriage is an economic as well as a social institution that its popularity is declining. The number of men aged between 15 and 64 who are in work has shrunk from nine tenths in 1973 to four fifths in 1993. More than half of all women work, and for those between 16 and 54 the figure is two thirds to three quarters. The Joseph Rowntree Foundation estimates that the average male contribution to the household budget shrank from three quarters in the early 1980s to less than two thirds ten years later. Women are finding that an increasing number of men, and particularly low-earning men, are not worth marrying. Significantly, for the last twenty years the rate of marriage of divorced men and widowers has increased faster than the rate of marriage of bachelors. Younger women are turning increasingly to older and better-established men to provide them with the income they need to rear children. The victims of this process are middle-aged women, particularly those with children, whom successful men do not wish to marry, and unsuccessful young men, whom younger women do not wish to marry. They have become dependent on the Welfare State, or crime.

It is also because marriage is an economic institution that previous generations saw the family, private property and pros- perity as mutually reinforcing. For this reason, the tax system always took account of the additional costs of rearing children and eschewed the temptation to tax inheritance. 'Home,' writes Roger Scruton, 'is the place where private property accumulates, and so overreaches itself, becoming transformed into something shared. There is no contract of distribution: sharing is simply the essence of family life. Here everything important is "ours". Private property is added to, and reinforces the primary social bond. It is for some such reason that conservatives have seen the family and private property as institutions which stand or fall together. The family has its life in the home, and the home demands property for its establishment. Whatever abstract arguments might be offered against that connection, it has a savour of irrebuttable common sense.'[50] It is the desire and the necessity, not just of supporting a wife and children, but of securing and enlarging their opportunities in life, which has given possessive individualism its capacity to endure.

These links between family, property and economic success are now better understood in the miracle economies of East Asia than in any Western society. So-called 'Asian values' have many objection- able features – lack of democracy and freedom of speech, systematic corruption, censorship, and abuses of human rights – but they are widely admired for combining economic growth with a strong family life. John Gray is convinced of the 'primacy of cultural forms', the historic accumulation of values, moral codes, perceptions, routines, attitudes, intuitions and collective memories that ensures the survival of institutions. He argues that the free market individualism of the West has undermined the family by 'disembedding' it from its supportive cultural context. 'It may be,' he writes, 'that the absence, or weakness, in these cultures of the romantic and individualist conception of married life that characterises Western bourgeois societies...in which family breakdown is most pervasive and extreme, may well go a long way toward accounting for their extraordinary economic achievements.'[51] This view is championed by Lee Kwan Yew, the former premier of Singapore. Like Gray, he believes that culture explains the resistance of East Asian family life to Western individualism. He says 'the fundamental difference between Western concepts of society and government and East Asian concepts is that Eastern societies believe the individual exists in the context of the family'.[52]

In East Asia, this view has facilitated the survival of authoritarian forms of government. Unfortunately, too many conservative thinkers in this country have also seen the family as the first in a series of concentric circles of obligation which are consummated in the Nation or the State. 'To be attached to the subdivision, to love the little platoon we belong to in society,' thought Burke, 'is the first principle (the germ as it were) of public affections. It is the first link in the series by which we proceed towards a love to our country and to mankind.'[53] In reality, the family is not the first rung in a State hierarchy but the main obstacle to the exercise of State power and the last bastion of individual privacy and liberty. Nor is the family one of the 'cultural forms' under threat from free market individualism. Possessive individualism is not the cultural destroyer of the family, but its parent and product.

This is why totalitarians and millenarians of every kind – Lenin, Stalin, Jim Jones, Pol Pot, the Reverend Sun Myung Moon and countless other despots and tyrants – have grasped that they must first break the family if they are to conquer the individual. But the modern liberal democratic State is a more formidable adversary of the family than any dictator or cult leader. It subverts the family imperceptibly. It milks it to subsidise the feckless; it legislates against it; it uses compulsory State education to mould people into useful citizens rather than warm relations; and it employs the resources of the Welfare State to release both the young and the old from economic and emotional dependence upon each other.[54] The State rescues the unhappy individual from an uncongenial marriage; it sets an age of sexual consent; and it grants children rights against their parents. In a series of notorious cases, from Teesside to the Orkneys, paid officials of the State seized children from their families and took them into 'care' pending an investigation into the private lives of their parents. In another infamous case nearly ten years ago, the judiciary upheld the right of the State to dispense contraceptives to a child irrespective of the wishes of the parents.[55] In family life, as in political life and economic life, it is the State, not the free individual, which is the enemy.

References

1   David Hume, *A Treatise of Human Nature*, Penguin Classics Edition, 1984, page 578.
2   Quoted in C. B. Macpherson, *The Rise and Fall of Economic Justice*, OUP, 1985, page
3   F. A. Hayek, *The Constitution of Liberty*, Routledge, 1960, page 62.
4   Michael Novak, *The Spirit of Democratic Capitalism*, Institute of Economic Affairs Health and Welfare Unit, 1991, page 164.
5   Karl Marx and Friedrich Engels, *The Communist Manifesto*, Penguin, 1978, page 101.
6   From *The Doctrine and Discipline of Divorce*, quoted by Ferdinand Mount, *The Subversive Family: An Alternative History of Love and Marriage*, Unwin Paperbacks, 1982, page 212.
7   See, for example, Lawrence Stone, *The Family, Sex and Marriage in England 1500–1800*, Penguin, 1990.
8   Michael Prowse, 'When the Cornflakes Bowl is Empty', *Financial Times*, 8 August 1990.
9   See Brigitte Berger, 'The Bourgeois Family and Modern Society', in *The Family: Is It Just Another Lifestyle Choice?*, Institute of Economic Affairs Health and Welfare Unit, 1993.
10 Matt Ridley, *The Red Queen: Sex and the Evolution of Human Nature*, Viking, 1993, pages 251-2.
11 Matt Ridley, *The Red Queen: Sex and the Evolution of Human Nature*, Viking, 1993, page 204.
12 Norman Dennis and George Erdos, *Families Without Fatherhood*, IEA Health and Welfare Unit, 1993, page 69.
13 An NOP poll in the *Sunday Times* in November 1993 found that 63 per cent of respondents thought it was vital for a child to be brought up by two loving parents if it was to be well-adjusted and avoid a life of crime. Although the majority is large, it is remarkable that as many as 27 per cent of people disagreed with the proposition.
14 Michael Novak, *The Spirit of Democratic Capitalism*, Institute of Economic Affairs Health and Welfare Unit, 1991, page 161.
15 David Willetts, *Civic Conservatism*, The Social Market Foundation, June 1994, page 31.
16 See, for example, John Gray, *The Undoing of Conservatism*, The Social Market Foundation,June 1994, page 23.
17 Quoted in Alasdair MacIntyre, *Marcuse*, Fontana, 1970, pages 87–8.
18 Anthony Sampson, *The New Anatomy of Britain*, Hodder & Stoughton, 1971, pages 148–9.
19 Arthur Marwick, *British Society Since 1945*, Penguin, 1990, pages 141–53.
20 Lawrence Stone, *The Road to Divorce 1530–1987*, OUP, 1990, page 422.
21 *The Road to Divorce 1530–1987*, page 387.

22 *The Road to Divorce 1530–1987*, pages 394 and 397.
23 *The Road to Divorce 1530–1987*, page 409.
24 *The Road to Divorce 1530–1987*, page 411.
25 Jon Davies, 'From Household to Family to Individualism', in *The Family: Is It Just Another Lifestyle Choice?*, IEA Health and Welfare Unit, 1993, page 100.
26 Lawrence Stone, *The Road to Divorce 1530–1987*, OUP, 1990, page 391.
27 Norman Dennis and George Erdos, *Families Without Fatherhood*, IEA Health and Welfare Unit, 1993, pages 60–l.
28 *Families Without Fatherhood*, pages 30–7 and page 17.
29 *Looking to the Future: Mediation and the Ground for Divorce*, H.M.S.O., Cm 2424, December 1993, page 1.
30 Lawrence Stone, *The Road to Divorce 1530–1987*, OUP, 1990, pages 398 and 401.
31 Arthur Marwick, *British Society Since 1945*, Penguin, 1990, page 148.
32 *British Society Since 1945*, page 148.
33 Lawrence Stone, *The Road to Divorce 1530–1987*, OUP, Iggo, page 409.
34 *Panorama*, 7 February 1994.

35 See *Next Steps Review 1993*, Cmnd 2430, page 108.
36 Department of Social Security, *The Growth of Social Security*, H.M.S.O., Table 11b, page 23.
37 *Sunday Telegraph*, 21 March 194
38 Central Statistical Office, *Social Trends*, 1994 Edition, H.M.S.O., page 37.
39 *Hamlet*, I, ii, 154–7.
40 Lawrence Stone, *The Road to Divorce 1530–1987*, OUP, Iggo, page 413.
41 Central Statistical Office, *Social Trends*, 1994 Edition, H.M.S.O., Table 2.11.
42 Table 11 is on page 100.
43 Table 10 is on page 87.
44 In the United States, the tax threshold for a married couple is $11,250. There is an additional tax allowance of $2,450 for each child. All mortgage interest on a principal residence can be offset against tax as well. Low-earning couples are entitled to a further tax credit on any monies owed up to a ceiling of $23,700. For a married couple with two children this would be worth $278. Married couples over 65 get an additional allowance of $2,450.
45 J. A. Kay and M. A. King, *The British Tax System*, Fifth Edition, OUP, 1990, page 42.
46 Fiscal Studies, *Institute of Fiscal Studies*, August 1994.
47 Patricia Morgan, *Farewell to the Family: Public Policy and Family Breakdown in Britain and the USA*, IEA Health and Welfare Unit, pages 164–5.
48 See Nigel Lawson, *The View From No. 11*, Bantam, 1991, pages 881–7.
49 Alan Macfarlane, *The Origins of English Individualism: The Family, Property and Social Transition*, Basil Blackwell, 1978.
50 Roger Scruton, *The Meaning of Conservatism*, Penguin, 1980, page 101.
51 John Gray, *The Undoing of Conservatism*, The Social Market Foundation, June 1994, pages 34-5-
52 From *Foreign Affairs*. Quoted in *Independent on Sunday*, I May 1994.
53 Edmund Burke, *Reflections on the Revolution in France*, Penguin, 1969, page 135.
54 See Allan Carlson, 'Liberty, Order and the Family', in *The Family: Is It Just Another Lifestyle Choice?*, Institute of Economic Affairs Health and Welfare Unit 1993.
55 Gillick vs West Norfolk and Wisbech Area Health Authority, October 1985.

CHAPTER THIRTEEN

The Death of Self-Government

The objections to government interference . . . may be of three kinds. The first is, when the thing to be done is likely to be better done by individuals than by the government. Speaking generally, there is no one so fit to conduct any business, or to determine how or by whom it shall be conducted, as those who are personally interested in it...The second objection is...[that] though individuals may not do the particular thing so well, on average, as the officers of the government, it is nevertheless desirable that it should be done by them, rather than by the government, as a means to their own mental education – a mode of strengthening their active faculties, exercising their judgment, and giving them a familiar knowledge of the subjects with which they are thus left to deal...The third, and most cogent reason for restricting the interference of government, is the great evil of adding unnecessarily to its power. Every function super added to those already exercised by the government, causes its influence over hopes and fears to be more widely diffused, and converts, more and more, the active and ambitious part of the public into hangers-on of the government, or of some party which aims at becoming the government.

John Stuart Mill, *On Liberty*[1]

The family is not the only social institution to be pulverised by the twentieth-century State. Before the holocaust of the Great War first raised the State to its present overpowering status, Great Britain was famous for the extent and variety of the voluntary clubs and organisations which collections of individuals, both small and large, had formed to pursue their hobbies or interests. These were not just chapel or church, but a host of associations, clubs, societies and business enterprises, which individuals joined without being coerced and in which they usually had a real personal influence. Sir Ernest Barker (1874–1960), a political philosopher and historian at both Oxford and Cambridge, devoted much of his long working life to an attempted reconciliation between individualism and his strong 'sense for the community'. He saw the State as providing the physical security in which Society, in the shape of countless voluntary organisations ranging from Church schools to the Marylebone Cricket Club, could flourish.

Barker even described the principal organs of the State, like the House of Commons and the Inns of Court, as merely varieties of what de Tocqueville considered the quintessential English institu- tion: the club. At the time he wrote, Dr Johnson's celebrated criticism of Sir John Hawkins – that he was a 'very unclubbable man' – was still among the worst insults one civilised Englishman could throw at another. Barker was convinced that the secret of the successful constitutional history of Britain was the benign nature of the dialogue which took place between these private institutions and the State:

> The development of England since 1688, and not least in the course of the nineteenth century, has been marked by two characteristics. One of them has been the parallel growth of Society and the State, of voluntary co-operation and political regulation, with one of them sometimes gaining on the other...but with both still moving and both still active. The other characteristic has been the interconnexion of the two growths – not divided into compartments, but mutually interfused and reciprocally interacting...Voluntary social groups, acting first in lieu of the State and men acting upon the State and then acting upon the State, can do an initial work of experimentation which will afterwards, if it is successful enough to merit general adoption, be 'endorsed' or 'taken over' by the legislation of the State . . . Here Society serves as a laboratory for the State.[2]

It is a more profound analysis than the *communitas communitatum* of the modern collectivists, but it is too sanguine by far. Writing in the 1930s Barker only dimly perceived the ratchet effect of the State 'taking over' previously voluntary social functions. He could not know that the coming war would so vastly accelerate the aggrandisement of private life by the State that it would more or less extinguish the voluntary Society he described. 'As at present, and under conditions of emergency,' he wrote in parentheses, 'the State would seem to be gaining.'[3] If he was alive today, Sir Ernest would probably agree with Margaret Thatcher that there is no such thing as Society any more. Today, Society is a synonym for the State.

The Nationalisation of Private Life

Some would argue that a myriad voluntary, private and independent associations and endeavours are thriving in Britain today. There are indeed, but a great many of them are wholly or partially reliant on the State for financial and legislative support. The pension funds – the most powerful private financial interests in Britain today – rest on a raft of unparalleled tax remission. The charity industry, which also relies heavily on tax concessions, is even less independent. In 1992–93 fees and grants from central and local government accounted for more than a fifth of the total income of the top 400 charities. Grants from the European Union accounted for another 7 per cent. Only just over half of the total income of the 500 biggest charities is purely voluntary.[4] Even the National Trust, which is apt to boast how little it has to do with the State, receives substantial sums in aid from public bodies like the National Heritage Memorial Fund, English

Heritage, the Forestry Commission, the Tourist Boards, the National Park authorities and the European Union. In 1991, for example, getting on for a tenth of the total income of the National Trust came from public sources. The Archbishop of Canterbury – one of whose predecessors was martyred rather than surrender ecclesiastical independence to the State – and whose cathedrals were granted £11½ million by the State in 1990, now wants State support for keeping churches open. There is virtually no ostensibly self-governing organisation in the country which is not either actually in receipt of taxpayers' money, or already lobbying actively for what it believes to be its share of the public purse. This was not the case in Victorian or Edwardian England, when total public expenditure had not yet exceeded a tenth of the national income.

The inhabitants of the towns and suburbs of England in that vanished age were the inheritors of a lively and entirely voluntary civic culture of Sunday schools and other church organisations, sports clubs, youth clubs, Boy Scout troops, Girl Guides, the YMCA, the Salvation Army, the Boys' Brigade, university exten- sion lectures, evening classes and even the first mass-membership political parties. The national team-games which emerged in the decades before the First World War – football, cricket and rugby - were underpinned at local level by a host of clubs, teams and minor leagues, school sides, factory sides and Sunday matches. The modern pursuits of hiking, rambling and cycling were all invented during this period too. But voluntary effort was the characteristic expression of nineteenth-century citizens not just in life and leisure. Charitable work was never more extensive or ambitious. A series of great new schools and universities were founded on private initiative alone. Even in the usually degraded profession of politics, popular movements like the Anti-Corn Law League or the Liberty and Property Defence League, or the Anti-Vivisection Society, sought to change the tide of laws, ideas and opinions by persuasion and propaganda. Their momentum derived from mass voluntary participation.

What Harold Perkin has called the 'entrepreneurial ideal' of Victorian England was formed in conscious opposition to the paternalism and idle property of the aristocratic centuries, which now find their last resting place in One Nation Toryism. It was an ideal which valued Property not as the privilege of the rentier but as the active Capital of the entrepreneur, creating new wealth. 'Mine,' wrote Richard Cobden, 'is the masculine species of charity which would lead me to inculcate in the minds of the labouring classes the love of independence, the privilege of self-respect, the disdain of being patronised or petted, the desire to accumulate and the ambition to rise.'[3] The entrepreneurial ideal valued hard work, thrift and self-help as the route to self-respect. It recognised the individuality of men and women, and refused to see them merely as objects of 'care' by the State. It propagated the virtue, just as E. F. Schumacher did for a later generation, of teaching people to help themselves rather than simply giving them what they needed.

The Thatcherite emphasis of the 1980s on individual character and 'vigorous' virtues struck a jarring note in a collectivist age. It was famously characterised by the impresario Jonathan Miller as 'catering to the worst elements of commuter idiocy'. But the Victorians saw no contradiction between individual vigour and collective welfare. 'The spirit of self-help is the root of all genuine growth in the individual; and exhibited in the lives of many, it constitutes the true source of national vigour and strength,' wrote Samuel Smiles, in the powerful opening to his best-selling Self-Help in 1859:

Help from without is often enfeebling in its effects, but help from within invariably invigorates. Whatever is done for men or classes, to a certain extent takes away the stimulus and necessity of doing for themselves; and where men are subjected to over-guidance and over-government, the inevitable tendency is to render them comparatively helpless. Even the best institutions can give a man no active help. Perhaps the best they can do is, to leave him free to develop himself and improve his individual condition. But in all times men have been prone to believe that their happiness and well-being were to be secured by means of institutions rather than by their own conduct. Hence the value of legislation as an agent in human advancement has usually been much over-estimated. To constitute the millionth part of a Legislature, by voting for one or two men once in three or five years, however conscientiously this duty may be performed, can exercise but little active influence upon any man's life and character. Moreover, it is every day becoming more clearly understood, that the function of Government is negative and restrictive, rather than positive and active; being resolvable principally into protection – protection of life, liberty, and property. Laws, wisely administered, will secure men in the enjoyment of the fruits of their labour, whether of mind or body, at a comparatively small personal sacrifice; but no laws, however stringent, can make the idle industrious, the thriftless provident, or the drunken sober. Such reforms can only be effected by means of individual action, economy, and self-denial; by better habits, rather than by greater rights.[6]

The wisdom of this passage is perhaps more apparent to a generation familiar with the demoralising effects of welfare dependency than it was to collectivists reared on Lytton Strachey's view of the Victorian age. The moral equivalent of Self-Help today is the 488-page Child Poverty Action Group guide to means-tested State benefits, which it issues to the new paupers of the Welfare State to help them negotiate the maze of different State organisations, benefits and regulations which separate them from the public purse. A book entitled How to Collect from the Government is available by mail order from an address in Essex. 'A new book,' runs the newspaper advertisement, 'tells how every UK citizen can collect their share of the £68 thousand million that will be handed out this year by the Government.'

Victorian values is now a term of abuse. They are routinely disparaged as skinflint and hypocritical, and Samuel Smiles is regarded as a figure of fun, but in reality the culture of self-help produced not a hard-faced disregard for the poor but a heightened sensitivity to suffering, great concern for others, a major and highly effective assault on public vices like drunkenness and prostitution, and a powerful code of ethics to which men and women could aspire. Self-help was always tempered by the realisation that not everybody could practise its virtues and that the privilege of wealth imposed a duty, not to patronise the poor but to help the less fortunate could help themselves out of poverty. The range and variety of Victorian philanthropy was phenomenal. Almost all of the best-known charities of today – the Salvation Army, the Royal Society for the Prevention of Cruelty to Animals, the Young Men's Christian Association, Barnardo's, even the Royal National Lifeboat Institution – date from the Victorian era. Dozens of missionary, Bible, temperance and anti-slavery organisations flourished. Anglicans, Nonconformists, Roman Catholics and Jews all had their own charitable funds. There were charity schools, hospitals, dispensaries, asylums, orphanages, reformatories and homes for prostitute

The Peabody Trust built and administered low-cost housing for the respectable working class, and Octavia Hill built and admini- stered model dwellings for the urban poor. Mary Carpenter founded ragged and industrial schools and reformatories for girls. A National Benevolent Institution paid pensions to gentlemen and professionals fallen on hard times. A survey of London charities in 1861 identified 649 – of which nearly a quarter were founded in the previous decade alone – with a total annual income of £2½ million, which was more than the State spent on administration of the Poor Laws in the capital. The Charity Organisation Society was founded in 1869 to try and bring some kind of order to a huge number of charities, and to replace their haphazard and unsophisticated methods by more scientific techniques. Drawing on the work of earlier 'visiting societies', it believed charities should assess needs and administer help directly. The willingness of the Society to distinguish between the deserving and undeserving offends the modern charitable conscience, but it was far more interested than its modern successors in the personal circumstances of individuals. Its emphasis on self-help and self-respect is also no different from the approach of many Third World charities to the question of sustainable development today. They were much influenced by E. F. Schumacher's dictum, which he borrowed as the central message of *Small is Beautiful*, that it is better to teach a poor man to make his own fishing tackle than it is to give him a fish or even a fishing rod. A similar approach is now being adopted by charities and voluntary groups working in the inner cities. 'Self-reliance,' as one enthusiast for modern self-help has put it, 'far from being a utopian, "soft" option...has come to be seen as a far more effective way of organising people's energies and their capacity to act as problem solvers than over-dependence on the wisdom and knowledge of civil servants and elected officials.'[7]

Working-Class Self-Help

Modern cynics, of course, have ascribed Victorian philanthropy variously to a fear of social revolution, guilt about inequality, social snobbery and even the need of the repressed bourgeois to find an outlet for unsatisfied emotional or sexual impulses. The oft-stated desire of Victorian philanthropists to reform the moral character of the poor is also considered disreputable, since it implies poverty was the fault of the individual rather than of an unjust social and economic system. But the culture of self-help permeated every level of society, not just the rich, and there is good reason to suppose that the percolation of its ideas throughout the social hierarchy was not so much a case of the embourgeoisement of the 'working class' as the rediscovery of the long-standing virtues of the English artisan. The earliest trade unions, for example, were not vehicles of class war but organisations of highly paid, highly skilled workers seeking to protect the interests of their members. They ran self-financing insurance schemes for their members, and helped and encouraged them to educate themselves and improve their skills and knowledge through the work of the Mechanics' Institutes, the Society for the Diffusion of Useful Knowledge and the Working Men's Union.

Much the same was true of the Co-operative movement. Although it began as a search for an alternative to capitalism, it was soon in the vanguard of self-help. Co-operators made regular contributions in order to buy food at cheaper rates, or on credit, and received in return a quarterly dividend from the funds invested. 'Modern co-operation,' averred a prize essay on the subject in the 1860s, 'means a union of working men for the improvement of the social circumstances of the class to which they belong...it is the working man's lever, by which he may rise in the world.'[8] And in its heyday Co-operation was a far more significant movement than trade unionism. Membership of co-operative societies rose thirteen-fold, from 627,000 in 1883 to 8.3 million by 1939.[9]

But it was the friendly societies which were the outstanding example of working-class self help. These self-governing associations – originally called 'box clubs', after the strongbox in which contributions were placed – included a multitude of different organisations. They ranged from simple dividing societies (which split the surplus among the members at the end of the year) through deposit societies (which paid interest on deposits) to accumulating societies like Hearts of Oak (which invested long-term). Some were little more than groups of individuals saving up for a Christmas feast, others hospital, medical or burial clubs intended to save the poor the indignity of the workhouse infirmary or a pauper's grave. But the largest and best of them provided comprehensive savings and insurance against the hard times occasioned by sickness, injury, unemployment, age and infirmity, medical care, funeral grants, financial support for widows and orphans and even job search allowances.

Some friendly societies grew in time into vast national federations like the Oddfellows or the Foresters. Because they emerged from the mutual tradition of the medieval guild and livery companies, which were much given to fellowship and conviviality as well as welfare and funerals, Freemason-like rituals and feasting were an integral part of friendly society life. The earliest societies were also intensely local and vigorously independent, and usually associated with a particular pub, factory or school. They built on the foundations of what was then a natural English aptitude for informal family and neighbourhood help. 'Every kind of witness in the first half of the nineteenth century,' wrote E. P. Thompson in *The Making of the English Working Class*, 'remarked upon the extent of mutual aid in the poorer districts. In times of emergency, unemployment, strikes, sickness, childbirth, then it was the poor who "helped every one his neighbour".'[10]

Friendly societies appealed to the self-respect of their members. Cooke Taylor, writing of the Lancashire cotton depression in 1842, observed that 'nearly all the distressed operatives whom I met north of Manchester...had a thorough horror of being forced to receive parish relief'.[11] An understandable desire to filter out bad risks and fraudsters meant the societies had to be obsessed with good character, self-reliance and moral probity. Members were fined for non-attendance, foul language, or talking politics or religion at meetings of the society. The Ancient Order of Foresters' initiation ceremony demanded of new members that they be faithful husbands, good fathers and steadfast friends. Criminals and philanderers could expect expulsion. Dissolutes, drunks and quarrelsome individuals were blackballed.[12] The friendly societies also taught men self-control, through the educative process of working with others for the benefit of others.

Of course, embezzlement by officials was not unknown. Fraudulent claims became increasingly common as the societies became less local and more anonymous, and their actuarial basis was often shaky, but for the most part the members still knew that if they took from the society they took from people they knew. This is not a sanction available to the Department of Social Security. And by the close of the Victorian age the friendly societies were larger and more important than any other voluntary movement. They had a million members at the time of Waterloo, and nearly 4 million by the 1880s. Numbers rose rapidly, to well over 5 million at the turn of the century and nearly 9 million at the outbreak of the Second World War.[13] At the height of their power in 1910 the 26,877 friendly society branches had 6.6 million registered members – against 2½ million trade unionists and 2½ million co-operators – and an unknown number of unregistered members.[14] The largest was the Manchester Unity of Oddfellows, which from its beginnings in a Salford pub grew into a nationwide organisation with half a million members by 1876.

The Displacement Effect of the Welfare State

The friendly societies remain in business today, but only as providers of orthodox savings and insurance products in competition with commercial and mutual suppliers of the same services, and many are now planning to incorporate. As Dick Atkinson has pointed out, their demise during the course of the twentieth century provides the most striking example of the displacement effect of the Welfare State:

> Although the 19th century saw a great flowering of charity and self-help organisations in schooling, retailing and health, the horrors of the dark satanic mill and mine ultimately encouraged people to call on the state to take on the main responsibilities for welfare and care. A more democratic culture came to see charity as at best inefficient and parochial and, at worst, as demeaning to the recipient. Local and central government came to influence most areas of social life until little stood between the individual and the state. Charity and a sense of responsibility became peripheral concepts. The unintended destructive potential of this change

was not at first apparent. Yet, gradually, it caused the state to take on from church, family and neighbour the responsibility for the care of others and absolved them from the need to take control of their lives.[15]

The State pulverises diversity. In pursuit of uniform national standards of public service – in the view of the central planner, diversity must mean inequity, it suppresses the variation which is the natural consequence of local and voluntary provision. This is the exact reverse of Ernest Barker's belief that local experiment is a useful laboratory for national schemes. The State also centralises control of any service it provides, issuing commands from Whitehall rather than involving local knowledge, expertise and experience. Self-reliance inevitably withers.

The friendly societies, which were consistently in the forefront of resistance to the nationalisation of pensions, health services and unemployment insurance from the 1880s onwards, are traditionally portrayed by the collectivist politicians and Whitehall bureaucrats who have written the history of the period as ill-informed and self-interested reactionaries. But their leaders were hostile to State interference not simply because they stood to lose business, but because they regarded themselves and their members not as a social service helping people to make do until the Socialist nirvana was inaugurated but as hard-working and prudent individuals making provision for their future. 'They strongly distinguished their guiding philosophy from the philanthropy which lay at the heart of charitable work,' writes one modern analyst. Any assistance was not a matter of largesse but of entitlement, earned by the regular contributions paid into the common fund by every member.'[16] Unlike the modern fiction of National Insurance, the members really had paid for their entitlements.

The friendly societies were still sufficiently powerful in the years before the First World War to persuade Lloyd George to use them (and the industrial insurance companies like the Prudential, the Refuge and the Pearl) as the agents of his new National Insurance scheme. But their absorption into it was the beginning of the end of the friendly society movement as the main agents of social welfare in Britain. The wide discrepancies in the value of the benefits provided by different societies proved intolerable to the craving for uniformity of the bureaucratic mind and the egalitarian-democratic conscience. They were, in the words of one civil servant, 'anomalous'.[17] Vainly, William Beveridge argued in favour of retaining the friendly societies as agents even after nationalisation of the welfare system, to ensure continued experimentation in methods of administering welfare. As he wrote, echoing Barker, in Voluntary Action:

> In a totalitarian State or in a field already made into a State monopoly, those dissatisfied with the institutions that they find can seek a remedy only by seeking to change the Government of the country. In a free society and a free field they have a different remedy; discontented individuals with new ideas can make a new institution to meet their needs. The field is open to experiment and success or failure; secession is the midwife of invention.[18]

The traditional friendly societies were killed off eventually by a combination of a monolithic Welfare State and fierce competition from the 70,000 door-to-door salesmen of the industrial insurance companies. They were a grievous loss to the ingenuity and flexibility of the welfare system in Britain.

The friendly society movement also gave rise to building societies. The earliest ones actually built houses for the contributors and were then wound up, and it was only later that they started lending depositors' money to people to build their own houses and became 'permanent' institutions. Although one historian argues that 'neither in terms of savings invested nor in terms of loans repaid can building societies properly be described as working-class financial institutions'– they were dominated by skilled workers, shopkeepers and office clerks – a lack of proletarian credentials is no reason to disparage them.[19] The building societies were highly representative of the mid-Victorian culture of self-help and self-improvement. At their Victorian peak in 1891 they had 646,000 members Significantly, home ownership was seen not only as a form of capital accumulation but, in an age when the right to vote was contingent on a property qualification, as the way to earn full political rights. By acquiring a house and starting to pay local authority rates, householders could gain a voice in the government of the country.

The savings banks, by contrast, were undoubtedly proletarian institutions. The Sunday Penny Bank started by the Reverend Joseph Smith of Wendover in 1799 inspired a number of Sunday and Penny Banks for the poor before Henry Duncan, a Scottish clergyman, founded what became the massive Trustee Savings Bank in his parish of Ruthwell in 1810. He was prompted to do so mainly by the prospect of the State taking over responsibility for poverty by extending the Poor Laws to Scotland. 'Compulsory benevolence,' he wrote in an age not yet familiar with Christian Socialism, 'is in fact a contradiction in terms.'[20] Duncan did not hesitate to turn away depositors whose moral character he doubted, and the trustees and managers of the banks he inspired were expected to take no remuneration. Trustee Savings Bank eventually spread all over Scotland and England, especially its northern and industrial parts.

By 1847 the savings banks, which were used mainly by domestic servants, agricultural labourers, mechanics, artisans, tradesmen and the like as an alternative to dependence on the Poor Law, had one million members.[21] They eventually suffered a fate similar to that of the friendly societies, especially after the State introduced attractive rivals for deposits in the shape of the Post Office Savings Bank and the National Savings Certificates issued to help pay for the First World War. According to one historian, friendly societies and independent savings banks controlled roughly two thirds of working-class financial assets in 1901, but less than one third by 1939. Industrial insurance companies and National Savings certificates accounted for half by the time of the Second World War. This gradual institutionalisation of personal savings, coupled with an increased willingness on the part of many people to rely on State hand-outs for unemployment and other personal calamities, foreshadowed the modern world of the Welfare State and the Corporate Economy.[22]

The Nationalisation of Health Services

The erosion of the friendly societies paved the way for the nationalisation of medical services too. Medical care in Victorian and Edwardian England was provided in a variety of ways. There were private fee-paying patients and contribution-based medical clubs organised by employers and doctors themselves, but free care was also available to the poor from the outpatient departments of the voluntary and local authority hospitals and the charitable dispensaries. But the friendly societies were easily the most important influence in the provision of health care. They paid doctors a retainer to attend members, appointed them to an approved panel of doctors who charged agreed fees or even employed them at friendly society medical institutes. Doctors had long disliked the ability of the friendly societies to agree lower prices for medical care for their members, and agitated continuously for higher fees. David Green has argued that doctors – or at least those who belonged to the doctors' trade union, the British Medical Association – welcomed the beginnings of the nationalisation of health services under the 1911 National Insurance Act as the best way to crush the power of the medical consumer over their pay, status and conditions of work.[23]

Since 1911, and especially since the formation of the National Health Service in 1948, doctors have merely redirected their complaints about low fees and harsh conditions from the consumer to the taxpayer. The campaign waged by the BMA against the proposed health services reforms in 1989, for example, was a cynical attempt by the doctors' trade union to preserve their pay and privileges by playing on public fears. Though many general practitioners have found they are actually better off as fund-holders, hospital consultants are still taking a reactionary stance. It was ever thus in the medical profession. It is popularly supposed, for example, that the hospital doctors of the 1940s were fiercely opposed to the National Health Service on principle, but in reality their complaints centred around fears that their standard of living would suffer as salaried employees of a monopolistic supplier of health services. 'I stuffed their mouths with gold,' was Aneurin Bevan's explanation of how he won the support of consultants for the establishment of the National Health Service. He let them keep some private beds in the nationalised hospitals – under a threat from consultants to set up private nursing homes – and paid them salaries for the first time too. Ironically, their initial fear that a monopoly employer would hold down their salaries was amply justified by the experience of the next 45 years. In the end, they sold their independence cheaply.

The Nationalisation of Education

In the field of education, the twentieth-century State has also crowded out spontaneous and self-governing voluntary activity and imposed a crushing uniformity. This was unexpected in England. State control of education was for nearly two hundred years unthinkable in a country where religious freedom was a major constitutional issue; compelling parents to send their children to school was regarded as a grave attack on the liberty of the individual; and suspicion of the tyrannical ambitions of the State ran deep. 'A general State education,' wrote John Stuart Mill in *On Liberty*, 'is a mere contrivance for moulding people to be exactly like one another: and as the mould in which it casts them is that which pleases the predominant power in the government, whether this be a monarch, a priesthood, an aristocracy, or the majority of the existing generation in proportion as it is efficient and successful, it establishes a despotism over the mind, leading by natural tendency to one over the body.'[24] Until the Education Act of 1870 empowered local authorities to set up secular schools financed out of the rates, and to compel all children aged under thirteen to attend them, State involvement in education was confined to the subsidisation and inspection of voluntary denominational schools. The Anglican 'National Society for promoting the education of the poor in the principles of the established church' was founded in 1811, and the Nonconformist British and Foreign School Society dated from 1814.

The religious division is widely held to have obstructed the development of an effective national system of education in Britain, since neither side was prepared to tolerate denominational teaching at the expense of the taxpayer. The Congregationalist Education Union, for example, was formed in the 1840s specifically to resist the nationalisation of education. But, in retrospect, this was a vital bastion against educational despotism. Despite its shortcomings, the voluntary system was more effective than its critics were inclined to believe. Between 1820 and 1883 the Church of England raised £12¼ million (about £600 million in modern prices) to build and maintain Church schools. The traditional public schools – founded over the centuries by a variety of rich aristocrats and philanthropists, and which relied entirely on a mixture of endowment income and fees – were thoroughly reformed during the early part of the Victorian era, and between 1840 and 1869 no fewer than 41 new fee-paying boarding schools were founded by private initiative for the education of the increasingly large and affluent middle class. Public school head-masters like Arnold of Rugby, Thring of Uppingham and Sanderson of Oundle were genuine educational innovators. Some public schools, like King's College and University College schools in London, were set up by reformers dissatisfied with the traditional schools and their methods. The diversity and variety of the system was its chief glory. It had 'gaps' of the kind which the tidy bureaucratic mind deplores, but there is no reason to suppose they would not in time have been closed by a mixture of voluntary initiative and a legal obligation on parents to educate their children.

Instead, impatient and avowedly practical men sought to accelerate the universalisation of education in order to 'keep up' with the Continentals. The first taxpayers' money – £20,000 for new school buildings – was provided in 1833, and split between the two denominational societies. It was a fatal mistake to accept it. State subsidies tend always to grow, and to bring in their wake the demand for political control. In this instance, the State provided a perverse incentive to schools to seek ever-larger sums of public money. Schools which accepted taxpayers' money were restricted in the amount of fees they could charge, and so tended as they grew to demand ever-larger subsidies. By the late 1840s the grant had quintupled. By 1856 there was a separate Education Department dispensing an annual budget of well over £500,000. A Bill to give local authorities power to finance schools out of the rates was first introduced in 1853, and later in the same decade the Newcastle Commission frankly recommended the formation of School Boards funded by the local taxpayers. Yet the system, by then only a few decades old, was not at all unsuccessful in terms of the ambitions policymakers had for education at the time. The Newcastle Commissioners estimated that in the late 1850s only 4½ per cent of children of elementary school age were not attending school, although they were admittedly pessimistic about the quality of the education received at some establishments. The system was also still relatively cheap for the taxpayer. Of the annual cost per child of 32–34 shillings, the State paid only half. Parental fees contributed a third, and endowments and subscriptions the balance. The voluntary system was cheap, reasonably comprehensive, self-governing and, above all, highly diverse.

The last chance to create a national system of secondary school education largely free of the deadening conformity of the State was lost in 1869. In that year the Taunton Commission recommended redistributing the endowment income of the public schools (which then amounted to the substantial sum of £336,201 a year) to create a national network of secondary schools, with any shortfall supplemented from the rates. Matthew Arnold, who had inspected the French, Dutch and Swiss educational systems, recommended that the new schools be called Royal Schools. A partially subsidised collection of endowed secondary schools might well have developed into a highly variegated national system of higher school education in Britain, but the proposal was sunk by the combined opposition of the established Church and the endowed schools. Leading politicians and officials were already tempted by the regimented uniformity of the Prussian system of education, which was thought to have contributed in some way to the rapid defeat of France in the Franco-Prussian war of 1870. The State was also being pressed to introduce a national system of secular education by one of the first great political lobbying machines, Joseph Chamberlain's National Education League. For once, the Nonconformist conscience abandoned its suspicion of the State in favour of 'practical' reform. 'I confess to a strong distrust of government action and a passionate love for voluntary action and self-reliance,' wrote Edward Baines, the Congregationalist editor of the *Leeds Mercury*, as he endorsed State education for the first time, 'but now as a practical man I am compelled to abandon the purely voluntary system.'[25]

The Education Act of 1870 was the biggest single extension of State intervention in the whole of the nineteenth century. It radically truncated individual freedom and led to a quadrupling of public expenditure on education (to a total of £4 million a year) by the 1880s.[26] The Act allowed local taxes to be levied for the foundation and maintenance of schools, and set up the first State schools to fill the gaps in private and voluntary elementary education. Building grants to voluntary schools were axed from the end of 1870, and replaced by maintenance grants from central government which were bound in the end to expunge the independence of the schools which accepted them. The value of State subsidies to schools and the payment of teachers' salaries had already been tied to the result of State-monitored tests since the 1860s. Where voluntary effort failed to fulfil the aim of the Act to educate all children between the ages of 5 and 13, elected School Boards were set up to levy special rates to build new schools. Although it was left initially to parents to decide whether to send their children to school, it was not long before the State decided to take that decision for them too. In 1880 full-time schooling was made compulsory up to the age of lo. The school-leaving age was gradually raised to 11 (1893), 12 (1899), 14 (1918), 15 (1947) and 16 (1973).

Religious teaching in 'formularies distinctive of any creed' was banned by the legislation of 1870, in the earliest and best example of the secularising tendencies of the democratic State.[27] Rising public expenditure on education gradually nationalised the entire school system. In 1891 elementary schools were made free of charge at the point of entry, giving the State sweeping powers over primary education. The Education Act of 1902 established local education authorities to manage State schools for the first time. Church schools were granted subsidies from local authority rates, and Board of Education grants were given to local education authorities willing to set up grammar schools for secondary education. The grammar schools were initially fee-paying, but from 1907 the State undertook to pay the fees of a quarter of their pupils. From 1906 the Treasury began to subsidise the provision of school meals, and from 1921 to supply free school milk to children in need. After the Second World Wr milk was given free to all children in State schools until 1971, giving the Nanny State a palpable form. Annual block grants for all State schools were introduced for the first time in 1917, and in 1918 attendance was made compulsory up to the age of 14. Between the wars, the State financed the establishment of secondary moderns to provide a vocational education for those who failed to pass the eleven-plus and get into a grammar school. During the war, the school meals service was universalised. Private and voluntary schools were quietly strangled by the State. By forcing up the school-leaving age, but restricting the amount of fees a subsidised school could charge, the State made it exceptionally difficult for schools to retain their independence.

By the time R. A. Butler introduced his Education Act in 1944, the State had almost complete control of schools. Even the public schools seemed likely to be absorbed into the State system. The Fleming Committee of 1944 recommended they take a quarter of their pupils from State primary schools free of charge, with a view to becoming wholly a part of the State-subsidised sector over a period of years. The Butler Act was anyway expected to wither them away by making the cheaper grammar schools the preferred route to university for middle-class children. Until successive Labour and Conservative governments wiped out the grammar schools in the 1960s and 1970s this did indeed look like becoming the case. Butler fixed the shape of State education in England for twenty years, suppressing educational innovation for a generation. The new State command over young minds was symbolised by the change in his own title, from President of the Board of Education to Minister of Education.[28] Under the 1944 Act, all State schools were free at the point of entry and financed by a mixture of local authority rates and central government grants. Primary and secondary education was divided by the eleven-plus examination, which was used to select which children went on to grammar schools and which to a technical school or a secondary modern. In effect, the State now dictated which children could look forward to a professional career and which were consigned to labouring, clerical or industrial occupations.

The 1944 Education Act was a depressing piece of legislation. Human talents undiscovered at the age of eleven were simply squandered.[29] Publicly aided schools were banned from charging fees, narrowing the potential range of parental choice and squeezing nine tenths of children into one of the three State-directed conduits. The proportion of children educated at independent, fee-charging schools fell to less than a tenth of the school population. The range, type and variety of schools – the chief virtue of the educational system in England, thought Matthew Arnold – were reduced to a tripartite uniformity, with only a struggling and expensive public school sector to provide experiment, innovation and diversity. The tripartite system was also bound to self-destruct, in the end demonstrating to perfection the egalitarian tendencies of the democratic State. It was the failure of the secondary moderns to achieve 'parity of esteem' with the grammar schools which launched the comprehensive holocaust on a wave of popular protest. It is often forgotten that comprehensivisation was a bi-partisan, highly popular political initiative, created entirely by the nationalisation of the education system. It was popular because it promised to end the stigma of failing the eleven-plus, and although it proceeded at first on a voluntary basis, democratic pressure eventually obliged the State to use coercion. The number of comprehensives rose steadily from 10 in 1950 to 175 in 1964, but in the following year the great philosopher of revisionist socialism, Anthony Crosland, became Minister for Education. His ambition, he told his wife at the time, was 'to destroy every fucking grammar school in England. And Wales. And Northern Ireland.'[30]

In his notorious Circular 10/65, Crosland 'requested' local authorities to go comprehensive, and set out a number of ways in which they might do so. He later blackmailed the recalcitrant by threatening to withhold grants, and built all new schools to the comprehensive pattern. The Education Act of 1976 finally compelled local authorities to turn their schools into comprehensives, a piece of legislation which the State was eventually forced to impose against the will of some local authorities by taking them to court. With almost the entire educational system under its control the State was free to impose its will on the schools. Labour governments tended to favour untried teaching methods. Lady Plowden's celebrated *Report on Children and Their Primary Schools*, published in 1967, was heavily influenced by psychological mumbo-jumbo. It advocated a 'child-centred' approach to primary school education which enabled children to 'discover' knowledge through play, activity and experience rather than by being taught. It was duly imposed on primary schools by the State. Millions of children have suffered from poor standards of literacy and numeracy as a consequence.[31]

The Conservative governments of the last fifteen years have abandoned trendy teaching methods, but they have proved just as ealous as their Labour predecessors in suppressing variety and experimentation in schools. In the last decade, teacher-training was taken over by the State; responsibility for teachers' pay was given to a quango; the schools examination boards were effectively nationalised; teachers were told what to teach and when to teach it by a new brand of national curriculum, backed by national tests at the ages of 7, 11, 14 and 16; schools were inundated with diktats and instructions on every aspect of the school day; a new class of grant-maintained schools funded directly from Whitehall was created to bypass undesirable local control; and the whole system of education was redirected not to the maintenance of civilisation and the realisation of the individuality of every child, but to the production of 'skills' for industry, the most bathetic echo of the symbiotic relationship between the Welfare State and the Corporate Economy. In the whole history Or modern British politics, the victimisation and impoverishment of the schools is the clearest and the most tragic example of the destructive and arbitrary nature of State power. It is in the schools that the State has come closest to realising John Stuart Mill's nightmare of a 'despotism over the mind, leading by natural tendency to one over the body'.

The Nationalisation of the Universities

The universities, another powerful centre of resistance to the State, were also nationalised during the twentieth century. The Colleges and Universities of Oxford and Cambridge, founded and endowed by a variety of benefactors over the centuries, did not accept taxpayers' money in serious quantities until after the First World War and then only with deep misgivings. As ever, it was the practical men who advocated the change. 'I dislike, and I suppose everyone here dislikes, the idea of receiving government money,' the Master of Trinity College, Cambridge, told the Senate in 1918, '[but] I am convinced that the only alternative is to lose the efficiency of the University, and much as I dislike the receipt of money from the government I dislike still more the idea of an inefficient university.'[32] At contemporary Oxford, two fifths of the dons in congregation voted against accepting government grants. What the universities would lose, they recognised, was their independence. They were not believed. Public subsidisation followed the usual pattern. It began timidly enough between the wars, but today the State accounts for nine tenths of the income of both Oxford and Cambridge.

The civic, or redbrick, universities were not the invention of the State either, though they are now its captives to an even greater extent. Dissenting Academies, which flourished during the eighteenth century, when Oxford and Cambridge were closed to Nonconformists, were the main source of innovation in higher education, especially in the sciences. In the nineteenth century the combination of the Nonconformist conscience and the new commercial wealth of the Industrial Revolution founded and endowed new universities at Birmingham, Bristol, Hull, Nottingham and Sheffield. Both University and King's Colleges in London were financed by the issue of shares in a joint stock company. Durham was the creation of the cathedral chapter and bishop. Holloway College was founded and lavishly endowed by Thomas Holloway, the patent medicines millionaire. Manchester University was founded in 1851 by a local plutocrat called John Owens, Sheffield by the steel tycoon Mark Firth and Hull by Thomas Ferens, managing director of the local manufacturing company, Reckitt & Colman. Southampton was endowed by the local eccentric and millionaire, Henry Robinson Hartley, and Newcastle University by the arms manufacturer William Armstrong. Aberystwyth in Wales was established by a house-to-house collection of money from the householders of South Wales.

The civic universities were never financially strong, though there is no reason to suppose they would not have become so as time wore on. After all, the colleges of Oxford and Cambridge took centuries to establish themselves. The new universities received their first infusions of public money in the 1880s, at the very beginning of the collectivist era. By the turn of the century their total subventions from the State amounted to £25,000. Today, when the civic universities share an overall annual income of £4¹/₂ billion, only Glasgow University receives more than one twenty-fifth of its revenue from endowment income. Almost the whole of the balance comes from the taxpayer. The universities are now effectively the property of the State. But they enjoyed their early years in the public sector. In the first two decades after the Second World War they were the darlings of the Treasury – which considered them vital to economic success, just as the schools were once perceived – and they enjoyed a compound annual increase in public subsidies of 7 per cent a year between 1945 and 1966. The numbers of universities, teachers and students expanded massively.

But enlargement merely increased dependence on the State, and increased dependence meant increased State control. The Treasury eventually ceded responsibility to the Department of Education and Science, and its subventions were fully subjected to the aims of public policy for the first time. The University Grants Committee began to control capital investment, staff numbers and salaries and academic developments. When the Treasury began to reduce the rate of growth of public expenditure on the universities in the 1980s, and the Department of Education started to force them to increase numbers at the expense of standards, questioned the validity of academic tenure and demanded more vocational and technical courses, dons reared on a diet of open-ended public funding naturally became resentful. In 1985 the academics of Oxford spitefully refused to award Margaret Thatcher an honorary degree, to protest about 'cuts' and 'under-funding'. It was left to one or two honest academics to face up to the truth. One of them was Kenneth Minogue, Professor of Government at the London School of Economics.

Minogue admitted in a newspaper article in September 1987 that the modern history of the universities was 'an object lesson on the perils of dependence on the State':

> In the course of the twentieth century, universities have lost, step by step, the considerable autonomy they had previously enjoyed. They lost it because they were bribed into becoming functionaries of national policy.

In the wake of the Robbins Report, they were showered with gold, new universities were founded, jobs opened up and delightful prospects of power and importance unhinged the wits of simple academics. They unhinged more than just the dons. Students, in the best Gadarene tradition, could not resist the temptation of imitating the Marxists of Berkeley and Paris. They rioted and protested in ways so repellent as to lose nearly all public sympathy. The result was to leave universities both financially and politically helpless before the next turn of Fortune's wheel.[33]

Oxford and Cambridge, which had survived (and usually thrived) in the private sector since the thirteenth century, surrendered managerial autonomy and academic freedom for the first time in the twentieth century. The civic universities were never as rich as their ancient rivals and perhaps had no choice but to surrender their independence, though the University of Buckingham and the endowment of a number of new colleges and universities by corporate wealth and sponsorship suggests otherwise. Inevitable or not, the nationalisation of such important citadels of academic excellence and independent thinking was a dreadful blow to spontaneity, diversity, culture, civilisation and liberty.

When they were independent institutions the universities used to provide education to undergraduates as a by-product of research. But the modern don is a State employee who is expected to train young men and women to become useful contributors to the Corporate Economy or the Welfare State. This has led to an increase in law, economics and business studies courses, and to a massive State-sponsored inflation of the number of places to study scientific subjects. Public money is also less discerning, allowing academics to pursue non-subjects like women's studies and green issues. The accompanying increase in academic specialisation within the universities has destroyed almost completely the humane and civilised idea of a university put so eloquently by John Henry Newman a century and a half ago:

> If the intellect is so excellent a proportion of us, and its cultivation so excellent, it is not only beautiful, perfect, admirable and noble in itself, but in a true and high sense it must be useful to the possessor and to all around him; not useful in any low, mechanical, mercantile sense, but as diffusing good, or as a blessing, or a gift, or power, or a treasure, first to the owner, then through him to the world.[34]

Politicians and bureaucrats mocked such a high doctrine of university education, regarding it as the source of the national economic 'inefficiency'. They forced the universities to abandon their historic role of transmitting to successive generations the common moral and cultural inheritance of Western civilisation.

Nationalisation has trapped dons in specialisms which are deaf to each other, and redirected them from the uninhibited pursuit of knowledge and truth into the humdrum tasks of processing degree-fodder for the Welfare State and the

Corporate Economy. They no longer contribute to the vitality, diversity and plurality of national life or play much part in the preservation of moral order. The dons have become, like everybody else who is paid by the State, just another collection of politicians milking the public finances for financial advantage. 'The successful politician,' wrote Hayek, 'owes his power to the fact that he moves within the accepted framework of thought, that he thinks and talks conventionally. It would almost be a contradiction in terms for a politician to be a leader in the field of ideas.'[35] Yet the universities were once the source of the ideas which shifted the framework of public discussion to Right or Left, or transformed the conception of the possible. That role has since passed to the multiplying 'think-tanks' which have not yet surrendered their independence to the State. The universities have ceased to be an alternative source of intellectual and moral power and ideas, or to contribute to the vitality of civilisation in Britain. That is a direct consequence of their dependence on the State.

The Nationalisation of Local Government

Local government, once another great source of new ideas and experiments in education, health and social security, has also learnt the perils of dependence on the State. A century ago the municipality was the principal way in which political power encroached on the private sector. In 1889 Sidney Webb mocked resistance to State intervention by claiming that collectivist solutions already pervaded everyday life, through the actions and investments of the local councils:

> The individualist town councillor will walk along the municipal pavement, lit by municipal gas and cleansed by municipal brooms with municipal water, and seeing by the municipal clock in the municipal market that he is too early to meet his children coming from the municipal school, hard by the county lunatic asylum and municipal hospital, will use the national telegraph system to tell them not to walk through the municipal park, but to come by the municipal tramway to meet him in the municipal reading-room by the municipal art gallery, museum and library where he intends to consult some of the national publications in order to prepare his next speech in the municipal town hall in favour of the nationalisation of canals and the increase of Government control over the railway system. 'Socialism, Sir,' he will say, 'don't waste the time of a practical man by your fantastic absurdities. Self-help, Sir, individual self-help, that's what made our city what it is.'[36]

The pejorative tag of 'gas and water socialism' reflected reality rather than aspiration. As recently as 1945 councils owned two thirds of electricity supply companies and one third of gas distribution.

Today, local government is little more than the agent of the centralised State at the local level. Its subordinate role was typified by the fate of a recent application by Wandsworth Borough Council to reintroduce grammar schools. It was simply rejected by the Secretary of State for Education. Of course, once the main objectives of the heroic age of local government – sewerage, gas and electricity, roads, health services, even housing – were accomplished, local councils had to switch in the 1950s and 1960s to the less onerous task of maintaining what their predecessors had built. But they also welcomed enthusiastically the new role assigned to them as agents of the centralised State, especially in the provision of welfare services. Most local responsibility for poor relief and health services was taken away by the Labour Government in 1948, and the role of councils in education much expanded . Municipal gas and electricity interests were nationalised at the same time. But once national standards were accepted in areas like education and social security, it was obvious that not every council would be able to finance services of the requisite standard from a local tax base. This was the beginning of the end of the independence of local government.

The drive for uniform standards of public service provision gave Whitehall and Westminster the substantial role they still enjoy today in the redistribution of resources from national taxpayers to council tax-spenders and from rich council districts to poor ones. It is often alleged that local autonomy was erased for ideological reasons by the Conservative governments of the 1980s. In fact, it was the culmination of a process which was already apparent to Peacock and Wiseman over thirty years ago:

> Local governments have shared in the growing acceptance of government intervention, which has encouraged the development of government activity as a whole. But within that activity, there has been a general shift in emphasis from relief of outright distress (e.g. in the provision of indoor poor relief) to the provision of public services on the basis of desirability (e.g. education) and a growing consciousness (undoubtedly related to transportation developments) of the state as one community to which common standards should apply.[37]

The old rates were effectively neutered in the 1930s when agricultural premises were de-rated, and industrial premises partially de-rated, by central government decree. The first general grant-in-aid from central to local government, the General Exchequer Contribution, was introduced in the 1930s. In the war which followed, it was the centralised State rather than the local authorities whose powers and resources were expanded. Central government spending has continued to grow faster than local government expenditure ever since.

As the centralised State enlarged its responsibilities, local government was obliged to implement a wider range of policies as the agent of the State at the local level. Because the grand projects of social engineering – to say nothing of the tidy bureaucratic mind and egalitarian outlook of the centralised democratic State – required uniform standards, this led ineluctably to an increasing reliance on grants from central government. The proportion of local government current expenditure financed from local taxation fell from 75 per cent of revenues in 1890 to 56 per cent in 1938 and 46 per cent in 1955.[38] In 1994–95 local authorities financed just 15 per cent of total expenditure of £72 billion from the Council Tax, charges, asset sales and other forms of self-financing. It was not ideology which extinguished the independence of local government but the combination of complex and important national responsibilities with a local tax base of trifling proportions. Until the State shrinks, or local government agrees to cede education, housing and some social services to the private sector, the scope for local political responsibility to expand will remain severely circumscribed.

The fate of the family, the charities, the friendly societies, the schools, the universities and the local authorities is a reminder that political power, unlike private wealth and initiative, is available in fixed quantities only. To the extent that the State expands, the scope for self-help, self-government, autonomy and liberty is diminished. Every function taken over by the State will cease to be performed by individuals or groups of individuals. The State, except where it assumes a task not previously done by anyone, always displaces the free or voluntary activity of individuals. There are countless examples of this syndrome. The first effect of the State-financed school feeding programme introduced in 1908, for example, was to reduce voluntary contributions to the same cause by 83 per cent.[39] The introduction of State insurance schemes against unemployment and sickness squeezed the friendly societies, whose membership began to stagnate as soon as the 1911 National Insurance Act was passed. The extinction of the independence of the voluntary schools, the civic universities and the municipal corporations were other examples of this displacement effect.

All of the 'established institutions' whose enfeeblement is usually ascribed to the destructive effects of Thatcherism – monarchy, Parliament, civil service, local government, schools, universities, historic hospitals, Oxbridge colleges – have only one characteristic in common: they are all almost wholly dependent on public money. At various times between 1760 and 1948 they elected to surrender their independence to the State, in exchange for regular infusions of taxpayers' money. All of the initiatives which these formerly autonomous institutions find so disagreeable – policy direction, financial constraints, closures, the loss of security of tenure, performance-related pay and market-based reforms – reflect the fact that they are now owned by the State. It is the purest cant to imagine that these once-great institutions are the last outposts of civilisation in a land laid waste by rampant economic individualism. They are merely the pitiful clientele of the modern centralised State, clambering over each other like hungry pigs to get their snouts in the public trough. It is not surprising that the people who live and work inside such institutions complain constantly of cuts' and demoralisation. It is the least they can do to persuade the voters to cough up some more.

References

1   John Stuart Mill, *On Liberty and Other Essays*, OUP, 1991, pages 121–2.
2   Ernest Barker, *Principles of Social and Political Theory*, OUP, 1951, page 50.
3   *Principles of Social and Political Theory*, page 50.
4   *Charity Trends 1993*, Charities Aid Foundation.
5   Quoted in Harold Perkin, *The Origins of Modern English Society 1780–1880*, Routledge, 69, page 225.
6   Samuel Smiles, *Self-Help*, John Murray, 1897, pages 1–2.
7   Dick Atkinson, *The Common Sense of Community*, Demos, 1994, page 5.

8   Harold Perkin, *The Origins of Modern English Society 1780–1880*, Routledge, 1 969, page 8.

9   Paul Johnson, *Saving and Spending: The Working Class Economy in Britain 1870–1939*, OUP, 1985, Table 4.6.

10   E. P. Thompson, *The Making of the English Working Class*, Pelican, 1977, page 462.

11   *The Making of the English Working Class*, page 463.

12   David G. Green, *Reinventing Civil Society: The Rediscovery of Welfare Without Politics*, IEA Health and Welfare Unit, 1993, pages 48 and 63.

13   Paul Johnson, *Saving and Spending: The Working Class Economy in Britain 1870–1939*,

14   David G. Green, *Reinventing Civil Society: The Rediscovery of Welfare Without Politics*, IEA Health and Welfare Unit, 1993, pages 31–2, 42 and 66.

15   Dick Atkinson, *The Common Sense of Community*, Demos, 1994, pages 10–11.

16   David G. Green, *Reinventing Civil Society: The Rediscovey of Welfare Without Politics*, IEA Health and Welfare Unit, 1993, page 30.

17   *Reinventing Civil Society: The Rediscovery of Welfare Without Politics*, pages 109 and 111–16.

18   *Reinventing Civil Society: The Rediscovery of Welfare Without Politics*, page 45.

19   Paul Johnson, *Saving and Spending: The Working Class Economy in Britain 1870–1939*, OUP, 1985, page 124.

20   Haldane, *150 Years of Trustee Savings Banks*, TSB Association, 1960.

21   H. Oliver Horne, *A History of Savings Banks*, OUP, 1947, page 116.

22   Paul Johnson, *Saving and Spending: The Working Class Economy in Britain 1870–1939*, OUP, 1985, Table 7.1.

23   David G. Green, *Reinventing Civil Society: The Rediscovery of Welfare Without Politics*, IEA Health and Welfare Unit, 1993, pages 70–87 and 98–9.

24   John Stuart Mill, *On Liberty and Other Essays*, OUP, 1991, pages 117–18.

25   Quoted in Derek Fraser, *The Evolution of the British Welfare State*, Second Edition, Macmillan, 1984, page 86.

26   About £250 million today.

27   See Chapter 10, page 251.

28   It remains to be seen if a change of title in the reverse direction at the Department of Trade and Industry also has a reverse effect on interventionist policy.

29   The private sector, by contrast, has always preferred to wait another two years before making the decisive selection.

30   Susan Crosland, *Tony Crosland*, Coronet, 1983, page 148.

31   In a recent survey of small employers by the British Chambers of Commerce, 39 per cent of respondents claimed to be suffering from a 'skills gap', with two thirds citing the literacy of recruits as the main problem. Reported in *Financial Times*, 26 September 1994.

32   Quoted in V. H. H. Green, *The Universities*, Pelican, 1969, page 186.

33   *London Evening Standard*, 30 September 1987. Quoted in Martin Holmes *Thatcherism: Scope and Limits, 1983–87*, Macmillan, 1989, pages 127.

34   Quoted in Owen Chadwick, *Newman*, OUP, 1983, page 56.

35   F. A. Hayek, *The Constitution of Liberty*, Routledge, 1960, page 112.

36   Quoted in Derek Fraser, *The Evolution of the British Welfare State*, Second Edition Macmillan, 1984, page 112.

37   A. T. Peacock and J. Wiseman, *The Growth of Public Expenditure in the United Kingdom*, OUP, 1961, page 119.

38   *The Growth of Public Expenditure in the United Kingdom*, Table 11, page 100, and Table A-18, page 197.

39   Bentley B. Gilbert, *The Evolution of National Insurance in Great Britain: The Origins of the Welfare State*, Michael Joseph, 1966, page 113.

CHAPTER FOURTEEN

The Demoralisation of the Individual

I know it has been found easier to please the people by holding out flattering and delusive prospects of cheap benefits to be derived from Parliament rather than by urging them to a course of self-reliance; but while I will not be the sycophant of the great, I cannot become the parasite of the poor; and I have sufficient confidence in the growing intelligence of the working classes to be induced to believe that they will now be found to contain a great proportion of minds sufficiently enlightened by experience to concur with me in this opinion, that it is to themselves alone individually that they, as well as every other great section of the community, must trust for working out their own regeneration and happiness. Again I say to them, 'Look not to Parliament; look only to yourselves.'

Richard Cobden, 1836[1]

The expansion of the State demoralises and poisons the life of the individual. No other remark by Margaret Thatcher provoked collectivists into quite such fulminating rage as her notorious comment that 'there is no such thing as society'. Yet it is the veracity of her statement, and not its insensitivity, which is striking when it is read in the context of her remarks as a whole:

I think we've been through a period where too many people have been given to understand that if they have a problem, it's the government's job to cope with it. 'I have a problem, I'll get a grant.' 'I'm homeless, the government must house me.' They're casting their problem on society. And, you know, there is no such thing as society. There are individual men and women, and there are families. And no government can do anything except through people, and people must look to themselves first. It's our duty to look after ourselves and then, also, to look after our neighbour. People heave got the entitlements too much in mind, without the obligations. There's no such thing as entitlement, unless someone has first met an obligation.[2]

Perhaps the most objectionable of all the collectivist fallacies is the belief that voting for the income and wealth of others to be redistributed by the State is an expressly moral action. Asking 'society' to take on the burden of caring for a vulnerable person is merely a euphemism for the coercion of some (usually a minority) by others.

Only the individual, choosing freely what to do with his money, can possibly be making moral choices. 'We can never have regard to the virtue of an action,' wrote David Hume, 'unless the action be antecedently virtuous. No action can be virtuous, but so far as it proceeds from a virtuous motive.'[3] Virtuous motives, he thought, did not include the love of mankind so often cited by socialists. This seems unarguable. Personal judgment must have a role in the life of the virtuous man which it cannot possibly have in the life of the man who is merely law-abiding. Yet in England today politicians and voters who promise to spend other people's money are routinely described as more 'caring' – in other words, more moral – than those who do not. If opinion polls are to be believed, a great many voters are genuinely under the illusion that voting for other people to pay higher taxes is an altruistic or even a moral action. But that is no excuse for important public figures to perpetuate their mistake.

Successive Circles of Moral Obligation

During the last general election campaign, the television celebrity Melvyn Bragg urged voters to support the Labour Party on the grounds that it was promising to raise taxes, many people had done well in the 1980s and that the wealthy owed it to themselves and to the State to pay more in taxes:

> [The Labour Party] leaders have presented and costed their policies openly, taking risks, gutsily, not fearing to name those who might feel themselves the injured faction, the well-off…those of us who did okay during the Thatcher years. But it ought to be no surprise to say that some of those so-called tax targets of my acquaintanceship will also be voting Labour. They believe, as I do, that there must be change. Change has to be paid for. Those who have earned a bit can afford to stump up. Besides, it is of no little real value to the well-off that Labour wins. What will happen to any lasting chances of prosperity if the infrastructure crumbles away? Or homelessness increases? Or unemployment grows? Or training budgets and research budgets are not increased? More depression, more loss, and more nastiness.[4]

Mr Bragg had indeed done well in the 1980S. He and his colleagues at London Weekend Television (LWT) benefited from a 'golden handcuffs' management share option scheme which was so generous that even the company's normally quiescent institutional investors balked at the initial version. The revised version of the scheme, realised when the company retained its television franchise, was still sufficiently generous to net Mr Bragg an estimated £2.87 million.[5] Lesser employees later embarrassed Bragg and the other managers into sharing a proportion of this windfall with them.

It is a measure of the demoralising effects of State intervention that champagne socialists see no contradiction between their private and their public behaviour. Throughout the 1980s there was nothing to prevent socialists who felt they should be paying higher taxes from sending a cheque to the Inland Revenue for whatever sum they considered appropriate. Many people do exactly that every year. A widow recently left £2 million to pay off the National Debt, as a mark of her gratitude for being a British citizen.[6] But there is no publicly recorded instance of any champagne socialist following the example of the Conservative Prime Minister, Stanley Baldwin, in using his personal fortune to pay off a part of the National Debt. The Victorian socialist William Morris was once asked by a heckler why he did not give his considerable fortune to the poor. 'I am not a rich man,' he replied, 'but even if I were to give all my money away, what good would that do? The poor would be just as poor, the rich, perhaps, a little more rich, for my wealth would finally get into their hands. The world would be pleased to talk about me for three days until something new caught its fancy. Even if Rothschild gave away his millions tomorrow, the same problems would confront us the day after.'[7] It is comforting for rich men to believe that individual gestures of charity are futile, but a great many of them – George Peabody, Henry Wellcome, Joseph Rowntree, Lord Leverhulme, Lord Nuffield, Lord Rank, Lord Wolfson, Garfield Weston, Charles Clore and the Sainsbury family, to name but a few – have taken a higher and harder view than that. It is also a rejection of the whole of the Judaeo-Christian tradition, which values the widow's mite as highly as the largesse of the millionaire.

Collectivists are simply too obsessed with man as a public rather than as a private individual to see any real connection between private and public morality. As State-worshippers, they naturally believe that the State – or what they sometimes call 'Society' or the 'Community' or, on the global stage, the 'International Community' – is the authentic vehicle of personal moral aspirations. It is in fact general or political altruism of this kind which is meaningless, not personal acts of charity. National or international taxation disconnects the individual from the essential condition of authentic activity in the moral sphere: that it present moral choices which the individual can judge, solve and make his own.[8] Useful and effective moral behaviour can occur only at the most intimate level of human activity. The individual can care properly only for himself, his family and his immediate circle of friends and acquaintances. He may also choose to devote time, energy and money to a particular charity. But in all these cases his duties towards other people are moral only in so far as they are particular and not general, and he must decide which of the needs he confronts are most important to him. 'People who devote time to charitable work, or give money to charity, do so voluntarily,' Nigel Lawson has observed. 'There is positive moral worth in this. But services provided by the State are funded from taxation, and the moral worth in complying with a legal obligation to pay income tax is hardly in the same league. In terms of the quality of life, the nationalisation of morality is debilitating.'[9]

Constant calls to fulfil obligations to abstractions like Society or the Community are bound in the end to blunt moral sensibilities altogether. They make it impossible to decide which moral responsibilities are truly the obligation of the individual and which are not. Collectives simply cannot make moral choices. This is made clear by a classic psychological study, showing how a lone bystander is more likely to help somebody in trouble than a crowd of onlookers. Collectivists do not believe this. They think that caring for only an immediate circle of individuals or a self-selected charity is not at all a form of morality, which must be based on universalism. But, as James Wilson has explained, 'morality governs our actions towards others in much the same way that gravity governs the motions of the planets: its strength is in inverse proportion to the square of the distance between them...Our natural sociability is reinforced by attachment to familiar others, and so we tend to value the familiar over the strange, the immediate over the distant; in common with most species, we are by nature locals, not cosmopolitans...Mankind is not devoid of moral sense if most of its members treat villagers better than strangers and family better than non-kin. On the contrary; unless people are disposed to favour the familiar face to the strange one, their natural sociability would not become a moral sense at all.'[10]

As Samuel Brittan has pointed out, a world in which mothers were responsible for all children rather than just their own would be one with universal neglect of children. He believes people are subject to 'successive circles of obligation', in which it is natural and right for people to care most for their nearest and dearest, to care more about the death of a neighbour than a Rwandan refugee and to grieve more over the death of an English soldier than his Iraqi opponent. 'Strangers do and should count,' he says, 'but we need not be ashamed to give most weight to those closest to us... Too many moralists have paid lip service to the idea of the whole human race counting equally and have then gone on to concentrate on policies affecting exclusively their own community. Ordinary people are then presented with the false choice of either giving equal value to every inhabitant of the earth or giving no value at all to those outside their immediate circle or country. The result of paying lip service to impartial benevolence is too often in practice the total neglect of those outside our own group.'[11] A cold relation, to invert the wisdom of Edmund Burke, is depressingly often a zealous 'citizen'.

How the Welfare State Shrinks Moral Opportunities

The fallacious collectivist belief that the Welfare State is the vehicle of authentic moral aspirations blinds State-worshippers to the fact that it is the displacement effect of the State, and not the false consciousness of capitalism, which is pulverising the moral faculties of the individual man and woman. When schools and universities are provided by the Department of Education, unemployment benefit and income support by the Department of Social Security and medical help by the National Health Service, the effect is not to enlarge the moral opportunities open to individuals but to narrow them. By widening the reach of its authority, to adapt a phrase of David Green, the State has narrowed the scope of individual conscience.[12] In its extreme form – totalitarianism – collectivist government leaves no room for individual initiative at all, destroying all moral sense. It is for this reason that the withdrawal of the State from areas of life that it had previously occupied to the exclusion of all other agents has led to such an explosion of criminality in the former Soviet Union.

But even in Britain the taxation needed to pay for public services has not only diminished the time and money available to individuals to expend on helping their fellow-men, but also blunted moral sensibilities. People have, in a sense, abdicated moral responsibility to the State. They believe that paying taxes is enough. It is a ritual complaint of the modern citizen that 'they should do something about it' or 'there should be a law against it'. It is uncanny how often the shrinkage of the area of moral choice is greeted with enthusiasm by ordinary people, as if they can no longer trust themselves to make the right choices. This syndrome is nowhere more obvious than in the unfailing public approbation of every increase in State power over the behaviour of motorists. The helmet laws, the seatbelt laws, the annual and increasingly hysterical Christmas propaganda campaign against drinking and driving, and the cameras and electronic notice-boards on the motorways, are all massively popular. The State now has the power to stop people eating eggs, and to keep them eating beef. Democratic man in England is unfolding exactly as de Tocqueville predicted he would a century and a half ago. 'Over this kind of men,' he wrote, 'stands an immense, protective power which is alone responsible for securing their enjoyment and watching over their fate.'[13]

This tutelary power is mirrored in the current shape of the British constitution. As Ferdinand Mount has pointed out, it has gradually shed its historic checks and balances and come to rest on the notion of unfettered executive power: 'The Constitution, we are told, is parliamentary supremacy and nothing but parliamentary supremacy. It admits no considerations of natural law or human rights, just as it admits no powers for subordinate or external law-making bodies.'[14] Today, even the judgments of the courts are not entirely secure from subsequent political correction. As de Tocqueville predicted, democracy necessitates the creation of a constitutional machine for translating the popular will into legislation, however ill-considered and damaging to natural rights. Britain is governed now by what Lord Hailsham once called 'an elective dictatorship'. The most melancholy consequence is the transformation of Parliament from the watchdog of the interests of the tax-payers into the poodle of the tax-eaters.[15] But it has also made Parliament so acutely sensitive to every wish and nuance of the electorate that no intelligent citizen can ignore the possibility that the legislature will save him the trouble of solving his own problem by drowning it in money or laws or regulations.

In a sense, the collectivist vision of man 'realising' himself through the State is close to accomplishment, but in a bastardised and prosaic form exceedingly remote from the high-flown language of German metaphysicians. David Green has described the new moral individual like this:

> Socialists have not seen the good person as someone who gave his own time and energy in the service of others, but as the individual who demanded action by the State at the expense of other taxpayers. This politicised interpretation of moral responsibility, far from increasing

consideration for others, tends to undermine the sense of personal responsibility on which an ethos of service truly rests.[16]

As the State has taken over the functions performed by the variety of non-political institutions, which once breathed life into the moral ideas of individuals and transmitted them down the generations, it has robbed people of the means of putting their moral beliefs into practice and turned them into mere litigants and politicians who claim civil and material 'rights' from the State.

The Citizen as Litigant

The modern citizen no longer sees liberty as duty, as men like Llewellyn Woodward did at the outbreak of the Great War.[17] Instead, he or she lay claims upon the State for cash, goods and services or compensation when it fails to supply any of these things. The State and the Individual are not fused or synthesised in the way that the metaphysicians predicted. Their relationship is reduced to what Carlyle or Marx might have called 'the cash nexus', a purely contractual and legalistic dialogue between supplier and customer devoid of any sense of moral or reciprocal obligation. In the popular mind, there is no longer even a distinction between moral and material claims. Politicians and officials exist to satisfy unmet needs, and all unmet needs have equal worth. After a cut in interest rates or a tax-cutting Budget, non-mortgage payers or non-taxpayers write to the Chancellor to complain that he has 'done' nothing for them. As people become accustomed to expect the State to provide everything for them; they are also inclined to blame all their misfortunes on the State. Doctors are sued for operations which fail or conditions which are untreatable, as if they had broken a contract between State and citizen.

The Army was sued recently for damages by a former female officer dismissed from the service when she became pregnant. She won damages of £299,51, with more to come from lost pension rights. A young woman suffering from cerebral palsy sued her local authority for allowing fellow-pupils at her school to stare at her. A photographer sued the council at Lyme Regis for allowing him to fall off the Cobb, and won £95,000. Workers made redundant as a result of privatisations are suing the State for failing to consult them first. A schizophrenic who killed a stranger on the London underground is suing the local health authorities for negligence in releasing him. Bizarrely, the widow of his victim agrees that the murder was not his fault: 'I don't blame [him] – I blame the authorities and their failure for my husband's death.'[18] A juvenile criminal sued Bolton borough council for failing to educate him properly.'[19] Since the criminal injuries compensation scheme was set up in 1964, the payment of compensation to victims of crime has become routine. As one solicitor familiar with the scheme describes it:

> The government took the view [in 1964] that if, say, you are mugged leaving the office, then that is a failure of society, a failure of policing and a failure of the State.[20]

When the decomposing corpse of a pensioner is found in a block of council flats, the neighbours blame not themselves but the social services for not discovering it sooner. 'Modern society,' Disraeli warned more than a century ago, 'knows no neighbours.'[21] It was a dark moment when the mother of one of the killers of little James Bulger blamed his actions not on his own depravity or his upbringing, but on social workers, teachers and policemen. The Citizen's Charter is the bathetic apotheosis of this outlook. Every branch of the State advertises ways in which the 'customer' can complain; the Department of Transport puts up signs by every set of roadworks saying 'sorry for any delay', and advertises 'hotlines' which irate motorists can telephone to complain about the number of cones obstructing their journey home; and British Rail and London Transport promise to pay compensation to passengers whose trains fail to run on time.

Collectivists call this 'citizenship'. In their view, the individual citizen acquires moral and material rights against other individuals merely by virtue of living in a Welfare State. This purely contractual view of the relationship between the Individual and the State is a symptom of the complete breakdown of consensus about the common moral rules and principles which underlie political obligation.[22] As the State has expanded, the scope for the exercise of the individual conscience has narrowed. 'Modern politics,' writes Alasdair MacIntyre, 'cannot be a matter of genuine moral consensus. And it is not. Modern politics is civil war carried on by other means...The truth on this matter was set out by Adam Ferguson: "We are not to expect that the laws of any country are to be framed as so many lessons of morality...Laws, whether civil or political, are expedients of policy to adjust the pretensions of parties, and to secure the peace of society. The expedient is accommodated to special circumstances"...The nature of any society therefore is not to be deciphered from its laws alone, but from those understood as an index of its conflicts. What our laws show is the extent to which conflict has to be suppressed...In any society where government does not express or represent the moral community of the citizens, but is instead a set of institutional relationships for imposing a bureaucratised unity on a society which lacks a genuine moral consensus, the nature of political obligation becomes systematically unclear.'[23] The constant shadow of the State has turned people not into the universal good neighbours of collectivist fiction, but into litigants and politicians. Morality has been nationalised, and all moral decisions politicised. 'We have all become politicians,' is the bleak conclusion of Martin Jacques.[24]

The Rise in Crime

As the Welfare State has aggrandised more and more of private life, and taken in tax the sums previously devoted to private pursuits, so the influence of the spontaneous and the non-political in the life of the British people has waned. All of the intermediary institutions which have traditionally socialised and civilised people – the nuclear family, the voluntary school, the universities, the friendly societies and so – have been attacked and destroyed by the State. And the process of destruction has long since passed the point at which it becomes self-fulfilling. As the State has expanded, so it has needed to expand further, just as Edmund Burke foresaw two centuries ago:

Men are qualified for civil liberty in exact proportion to their disposition to put moral chains upon their own appetites – in proportion as their love of justice is above their rapacity – in proportion as their soundness and sobriety of understanding is above their vanity and presumption – in proportion as they are more disposed to listen to the counsels of the wise and good, in preference to the flattery of knaves. Society cannot exist, unless a controlling power upon will and appetite be placed somewhere; and the less of it there is within, the more there must be without. It is ordained in the eternal constitution of things, that men of intemperate minds cannot be free. Their passions forge their fetters.[25]

As informal methods of social control have broken down during the twentieth century, the State has been drawn into increasingly arcane corners of the moral domain. In commerce, declining honesty has multiplied regulation; in health, a lack of temperance has led to advertising restrictions, increased police powers to stop and search motorists and ceaseless propaganda about diet and exercise; and illegitimacy and fecklessness have bloated the range, scope and expense of the social services.

But in no area of public policy is the cycle of State destruction and intervention more vicious than that of criminal justice. It is richly ironic that law and order, the one area of political life where the coercive power of the State impinges most rightly and obviously on the life of the free Individual, is where the State is now experiencing its greatest and most prolonged defeat. Over the past fifteen years, public expenditure on law and order and protective services has more than doubled in real terms to £14.4 billion. There are nearly 1,000 more uniformed police of icers and over 13,000 more civilians working in the police service, equipped with more cars, computers and other equipment than at any previous time. The average number of people in custody or prison in England and Wales has increased by nearly a tenth to over 46,000, a figure higher than the total capacity of the prison system despite a doubling of expenditure on prisons and the prison service. Even informed observers have lost count of the quantity and content of the stream of criminal justice legislation which has been enacted since 1979. Yet, as Table 19 shows, the country has experienced during the same period an unprecedented and apparently uncontrollable epidemic of crime.

No amount of statistical manipulation, redefinition of categories or excuses like the increased willingness to report crimes can wholly dissolve the brute fact that since 1979 recorded crime has more than doubled.[26] The overall increase conceals some disturbing trends in particular types of crime. There were 6,300 robberies in 1970, but in 1992 there were 63,000. Violent crimes against people have doubled since 1979, to over 200,000 offences in 1992. As two recent authors have put it:

When every known and correctable defect of the figures has been attended to; when every reasonable estimate has been made for defects the magnitude of which can only be intelligently gauged; and when the benefit of every doubt is given to those whose elitist speculations are directed at showing that the ignorant and misguided population at large suffers under an illusion that crime has increased, what is left is a massive increase in criminal activity in British society.[27]

Citizens concerned about crime are not merely drunk from a surfeit of *Crimewatch* or the indescribable horror of watching on television the abduction and murder of a two-year-old by two Liverpool schoolboys. They can see and hear the unarguable evidence of unceasing criminality in the prosaic surroundings of their everyday life. The shattered glass of car windows lies in the gutter, ringing burglar alarms break the silence of the night, cars screech past the drawing-room window, neighbours and shopkeepers barricade their property with iron grilles and metal shutters, the parish church is locked and the offices, factories and warehouses are patrolled by security guards and dogs and surrounded by barbed wire fences and broken-glass capped walls.

Table 19   Notifiable Offences Recorded by the Police
                     in England and Wales (1000s)

	1979	1992	Percentage Increase
Violence against the person	95.0	201.8	+ 112.4%
Sexual offences	21.8	29.5	+35.3%
Burglary	544.0	1,355.3	+149.1%
Robbery	12.5	52.9	+323.2%
Theft and handling stolen goods	1,416.1	2,851.6	+101.4%
Fraud and forgery	118.0	168.6	+42.9%
Criminal damage	320.5	892.6	+178.5%
Other offences	8.8	39.4	+347.7%
Total	2,536.7	5,591.7	+ 120.4%

Source: *Annual Abstract of Statistics*, 1990 and 1993.

Why Crime Rises

Before this explosion of wickedness, some of the greatest superstitions of the twentieth century – sociology, criminology and psychology – lie prostrate. At various times they have advanced prosperity, adversity, affluence, deprivation, poverty, wealth, relative deprivation, relative poverty, full employment, unemployment, urbanisation, mobility, immobility, anonymity, alienation, boredom, lack of challenge, bad housing and countless other socio-economic explanations as the cause of the rising rate of crime. Their current explanation of the crime epidemic, much admired in police canteens as well as collectivist think-tanks, is that the economic individualism of the 1980s unleashed a torrent of greed which the young, unskilled and materially deprived inhabitants of the cities were able to satisfy only by a life of crime. 'It is only by the exercise of heroic powers of self-deception, or else by simple dishonesty, that British

Conservatives can fail to discern the links between levels of criminality that are unprecedented in recent generations and policies of marketisation, pursued for a decade and a half, which have ridden roughshod over settled communities and established expectations,' declares John Gray.[28] In fact, as David Willetts has rightly observed, most crime is committed by young males and it is generally a group activity rather than an individual enterprise. 'They hunt and fight in gangs, are influenced by their friends, and will engage in extraordinarily risky behaviour in order to impress them,' writes Willetts. 'The trouble is not therefore that they are more self-centred, the problem is that their natural sociability and desire to be regarded by others is not being expressed constructively or creatively.'[29]

One obvious obstacle to curing crime driven by peer group pressure is idleness. The connections between crime, unemployment and economic need are hotly disputed. Some reject the idea of a direct link between joblessness and crime altogether, not least because the exceptionally high unemployment and dreadful poverty of the inter-war years was not characterised by a similarly large increase in criminal activity.[30] Crime does seem to have risen fastest during the full employment and rising living standards of the 1950s, suggesting there may even be some truth in the idea of the greedy individual. It would certainly be foolish to discount economic motives altogether, if only because the unemployed are more likely to encounter criminal opportunities. In crowded and prosperous cities there is more property to steal, and the unemployed have the leisure to steal it. Many of them undoubtedly do find the wide and obvious disparities between rich and poor distressing, and the greater mobility and anonymity of urban living allows them to gratify their envy without feeling that they have caused personal offence. Criminals often cite the fact that an item is insured as evidence that its owner can obtain a replacement at little cost to himself. These suppositions certainly fit the fact that crime has increased in line with material prosperity in every industrialised country except Japan over the last eighty years.

There is undoubtedly also such a character as the rational 'economic criminal', who chooses to break the law because it is more remunerative than to keep it. It is undeniable that in some cases theft, drug-dealing (and, of course, terrorism) have become alternative 'careers' for people who could not hope to enjoy an equivalent level of material success from a legitimate occupation. Even petty crime is often economically motivated. People without a job or readily marketable skills, or in a low-paid job with little hope of social and economic elevation, limited access to social security benefits and little or no savings – in short, the unskilled and often young people who make up the majority of minor criminals – are more likely to consider a criminal career a rational economic choice. Although there is no direct link between unemployment and the crime rate, at least on the available statistics, historians have identified some historical correlation between recession, inflation and unemployment and peaks in criminal activity by those on the nlargills of a steady economic life.[31]

But, as James Wilson has pointed out, the extraordinary thing is how *uncommon* it is for people to turn to crime. Most people in straitened circumstances do not turn to crime, and nor do most rich or greedy people.

'Having thought about the matter for many years, I can find no complete explanation for the worldwide increase in crime rates,' writes Wilson, 'that does not assign an important role to a profound cultural shift in the strength of either social constraints or internal conscience or both, and I can find no complete explanation of that cultural shift that does not implicate to some important degree our convictions about the sources and importance of the moral sentiments...Over the course of the last hundred years the world has experienced a shift from an era in which crime chiefly responded to material circumstances to one in which it responds in large measure to cultural ones. That shift had many causes, but one is the collapse in the legitimacy of what once was respectfully called middle-class morality but today is sneeringly referred to as "middle-class values".'[32] If he is right, and it seems likely that he is, the State is the ultimate cause of the increase in crime. Over the course of the twentieth century it has directly and indirectly undermined and even destroyed those institutions – the family, denominational and voluntary schools, private housing estates, the friendly societies and other informal networks of social control, even the village policeman paid out of the rates – which upheld and transmitted 'middle-class values' to successive generations of young people.

History, and the contemporary experience of modern Japan, lends some support to this thesis. Between the Great Exhibition and the outbreak of war in 1914 – a period in which both the national income and the urban population trebled, and social and economic inequalities were wider than at any time in history – serious criminal offences per 100, 000 inhabitants of England and Wales declined by between a third and two fifths, and acts of theft and violence fell even more steeply. As Table 20 shows, crimes recorded per 100,000 of the population fell by roughly two fifths between 1860 and 1911. In other words, there is no necessary connection between crime and the marginalisation of some people at a time of rising prosperity. Historians of crime are confident that the Victorian and Edwardian achievement is not a mere quirk of statistics.[33] The fall in the crime rate was as obvious to contemporaries as the increase is to observers today. 'There never was, in any nation of which we have a history, a time in which life and property were so secure as they are at present in England,' claimed L. O. Pike, author of the *History of Crime in England*, in 1879. In 1887 Conan Doyle had Sherlock Holmes complain that there were not enough crimes and criminals to excite his interest.[34] 'We have witnessed,' agreed the Criminal Registrar in 1901, 'a great change in manners: the substitution of words without blows for blows with or without words; an approximation in the manners of different classes; a decline in the spirit of lawlessness.'[35] Somehow, the late Victorians and Edwardians managed to defeat crime.[36]

How the Edwardians Defeated Crime

How did they do it? Most obviously, by increasing the efficiency and effectiveness of the police, the criminal law and the court system. A salaried national police force was gradually introduced and expanded in quality and numbers between 1829 and 1856. The criminal law, which in the Georgian age was notorious for the sloppiness of its drafting, was in the Victorian period amended to facilitate the prosecution of criminals. Salaried magistrates and prosecutors were introduced; summary trials without jury were greatly extended; and prisons were built.[37] The detection, arrest, conviction and punishment of criminals improved commensurately, incapacitating habitual offenders through incarceration and deterring would-be criminals. Importantly, the new techniques and institutions were also adequate to the task they faced. Victorian and Edwardian criminals were unskilled, unsophisticated and unorganised by comparison with their modern counterparts. Most were casual thieves, using larceny to supplement an inadequate or insecure income from employment, rather than well-organised bank robbers or gangs of drug-dealers or muggers. Their knowledge of the law, and of their rights under it, was slim.

Table 20 Notifiable Offences Recorded by the Police in England and Wales (e)

Year	(a)(b)	(a)(c)	(d)	(a)(b)'	(a)(c)'	(d)'
1861	88,000			437		
1871	82,000			360		
1881	97,105			373		
1891	79,734			274		
1901	80,962			248		
1911	97,171			269		
1921	103,258			272		
1931	159,278			398		
1941	358,655			859		
1951	524,506	549,700		1,197	1,255	
1961	806,900	870,900		1,747	1,885	
1971		1,665,700			3,389	
1981	5,971	2,794,200	2,963,760		5,630	5,971
1991	10,942	5,075,300	5,276,173		9,932	10,325

1 Crimes per 100,000 of the population.
(a) Excludes criminal damage valued at £20 and under. These offences were not recorded before 1977, and inflation increased the incidence.
(b) As originally recorded before the Theft Act 1968, which fundamentally redefined a large number of offences. The figures for 1861 and 1871 are approximate and for the year ending 29 September.
(c) The figures before 1972 are adjusted to take account of changes in legislation, notably the Theft Act 1968. Data are rounded.
(d) Includes all criminal damage.
(e) There are some changes over time in the exact definition of population used.
Sources: Criminal Statistics, England and Wales Annual Command Papers; B. R. Mitchell, *British Historical Statistics*, pages 12–14; *Annual Abstract of Statistics 1994*, Table 2.1; *Monthly Digest of Statistics May 1994*, Table 2.1.

The mental world of the Victorian or Edwardian criminal harked back to the eighteenth century, when the risk of detection and prosecution was minimal, the authorities relied largely on the deterrent effect of ferocious and exemplary punishment and some forms of criminal activity (like rioting) were regarded as a semi-legitimate social safety valve. In the nineteenth century, an arrest often followed a simple visit to the pawn shop to ask who had deposited a stolen item.[38] Nor were the police particularly fastidious about assembling the evidence to make an arrest, frequently charging a suspect with several offences in the hope that at least one would stick. But the organisation and technology of the authorities was anyway superior to that of the criminals. The police presence on the streets, the use of plain-clothes detectives for surveillance, the invention of the telegraph and telephone, fingerprinting techniques, better street lighting, photography, cheaper and more efficient court procedures, extradition treaties, and new prisons and juvenile reformatories were a formidable battery of weapons to train on an unsophisticated criminal fraternity. Methods of countering or outwitting the authorities – like firearms, safe-breaking and white-collar fraud – do not seem to have developed until much later. 'The police and courts cut into the criminal world as a result as much of the relative defencelessness of that world as of their own intrinsic potency,' as one historian has put it.[39]

The police were especially effective in penetrating the previously closed fraternities of friends, shopkeepers, publicans, peers, receivers of stolen goods, gangsters and the like into which criminals traditionally retreated. They persuaded neighbours and shopkeepers to pass on intelligence about criminal activity to the police, and the willingness to report crime greatly increased. As the fear of reprisals receded, even juries showed an increasing willingness to convict (at least in cases which did not carry the death penalty). Suspicion of the police – particularly among the poor – was always strong. In the eighteenth century, all classes regarded an organised police force as the chief characteristic of the Continental tyrannies Britain periodically engaged in war. A salaried police force was considered n unthinkable offence to historic English liberties.[40] But by the 1870s the police had won what is described as 'a certain grumbling acquiescence' in their authority. This was largely because they acquired a legitimacy disconnected from the attack on crime, through regulating the slum landlords, vagrants, drunks, prostitutes, beggars and other deviants which disfigured the Victorian urban neighbourhood.[41] The increasingly prosperous middle classes, with more possessions and a strong distaste for deviancy, became especially enthusiastic about the police. In short, the police won the confidence and consent of the policed and received information and support in return.

These explanations are nevertheless inadequate to explain the whole of the fall in crime. At bottom, far subtler forces of inner compulsion and social control were at work. The discipline of factory and school, and better and more secure housing, reduced the time and opportunities for the commission of crime. More importantly, Victorian England had accomplished a moral revolution which transformed the conduct of almost every individual towards every other individual, and created a remarkably stable, pacific and well-integrated society. According to the social historian Harold Perkin, a combination of Nonconformism, Evangelicalism, Benthamism, Cobdenism and working-class education and self-improvement captured the hearts and minds of all ranks of society and effected a profound change in the national character:

> Between 1780 and 1850 the English ceased to be one of the most aggressive, brutal, rowdy, outspoken, riotous, cruel and bloodthirsty nations in the world and became one of the most inhibited, polite, orderly, tender-minded, prudish and hypocritical.[42]

This transformation was accomplished not through the organs of the State, but through a host of private and voluntary businesses, associations and institutions.

The most important of these was obviously the nuclear family, strong in an age still unfamiliar with divorce and co-habitation and which was lightly taxed if it was troubled by the State at all. But the churches and chapels, and the Sunday schools and Church-controlled schools dispensed religious and moral instruction as well as useful knowledge. One analyst even claims to have found a clear correlation between the rise in Sunday school enrolments and the fall in crime between 1850 and the outbreak of the First World War.[43] 10,000 private schools were in existence by 1864. At the workplace, it was not unknown for the owner-manager to instruct his workforce in the evenings. Provincial newspapers, political pressure groups, trade unions, Mechanics' Institutes, the university extension movement, employers' associations, charities, voluntary organisations, working men's clubs, the workers' educational associations, the temperance movement, football teams, cycling clubs, friendly societies, co-operative societies, building societies and dozens of other 'mediating institutions' all inculcated restraint, self-control, self-help, virtue and discipline. At bottom, the potential criminal was not intimidated or incarcerated by the State police but socialised by a strong, confident, progressive, highly pervasive, consensual and seemingly permanent new moral order.

The Role Played by the Collapse of the Family

The contrast with today could scarcely be greater. The family is in wholesale retreat. The traditional family of two parents living together with dependent children is now a minority among households. In 1961 over half the population lived in traditional families. By 1992, less than two fifths did. Between 1961 and 1992 the proportion of the population living in one-parent families increased fourfold to over a tenth. There are now an estimated 1.3 million single-parent families, containing approximately 2.2 million children. Twenty years ago there was just over half a million one-parent families, and a quarter of them were headed by widows. By 1991, only one sixteenth of them were headed by widows. The divorce rate is also high, so even those children who start out in a married home may not continue in it. Thirty years ago roughly two in every thousand married couples divorced; today, over thirteen in every thousand do. Between a third and two fifths of all marriages fail. In England and Wales over 150,000 couples are getting divorced every year, the second highest rate of marriage failure in Europe. The high rate of divorce is driving up the number of second marriages. In 1961 only one in ten marriages was a re-marriage for either or both parties. Today, one in three is. These introduce the alien influences of a step-father or step-mother, and perhaps separate children from one parent, with attendant conflicts of loyalty. Second marriages also tend to fail more often.

Co-habitation and illegitimacy are more popular than ever. Nearly a fifth of unmarried men and women aged between 18 and 59 are living together, leading to an increase in illegitimate births. Nearly one in three children is now born out of wedlock, against a long-standing trend (outside wartime) of one in twenty until the 1960s. Births outside marriage doubled in the 1980s alone. Even a secular Scandinavian nirvana like Denmark, which has a higher divorce rate, does not have as many single parents as Britain today. Illegitimacy is heavily concentrated among poor or low-earning parents. Charles Murray believes that illegitimacy is the best indicator of the emergence of an 'underclass' – a group of young, healthy and mainly male individuals living in cities without much work or money and who do not share the values of those around them – akin to that which has developed in the United States. Murray has written:

> Illegitimacy is the purest form of being without two parents – legally, the child is without a father from day one; he is often practically without one as well. Further, illegitimacy bespeaks an attitude on the part of one or both parents that getting married is not an essential part of siring or giving birth to a child; this in itself distinguishes their mindset from that of people who do feel strongly that getting married is essential.[44]

Some do not even trouble to have the child. Nearly a fifth of all conceptions end in abortion, three quarters of them endured by unmarried mothers. As illegitimacy and co-habitation increase, more and more children are being brought up outside the context of an orthodox nuclear family. They lack fathers to emulate; mothers to care for them; and grandparents to help them. It is more difficult for them to grow up into polite, well-adjusted, respectful, hard-working and law-abiding adults. 'The habitual criminal,' says Murray, 'is the classic member of an underclass. He lives off mainstream society without participating in it.'[45]

Research into the effects of the breakdown of the family is gradually making clear what was always obvious to common sense. The sudden deprivation of a father, the sale of the family home and the possible lapse into unaccustomed poverty are damaging to children. Their fathers are usually absent altogether; their mothers probably work; the extended family is truncated; their mothers get irritated and cross with them; they move house more often; their food, washing and cooking facilities are always worse; they often end up in the care of local authorities; they die in childhood more often; they do less well at school; they are more likely to take drugs; and they are more likely to turn to crime.[46] As Professor A. H. Halsey has put it:

> The children of parents who do not follow the traditional norm (i.e. taking on personal, active and long term responsibility for the social upbringing of the children they generate) are thereby disadvantaged in many major aspects of their chances of living a successful life. On the evidence

available such children tend to die earlier, to have more illness, to do less well at school, to exist at a lower level of nutrition, comfort and conviviality, to suffer more unemployment, to be more prone to deviance and crime, and finally to repeat the cycle of unstable parenting from which they themselves have suffered...The evidence all points in the same direction, is formidable, and tallies with common sense.[47]

There is a staggering weight of sociological, psychological and biological evidence to support the contention that a child which comes from a loving family is less likely to develop into a criminal. Parents who are loving, consistent and firm tend to bring up children who become sociable, morally responsible adults. 'The family,' writes James Wilson, 'is a continuous locus of reciprocal obligations that constitute an unending school for moral instruction.'[48]

In particular, the family is the main mechanism for the socialisation of the naturally aggressive young male. It is often forgotten that crime is predominantly a male phenomenon. Most crime is committed by young, urban males without much foresight or planning, and with little resort to organised gangs or personal violence. This reflects the fact that the demise of the traditional family has spawned a new kind of rogue male, who is young, inadequately socialised, personally irresponsible and lacking in self-control children over several decades, fatherless working-class males roam the new slums of the modern housing estates, preying on respectable folk. They lack what James Wilson has called 'the moral sense' – his updating, with a wealth of evidence from fields as diverse as biology and game theory, of the long-standing belief that morality is due to some natural or intuitive quality in humankind.[49]

Wilson believes this answers his own questions about why most people, despite sometimes desperate circumstances, do not turn to crime. The reluctance to commit crime is due, he thinks, to an 'an intuitive or directly felt belief about how one ought to act when one is free to act voluntarily that is, not under duress)'.[50] This moral sense is characterised by four distinctive qualities – sympathy for others, a natural sense of fairness, a capacity for self-control rather than acting always on impulse, and the disposition to honour obligations even when there is no hope of reward or fear of punishment, or what used to be called conscience. These are inculcated in the individual through a mixture of human nature (his evidence suggests the moral sense appears almost at birth, and certainly before language is available to conceptualise it) and family upbringing (moral actions begin in family settings for the simple reason that sympathy is more easily aroused within the family). In other words, the Nurture of the family completes the inculcation of the moral sense implanted by Nature. Where the family is absent, the moral sense is naturally blunted. One result is a propensity to commit crime.

The State Criminal Factories

But the family is not the only informal social control which is disappearing from the lives of many young people. It was not until after the Second World War that the rich Victorian and Edwardian working-class urban culture began to disappear under the crushing impact of post-war social engineering and urban planning by the State. The persistence of this culture may explain why the undoubted hardships of the inter-war years did not result in an explosion of criminality.

The contrast with the culture of the inner cities today is immense. The modern urban, unskilled, working-class male faces a tax and benefits system which forces him into prolonged unemployment, or into the black economy. He lives in a concrete council-built tower block, where the lifts do not work and the stairwells are covered in graffiti, rubbish, excrement and discarded needles. His neighbours are probably afraid of him, if he is not afraid of them. He attended a State comprehensive school, where he learnt little except how to intimidate adults and write 'Fuck off, Miss' in his exercise book. He left school without qualifications and, after going on a State-subsidised training programme, he worked for a time for the State as a hospital porter or a dustman. Then he went on to the dole. He will be familiar to the police, and one day he may go to jail for stealing a car radio, or breaking into a house, or killing children while joy-riding a stolen car. Throughout his life the State has housed him, nurtured him, educated him, trained him, employed him, criminalised him and finally incarcerated him. He never had a chance, as Charles Murray has put it, to make sense of the world around him. He never governed himself, or developed himself, or owned anything himself. Because the State never let him control anything, he failed in the end to control himself.

In 1957 Michael Young and Peter Willmott published their classic study, *Family and Kinship in East London*, which predicted the failure of the rehousing experiments which were then getting under way. But the State authorities ignored their warnings, and persisted for twenty-five years in a policy of bulldozing the low-level housing which played host to a wide variety of informal social networks among families and friends. They replaced them with anonymous and alien high-rise tower blocks. This policy – described now by Wilmott and Young as a form of 'collective madness' – was driven by a variety of factors. Among them was a misplaced enthusiasm for modern architectural visions and new building techniques and, according to one view, a cynical compact between the major political parties to prevent their respective electoral support from being dissipated. But at bottom high-rise housing is just another example, albeit a particularly brutal one, of the many ways in which the bureaucratic intelligence of the twentieth-century State has pulverised the informal networks of families and individuals which once helped to socialise and civilise the young urban male. Almost all of the eyesores which despoil the modern urban environment – shopping centres, motorways, one-way systems and bypasses, as well as tower blocks – are the actions of elected or unelected officials of the State. 'It is the reach and power of the public domain,' wrote Ferdinand Mount, 'which today are the prime uprooting and alienating factors, not the dehumanising nature of factory work or the cash nexus.'[51] The result of the efforts of the State to plan new 'communities' of the future is the desolation, fear, crime, drug-taking and random violence of many inner cities today.

'Boredom' is the usual excuse offered by young men as the cause of their drug-taking or criminal activities. The State has deprived them of the other options – church and chapel, friendly societies, trade unions, football clubs and the rest of it – and the culture of self-improvement which were developed by their forebears. Instead, the young urban working-class male of today haunts a desolate world of high-rise concrete, underpasses, theme pubs, karaoke bars, discotheques and drive-in fast-food outlets, watches mind-numbing and violent videos, listens to rock groups with depraved and sometimes frightening lyrical suggestions, flaunts his disrespect for all forms of authority and pursues a life of reckless hedonism.[52] According to Social Trends, less than one in twenty people have taken part in a political campaign; only 15 per cent go to any church; 75 per cent of the population has done no voluntary work; and the average citizen spends 27 hours a week watching television, on which advertisers, producers and journalists pander remorselessly to the worst instincts of the viewers without much regard to right and wrong. Countless surveys – usually conducted at the expense of television companies – record a growing insensitivity to sex, violence and bad language on ordinary, cable and satellite-based television.

Martin Jacques has depicted modern Britain as 'the pick-and-choose society... the hypermarket society' in which the State is increasingly irrelevant to people more interested in choosing clothes, CDs and sexual orientations than which political party to support. 'Power,' he thinks, 'has... drained away from the State into, quite literally, thousands of groups within civil society.'[53] It is an odd view. Even the power which people exercise in the marketplace every day as consumers is circumscribed by a State which still takes between two fifths and a half of the national income. Many people are wholly or partially dependent on State-owned or State-subsidised housing, education, social security and health services. People are not alienated from the State because it is irrelevant to their daily life; they are alienated from each other because it plays too large a role in their life. 'The alternative I advocate,' writes Charles Murray, 'is to have the central government stop trying to be clever and instead get out of the way, giving poor communities (and affluent communities too) a massive dose of self-government, with vastly greater responsibility for the operation of the institutions which affect their lives – including the criminal justice, educational, housing and benefit systems in their localities. My premise is that it is unnatural for a neighbourhood to tolerate high levels of crime or illegitimacy or voluntary idleness among its youth: that, given the chance, poor communities as well as rich ones will run affairs so that such things happen infrequently... Money isn't the key. Authentic self-government is.'[54]

It is certainly worth trying. The State is, by its nature, an impersonal and anonymous bureaucracy, quite without the human characteristics which might cause people to value its generosity or respect its principles and its liberality. Its officials are guided not by personal knowledge of the poor and the sick, but by statistics which show where poverty or sickness or unemployment or crime is going up or going down. Numbers, not people, are the currency of the collectivist State. Hidden from the view of the minister and the bureaucrat, behind the dry, computer-generated statistics, are the individual stories of suffering and of joy which the telescopic philanthropy of the Welfare State cannot possibly see. 'Man's trick is always to put forward numbers,' observed Kierkegaard, 'so that one can hide in them.' Social security claimants, filling in endless forms and tagged as much by numbers as by names, know this best of all. They are forced to deal with several different bureaucracies, some local and some national, and negotiate a maze of four different benefits – unemployment benefit, income support, family credit and housing support – which may vary according to personal and family circumstances.[55]

Humiliated, depersonalised and often angry, but bludgeoned by decades of State propaganda into thinking that they are entitled to free goods and services by virtue of having paid a fictional national insurance premium, or through the plain good luck of being born in a Welfare State, the clients of the State are not slow to resort to violence and abuse when the 'Community' or 'Society' lets them down. According to one report, twenty health service staff are assaulted every week.[56] Another reveals that traffic wardens are learning karate to defend themselves from irate motorists.[57] In 1991 a planning officer in County Durham was shot dead by a man he had accused of offending building regulations. Housing and social security officers are frequently attacked by disgruntled claimants, in the streets and in their homes as well as at work. Trading standards and environmental health officers, and even librarians, can all expect to be punched occasionally. A 1992 survey by a telephone training and monitoring organisation named the Department of Social Security as the organisation most detested by its clients. Last year the Social Security Benefits Agency had more complaints submitted to an ombudsman than any other government body.[58] The increase in begging on the streets is due at least in part to an unwillingness on the part of the disadvantaged to deal with the bureaucrats of the Department of Social Security. There is not so much an 'underclass' in the inner cities as an outcast society, in which people have given up struggling with a State system which is so impersonal that it cannot but appear to be hostile.

Martin Jacques believes television and the tabloid newspapers are the most accurate gauges of the condition of the country today. They are, he says, 'the mirror, the interlocutor, the enabler of this new society…the source of information and opinion, symbols and humour…the template of society, defining success and failure in everything from sport to politics, from entertainment to ideas'.[59] It is a platitude that people get the newspapers they deserve, but it is probably true. The *Sun*, for example, is described by its biographers as 'a sophisticated and extremely high-quality product, carefully tailored for its market'.[60] The absorption of its readers in sexual intercourse, television celebrities and sport reflects a country in which millions of people are leading stunted and demoralised lives, which they have lost the will to escape or improve. Their newspapers gratify their desire to belittle all great men and women, all high endeavours, great causes and original ideas, and to judge them by the standards of ordinary men. The popular press is a reflection of a society which fears adventure, enterprise, change, individuality, knowledge, achievement and civilisation, the society which Correlli Barnett called 'New Jerusalem itself, a dream turned to a dank reality of a segregated, subliterate, unskilled, unhealthy and institutionalised proletariat hanging on the nipple of state maternalism'.[61] Far from wishing to become the author of his own life, the archetypal inner-city inhabitant of today is a cynical, alienated, dependent and materialistic couch-potato battered into imbecility by television and tabloid journalism.

But it is not the consumer society of collectivist legend which did this to him. It is the State, which has housed him in soulless tower blocks, subjected him to failed educational and egalitarian experiments and narrowed to vanishing point his opportunities for self-government, self-improvement, self-help, spontaneity, diversity and individuality. It is worth recalling the warning which John Stuart Mill issued in the closing words of his great essay, *On Liberty*:

> A government cannot have too much of the kind of activity which does not impede, but aids and stimulates, individual exertion and development. The mischief begins when, instead of calling forth the activity and powers of individuals and bodies, it substitutes its own activity for theirs; when, instead of informing, advising, and, upon occasion, denouncing, it makes them work in fetters, or bids them stand aside and does their work instead of them. The worth of a State, in the long run, is the worth of the individuals composing it; and a State which postpones the interest of their mental expansion and elevation, to a little more of administrative skill, or that semblance of it which practice gives, in the details of a business; a State which dwarfs its men, in order that they may be more docile instruments in its hands even for beneficial purposes – will find that with small men no great thing can really be accomplished; and that the perfection of machinery to which it has sacrificed everything, will in the end avail it nothing, for want of the vital power which, in order that the machine might work more smoothly, it has preferred to banish.[62]

Unless the State begins to yield territory to the individual once more, there is nothing that stands between Britain today and a terrifying descent into barbarism.

References

1 Quoted in J. A. Hobson, *Richard Cobden: The International Man*, Ernest Benn Limited, 1968, page 393.
2 Interview, *Woman's Own*, 31 October 1987. Quoted in David Willetts, *Modern Conservatism*, Penguin, 1992, pages 47-8. When asked by a young Conservative, Mark Mason, to reproduce this infamous quotation for him, she paraphrased it in her own hand like this: 'There is no such thing as Society. There are only individuals. It is we who bear the responsibility.'
3 David Hume, *A Treatise of Human Nature*, Penguin, 1984, page 532.
4 *Sunday Times*, 22 March 1992.
5 *Financial Times*, 27 August 1993.
6 *Sunday Times*, 1 January 1995.
7 Fiona MacCarthy, *William Morris: A Life for Our Times*, Faber & Faber, 1994, page 542.
8 Paradoxically, collectivists generally recognise this in areas of self-expression like

sexuality, art or pornography. It is only areas like charity or economics that they favour an increase in State compulsion.

9   Nigel Lawson, *The Fourth Arnold Goodman Lecture*, 2 June 1987, published by the Charities Aid Foundation, page 13.

10 James Q. Wilson, *The Moral Sense*, The Free Press, 1993, pages 191-3.

11 Samuel Brittan, 'There Is No Such Thing as Society', J. C. Rees *Memorial Lecture, University College of Swansea*, 9 November 1992, pages 29–32.

12 'To narrow the reach of authority is to widen the scope of conscience.' See David G. Green, *Reinventing Civil Society: The Rediscovery of Welfare Without Politics*, IEA, 1993, page 26.

13 See Introduction, page 15.

14 Ferdinand Mount, *The British Constitution Now*, Mandarin, 1993, pages 32–3.

15 See Chapter 5, pages 101–7.

16 David G. Green, *Reinventing Civil Society: The Rediscovery of Welfare Without Politics*, IEA, 1993, pages 2–3.

17 See above, page 260.

18 *Sunday Times*, 13 November 1994.

19 *Sunday Times*, 16 October 1994.

20 Ian Walker, quoted in *Sunday Telegraph*, 25 September 1994.

21 Quoted in Charles Handy, *The Empty Raincoat*, Hutchinson, 1994, page 248.

22 It is not surprising that two of the most profound thinkers about modern politics Robert Nozick and John Rawls, had to revert to social contract and natural rights theory in order to devise a new set of rules of the political game. Rawls proposed a 'veil of ignorance' behind which free and rational individuals would choose the principles by which they would like their State to be run. The most important of the principles chosen in this imaginary thought-experiment was the so-called 'maximin' principle, according to which the State is entitled to redistribute wealth up to the point where any further redistribution would so damage the economy that even the poorest people would no longer gain. The libertarian Robert Nozick, by contrast, argued that individuals are the only true political entities and that inequalities can be effaced only by violating the right of individuals to keep wealth and property which they have acquired justly. 'The State,' he writes, 'may not use its coercive apparatus for the purpose of getting some citizens to aid others.' As Alasdair MacIntyre has pointed out, these contradictory arguments are symptomatic of the difficulties of devising a new moral consensus for politics.

23 Alasdair MacIntyre, *After Virtue: A Study in Moral Theory*, Second Edition Duckworth, 1993, pages 253-4.

24 'The End of Politics', *Sunday Times*, 18July 1993.

25 Quoted by John O'Sullivan, *Introduction to The Loss of Virtue: Moral Confusion and Social Disorder in Britain and America*, Social Affairs Unit, 1992, pages xiii-xiv.

26 The Home Office argument that British Crime Surveys show crime is less prevalent than people think, and that all that is happening is an increase in reported crime, is not persuasive. There may even be an increase in unreported crime, due to declining confidence in the police and judicial system. And even if it is a 'moral panic' the fact that people are panicking still reduces the quality of their lives. See Norman Dennis and George Erdos, *Families Without Fatherhood*, IEA Health and Welfare Unit, 1993, pages 74–6.

27 Norman Dennis and George Erdos, *Families Without Fatherhood*, IEA Health and Welfare Unit, 1993, page 78.

28 John Gray, *The Undoing of Conservatism, The Social Market Foundation*, June 1994, page 9.

29 David Willetts, *Civic Conservatism, The Social Market Foundation*, June 1994, page

30 Norman Dennis and George Erdos, *Families Without Fatherhood*, IEA Health and Welfare Unit, 1993, pages 891.

31 It seems a general feeling of economic insecurity also encourages victims to report crime more readily and the authorities to attack It more vigorously. See V. A. C.

Gattrell, 'The Decline of Theft and Violence in Victorian and Edwardian England', in Crime and the Law: The Social history of Crime in Western Europe Since 1500, Europa Publications, 1980, pages 307–15.

32 James Q. Wilson, The Moral Sense, The Free Press, 1993, pages 9–10.

33 See V. A. C. Gattrell, 'The Decline of Theft and Violence in Victorian and Edwardian England', in Crime and the Law: The Social History of Crime in Western Europe Since 1500, Europa Publications, 1980, pages 241–9.

34 Quoted in Norman Dennis and George Erdos, Families Without Fatherhood, IEA Health and Welfare Unit, 1993, page 81.

35 Quoted by V. A. C. Gattrell, in 'The Decline of Theft and Violence in Victorian and Edwardian England', in Crime and the Law: The Social History of Crime in Western Europe Since 1500, Europa Publications, 1980, page 241.

36 Crime clearly cannot be eliminated, even in a totalitarian state. But it can be said to be defeated when people feel the authorities are dealing effectively with the forms of crime which are feared and perceived. This is manifestly not the case today, when the fear of crime vastly exceeds its prevalence.

37 See David Philips, 'A New Engine of Power and Authority: The Institutionalization of Law-Enforcement in England 1780–1830', in Crime and the Law: The Social History of Crime in Western Europe Since 1500, Europa Publications, 1980, pages 155–89.

38 V. A. C. Gattrell, 'The Decline of Theft and Violence in Victorian and Edwardian England', in Crime and the Law: The Social History of Crime in Western Europe Since 1500, Europa Publications, 1980, page 277.

39 V. A. C. Gattrell, 'The Decline of Theft and Violence in Victorian and Edwardian England', in Crime and the Law: The Social History of Crime in Western Europe Since 1500, Europa Publications, 1980, page 261.

40 Frank McLynn, Crime and Punishment in Eighteenth Century England, OUP 1991.

41 V. A C. Gattrell, 'The Decline of Theft and Violence in Victorian and Edwardian England', in Crime and the Law: The Social History of Crime in Western Europe Since 1500, Europa Publications, 1980, page 250.

42 Harold Perkin, The Origins of Modern English Society 1780–1880, Routledge, 1969, page 280.

43 Christie Davies, 'Moralisation and Demoralisation: A Moral Explanation for Change in Crime, Disorder and Social Problems', in The Loss of Virtue: Moral Confusion and Social Disorder in Britain and America, Social Affairs Unit, 1992, Table 1, page 11.

44 Charles Murray, The Emerging British Underclass, IEA Health and Welfare Unit, 1990, page 5.

45 The Emerging British Underclass, page 13.

46 Norman Dennis and George Erdos, Families Without Fatherhood, IEA Health and Welfare unit, 1993, pages 37–47.

47 A. H. Halsey, Foreword to Norman Dennis and George Erdos, Families Without Fatherhood, IEA Health and Welfare unit, 1993, page xii.

48 James Q. Wilson, The Moral Sense, The Free Press, 1993, pages 141–65 and page 163.

49 David Hume, for example, argued that 'the final sentence, it is probable, which pronounces character and actions, amiable or odious, praiseworthy or blameable; that which stamps on them the mark of honour or infamy, approbation or censure; that which renders morality as active principle and constitutes virtue or happiness or vice and misery – it is possible, I say, that the final sentence depends on some internal sense or feeling which nature has made universal in the whole species'. Quoted In Alasdair MacIntyre, After Virtue: A Study in Moral Theory, Second Edition, Duckworth, 1985, page 230.

50 James Q. Wilson, The Moral Sense, The Free Press, 1993, page xii.

51 Ferdinand Mount, The Subversive Family: An Alternative History of Love and Marriage, Unwin, 1982, page 171.

52 See Norman Dennis and George Erdos, Families Without Fatherhood, IEA Health and Welfare Unit, 1993, pages 98–108 and 128–30.

53 'The End of Politics', Sunday Times, 18 July 1993.

54   Charles Murray, *The Emerging British Underclass, IEA Health and Welfare Unit, 1990,*
      page 34.
55   Unemployment benefit is to be replaced from April 1996 by a new Jobseeker's
      Allowance, payable for six months rather than twelve. If the recipient does not find
      a job, he or she will still revert to means-tested benefits. Typically, the new
      Allowance will be administered by two government departments – Employment and
      Social Security – rather than one.
56   *Independent on Sunday,* 18 October 1992.
57   *Sunday Times,* 20 November 1994.
58   *Independent on Sunday,* 10 April 1994.
59   'The End of Politics', *Sunday Times,* 18 July 1993.
60   Peter Chippindale and Chris Horrie, *Stick It Up Your Punter! The Rise and Fall of The
      Sun,* Mandarin, 1992, page xi-xii.
61   Correlli Barnett, *The Audit of War: The Illusion and Reality of Britain As a Great
      Nation,* Macmillan, 1986, page 304.
62   John Stuart Mill, *On Liberty,* paperback edition, OUP, 1991, pages 127.

Conclusion

CHAPTER FIFTEEN

What Is to Be Done?

The democratic, property-owning rentiers of the twenty-first century will look very different from their hierarchically structured and highly enterprising ancestors. But perhaps they will manage to preserve the one characteristic which marked them out among the nations. Perhaps they will retain the ability to tolerate variety and will once again come to respect the rights of the individual: the rights not of Man but of English men and women.

Geoffrey Elton, The English[1]

A practical scheme is either a scheme that is already in existence, or a scheme that could be carried out under existing conditions. But it is exactly the existing conditions that one objects to; and any scheme that could accept these conditions is wrong and foolish.

Oscar Wilde, The Soul of Man Under Socialism[2]

'We must recollect,' Pitt told the House of Commons on the resumption of the war with Napoleon in the summer of 1803, 'what it is we have at stake, what it is we have to contend for. It is for our property, it is for our liberty, it is for our independence, nay, for our existence as a nation; it is for our character, it is for our name as Englishmen, it is for everything dear and valuable to man on this side of the grave.' The classical liberal tradition is rightly suspicious of patriotism, which it judges to be an enemy of the sovereign propriety of the individual and a cloak for the unwholesome chauvinism of continental despots. But there is abroad today a deep and justified feeling that a historic way of life is once again at risk. The glowering presence of the State, with its laws and regulations and taxes and officials and policemen, darkens every club house and pub, lurks by the roadside and on the bridges, sits in the window of the car and waits at the airport, slips through the letterbox in its customary brown envelope, issues forms to the supplicant and interrogates the taxpayer, inspects the kitchens or the books, tells teachers what to teach and people what to learn, converses through the P45 and the UB40 and the National Insurance number, rifles through the boot of the car, and follows people home to peer over the fence at the conservatory or the car.

If there is a leitmotif which runs through the history of England from the Conquest to the third Reform Act, it is a toleration of diversity and a respect for individuality. It is the triumph of the collectivist State of the twentieth century to have taken a myriad rival and incompatible conceptions of the good and useful life – tens of millions of different choices, opinions and preferences, which in the natural order of things can survive quite happily alongside each other – and made them the subject of crude political or judicial arbitration. The State has replaced the spontaneous order of private life with a formal world of contracts and forms and laws and regulations and taxes and officials. It has broken up what Alasdair MacIntyre has called 'the moral community of the citizens', in which people tolerate and respect each other and co-operate with others precisely because formality and enforcement are absent.

In the gloomy closing paragraph of his great work, *After Virtue*, MacIntyre compared the demoralised condition of Western civilisation today with that of Rome at the time of the Fall:

> A crucial turning point in that earlier history occurred when men and women of goodwill turned aside from the task of shoring up the Roman *imperium* and ceased to identify the continuation of civility and moral community with the maintenance of that imperium. What they set themselves to achieve instead – often not fully recognising what they were doing – was the construction of new forms of community within which the moral life could be sustained so that both morality and civility might survive the coming age of barbarism and darkness...For some time now we too have reached that turning point. What matters at this stage is the construction of local forms of community within which civility and the intellectual and moral life can be sustained through the new dark ages which are already upon us. And if the tradition of the virtues was able to survive the horrors of the last dark ages, we are not entirely without grounds for hope. This time however the barbarians are not waiting beyond the frontiers; they have already been governing us for some time. And it is our lack of consciousness of this that constitutes part of our predicament. We are waiting not for a Godot, but for another – doubtless very different – St Benedict.[3]

The task of the new Benedictines is simply stated. It is to liquidate the State. Until its obtrusive bulk is banished from the private lives of English men and women there will be no moral opportunities to seize, or needs to be met, or institutions or associations to be founded, which the State has not already corrupted or crowded out.

Cutting Public Expenditure

The liquidation of the State cannot be accomplished without a drastic reduction in public expenditure. Only this will create the room for the dramatic reductions in the burden of taxation which will, by allowing people to keep and spend more of their own money, rebuild the family and recreate some of the myriad independent, private and voluntary associations on which the free and lively 'civic culture' or 'moral community' (which even the collectivists now claim they want) must ultimately depend. The experience of the last fifteen years shows how hard it is to contain the rate of increase in public expenditure, let alone effect real cuts in departmental programmes. The inexorable rise in public spending over the last one hundred years has created an array of vested interests, which include public sector producers as much as their clients.

The sensitivity of the democratic mechanism to any alterations in the distribution of State patronage and subsidies is such that any disturbance of the status quo creates a political momentum against even minor proposals for change. The only way to break the deadlock is to combine dramatic, immediate and sweeping reductions in public expenditure with a wholly new political vision of the future of the country which is capable of capturing the imagination and enthusiasm of the electorate. This was precisely the technique the collectivists used in 1945 to *increase* public expenditure, and it can be used again today to liberate the individual from the despotic State they created as a result. 'A revolutionary moment in the world's history,' as the Beveridge Plan put it, 'is a time for revolutions, not for patching.'

As Table 21 shows, the Welfare State, in the shape of the budgets for social security, health and education, accounted for over half of public expenditure in 1993–94. Once defence is added, these four programmes account for nearly two thirds of total public spending. Clearly, any serious plan to reduce the role of the State in the life of the individual will have to address the question of how to reduce the scale of these four liabilities. In the case of defence, the budget is best left untouched. Defence is one of the classic public goods which will always be provided by the State, because no individual or group of individuals has an incentive to supply it.[4] The world is less stable today than it was during the period of the Cold War, and the defence economies which have taken place may well have cut too deep already. There is also a powerful case for making the National Health Service (NHS) immune from any restructuring of public expenditure.

This is not to say that there are not some profound objections to the NHS. It was implemented from 1948 at the expense of a variety of highly effective health schemes invented by friendly societies, medical institutes, industrial insurance companies and other organisations. The nationalisation of medicine also put the supply of health care firmly in the hands of the producer (the doctors) rather than the consumer (the patients), but as a near-monopoly employer of medical labour the State does at least have the advantage of being able to keep wage and salary costs under strict control. The role of the patient as consumer in choosing treatments (as opposed to financing them) is anyway limited. In an area of life where the demand for services is potentially limitless, but its restriction by price alone would be morally objectionable, it is arguably far more acceptable to ration the supply of medical goods and services by the present methods: queuing and the explicit denial of treatment to people whom doctors believe will not or cannot benefit from it.

Patrick Hutber once laid it down that it is no more possible to make a nationalised industry mimic market disciplines by rewriting the rules than it is to turn a mule into a zebra by painting stripes on its back. But the current experiment within the NHS, which uses fund-holding family doctors as surrogate consumers of hospital services supplied by NHS Trusts, does appear to be achieving modest success in reducing costs and increasing efficiency, albeit at what appears to be an excessive cost in managerial overheads. But the main argument for retaining the NHS in its current form is the cost of the alternative: a fully private, insurance-based system. Compared with that, the NHS is a bargain. The United States spends more than twice as much of its national income on health as the United Kingdom, but Americans gain nothing in terms of life expectancy and actually have a worse record in infant mortality.

Table 21   CGE(X) by function (a)
Estimated outturn 1997/98

Function	£ billions	Percentage of Total
Social Security	98.6	31.5
Health	42.6	13 6
Education	33.7	11.8
Debt interest	23.8	7.6
Law, order & protective services	17.0	5.5%
Adjustments (b)	13.3	4.3
Personal social services	10.7	3.4
Other environmental services	9.7	3.1
Transport	9.1	2.9
Trade, industry, energy, emply't & training	8.8	2.8
Central administration (c)	6.4	2.1
Agriculture, fisheries & food	5.2	1.7
Housing	3.5	1.1
Int development & other int. services	3.4	1.1
Culture, media & sport	2.7	0.9
Total	312.6	100.0

Notes: (a) General government expenditure less privatisation receipts, lottery funded expenditure and interest and dividend receipts.

       (b) Amount necessary to reconcile public expenditure data to national accounts concepts. Including allowance for shortfall.

       (c) Including net contributions to EC budget.

Source: HM Treasury, 'Public Expenditure Statistical Analyses 1998/99, Cm 3801 table 3.5

American doctors are better off because they are able to pass on their high costs to insurers, which in turn pass them on to the consumer as higher premiums. This rations health care by price and the refusal of health-insurance coverage, which means some people go without. The uninsured population is the main reason why the overall health record of the United States is inferior to that of this country.

Earmarking Taxes

Health is one area where a universal taxpayer-financed service free at the point of use is the cheapest and least objectionable of two invidious alternatives. However, there may be a case for funding increases in health spending from a hypothecated tax rather than out of general taxation.[5] The hypothecation, or earmarking, of taxes is the designation of particular tax revenues to particular areas of public expenditure.[6] The practice is not unknown in Britain. Local authorities used to charge a separate rate for each service – water, gas, electricity, roads and so on – before they were combined in the 1930s into a single 'rate'. The BBC Licence fee is an earmarked poll tax. The Road Fund was invented as an earmarked tax for spending on the road network. National Insurance contributions were originally intended to sustain a designated National Insurance fund, on which people would draw when they were sick, unemployed or retired. They were even introduced at a flat rate, to remind employers and employees that benefits were being earned through their contributions. The Redundancy and Maternity funds also started as earmarked taxes.[7]

The subsequent history of all these earmarked funds is a reminder of the vulnerability of all earmarked tax revenues to the shifting enthusiasms and electoral needs of politicians. The hallowed 'contributory principle' of National Insurance is now little more than a cloak for a surrogate income tax. It remains authentic to the extent that gaps in contributions lead to gaps in benefits – as in the exclusion of Class 2 self-employed contributors from unemployment benefit – but the introduction of earnings-related contributions in 1961 effectively subsumed National Insurance in a progressive system of income taxation. Today, 99 per cent of the expenditure of the Department of Social Security is funded from a mixture of general taxation and employers' and employees' National Insurance contributions, and just 1 per cent from the investment income of the National Insurance fund. The road and other earmarked funds were soon raided for general spending purposes too. It is precisely because they are awkward and inflexible that the Treasury has never favoured earmarked taxes. They make it difficult to tax people in politically cost less ways, and especially difficult to finance unpopular spending programmes. They also complicate the task of adjusting fiscal policy to changed circumstances, the ups and downs of the trade cycle or external economic shocks.

But these are exactly the sort of objections which entrench the existing pattern of taxation and public expenditure. One of the attractions of hypothecation is that taxes would rise and fall in line with the business cycle rather than some bureaucratic definition of need. Another is that voters could vote to reduce or even abandon spending programmes they disliked or disapproved of. At the moment the political system has no means of registering the vastly different preferences individuals have in matters of taxation and expenditure. Financing public services out of general taxation forces voters to 'buy' a bundle of tax-financed goods and services at periodic local and general elections from the party whose programmes correspond most closely to their own preferences, but which will rarely if ever meet them exactly.

Voters are even further removed from the political horse-trading between the elected members of the majority party which determines the exact size of the budget, the mixture of taxation and borrowing needed to finance it and the precise goods and services on which the money raised will be spent. Expenditure and taxation decisions are still reached independently of each other – despite the ostensible unification of tax and spending decisions from November 1993 – and according to different criteria. Because ministerial and official careers are advanced by spending money rather than not spending it, and it is an inflexible law of democratic government that the party in office must shower its supporters with money, public expenditure tends inexorably to rise at a faster rate than finance. Of course, finance is obliged eventually to catch up. Treasury ministers attempt to exert some control over the rate of increase of public expenditure and taxation but even when their differences with a department prove irreconcilable, they invariably end up by splitting the difference.

The overall outcome of the process is unpredictable, paradoxical and frequently perverse. It is therefore not surprising that taxes are paid less willingly than any other form of payment to the State. This is because taxpayers do not know what they are being asked to pay for, and they almost always receive nothing immediately identifiable in return. Yet, paradoxically, taxation continues to rise precisely because people do not know how much they are paying or how little they are getting. As the Poll Tax fiasco showed, once people grasp directly how much it is they are having to pay for a particular service they tend to resist vehemently. But under the present system of national taxation, ignorance of how taxes are raised and where they are spent is so widespread that people can pay a great deal of tax or none at all and still feel free to complain that a particular public service is 'underfunded'.

The National Health Service is the classic illustration of this syndrome. Opinion polls continually find a large majority of the electorate in favour of increased expenditure on the NHS. Under the present system, health has to compete with education, defence, social security and all the other demands on the public purse for a share of available tax revenues. A hypothecated health tax would, to put it crudely, oblige voters for the first time to put their money where their mouth is. But there are legitimate doubts about how well hypothecation would work in the Corporate Economy. In Britain today most direct and indirect taxes and National Insurance contributions are paid by employers. Employees still have to pay in the end, as the taxes are passed on to them in lower wages or higher prices in the shops, but the automatic nature of the deductions will make it difficult for people to attach a price to increases in health expenditure.

But by establishing any sort of direct connection between the taxpayer and the health service, a hypothecated tax should encourage doctors and nurses to improve the quality of the service in the hope of attracting more money. One analyst has described what happens instead under the present system:

> The easiest route to prosperity for these producers is to secure an increase
> in government spending; this is a genuine interest for government-sector
> producers. They are often supported in their pressure for increased

government spending by elements of consumer opinion which are either under the illusion that goods provided 'free' at the point of consumption impose no costs elsewhere or else have in any case no means of assessing the marginal cost imposed on themselves (as they can very accurately in everyday purchases). Decisions are both centralised and politicised. This is the road to economic inefficiency...since the quality of information at the centre cannot match its quality at the level of the individual consumer and since the motives of the economic agents are in any case distorted by the system. It is also the road to overprovision, although this overprovision is masked by inefficiency and underperformance.[8]

A good recent example of the perverse consequences of centralised planning and the lack of any means of registering specific consumer preferences was the Tomlinson Report on London hospitals, in which social planners attempted to predict the demand for health services in London. Politicians then selected which hospitals to retain and which to close, largely on the basis of the effectiveness of the lobbying by the various producer groups. Thus St Thomas's Hospital, despite its widely perceived inferiority in most medical disciplines to the nearby Guy's Hospital, was kept open.

The only surprising aspect of this process was that people found the perversity of the outcome surprising. An earmarked health tax or taxes could prevent politicians and bureaucrats frustrating popular demands in this way. It could also limit the ability of politicians to increase public expenditure as a whole by obliging them to justify and secure public assent to each increase in health spending. An earmarked tax is also preferable to means-testing free health care, since it escapes the inequity of obliging some taxpayers to fund a service to which they are not entitled.[9] The principal danger in earmarking a tax for health purposes is that it would be used as an additional rather than an alternative source of public funding for the NHS. The precedent of the National Lottery, which it was thought would be politically unsaleable as a substitute for existing forms of taxation, is in reality an additional tax.

Similarly, if NHS patients were obliged to pay for more of the goods and services they consume, there is a danger that the charges would become an additional tax rather than a substitute for existing expenditure. The idea of using a referendum to approve an earmarked tax is particularly susceptible to degenerating into a search for a popular mandate for an extra tax. It is a danger to which some advocates of hypothecation are alive.[10] Yet, if they were properly designed, earmarked taxes and charges could simultaneously reduce the demand for health services (through the deterrent effect of an identifiable personal cost of using them) and increase the supply (by removing the general public expenditure constraint on a particular service). By improving the allocation of health resources they should also enable the overall burden of taxation to be reduced, not least by improving the rate of growth of the economy.

Reforming the Police

Law and order is the second of the classic public goods. Like defence, it is a service which only the State can supply. The scope for immediate economies is limited. The Sheehy Inquiry into Police Responsibilities and Rewards, which reported in the summer of 1993, identified recurrent annual savings on various forms of police remuneration which it estimated would be worth £107 million within five, years of implementation.[11] These savings were unfortunately lost to a producer propaganda campaign orchestrated by the Police Federation. Despite the vehemence of the campaign against them, the savings were also of the most trifling kind, amounting after five years to much less than one per cent of the total budget on law and order and protective services in 1993-94. A much more unfortunate collateral loss was the series of sensible proposals for the reform of the management and remuneration of police officers put forward by the Inquiry. These might well have improved the effectiveness of the police service in deterring crime, catching criminals and securing a higher rate of convictions.

Certainly something is wrong with the police force. In the last fifteen years expenditure on law and order has doubled. The government has made strenuous efforts to ensure that the police are well-equipped, and that they and the courts have statutory support appropriate to the threats the face. During the 1980s the police acquired a range of riot control equipment, camera and computer systems, cars and helicopters. The number of armed policemen has increased dramatically to take account of the rising use of firearms in criminal enterprises. The police are even now acquiring Porsche sports cars to give them a better chance of catching ram-raiders and joy-riders speeding on the motorways. But all this expenditure and equipment has had no perceptible effect on crime. The rate of recorded crime has doubled as well.[12]

The police and prison services, of course, argue that a doubling of their resources was the minimum required to cope with a doubling of the rate of recorded crime. It is undeniably true that there are as yet no solutions to a range of modern crimes which are both effective and consonant with liberty. The obstacles to the successful commission of a car crime, for example, are notoriously easy to circumvent. The apparatus of the Victorian and Edwardian police and criminal justice system was certainly much better adapted to the criminal threats it faced.[13] Doubtless there are further technological improvements which could be made – automatic vehicle location systems, for example, would make it much harder and less rewarding to steal a car – but the real lesson of the late Victorian and Edwardian success in the battle against crime was not money or technology, but intelligence. The forces of law and order had the confidence of the public, which repaid them with intelligence about the activities of criminals .

The modern police service, by contrast, is increasingly alienated from the public it serves and relies upon for criminal intelligence. A crime is hardly ever solved by sleuthing, or old-fashioned police work, as the seemingly endless television programmes on real-life crimes never cease to illustrate. Most crimes are solved by intelligence-gathering among the general public, as well as the criminal fraternities. The abnormally low rate of crime in modern Japan – the one major industrial country to escape a crime wave, so far – is due in large part to the remarkably good relations between the police and the public. The country is covered not by brick and concrete fortresses from which the police venture forth in motor cars to harass innocent passers-by, but by a network of 15,000 tiny police stations manned by two or three friendly policemen prepared even to lend passers-by the bus fare home.

Many of these mini-police stations double as home to one of the police officers. Home visits are a routine aspect of police work, and not an unwelcome necessity which follows the commission of a crime. Older policemen, whose experience gives them a less suspect judgment than their younger colleagues, are often used specifically to win the confidence of local people. The English home beat officers and Neighbourhood Watch schemes, by contrast, tend never to develop an adequate range of personal contacts. In Japan, petty offenders are usually released after signing a written apology, confirming public faith in the decency of the criminal justice system in a way that the notorious British 'caution' somehow fails to achieve. This integration into the daily lives of the people they serve has ensured the Japanese police receive a steady flow of intelligence about the criminal fraternity.

As the police have forfeited the confidence of their fellow countrymen, the volume of criminal intelligence they receive has naturally dried up. The police have only themselves to blame. A habit of taking short-cuts to secure convictions has led to a number of well-publicised miscarriages of justice, which have reduced the willingness of juries to convict and increased the burden of procedure and paperwork on all police officers. As their success rate declines in line with shrinking intelligence, public confidence in the police dips still further. As a result, an increasingly large number of businesses and individuals are turning to private security and vigilante groups. Declining public confidence and respect makes the police service feel beleaguered, demoralised and unwilling to make arrests, especially when juries suspicious of the police are so unwilling to convict.

In a sense, the police are also victims of the over-mighty State. They have the difficult and dangerous task of protecting property and maintaining order in a society in which a significant minority of people have lost all capacity for self-control. This has obliged the government to increase their numbers and powers, further alienating them from the public they serve. The extent of that alienation varies in different parts of the country, and especially between urban and rural areas. Most rural police forces remain popular with the public. But in the inner cities, too many policemen now see themselves as lone crusaders grappling single-handedly with an epidemic of crime without the sympathy or the support of the general public or the criminal justice system. Some urban police officers, particularly in the junior ranks, have become openly contemptuous of the public. By being rude, offhand and occasionally threatening even to respectable members of the public, they have further reduced support for the police. The account given by a national newspaper editor, John Junor, of how he was twice driven off the road in a revenge attack by officers he had offended is only a particularly dramatic example of the kind of incident which is becoming alarmingly common.[14] In July 1994 a peer of the realm, Lord Pearson of Rannoch, was so fed up with police harassment that he preferred a £500 fine and a year's driving ban to taking yet another gratuitous breath-test. It is obvious that the police are unlikely to regain the public trust they have lost without a searching reform of their recruitment, training, management and remuneration. The government would be wise to return to the question of the reform of police management, before bad habits spread to rural police forces as well.

A Basic Income for All

Any programme which aims to reduce public expenditure cannot ignore the social security budget. It is the biggest single departmental spending programme. Since the inception of the Welfare State in the 1940s, expenditure on social security benefits has grown roughly eight-fold in real terms to a total in 1993–94 of £85½ billion, or about one third of total public expenditure. The Department of Social Security alone employs almost 99,000 officials in seven different bureaucracies, administering 26 different benefits to an average at any one time of nearly 46 million claimants.[18] In 1993–94 the Department spent around £4½ billion merely on running itself, or an average of of nearly £45,000 per bureaucrat.[19] The costs are even higher, once the impact of incoherent welfare policies on other government departments is taken into account. The costs of the housing and local government policies of the Department of the Environment, for example have to be relieved by the Department of Social Security. As Table 22 shows, despite this vast expenditure of money and manpower, poverty has not been eradicated and is still increasing. Since the Conservative government was first elected in 1979 expenditure on social security has increased by 7 per cent In real terms, but the standard of living of the poorest third of the population has actually gone down. The present system is clearly not working.

The concept of poverty has changed. It is now a relative rather than absolute concept, as the Duke of Edinburgh was reckless enough to point out, but the fall in the net income of the bottom third since 1979 was in absolute terms. A relative decline does not make poverty any less bitter anyway. It may even make it more so. Poverty is a deeply demoralising and debilitating condition which, if it is left unattended, threatens the security of liberty and property.

'Poverty,' as Dr Johnson pointed out, 'is a great enemy to human happiness. It certainly destroys liberty, and it makes some virtues impracticable, and others extremely difficult.' It makes it difficult or even impossible to lead a full, free and virtuous life. No true individualist can be indifferent to that fact. Those who argue that the lives of the poor are incomparably richer than those of the wealthy are deluding themselves.

This is not an argument for equality. A large and unpredictable measure of inequality is a feature of a successful capitalist economy which cannot be eradicated without sacrificing the prosperity it creates. People can be too poor to enjoy their liberty, which will mean less to them than getting something to eat.

But to be free is not necessarily to be rich. That is to confuse two entirely different values. Prince Charles, for example, is a wealthy man, but the range of choices he can freely make is heavily restricted. To be truly free is to be free to starve. Equality and welfare are entirely different propositions. The essential question in the field of social security is not whether there should be 'more' equality or less, or even whether there should be a national minimum standard of living at all, but how that minimum can best be organised.

Table 22   Net Real Income After Housing Costs

	Percentage Increase/(Decrease)	
	Including Self-Employed	Excluding Self-Employed
Bottom Tenth	(17%)	(9%)
Next Tenth	(0)%	(0%)
Next Tenth	(6)%	(5%)
Next Tenth	16%	15%
Next Tenth	23%	22%
Total Population (Mean)	36%	35%

Source: Department of Social Security, *Households Below Average Income: A Statistical Analysis 1979–1991/92*, H.M.S.O., 1994, Table A1

The current system is manifestly ineffective in preventing or even relieving poverty. It is also expensive, bureaucratic and riddled with anomalies and perverse incentives. In 1994 an unemployed man was paid £45.45 a week, a sick one only £43.45 but an invalid £57.60.[20] It is not surprising that so many people have opted in recent years to quit the unemployment register and claim Invalidity Benefit instead. According to the Department of Social Security, the number of Invalidity Benefit claimants has increased from 600,000 in 1978–79 to over 1.6 million today.[21] The increase is due in part to the fact that, at a time of chronically high unemployment, many people are choosing to stay on Invalidity Benefit for longer periods than they would ordinarily choose to do. But many people have also responded to an obvious cash incentive. In 1994 an invalid was £13.15 a week better off than an unemployed one, and £14.15 better off than a sick one. There are other anomalies. Invalidity Benefit was paid at the same rate as the Retirement Pension, but a widow claiming a pension under the Widow's Benefit rules might have got anything from £17.28 to £53.57 a week, depending on her age. A widower, by contrast, got nothing at all. Those who make any sort of provision for hard times are immediately penalised. A modest amount of savings (just £8,000) or a spouse at work disqualifies people from claiming means-tested benefits immediately, penalising the prudent and rewarding the feckless. Retired people with a small occupational or personal pension, for example, can easily lose entitlement to benefit as a result.

The cost of administering means-tested benefits is thought to be up to ten times that of universal benefits like the Retirement Pension and Child Benefit.[22]

Yet they are remarkably inefficient, often failing to reach those who need them most, subsidising some who do not need them at all and involving all potential recipients in humiliating bureaucratic interrogations. In 1994 the Benefits Agency identified just 312,000 people who had submitted false claims for benefits, less than a fiftieth of the number on means-tested benefits, but to catch them involved combing through the records of up to 17 million claimants.[23] Universal benefits are costly for a different reason. They take money from some people only to give it back to them later, minus a small charge for administrative costs.[24]

But the most perverse of all the effects of the social security system is its interaction with the tax system. Increasing numbers of working people who are poor enough to be in receipt of State benefits are still liable to income tax, National Insurance contributions and council tax. Many households paying substantial amounts in tax are then expected to claim means-tested benefits to make good part or all of the loss.

The ineradicability of these absurdities is a direct consequence of the sheer size of the State taxing and spending machine. It makes the obvious solution – raising the tax threshold to the point where no one who is poor is liable to pay income tax – expensive in terms of lost revenue. It is expensive because the benefits of the higher threshold are given to every taxpayer, including those who are not poor. Yet the difficulties caused by taxation at such low levels of income are well known. One is the poverty trap, in which the withdrawal of means-tested benefits as income rises means some people in work are no better off, or even worse off, as they earn more. Until the reform of the social security system in 1988 – when entitlement to means-tested benefits was based on post-tax rather than pre-tax income – the implicit rate of tax payable on extra earnings was, in some cases, over 100 per cent. But the reform has only alleviated the problem, not solved it. Implicit marginal tax rates of 97 per cent are still not uncommon, and many of the low paid experience marginal tax rates of over 70 per cent. Similarly, for those out of work the withdrawal of income support or unemployment benefit when they start work can create an unemployment trap in which it is not worthwhile to take a job.

Friends of an unreconstructed Welfare State depict it now as a savings bank, into which all pay and from which all ultimately withdraw an average of two thirds of their contributions over the lifecycle. But in reality the Welfare State is increasingly becoming a safety net for those who cannot help themselves rather than a universal source of material security. The cost and inefficiency of the system is leading inexorably to a means-tested or residual Welfare State. David Willetts – who happily continues to describe the Welfare State as 'first and foremost a mutual insurance scheme to which we all contribute when times are good and from which we all expect to draw when times are not so good' – nevertheless argues that social security expenditure is being spread too thinly across rich and poor alike, and that the government is right to try and aim its largesse at the genuinely poor, partly by setting more rigorous qualification criteria.[25] This is what is now happening. Some universal benefits, like maternity and death grants, have disappeared altogether; contributory benefits like unemployment and sickness benefit are no longer earnings-related; all benefits are linked at best to prices rather than earnings; the State Earnings Related Pensions Scheme (SERPS) was pruned; and the eligibility criteria for claiming any benefit are being tightened all the time. One effect is to increase private provision against destitution. This is rightly seen as a desirable step in an increasingly affluent and consumer-driven economy. But it is marooning a growing class of poor people – some of them retired, many unskilled, and increasing numbers of single parents – without a job because of their reliance on means-tested benefits. The real answer to poverty is to get these people back to work.

The introduction of a Basic Income scheme, or what some people call a Citizen's Income, would help to achieve that. If all existing tax allowances, reliefs and social security benefits, student grants and training allowances were scrapped and replaced by a single cash payment to each adult, made without deduction of income tax and paid regardless of economic circumstances, the social security system would achieve three desirable objectives. It would be economically efficient, enabling people to work rather than live off welfare. It would also free millions of poor people from the humiliating inquisitorial activities of the State. Lastly, a Basic Income payment would be cheaper to administer. Each individual would be guaranteed a minimum sum of money each year, which most people earning more than the minimum would receive as a tax credit. Those people with no other income would receive a cheque totalling the minimum amount in twelve monthly instalments or fifty-two weekly payments. The entire scheme could be administered through the computer systems at the Inland Revenue, enabling the staff of the Department of Social Security to be retired.

In a Basic Income scheme, all personal income tax allowances and reliefs would disappear and income tax would be payable at a single proportional rate on all income other than Basic Income.[26] National Insurance contributions would also be abolished, but indirect taxes such as VAT and excise duties and council taxes would remain as they are. The State Earnings Related Pensions Scheme (SERPS) would also be retained. By making an unconditional minimum payment to all citizens, whether they are rich or poor, healthy or sick, employed or unemployed, young or old, Basic Income would guarantee every adult in Britain a minimum level of income. It would tackle poverty directly, plugging the gaps in the present means-tested safety net caused by the incomplete take-up of benefits, various disqualifications and the inability of even the most complicated social security system to take account of the personal circumstances of every individual. Take-up of a universal benefit like Child Benefit, which is akin to a Basic Income, is close to 100 per cent.

Basic Income would also eliminate the army of social security bureaucrats devoted to the assessment of contribution records and the investigation of personal means, since the scheme could be administered without difficulty by the existing Inland Revenue bureaucracy. Above all, by integrating the tax and social security systems it would eliminate the poverty and unemployment traps. It would also replace the 'malign churning' of public money, by which wealthy taxpayers also receive social security benefits, with a 'benign churning' of redistribution through the tax system. This would gradually reduce the cost of the Welfare State by removing the present disincentives for those on means-tested benefits to accept low-paid jobs and increase the incentive to take jobs where the income or security of tenure was uncertain. Unlike the modern Welfare State, a Basic Income would alleviate poverty efficiently, reduce the cost of government, enlarge liberty, increase the incentives to work and enhance the flexibility of the labour market.

The idea of providing every citizen with a minimum income is not new. At the turn of the century Charles Booth and Seebohm Rowntree both advocated a 'national minimum', and so did William Beveridge.[27] But it is not the property of the collectivists. The classical economist and inventor of welfare economics, A. C. Pigou, recommended 'minimum conditions in every department of life' as early as 1914.[28] The notion of a Basic Income was put forward as an alternative to the Beveridge Plan by Lady Juliet Rhys-Williams in *Something to Look Forward To*, published in 1943, mainly because she thought denying the working poor any assistance would undermine the incentive to work.[29] Her ideas were taken up by the Nobel Prize-winning economist James Meade in *Planning and the Price Mechanism*, his powerful attack on collectivist planning published five years later. He has advocated them repeatedly in many subsequent books and papers. Even Milton Friedman endorsed the idea, in the shape of a negative income tax, in *Capitalism and Freedom*, published in 1962.[30]

As Samuel Brittan has argued, a Basic Income guarantee does not have to be seen as a State handout. Properly constituted, it can be viewed as a property right equivalent to the inheritance or trust funds of the rich or the imputed rental income of the owner-occupier. 'The clue to legitimising some Basic Income Guarantee is to see it not as a handout, but as a property right,' writes Brittan. 'What is or is not a property right depends on custom, attitudes and psychology, as well as law...It is therefore unfortunate that the subject is usually treated purely as an aspect of social security reform...It would be just as valid to see the Basic Income aspect as an inalienable part of the return on the national capital...Basic Income would be the equivalent of an inherited, modest competence available in the middle and lower, as well as upper, reaches of the income scale...The only thing wrong with unearned income is that too few have it.'[31] A Basic Income is not necessarily at odds with the ideal of a prosperous and property-owning nation of inheritors. Twenty years ago wages and salaries accounted for well over three quarters of personal income but today income from work or self-employment accounts for only two thirds of personal incomes. The balance comes from rents, dividends and interest on capital or property (8 per cent), private pensions or annuities (11 per or social security or other public and private grants (15 per cent).[32] Basic Income would make every adult a rentier.

A common objection to Basic Income is that, even if it solved poverty, it would not solve unemployment. Beveridge rightly argued in 1944 that 'Idleness is not the same as Want; but a separate evil which men do not escape by having an income. They must also have the chance of rendering useful service and of feeling that they are doing so.' But it would be perverse to reject a Basic Income on these grounds. By solving the problem of the unemployment trap a Basic

Income is more likely to alleviate joblessness than the current range of means-tested benefits. By topping up the income of low-paid jobs it would also entice people to take work which paid too little to offer an acceptable standard of living. The low and falling value the modern market economy accords to male, unskilled labour would be overcome. Unlike the present system of social security, which encourages people not to upgrade their skills by withdrawing benefit as soon as they spend more than a few hours a week on a training course, a Basic Income would also enable people to study and to train. Others would be free to take a part-time job, or do voluntary work, or spend more time looking after their family.

A Basic Income can reduce but not remove the moral hazard of pauperism. Some people, like the so-called 'travellers', undoubtedly will choose to opt out of economic life to live on the subsistence offered by a Basic Income. But in most cases the feckless are already idle or dependent, and no free or even humane society would prefer to see them either utterly impoverished or coerced into State-organised make-work schemes instead. Provided marginal tax rates were properly adjusted, everyone would be better of with a job than without one, even if some people chose to remain idle. That would enable the welfare system for the first time to meet the objective Beveridge set in his 1942 blueprint for the Welfare State, *Social Insurance and Allied Services*:

> The State in organising security should not stifle incentive, opportunity, responsibility; in establishing a national minimum, it should leave room and encouragement for voluntary action by each individual to provide more than that minimum for himself and his family.[33]

Most importantly, by subsidising jobs which pay wages below market-clearing rates it will price people – and especially the unskilled male unemployed – back into work.

'The challenge for economic and social policy,' as Samuel Brittan has explained, 'is to find a way of obtaining as much as we can of the benefits of an American-style labour market, without incurring the cost of American-style poverty.'[34] A Basic Income is a way of achieving that goal without coercion. It works with the grain of a labour market in which people are shifting from salaried employment into self-employment, job changes are frequent and many people are doing part-time or lowly paid work. Ideally, the old distinctions between the employed, the self-employed, the unemployed, the sick and the retired would start to disappear. In this way a Basic Income will not only alleviate poverty and make the labour market work better but it will also oblige the State to give up its pointless campaign to harass the work-shy and stigmatise the pauperised. It will allow people to choose to do a lot, a little or nothing at all. By creating a new class of rentier, it will make another modest contribution to the liquidation of the coercive State.[35]

A more serious objection to a Basic Income is its alleged unaffordability. The greater coverage of Basic Income means that it could easily cost more than the present systems of social security and income tax allowances, and the wider its coverage the more it will cost. If it is set too high, the tax costs will be insupportable, but if it is set too low the Basic Income will be inadequate for those with no other means of support. One analyst reckoned a Basic Income equal to one third of average earnings would require an Income Tax rate (about £115 a week today) of between 68 and 86 per cent to finance, depending on the curtailment or otherwise of the non-personal income tax reliefs.[36] Even a modest scheme devised by another analyst, and limited to families rather than individuals, implied an Income Tax rate of 49 per cent and a total tax burden of 70 per cent of gross personal income.[37] These seem too pessimistic. The exact cost in tax terms depends on the level of the payment, and whether it is used to replace existing benefits or added to them. An affordable scheme will replace all existing benefits. It will also be set sufficiently low to maintain a large gap between the Basic Income and the national income per head, to avoid pitching the entire working population into a poverty trap.[38]

Table 23   The Cost of Paying a Basic Income
                  to Every Adult in the United Kingdom

	Weekly Cost £	Annual Cost £	Indicative Cost £bn
Personal Income Tax Allowance	67.79	3,525	162
Incapacity Benefit	59.15	3,076	141
Unemployment Benefit	46.45	2,415	111
Income of Poorest Tenth[1]	53.00	2,756	127
Third of Median Income[1]	53.33	2,773	128
Income Support[2]	36.52	1,899	88
Average	52.70	2,740	126

1 Single adult, after tax but before housing costs, in 1991–92.
2 Half Income Support for a couple (£73.05).

A sensible rule-of-thumb suggests that the Basic Income should not exceed one third of average post-tax income, currently well under £3,000 a year or about £53 a week. This is less generous than other measures or implicit measures of an individual subsistence income, such as the personal allowance for income tax or the retirement pension. The implications of the various measures are set out in Table 23, which suggests a weekly income of about £53 a week or £2,756 a year would be an appropriate level for the Basic Income. To pay this sum to each of the adults in the United Kingdom aged over 16 would cost just under £123 billion a year.[39] This seems a substantial sum of money, but it is in fact much less than half of projected government expenditure of £286 billion in 1995-96. Over two thirds of the sum required would be contributed by the existing social security departmental budget of £86½ billion. Most of the balance is accounted for by the existing personal tax allowance which was equal to over £25.9 billion in tax forgone in 1994-95 even before the cost of dozens of other tax reliefs and cuts in expenditure programmes are taken into consideration. This leaves another £9.6 billion to be found from tax increases or cuts in other government expenditure programmes. If it was decided to retain some personal tax reliefs, almost the whole of this sum could still be retrieved from the surrogate social security spending of the Departments of Employment, Education and Environment.[40] Computer modelling shows that it is perfectly possible to introduce a Basic Income payment of £53 a week at a single proportional Income Tax rate of 37.9 per cent. This is substantially below the current marginal rate of taxation for most people in 1995–96 of 44.1 per cent. Reducing the Income Tax rate to 30 per cent would still enable a payment of £39.47 a week to be made.

The cost of a Basic Income scheme will also be offset by the fact that some of the unemployed currently on means-tested benefits will go back to work and pay taxes. This effect should increase over time as people get used to using Basic Income as an employment subsidy. Tax rates could even be levied at a relatively high rate on initial earnings, and then fall as more is earned in order to give people more incentive to carry on working, but this would undermine the symmetry and fairness of a single proportional rate of income tax.[41] A scheme of this kind is clearly affordable.

Some argue that for some individuals – like single mothers, some pensioners and the chronically sick or disabled – a Basic Income of £53 a week would not amount even to subsistence. This is why they argue that a Basic Income has to be supplemented with means-tested or discretionary benefits or set at a much higher level and withdrawn at savage rates from the working population through the income tax system. But it is not clear that £53 a week is too low. It will scarcely pay for a sybaritic lifestyle, but the evidence suggests it is adequate for subsistence. A lone mother on Income Support will receive £46.55 a week in 1995–96, a couple £73.05, or £36.53 a head. The Family Budget Unit has estimated that it is possible to subsist on about £40 a week. Of course, the material needs of different types of individual vary enormously. The Family Budget Unit estimates, for example, that a grandmother living alone in York needs a gross income of roughly £142 a week to sustain a modest but comfortable standard of living but a family of four in the same city needs £393 a week. There is no reason why a Basic Income should not, within an overall budget constraint, be higher for old people than young ones or for sick people than healthy ones, while leaving the average cost at £2,756 a year.

But the most telling criticism of many Basic Income schemes is their refusal to address the distributional effects. 'These schemes,' writes one critic of Basic Income proposals, 'always seem to avoid addressing the crucial distributional question of who gains and who loses and why.'[42] The introduction of a Basic Income scheme which is revenue-neutral – in other words, which does not add to or subtract from existing levels of public expenditure – will obviously re-distribute income among individuals, because it replaces means-tested benefits with a single universal payment. A computer analysis of a Basic Income payment of £53 a week suggests that, although the poorest tenth of the population will be considerably better off, five out of the six poorest deciles will actually be worse off. Three out of the four richest deciles actually gain, and only the richest tenth of the population stand to lose. Slightly over a quarter of the poorest tenth are more than £10 a week worse off. These effects, which do not differ markedly when the scheme is tested with both lower and higher basic income payments, reflect two main factors. One is that a Basic Income scheme of this kind takes no account of the extra costs of housing and of bringing up children. In the present welfare system, some people receive means-tested housing benefit and every mother receives weekly child benefit. Help with the costs of housing and raising children is also dispensed through the income support system. The second is that the sharp improvement in the standard of living of the poorest tenth is partly attributable to the fact that many of the poorest people in Britain do not take up their full entitlement to means-tested benefits. The positive effects of introducing a universal payment would not be so dramatic if they did, however unrealistic that prospect might be.

Distributional consequences of this kind have driven most advocates of Basic Income schemes to favour the means-testing of payments, or the taxation of payments at progressive rates, or to provide separately for the costs of children and housing. The retention of the existing child benefit and housing subsidy budgets would cost another £12 billion a year, and the retention of income support more than half as much again. These costs are not intolerable, in the context of a total public expenditure budget of nearly £300 billion, but in the absence of compensating cuts in public expenditure they would imply a significant increase in the single proportional rate of taxation to 40–50 per cent. One solution is to reintroduce progressive tax bands, but the interpolation of complications of this kind sharply reduces the attractiveness of Basic Income schemes. A surfeit of different taxes or tax bands, or even discretionary grants for the costs of children and housing, would badly erode the elegance and simplicity of the scheme. They would also undermine the incentive effects of Basic Income, which are its principal attraction. A Basic Income payment would make more lower-paid jobs worth taking, lifting many of the poorest people out of the poverty and unemployment traps. A computer model cannot predict the scale of the decrease in unemployment and the rise in tax revenues which would result but, provided the scheme is not so generous that it closes the gap between Basic Income and the wages of the lowest-paid jobs, they are likely to be substantial. The incentive effects naturally diminish in line with the generosity of the scheme, particularly if it necessitated a heavy rate of taxation. In particular, too steep a withdrawal of Basic Income through the tax system would create a 'Why Work?' disincentive of precisely the kind the scheme is designed to rectify. 'Proposals that begin as fundamental reforms,' observe John Kay and Mervyn King, 'tend to become modified in ways which lead to results not necessarily much less complex than, or different from, the present system.'[43]

Trimming of this kind is probably an unavoidable feature of any democratic political system. The distributional consequences of a straightforward Basic Income scheme may be so intolerable, even after taking incentive effects into account, that it becomes politically impossible to implement. In these circumstances, the task for policymakers is to devise a politically achievable scheme which is neither ruinously expensive nor hopelessly compromised. Given that it is arithmetically impossible to abolish all means-tested benefits and keep the income tax rate at an acceptable level and create no losers, this means either reducing the number of beneficiaries or paying some recipients more than others. One option is to reduce the coverage of the scheme. Many people would argue, for example, that it is over-generous to pay Basic Income to sixteen and seventeen year olds. Another solution is to introduce a means-tested provision to cover housing costs, though means-testing is objectionable on both philosophical grounds and in terms of incentives. Housing is best dealt with separately. The most sensible adjustment is to concentrate spending on the principal losers of the switch to a single Basic Income payment of £53 a week. Computer analysis identifies these as poorer (though not the poorest) families with children, and their difficulties can be ameliorated by a relatively simple adjustment. It would be possible, without any increase in the single proportional rate of Income Tax of 37.9 per cent, to pay a single rate of Basic Income to every adult of £49 a week and an extra payment of £15 a week for each child.[44] Many other permutations are possible. But any Basic Income scheme which aims to solve poverty by getting people back to work, and to enlarge liberty by putting an end to offensive personal inquisitions by State bureaucrats, can never insulate everybody from the change. Gaps in social provision are a weakness Basic Income shares with the current Welfare State. But by creating room for personal initiative, and increasing the scope for charitable work by individuals and voluntary organisations, Basic Income may well create a safety net with fewer holes than the existing system. The costs of Basic Income will be difficult to contain when there is a chronic temptation for politicians to seek votes by offering to raise the rate of Basic Income or to supplement it with a variety of new cash benefits. The electorate will set limits to this redistribution of wealth, just as it already limits the scope for tax increases, but experience suggests that the ultimate effect of the democratic process in a welfare state is to increase public expenditure and taxation. It is difficult to see how this problem can be circumvented completely. The answer which earlier generations might have given – denying recipients of Basic Income the franchise – is clearly unthinkable. But a Basic Income does have one further advantage over the existing system: it makes explicit the squalid nature of the political competition for votes.

Reform of the Tax System

It is important to bolster that novel feature with a reform of the system of taxation which would reacquaint ordinary voters with exactly how much it is that they are paying in tax. Pay As You Earn, or PAYE, was introduced during the Second World War as the most convenient method of paying income tax. It was also the most cunning device for the coercion of the individual which the State has ever invented. Most salaried employees think of their income in gross terms, but are content actually to receive them net. In other words most people do not enjoy even temporary use of somewhere between a third and a half of their own income. It disappears painlessly, without most of them knowing how it is done or even how much it is. About three quarters of income tax is collected automatically under PAYE, and all but a tenth or so of the rest is deducted at source from gilt-edged securities, bank accounts, company dividends and the like. It is principally its acquiescence in this astonishingly efficient and uncontroversial expropriation of private income and wealth which has made the Corporate Economy such a valued friend of the high-spending and high taxing State.[45] Even increases in indirect taxes like VAT and excise duties – which are arguably far less visible and certainly less inquisitorial than their direct counterparts – seem to arouse the ire of the taxpayers to a far greater extent than the incessant but silent picking of their pockets by the system of PAYE.

Even those taxpayers interested, intelligent or organised enough to take an interest in such matters are happy to be bought off with a variety of tax privileges or perks or avoidance strategies which never confront directly the underlying reality. Indeed, tax privileges have the habit of developing into property rights. They acquire what Charles Adams has called 'aristocratic status', and a great deal of energy and venom is devoted to defending them because taking them away brings home the reality of confiscation by the State in a way that PAYE does not. The overall effect of a system with high overall rates of taxation, plenty of exemptions and PAYE is to entrench excessive rates of public expenditure and taxation by keeping taxpayers confused and encouraging them to divert their energies into defending privileges which the State in equity has no right to grant anyway. If it is immoral for any taxpayer to evade tax, it is equally immoral for the State to grant exemptions from tax to favoured interest groups: in equity, exemptions must apply to all or to none. Yet the Treasury estimates that the overall cost of the principal tax expenditures and structural reliefs in 1993–94 was slightly over £118 billion, one and a half times the total raised by the Inland Revenue.[46]

As long as the State concentrates on granting and eroding tax reliefs and inventing new taxes, and the taxpayers expend all their energy resisting attacks on their tax privileges, it is likely that the overall burden of tax will at best remain static. 'It remains difficult to resist the conclusion,' write John Kay and Mervyn King, 'that the Inland Revenue does not feel its work could be helped if the taxpayer had a better understanding of the basis or methods of collection of the taxes involved.'[47] Elected governments have little incentive to devise a readily comprehensible system of taxation. They are also overly influenced by political rather than rational considerations. The weakness of the tax cuts of the 1980s, for example, was that there was no corresponding reduction in the functions of government, for fear of offending the various lobbies dependent on State subsidies. The rate of increase in public expenditure was contained, at some cost in lost capital expenditure, and the cuts in income tax were financed through a mixture of asset sales and economic growth. Nothing fundamental was changed.

The tax increases of the early 1990s were a response to the same political incentives. They introduced some desirable changes (like the withering of mortgage tax relief), some undesirable changes (like the reintroduction of capital allowances) and even some completely arbitrary new taxes (like those on mobile telephones and airport departures) without any attempt to piece together a coherent strategy of reform. The purpose, it is quite obvious, was not to reward virtue and punish vice but to raise the most revenue at the least political cost by hiding part of the pain in technical changes and spreading the rest as thinly as possible, using fresh subsidies where the political cost was felt to be too high.

Short of a major constitutional upheaval, which restored Parliamentment to its traditional role as the guardian of the taxpayer, the only hope of achieving neutrality in the tax system and increasing the political resistance to taxation is to introduce an *expenditure tax* of the kind recommended by James Meade. The name is actually something of a misnomer.[48] In practice it would not be levied on spending as such but on a measure of income best described as net cash flow or consumed income. In essence, the tax base for individuals would be income net of business expenses plus net cash flow from financial transactions. The sale of financial assets, or borrowings, would increase the tax liability while savings, or purchases of shares or bonds, would reduce it. Businesses would also pay taxes based on cash flow, the corporate tax base being sales revenue minus business expenses. The taxation of individual and corporate income in this way could be at progressive rates, but it is best if the tax is proportional. One advantage of an expenditure tax is that it obviates the many difficulties, injustices and absurdities of attempting to measure individual incomes and real returns on business assets for tax purposes. At present an army of lawyers and accountants is engaged in devising tax avoidance and arbitrage strategies, of which the best-known is turning income into capital gains.

A second advantage of an expenditure tax is that it encourages saving, penalising spendthrifts and rewarding the prudent. Under the present system of taxation, most kinds of savings are taxed twice – they are mostly made out of net income, and income from them is taxed as well – while borrowing is tax-deductible. An expenditure tax would eliminate the discrimination between savings vehicles, and especially the tax-driven tendency to save through institutional pension funds. It should therefore increase the personal ownership of financial assets. An expenditure tax would tax the self-employed and the small businessman only on the income he or she consumed, further encouraging reinvestment and the accumulation of capital. Importantly, it would oblige every taxpayer to maintain a personal balance sheet and profit and loss account. This will not only encourage people to manage their income and expenditure more sensibly over their life cycle but – by reminding them of where their money and wealth come from and where they go, and obliging them to write out a cheque to the Inland Revenue twice a year – reinforce resistance to expropriation by the State.

The conventional objection to an expenditure tax is that it would be impossibly bureaucratic. Nigel Lawson summarised the case against it as follows:

It would not be directly levied on personal spending at all but on income – after various complex subtractions and additions designed to exempt all savings and to tax drawings of capital. In its fully fledged form, all forms of saving would have to be registered, as would all capital disposals, including sales of pictures, homes, withdrawals of savings from the Post Office, even in principle the sale of second-hand furniture. In practice there would have to be many exemptions for small transactions and volumes of legislation to avoid cheating. The administration and information required would be similar to that needed for the Wealth Tax, which even the 1974–9 Labour Government decided to drop.[49]

An expenditure tax which attempted to measure the value of personal possessions in such a way would indeed be objectionable – though adequate information is usually readily available from insurance valuations – and awkward to administer.

But, as Nigel Lawson himself indicates, there is no need to introduce the tax in its fully-fledged form. Net income from asset sales could be confined to financial assets, exempting houses and heirlooms and restricting the pain of the period of transition to the wealthiest taxpayers, who have accumulated a large number of financial assets. A sensibly designed expenditure tax would then oblige taxpayers to do no more than keep cash books equivalent to those maintained by millions of self-employed people already, on the basis of which they would then assess their own tax liabilities and agree them with the Inland Revenue. There is no reason why it should make tax collection any more awkward than it already is, though the Inland Revenue would certainly lose the enormous advantage of being paid in advance. There is no PAYE in the United States, where every taxpayer is obliged to fill in a tax return, but it seems that British taxpayers are in correspondence with the Inland Revenue more often than their American counterparts.[50] If the tax made life more awkward for the Inland Revenue, most people would count it a blessing. Reinforcing the mechanisms that encourage public finance to determine public expenditure rather than the other way round – in other words, making tax more difficult to collect – is a vital element in the gradual reduction of the intrusion of the State into private life.

The Liquidation of State Education

In no area of public endeavour has the State inflicted as much damage as in the field of education. Schools and universities were gradually nationalised, not to help individual personalities find their fullest expression but to enhance the competitiveness of the economy, and advance science and national security. The same kind of thinking still contaminates education today, with politicians, businessmen and 'educationalists' fussing over whether the schools and universities are producing the 'skills' and 'scientific manpower' needed by industry. But after over one hundred years of State involvement in schools, overall standards of literacy and numeracy are lower than those of any other major country and lower than they were at the turn of the century. A reckless expansion of the numbers of undergraduate students has swamped the universities. The State has created for the first time in Britain a Continental-style university system, with large numbers of students, less personal supervision, more questionable disciplines and qualifications, a much higher rate of failure and an obsession with justice rather than excellence.

Pitifully, deteriorating educational standards have encouraged more State intervention rather than less. It is true that the schools reforms of the last six years were not a complete disaster. Parents were given more choice over schools through open enrolment, and more information on which to base a decision. Schools were given control of their own budget and the opportunity to escape local authority control by opting for a central government grant. One entirely new kind of school – the City Technology College, sponsored by industrial companies – emerged, with government blessing. But these potentially desirable reforms were utterly compromised by a concomitant increase in State control of teacher training and appraisal, examinations and the curriculum. The reforms are reminiscent in some ways of the attempts once made to raise the performance of the nationalised industries by setting them attainment targets. At the universities – now much expanded by the elevation of polytechnics to university status – the government is trying to raise standards by linking block grants specifically to the number of students a university attracts and the quality of its teaching and research. It is not unlike the method adopted for the funding of elementary schools in the 1860s by that famous reactionary, Robert Lowe. He tied public grants to performance tests in reading, writing and arithmetic. The main effect so far seems to be an expansion of student accommodation.

Educational standards and diversity cannot be recovered until the State withdraws from education altogether, including standard-setting. School budgets, even if they are now controlled in some cases by the headmaster, are still ultimately set by the State. Opting out of local authority control only transfers dependence from the local education authority to the Secretary of State for Education. It has failed to take off anyway. At the beginning of 1994 just 507 out of 18,905 primary schools had held ballots on grant-maintained status, and only 398 voted for it. Of the 3,655 secondary schools, 827 held ballots and 648 opted to leave local authority control.[51] By failing to set education free from the State, the reforms have more or less guaranteed that an incoming collectivist government will return control of education to a mixture of ideological politicians, departmental 'educationalists', local councils and the militant teachers' trade unions. They have not only failed to create the room for the emergence and development of the many new kinds of school which are needed to make a reality of variety and choice for parents and employers, but may actually have narrowed it through the nationalisation of the curriculum. They have postponed yet again the emergence of a system of schooling which will equip children with the ability to read, write and add up and give them a sound moral and cultural understanding. Too many children are still trapped in a State system which fails to help their gifts find their fullest expression.

The conventional market solution to the failure of State education is to give parents, schoolchildren and students more control over their choice of schools and universities, in the expectation that a system will eventually emerge which reflects as far as possible the needs of all the individuals using it. Parents, it is thought, can be equipped with State vouchers encashable at the school of their choice. Likewise, it is often argued that a system of student loans rather than grants would force young people to think more carefully about the investment they are making in their own human capital, raise standards and eliminate nonsensical courses. But the whole history of education in Britain shows that as long as the State is subsidising education, it will seek to control it. Only true financial independence can free schools and universities from the threat and the reality of coercion by the State. The most obvious way to achieve this is to make parents, or parents and students, pay fees, or at least bear a greater share of the costs of education directly. There is clearly a place for increased fee-paying in a reformed educational structure and tax system. It would not be politically popular, and would have to be phased in.

But it could be combined with a reform which would be popular. This is to equip schools and universities with an endowment of capital which would yield each institution an income sufficient to free them from dependence on the taxpayer. This is obviously not achievable immediately. In 1993–94 the State spent £19.3 billion supporting schools, and another £1 billion on capital projects. Securing an income of that magnitude at current long-term gilt rates of $8\frac{1}{2}$ per cent would require an investment of nearly £240 billion. Another £11 billion or so was spent on further and higher education (including £3.4 billion on student grants and fees), which would require another £130 billion. A total of £370 billion is more than one and a half times total public expenditure in 1993–94, or more than half the national income in that financial year. Even if the taxpayer was prepared to put up £50 billion today for the endowment of education it would still take twenty-five years, at current long-term interest rates of $8\frac{1}{2}$ per cent, to build up a fund of sufficient size to cover the current and capital costs of school and higher education today. Freeing educational institutions from the grip of the State is clearly a long-term project, achievable over two to three decades rather than two to three Parliaments.

But independence is certainly achievable, especially if the creation of endowment funds by the State is combined with an increase in fee-paying by parents and students. The accumulation of endowment funds would create an investment income which could be used gradually to displace State funding. Some rough calculations illustrate how such a gradual liquidation of the role of the State in education might work. The State could, for example, undertake to create endowment funds for schools with a collective value of £240 billion in thirty equal annual instalments of £8 billion. If these were invested at the current long-term gilt rate of $8\frac{1}{2}$ per cent they would after a dozen years produce sufficient income to offset any extra borrowing by the State to fund the purchase of financial assets by the schools. During those twelve years the State would have to borrow an extra £43 billion, or just £3½ billion more a year, with the associated extra interest costs. After thirty years there would be sufficient assets to fund the whole of the £20 billion currently spent on the schools by the State. If parents were prepared to cover slightly over a third of the cost of schooling, or about £800 a year extra for every household with children of school age, the same results could be achieved without any extra borrowing by the State. Similar results could be achieved for the universities more cheaply. Endowment funds for the universities worth £130 billion could be created in thirty equal annual instalments of £4.3 billion, funded by an extra £23 billion or so of additional borrowing over the first twelve years. If slightly over a third of university costs were covered by fees, the same results could be achieved without extra State borrowing.

The endowment of schools and universities offers the prospect of complete State disengagement from education within thirty years even if there is no additional income from fees. But the process could be accelerated rapidly through the greater use of fees and, in the case of university students, greater use of loans rather than grants and automatic fee payments. Schools and universities could also seek to build up their own endowment funds through private and charitable donations. Some institutions already have substantial endowments. Few State schools – unlike a tiny minority of private schools – do, but some universities are in a much stronger position. The Oxford and Cambridge colleges already generate a tenth of their income from historic endowments, and have a system of internal taxation to redistribute wealth from richer colleges to poor ones. Another third comes from various private sources, fees, grants, rents and services.

Oxford and Cambridge universities probably own net assets of £1 billion apiece, even before works of art and the assets of the colleges are added to the total. The colleges own historic endowments which have a collective value of another £800–900 million at each university, even if priceless artistic assets are left out of the equation. Oxbridge also remains uniquely attractive to individual and corporate benefactors at home and abroad, making complete independence of the State a real possibility even in the short term. The redbrick universities are not as rich as Oxford and Cambridge, but neither are they as poor as they often make out. In 1992 they had estimated net assets of over £4 billion, though roughly four fifths of this was accounted for by land and buildings rather than income- yielding cash and securities.[52] But, on average, the redbrick universities already raise about a third of their income from the private sector through asset sales, renting buildings, selling courses and undertaking research and development projects for the private sector. The withdrawal of the State would create room for that kind of private funding to increase significantly, especially if gifts were fully deductible for tax purposes.

What Can Be Cut?

The idea of endowing institutions to secure their independence from the State is capable of extension beyond the schools and universities. Hospitals are an obvious example. The many branches of the heritage industry are another. Environmental projects currently funded by the State could be privatised in the same way. Public housing, and even roads, could be similarly endowed. But even on the most generous interpretation of the public finances, the gradual liquidation of the State in this way will be a prolonged business of the kind democracies are rarely adept at pursuing. If the process of endowment is not to be impossibly lengthy or expensive, it will be necessary to make radical cuts in public expenditure elsewhere to finance the initial endowments.

The long-term objective should be to reduce public expenditure to 15-20 per cent of Gross Domestic Product, or less than half its present level, over the next thirty years. It has become obvious over the last fifteen years that an incremental approach to cutting public expenditure will be totally ineffective in achieving cuts, as opposed to restraining the rate of increase. But in the context of a genuinely radical programme of social reform, the political possibilities are much enlarged. In an atmosphere of upheaval it should be possible to close down entire departments of State and withdraw from whole areas of State activity, rather than rely on chipping away steadily at monolithic and well-established spending departments.

Table 24 How to Cut £20 Billion From Public Expenditure

Budget	Estimated Outturn in 1993–94 (£ m)
Overseas Aid	2,095
Agricultural Subsidies	3,048
Agricultural Research & Advisory Services	789
Privatisation of Forestry	94
Industrial Subsidies	747
Police Service	107
Central Government Housing Subsidies	1,097
Student Grants	3,358
Student Loan Subsidies	330
Department of National Heritage	2,709
Contributions to the European Union	1,778
Employment and Training Subsidies[1]	3,573
Economies at the Foreign Office	200
Compulsory Manpower Cuts at all Departments	75
	20,000

1 Assuming implementation of Basic Income scheme.

Table 24 lists a series of immediate cuts which could be made in public expenditure. None can be made without howls of outrage from the vested interests which they affect, but there is a respectable case against each of them. Overseas aid would be better replaced by the removal of tariff barriers against imports from the developing world. The principal beneficiaries of agricultural protectionism are farmers, who are now also subject to such an intense degree of State subsidisation and direction that the industry is effectively nationalised. And the victims of this indefensible web of protection and subsidy are consumers and taxpayers, who can be expected to applaud its disappearance. The arguments against the privatisation of the Forestry Commission – that privately owned forests will be closed to the public, and environmentally despoiled – are simply untrue. State ownership and management of the forests is a disaster for the landscape and the natural environment. The Commission itself has covered much of the countryside with unsightly conifers, rather than the broad-leafed trees now in favour among environmentalists. Many private forests of conifers were also planted with State help, in the shape of a tax subsidy. And several of the forests sold by the Commission in recent years went not to selfish landowners but to the State, which promptly built motorways across them. The whole history of land management in Britain demonstrates that the natural environment is safer in private hands than public ones. And it would be completely straightforward to sell forests subject to the proviso that public access is preserved. After all, plenty of private forests are in exactly that position already.

The case against industrial subsidies is so compelling that it is surprising to find that any are still being paid. Housing is a classic instance of the fallacious view that, if the market fails, the only alternative is the State. The budget can be cut by £1 billion without affecting local authority and housing corporation expenditure. Turning student grants into loans has proved politically awkward, but those on Basic Income would be better off than they are today. It is also inequitable for poorly paid taxpayers to subsidise the studies of university students who can expect to enjoy far higher lifetime earnings. Accordingly, linking loan repayments to salary levels obviates the risk that some individuals will pay an excessive proportion of their post-graduation salary in interest and capital payments on loans taken out while they were students. Likewise, employment and training subsidies could be phased out once every adult was receiving Basic Income.

The Department of National Heritage is the ironic creation of the excessive taxation of the twentieth century. Having taxed wealthy families into penury, the State now obliges the taxpayer to subsidise their land and houses and the museums which house those of their possessions 'saved for the nation'. There are also powerful arguments, on grounds of equity and incentives, against State subsidisation of the arts. The Department should be abolished. The Diplomatic Service is one of the core functions of government, but it is in need of radical restructuring. Many of its diplomatic methods are anachronistic in the age of instant electronic communication; the benefits of its support to British industry competing for business abroad are frequently exaggerated; and it possesses a propertied estate which is far larger than it needs, and which is probably worth at least £1 billion. Trimming less than a fifth from its annual budget of £1.2 billion is unlikely to reduce the effectiveness of the Diplomatic Service, and may even increase it.

The conventional solution to the current moral and political crisis is a constitutional one. Regional assemblies, the restoration of local government, federalism, proportional representation, an elected upper house, plebiscites, direct electronic democracy, immersion in the European Union, and various other bits and pieces of new and old constitutional machinery are now being put forward by the collectivist parties. This is only to be expected. Collectivists sense the disillusionment with politics and politicians and with the State they still worship, albeit in these more enlightened days as 'enabler' rather than wielder of the sword of 'social justice'. But they are only seeking new ways to legitimise the status quo, not to change it, and new arguments to justify the power of the State rather than to reduce it. They want, in the cant phrase of the times, to make the

State 'accountable' to the people. But the country cannot be resurrected – morally, socially, politically, or economically – by creating more political assemblies and more politicians. The task is to set the British people free again.

Freedom hinges not on making the State accountable to the people, but upon dissolving what Michael Oakeshott called 'overwhelming concentrations of power'. Fortunately, power is not available only in its political form. It is available in economic form too. Individuals, companies, schools, universities, clubs, hospitals and charities can all be made free with an endowment of economic power. Unlike political power, economic power is not available in fixed quantities only. A millionaire is not wealthy because he impoverished a beggar, but Parliament is weak because the Cabinet is strong. An endowed school is not independent because a State school is not, but local government is impotent because central government is omnipotent. One individual is not free because another is enslaved, but Westminster is less powerful because Brussels has taken its powers away. Edinburgh is weak because London is strong. Unlike State power, economic power places no limits on human aspirations. It was obvious to the outstanding jurist of an earlier age, Sir Henry Maine, that men have as much to gain from new contractual relationships with each other as they do from registering preferences through the voting system. Free individuals and free associations of individuals can use property – in the shape of voluntary donations or income from endowments – as an aid to widespread self-government, or the dispersion of power without the need for it to be intermediated by the political system.

The widest possible endowment of property will disperse all forms of power and enhance all kinds of freedom by enabling economic power to offset political power.[53] As Milton Friedman explained more than thirty years ago:

> Economic power can be widely dispersed. There is no law of conservation which forces the growth of new centres of economic strength to be at the expense of existing centres. Political power, on the other hand, is more difficult to decentralise. There can be numerous small independent governments. But it is far more difficult to maintain numerous equipotent small centres of political power in a single large government than it is to have numerous centres of economic strength in a single large economy. There can be many millionaires in one large economy. But can there be more than one really outstanding leader, one person on whom the energies and enthusiasms of his countrymen are centred? If central government gains power, it is likely to be at the expense of local government. There seems to be something like a fixed total of political power to be distributed. Consequently, if economic power is joined to political power, concentration seems almost inevitable. On the other hand, if economic power is joined to political power, it can serve as a check and a counter to political power.[54]

By making people and institutions independent once more economic power will imbue society with a new civil and moral power: that of autonomous institutions and free individuals. The true ideal is not 'democratic accountability' but a plural society, or what George Bush once called 'a thousand points of light'.

'Pluralism,' wrote Isaiah Berlin, 'with the measure of' negative liberty" that it entails, seems to me a truer and more humane ideal than the goals of those who seek in the great, disciplined, authoritarian structures the ideal of "positive" self-mastery by classes, or peoples, or the whole of mankind.'[55] This book has set out some of the steps by which the British people can begin to recreate that plural society. It will, of course, be objected that the programme is impractical. It will be argued that it runs against interests too deeply entrenched to dislodge. Lists of minor objections will be enumerated and advanced, by those who know that even to attempt to address them is to risk wrecking the enterprise in its entirety. It is unlikely that any scheme of political improvement can be achieved in its entirety but, as John Stuart Mill pointed out, 'the first object in every practical discussion should be to know what perfection is'.[56]

References

1   Geoffrey Elton, *The English*, Blackwell, pages 234-5.
2   Oscar Wilde, 'The Soul of Man Under Socialism', in *De Profundis and Other Writings*, Penguin Classics Edition, 1986, page 48.
3   Alasdair MacIntyre, *After Virtue: A Study in Moral Theory*, Duckworth, Second Edition, 1985, page 263.
4   Though see above, Chapter 3, pages 60–4.
5   See below, pages 399–401.
6   Earmarking is not the same as labelling, in which taxpayers are merely informed how much a particular public service is costing them. Nor is it the same as charging for public services, because charges are not paid into a separate fund.
7   Ranjit S. Teja and Barry Bracewell-Milnes, *The Case for Earmarked Taxes: Government Spending and Public Choice*, Institute of Economic Affairs, 1991, pages 573 and Appendix.
8   Ranjit S. Teja and Barry Bracewell-Milnes, *The Case for Earmarked Taxes: Government Spending and Public Choice*, Institute of Economic Affairs, 1991, pages 44–5.
9   This is a powerful objection to all forms of so-called 'targeting'. According to welfare analysts at the London School of Economics the average taxpayer already receives back m benefits only 62 per cent of what he pays in taxes (the other 38 per cent is redistributed to others) and much even of the 62 per cent is contingent on future governments honouring unemployment and pension commitments. See Geoff Mulgan and Robin Murray, *Reconnecting Taxation*, Demos, 1993, page 9 and footnote 8, page 48.
10 Geoff Mulgan and Robin Murray, Reconnecting Taxation, Demos, 1993, page 9 and footnote 8, pages 28–9.
11 *Inquiry Into Police Responsibilities and Rewards*, Cm 2280.I, H.M.S.0., Volume 1, June 1993, page 165.
12 See Table 19, page 375.
13 See pages 378–82.
14 John Junor, *Listening for a Midnight Tram*, Pan, 1991, pages 268–72.
15 Quoted in Frank McLynn, *Crime and Punishment in Eighteenth Century England*, OUP, 1991, page 186.
16 *Financial Times*, 7 April 1994.
17 See Introduction, page 15.
18 Some of the 46 million are, of course, the same people claiming different benefits in various guises. Department of Social Security, *Facts and Figures 1994* and *The Growth of Social Security*, H.M.S.O., 1993, page 34.
19 Department of Social Security Departmental Report, *The Government's Expenditure*

Plans, Cmnd 2213, H.M.S.O., 1993, March 1994.

20 From April 1995 unemployment benefit for a single man will rise to £46.45. Invalidity Benefit and Sickness Benefit will be replaced by a new Incapacity Benefit of £59.15 a week.

21 Incapacity Benefit will be subject to a more stringent medical test.

22 J. A. Kay and M. A. King, *The British Tax System*, Fifth Edition, OUP, 190, page 71.

23 The Department of Social Security estimated in 1993 that 16.7 million people were on income-related benefits at any one time. See *The Growth of Social Security*, H.M.S.O. Table 15, page 37.

24 Universal benefits like Child Benefit and the Retirement Pension are administratively cheap, at around 2 per cent of the sums dispensed, but income-related benefits can consume up to 25 per cent of the money involved once the cost of the various interrogations and inquiries is taken into account.

25 David Willetts, *Civic Conservatism*, The Social Market Foundation, June 1 994, page 42.

26 The cost of the scheme can be increased or reduced by accelerating the rate at which it is offset through the tax system, and Basic Income can also work with progressive rates of tax. At present benefits are offset very rapidly by the tax system. As net income rises, Income Support is reduced pound for pound and Family Credit by 70p per pound.

27 The Speenhamland system invented by Berkshire Justices of the Peace in 1795 was a basic income guarantee, in which taxpayers made up the wages of agricultural labourers to a minimum level, but it was means-tested.

28 Quoted in Harold Perkin, *The Rise of Professional Society: England Since 1880*, Routledge, 1989, page 130.

29 See Hermione Parker, *Instead of the Dole*, Routledge, 1989, pages 121–2.

30 In a negative income tax scheme anybody receiving more than the personal tax allowance (currently £3,525) would pay tax on it. Anybody receiving less than the personal allowance would receive a cash subsidy. The value of the subsidy can be adjusted like a tax rate. If the subsidy rate was set at 50 per cent, for example, and a man earned £2,525, he would receive a cheque for £500. This is different from a Basic Income, though both the principle and the practice are the same if the subsidy rate is assumed to be 100 per cent. See Milton Friedman, Capitalism and Freedom, University of Chicago Press, 1962, pages 190–5.

31 Samuel Brittan and Steven Webb, *Beyond the Welfare State: An Examination of Basic Incomes in a Market Economy*, David Hume Institute, Aberdeen University Press, 1990, pages 3–4 cent.

32 Central Statistical Office, *Social Trends 1994*, H.M.S.O., Table 5.3, page 68.

33 *Social Insurance and Allied Services*, Cmnd 64c4, H.M.S.O., 1942.

34 Samuel Brittan, *A Restatement of Economic Liberalism*, Macmillan, 1988, page 301.

35 John Gray has criticised Basic Income (or at least a negative income tax) as a 'technical fix' which ignores the fact that the 'underclass' is a cultural rather than a financial problem, caused by a breakdown in familial and moral traditions. If a Basic Income was not part of a number of policies designed to recreate the nuclear family and the spontaneous institutions of what some call the 'moral community', mainly by withdrawing the State as an active agent in people's lives, this criticism would probably be true. But it is difficult to find it helpful. See John Gray, *Beyond the New Right*, Routledge, 1993, page ix and pages 53–4. Gray has since partially resiled from this view, arguing in a recent pamphlet that 'proposals for a basic or citizen's income, where that is to be distinguished from the Neo-Liberal idea of a negative income tax, and for a better distribution of capital among the citizenry, need reconsideration – despite all their difficulties – as elements in a policy aiming to reconcile the human need for economic security with the destabilising dynamism of market institutions. See John Gray, *The Undoing of Conservatism*, The Social Market Foundation, June 1994, page 42.

36 Hermione Parker, *Instead of the Dole*, Routledge, 1989, page 134.

37 Steven Webb, 'Some Illustrative Schemes', in Samuel Brittan and Steven Webb *Beyond the Welfare State: An Examination of Basic Incomes in a Market Economy*, David Hume Institute, Aberdeen University Press, 1990, pages 23–44.

38 The weakness of the Speenhamland System – which made up from parish rates deficiencies in the income of agricultural labourers – was that it failed to maintain a sufficiently large gap between working and non-working incomes and so encouraged farmers to cut wages and collect the subsidy, encouraging pauperism. All means-tested benefits tend to have this effect, unless wages at the bottom of the income scale are high .

39 Estimate derived from POLIMOD, the tax and benefit computer model run by the Cambridge University Department of Applied Economics. See Table 24.

40 See page 433

41 For a discussion of the relative merits of proportional and progressive taxation of incomes see Chapter 4, pages 96–100. A proposal for an Expenditure Tax, levied at a single proportional rate, is included in this chapter. See pages 423–7.

42 David Willetts, *Civic Conservatism*, The Social Market Foundation, June 1994, page 39

43 J. A. Kay and M. A. King, *The British Tax System*, Fifth Edition, OUP, 1990, page 73.

44 The projections assume that all social security benefits, training allowances and student grants are abolished; all tax allowances and reliefs are abolished; a single proportional rate of income tax is payable; National Insurance contributions are abolished, indirect and council taxes are retained, SERPS is retained; and a flat-rate Basic Income payment is made to every adult aged sixteen or over. The computer modelling for these projections was carried out using POLIMOD, the tax-benefit model owned by the Microsimulation Unit of the Department of Applied Economics at the University of Cambridge. POLIMOD uses data from the Family Expenditure Survey, made available by the Central Statistical Office (CSO) through the Economic and Social Research Council Data Archive (ESRC). Neither the CSO, nor the ESRC nor Holly Sutherland, Director of the Microsimulation Unit, bear any responsibility for the analysis or interpretation of the data reported here.

45 See Chapters 7 and 8.

46 H. M. Treasury, Tax Ready Reckoner and *Tax Reliefs*, July 1993 Table 9, pages 8–10.

47 J. A. Kay and M. A. King, *The British Tax System*, Fifth Edition, OUP, 1990, page 54.

48 It is called an expenditure tax because the tax is levied on the sources of expenditure (i.e. income) rather than the expenditure itself. Since all expenditure ultimately has to be financed out of income, expenditure plus net assets must ultimately equal income from all sources.

49 Nigel Lawson, *The View From No. 11*, Bantam, 1992, pages 344–5.

50 J. A. Kay and M. A. King, *The British Tax System*, Fifth Edition, OUP, 1990, page 53.

51 *Hansard*, 20 January 1994, Cols 729–32.

52 *University Statistics*, Volume III: Finance, Table, page 5, net of figures for Oxford and Cambridge.

53 Milton Friedman, *Capitalism and Freedom*, University of Chicago Press, 1962, page 9.

54 Capitalism and Freedom, page 16.

55 Isaiah Berlin, *Four Essays on Liberty*, OUP paperback edition, 1992, page 171.

56 John Stuart Mill, *Principles of Political Economy*, Penguin Classics Edition, 1985, page 155.